EUGENIO

LATERAL EXCHANGES
Architecture, Urban Development, and Transnational Practices
A series edited by Felipe Correa and Bruno Carvalho

EUGENICS IN THE GARDEN

Transatlantic Architecture and the Crafting of Modernity

FABIOLA LÓPEZ-DURÁN

UNIVERSITY OF TEXAS PRESS   AUSTIN

Illustrations in this book were funded in part or in whole by a grant from the SAH/Mellon Author Awards of the Society of Architectural Historians.

An earlier version of the first chapter (copyright © 2013 by Fabiola López-Durán) was published in Spanish in *Utopías urbanas: Geopolíticas del deseo en América Latina*, edited by Gisela Heffes (Madrid, Spain, and Frankfurt, Germany: Vervuert Verlag, 2013).

A brief excerpt from the second chapter will appear in a chapter on Brazilian modernism by Fabiola López-Durán for the forthcoming book *A Companion to Modern and Contemporary Latin American and Latino Art* (Blackwell Companions to Art History Series), ed. Alejandro Anreus, Robin Greeley, and Megan Sullivan). Copyright © by Wiley and Son. Used with permission.

Portions of the fourth chapter (copyright © 2016 by Fabiola López-Durán) appeared in *Across Space and Time: Architecture and the Politics of Modernity*, edited by Patrick Haughey (New Brunswick, New Jersey, and London: Transaction, 2016).

♾ The paper used in this book meets the minimum requirements of ANSI/NISO Z39.48-1992 (R1997) (Permanence of Paper).

LIBRARY OF CONGRESS CATALOGING-IN-PUBLICATION DATA

Names: López-Durán, Fabiola, author.
Title: Eugenics in the garden : transatlantic architecture and the crafting of modernity / Fabiola López-Durán.
Description: First edition. | Austin : University of Texas Press, 2018. | Series: Lateral exchanges: architecture, urban development, and transnational practices | Includes bibliographical references and index.
Identifiers: LCCN 2017025394
    ISBN 978-1-4773-1495-1 (cloth : alk. paper)
    ISBN 978-1-4773-1496-8 (pbk. : alk. paper)
    ISBN 978-1-4773-1497-5 (library e-book)
    ISBN 978-1-4773-1498-2 (non-library e-book)
Subjects: LCSH: Architecture and society—History—20th century. | Architecture, Modern—20th century. | Eugenics—History. | Social change—Environmental aspects. | City planning—20th century.
Classification: LCC NA2543.S6 L66 2017 | DDC 724/.6—dc23
LC record available at https://lccn.loc.gov/2017025394

doi:10.7560/314951

For my parents, Néstor and Livia,
my earliest and constant mentors.
You taught me the power of research and curiosity,
along with the value of work and kindness.
In a certain way, this story began long ago,
in your laboratories in the Venezuelan Andes.

And for Pelayo, always.

CONTENTS

ACKNOWLEDGMENTS

This book was inspired by the interdisciplinary teaching and transnational approach of the faculty at the School of Architecture's History, Theory, and Criticism of Architecture and Art (HTC) program at the Massachusetts Institute of Technology (MIT), where I received my PhD. My seven-year tenure there changed the way I look at the world. There, I learned that art and architecture are not impermeable, that is, they are not hermetically sealed aesthetic structures but rather porous inquiries into issues of power, inequality, and bigotry—understood not as natural disasters that must be endured but rather as symptoms of deeply rooted structures that must be interrogated, challenged, and even changed.

At MIT, I must first acknowledge my dissertation committee: Arindam Dutta, who taught me what critical and innovative thinking really means; Mark Jarzombek, who expanded my way of thinking to a bigger arena; and Robin Greeley, who taught me to scrutinize the tiniest details of my writing and thinking and who challenged me to examine my own biases and sensitivities as a relatively privileged Latin American in a challenging global context. I owe an intellectual and personal debt to many other professors, colleagues, and staff at MIT. Among them, I would like to especially thank Caroline Jones, whose supportive close reading and always meaningful criticism was invaluable to me; my colleagues and friends Deborah Kully, Lydia Kallipoliti, Winnie Wong, Patrick Haughey, and Tali Hatuka, who at different stages of this work provided sustaining intellectual and emotional support; and Steve Strang and his extraordinary team at the MIT Writing Center, who taught me all I know about writing in English, especially Marilyn Levine, who accompanied me in this journey from its very first lines. I hope this book reflects the extraordinary input I received from all of them.

This book also benefited from another community, the History of Art Department at the University of California, Berkeley, where I was lucky enough to spend two amazing years as a Mellon postdoctoral fellow revising my dissertation into a book under the inspiration of its brilliant faculty, especially Darcy Grimaldo-Grigsby, T.J. Clark, and Todd Olson. I am also indebted to the astute students in my "Nature In-Vitro" seminar, who read and intelligently critiqued early versions of my chapters. In particular, I am thankful to Sarah Cowan, Elizabeth Smith, Lawrence Schear, Steven Bernard, and Katalina Gallo, whose inquiries made me rethink my work in an innovative way. This was one of the most memorable courses I have ever taught.

During the years of archival research and writing, this book took me to different countries, where I had the guidance and support of many colleagues, friends, librarians, and archivists: In France, I found inspiration and joy from my colleagues Jennifer Grotz, Barbara Diefendorf, and Karen King-Aribisala at the Camargo Fondation in Cassis; and from Felice Varini, Isabel Hérault, Yves Arnod, and Manuel Bello in Paris. In Brazil, Gisele Sanglard, Ana Luiza Nobre, Otavio Leonídio, Rosa Costa Ribeiro in Rio de Janeiro and Ana Maria Tavares, Roberta Saraiva, and Martin Grossmann in São Paulo offered invaluable resources and a remarkable sounding board for my ideas. In Argentina, Alicia Novick generously opened her personal archives for my examination, and Cécile Duret was my companion during my French readings and travels between Rio and Buenos Aires. I have also benefited from many archivists in these countries and the United States. I am particularly thankful to Cristina Zappa at the Instituto Moreira Salles and Michele Silva Moraes at the Academia Nacional de Medicina in Rio de Janeiro; and to the librarians at Widener Library, Houghton Library, Frances Loeb Library, and Countway Library of Medicine at Harvard University.

Throughout the making of this book, I received significant financial and institutional support from MIT; Harvard University; the University of California, Berkeley; Rice University; and other organizations. Early fellowships from MIT and Harvard, such as the MIT Royal Fund, the MIT Schlossman Research Award, MIT-France, and Harvard University's Center for European Studies Fellowship, funded the very first periods of research in Paris, where this story began. A CLIR

Mellon Fellowship for Dissertation Research in Original Sources, the Charlotte W. Newcombe Doctoral Dissertation Fellowship from the Woodrow Wilson Foundation, the Dedalus Foundation Dissertation Fellowship, and fellowships from the Camargo Foundation and the Samuel H. Kress Foundation in the History of Art helped fund the research that later informed this book. More recently, the Mellon Postdoctoral Fellowship in the Humanities at the University of California, Berkeley, and a Humanities Research Center Faculty Fellowship at Rice University contributed to the process of refining my arguments and completing the manuscript.

The core ideas of this book were initially presented as talks, and the feedback obtained during these presentations was invaluable to the crafting of this book. I would like to especially thank: in France, the École Spéciale d'Architecture de Paris (ESA), the École Nationale Supérieure d'Architecture de Saint-Étienne, and the Camargo Fondation, Cassis; in Switzerland, the Swiss Federal Institute of Technology (ETH), Zürich, and Franklin College, Lugano; in Canada, the University of British Columbia, Vancouver; in Brazil, the Universidade de São Paulo and the Pontifícia Universidade Católica do Rio de Janeiro; in Venezuela, the Universidad Simón Bolívar, Caracas; and here in the United States, Harvard University; MIT; Savannah College of Art and Design; Vanderbilt University; Florida Atlantic University; Brandeis University; Syracuse University; University of California, Berkeley; University of California, San Diego; and Rice University. This study was also enriched by contributions from the audiences at academic conferences where I presented sections of this book, especially at the New England Society of Architectural Historians (NESAH), the Latin American Studies Association (LASA), and the European Association of Urban History (EAUH).

Rice University has been the perfect environment for me to write this book: incredibly stimulating, interdisciplinary, and intellectually challenging. Gordon Hughes, Luis Duno-Gottberg, and Gisela Heffes read sections and then offered brilliant insights. I gained new perspectives at regular meetings with colleagues at the Humanities Research Center during our year as fellows: from Alida Metcalf and Fares El-Dahdah, I developed a better understanding of the historical urban transformation of Rio de Janeiro; from Reto Geisser, Mariola Alvarez, Elizabeth Farfán Santos, Julie Fette, Sarah Stevens, Marcia Brennan, and Manuel Gutiérrez, I learned how to interrogate my own research from different angles. I am forever grateful to friends and colleagues at Rice University who generously gave their time and attention to me and my work, including Shirine Hamadeh, Graham

Bader, Lida Oukaderova, John Hopkins, Lisa Balabanlilar, James Sidbury, Sarah Whiting, and Beatriz González-Stephan, and especially Linda Neagley for her unwavering support as department chair. Likewise, I owe many thanks to the undergraduate and graduate students in my seminars, who brought to my attention work that contributed to the improvement of this book, read draft chapters, and inspired me to revise them under a different light.

At Rice, my heartfelt gratitude goes to two PhD candidates in particular: Nikki Moore and Olivia Wolf. Nikki Moore has collaborated with me on countless projects, both at MIT, where she received her master's degree, and at Rice, where she was again both my student and, in another sense, my colleague. Like collaborating scientists, Nikki and I coauthored articles that drew from my work on eugenics and hers on sustainability, and my work on biopolitics and hers on agriculture. Through this partnership, I came to more fully value interdisciplinarity and intellectual dialogues. In her thoughtful reading of my manuscript, Nikki brought her political and social sensitivity to bear on her discussions with me, always deepening my investigations and analyses. And Olivia Wolf went beyond navigating archives in Buenos Aires, where she found missing plans and relevant documents, strengthening my understanding of early-twentieth-century Argentine literature and supporting me in the arduous job of building a bibliography and finding images and their copyrights.

Many different skills are needed to transform a manuscript into a book, and I would like to thank the editorial team at the University of Texas Press, in particular my editor Robert P. Devens, for his lively and early interest in my work, for his sensitive commentary, and for turning this arduous task into a real joy; Sarah McGavick, for her support throughout the process of revising texts and evaluating images; and Lynne Chapman and Nancy Warrington, for the meticulous process of copyediting this book. My gratitude also goes to Sophia Beal, whose insightful remarks on the porous frontiers between fiction and reality, and culture and science, in modern Brazil were simply invaluable, and to Christina Cogdell, whose expertise in the field and sharp criticism deeply enriched my book. Both reviews made my book much better. My thanks also go to Bruno Carvalho at Princeton University and Felipe Correa at Harvard Graduate School of Design, the coeditors of Lateral Exchanges: Architecture, Urban Development, and Transnational Practices, the new series that this book inaugurates, for their complicity and support during this process. I celebrate their initiative to make us rethink our preconceived maps of the world—the geopolitical hierarchies that omit influential regions such as Latin America from our understanding of the global project of modernity.

I would be remiss if I did not also thank Dianne Harris, dean of the College of Humanities at the University of Utah, and Abby Collier, editor in History and Philosophy of Science, Architecture/Built Environment at Pittsburgh University Press, whose interest in my work was a meaningful part of this process. I also extend my thanks to William Howze for his resourceful assistance finding copyrights and images for this book. I am particularly honored to have received the SAH/Mellon Author Award from the Society of Architectural Historians to help fund image licensing and reproduction costs.

On a personal note, I would like to thank a group of dear friends and family members who provided critical support at different stages of what has, at times, been a difficult process. I feel moved and proud to mention Mierta Capaul, Benjamín Caballero, Luis López-Durán, Alicia Molero, Phillipa McDonald, Gabriela Gamboa, Nancy Bulkeley, Tom Bulkeley, Susan Goldman, Manuel Delgado, Olivier Humbert, Lisette Avila, Juan Carlos López-Durán, Caroline Reeves, Ignacio Inglessis, Isabella Bulkeley, and María Inés Sicardi. I will never forget the generous support given to me by my youngest brother, Néstor López-Durán. I do not know the precise moment when he went from being my little brother to being my guide, the scholar and the person I am most proud of in the world. And finally, to the López-Durán clan, my family, my intimate circle of love and support: it has been a joy to have each of you feeling so close during the long making of this book.

This book would not have happened without:

my life partner, Carlos Pelayo Martínez, an endless source of love, friendship, and unconditional support. He inspires me every day with his intelligence and humor. He is, without a doubt, the main source of my joy, my beloved refuge, my resting place. Thank you for accepting this work as part of our life together.

and

my soul sister, Marilyn Levine, who will always remain my intellectual compass, the best interlocutor a researcher could have, a narrative voice I have internalized, and the best present this work brought to my life.

This accomplishment is as much theirs as it is mine.

EUGENICS IN THE GARDEN

Q. Similes Lundi à midi   meme grandeur, ils
                                           representant au Sommet,
                                           quelus le dessin, la plume
                                           et sujlet du but au Sommet de la Sphere

                                                              Barteplet

INTRODUCTION

*. . . to make nature herself an accomplice
in the crime of political inequality.*

—NICOLAS DE CONDORCET

For the World's Fair at the turn of the twentieth century, the geographer and anarchist Élisée Reclus proposed the construction of an enormous globe at the border of the Seine that would represent the inevitable interaction between the natural milieu of living beings and the dynamics of heredity. Complementing the two monumental symbols of technology and industry—the Tour Eiffel and the Gallery of Machines—built for the 1889 World's Fair in Paris, the globe of 1900 was conceived as a temple to science itself, offering both an accurate representation of the earth's spherical surface and a panorama of its human evolution. At a scale of 1:100,000, Reclus' model would display the earth's relief with its continents and seas, with its mountains, rivers, and plains.[1] Rising from the bottom, two curved elevators and a serpentine ramp circling the globe would allow visitors to progressively traverse the various landscapes of the earth, from pole to pole and hemisphere to hemisphere. Emerging from the center of the spiral ramp, a vertical elevator would take visitors directly to the interior of the earth—to a panorama of human evolution. Just as the 1889 Eiffel Tower offered a 360-degree view of the city, Reclus' great globe would offer an accurate view of the entire landscape of the earth to inaugurate a new century. In Reclus' words, this "scientific" view of nature, "in perfect accordance with reality," would also offer to each visitor a sense of participating, of feeling "at home," a sense of belonging to "the same family."[2] Yet the colossal globe was not a simple testament to human beings' capacity

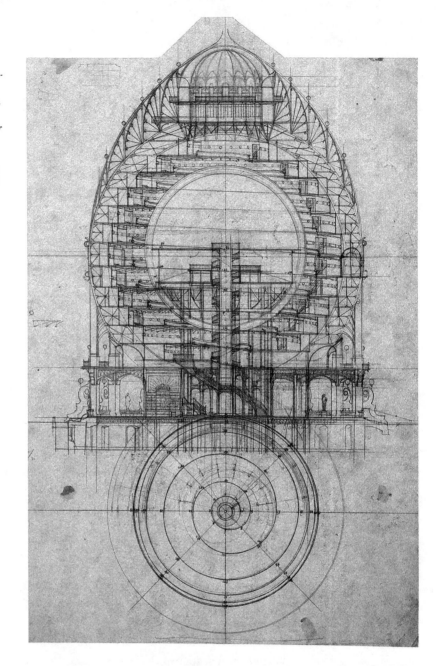

to re-create nature, themselves included. In fact, an aerial view of the earth provided by the globe's spiral ramp forecast a new form of seeing and control that, some years later, would inspire Le Corbusier (as we shall see in chapter 4) to cultivate this new understanding of the interaction between society and the environment—one in which society is seen as an abstract subject without history and culture, and land itself exists under surveillance and management.[3] This very social and environmental interplay would come to embody the driving force of a particular form of eugenics—the social and biological movement that strove for nothing less than the "improvement" of the human race, implicating heredity and the environment as its primary tools.

This book examines the dynamics of this form of eugenics, which first appeared in France and then spread throughout Latin America—the only region in the "developing" world where eugenics was systematically implemented and institutionalized.[4] By targeting the newly wrought confluence of evolutionary theories and the environment that Reclus' globe championed, this book investigates a form of eugenics based on Jean-Baptiste Lamarck's theory of the "inheritance of acquired characteristics" that conceptualized evolution as driven by adaptation to environmental changes, in stark contrast to mainstream eugenics, which viewed evolution as impervious to the environment, driven solely by control over breeding.[5] By "mainstream," I refer to the form of eugenics based on Mendelian genetics, which asserted that hereditary information repeats itself from generation to generation, thereby being fixed and impermeable to environmental influence. Yet it was the transformative capacity of the environment at the center of Lamarck's theory—at the time largely discredited by a significant segment of the European and US scientific community—that appealed so profoundly to the modernizing agenda of Latin American nations. Thus, eagerly adopted by Latin American elites, these Lamarckian discourses—an invitation to social engineering—set the stage for a particular orientation toward environmental-genetic interaction,

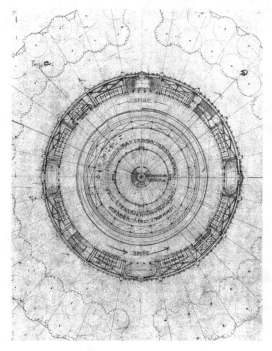

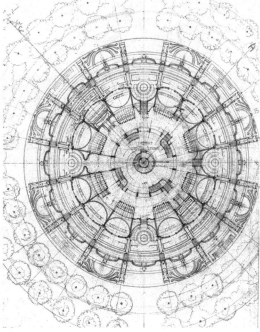

empowering an apparatus that made race, gender, class, and the built environment critical measurements of modernity and progress. This new science mesmerized intellectuals and technocrats on both sides of the Atlantic, from physicians and architects to reformers and urban planners, permeating almost every aspect of human life.[6]

As a remarkable foreshadowing of Lamarckian eugenics, Reclus carefully selected an all-star multidisciplinary team to design the globe. He first invited the French architect Louis Bonnier (1856–1946), the director of architectural services and public projects for the city of Paris, who would become an active member of the Musée social, a politically conservative institution created to investigate the social problems of modern France.[7] To design the globe's panorama, "Documentaire de l'évolution humaine," he invited the scientist Étienne-Jules Marey (1830–1904), who in his early preoccupation with the movement of blood, as well as human and animal locomotion, invented the technique of chronophotography—instrumental to the development of the first X-rays and to the advent of cinematography.[8] The team also consulted with the naturalist Alfred Russel Wallace, who, along with Charles Darwin, had developed the theory of evolution by natural selection; and with the botanist, sociologist, and urban planner Patrick Geddes, Reclus' close friend, who viewed society and

FIGURE 0.5.
Élisée Reclus, Louis Bonnier, and Étienne-Jules Marey, The Great Globe, *1900. Elevation showing the silhouette of the antique Trocadéro. Project 1897–1898. Fonds Louis Bonnier 035. SIAF/Cité de l'architecture et du patrimoine/Archives d'architecture du XXe siècle, Paris.*

ROUNDING EIFFEL TOWER

ROUND EIFFEL TOWER

FIGURES 0.6–0.7.
Brazilian aviator
Alberto Santos-Dumont
flying around the
Eiffel Tower, October
1901. Published in
Alberto Santos-Dumont,
My Airships: The Story
of My Life *(London:*
G. Richards, 1904).

the city from a biological standpoint, acknowledging the eugenic position that "social heritage provides another means by which human beings can inherit the results of earlier generations' interaction with the environment."[9] It was clear that evolutionary thoughts formed the ideological groundwork for modernists worldwide. However, in France during the turn of the century, it was not Darwin but Lamarck, the evolutionist—convinced that changes induced by the environment were biologically transmitted from generation to generation—who forecast a dominant axiom that brought architecture to center stage: change the environment, change the person.[10] By the early twentieth century, Lamarckian ideas had moved from scientific theories to social policies and to the very center of the construction of the modern built environment. It is thus evident that the great globe was not only a unique visual machine designed for the 1900 World's Fair, to display the geography of the earth, as noted, with a higher degree of accuracy than previously achieved, or to forecast that new form of seeing brought about by aviation; it was also the very embodiment of a new codependent alliance between humans and physical space, which together became the core technological agenda of modernity in Latin America and its ultimate instrument: eugenics.

THE COMPLICITY OF MEDICINE AND ARCHITECTURE
AS THE HANDMAIDENS OF EUGENICS

Arguing for a reconsideration of our understanding of eugenics and its reverberating influence, I explore in this book the international prolif- eration of a particular strain that moved from the realm of medicine to architecture and urban planning, becoming a critical instrument in the crafting of modernity in France during the Third Republic (1870–1940) and in the culturally and scientifically influential nation- states of Latin America. In the Latin world, eugenics—the so-called science of race improvement—gave scientific authority to social fears, respectability to class and racial prejudice, and extraordinary power to the construction and management of the built environment. As such, eugenics was understood and accepted as a science that lent credibility and legitimacy to modernists' anxieties about social and biological degeneration. In France, eugenics ideas and practices took root well before Darwin, and even before the moment in 1883 in which the British scientist Francis Galton coined the term "eugenics" (from the Greek εὐγενής, meaning "well born"), to define the modern "sci- ence" that "deals with all influences that improve the inborn qualities of a race; also with those that develop them to the utmost advan- tage."[11] Fueled by increasingly urgent fears of degeneration, French physicians visualized medicine as the apparatus capable of regulating reproduction and disciplining society. In Latin America, during the last decades of the nineteenth and the first decades of the twentieth centuries, medicine became "a rallying cry for the modern secular elite."[12] In other words, medical science was embraced as a form of progressive knowledge that viewed positivism, the political philoso- phy that sought to solve all of society's ills through science, as a way to bring the "order and progress" deemed necessary to transform Latin American countries into modern nations.[13] In Latin America, while the adoption of positivism changed from country to country and dif- fered from thinker to thinker, positivism was reformulated in the light of Darwinian and Lamarckian evolutionary theories, explaining social and political problems in biological and racial terms and affirming the inevitability of social evolution and progress.[14] Although this influen- tial doctrine was not uniform in the ways it was adopted across Latin America, the thrust toward both medical science and the physical en- vironment was a constant. Investigating this profound connection at the center of Lamarckian eugenics, I introduce an interrogative model that brings together two modern concepts—*milieu* and *biopower*— associated with an ongoing Latin-European preoccupation, *biopoli- tics*.[15] First, the notion of milieu was borrowed by Auguste Comte, the founder of positivism, from Lamarck's evolutionary theories and then transformed into a comprehensive system that brings together society and space in a state of contingency.[16] Historically, milieu, as defined by the French philosopher of science Georges Canguilhem, was a relational and variable system that, in the eighteenth century, mutated from physics to biology, and then, during the nineteenth century, from biology to sociology, then to geography, and finally, at the turn of the twentieth century, to urban planning, persisting today in the field of architecture through a global fixation on sustainability. In this conception of milieu, Canguilhem follows Lamarck to identify the absence of an intrinsic harmony between living beings and their surroundings, and a consequent mutual process of struggle and adaptation.[17] This socio-spatial struggle becomes highly discernible when we consider how positivist discourses, invested with "apolitical" scientific authority promising progress and discipline, penetrated the modern conception of physical spaces—natural and architectural. Second, the notion of biopower refers to a political technology whose goal was to intervene in human life. As observed by Michel Foucault, this technology was developed as a dualistic technique: one based on the "anatomo-politics" of the human body in order to achieve its optimization in a system of production; and the other based on the biopolitics of populations to regulate the basic mechanisms of life: birth, morbidity, and mortality.[18] Building on Foucault's work, the Italian philosopher Roberto Esposito defines biopolitics as a regime that has "no other object than the maintenance and expansion of life."[19] By exposing the complexity of the biopolitical lexicon and Foucault's indistinction between the terms "biopower" and "biopolitics," Esposito asks: "How are we to comprehend a political government of life? In what sense does life govern politics and in what sense does politics govern life?" Identifying biopolitics as "politics in the name of life," and biopower as "life subjected to the command of politics," Esposito shows how the pursuit of biological wellness implies a constant extermination or segregation of others: those who represent a threat, the source of disease, corruption, and degeneration.[20] Brought together at the end of the nineteenth century, to manage both the individual and the collective body, these two mechanisms of biopower and biopolitics became the main targets of the state's regulation of health, hygiene, welfare, and space. It is precisely the critical connection between milieu and biopower/biopolitics, as manifested in a new form of hygiene called social hygiene, that I interrogate in this book. It is important to keep in mind that this form of hygiene, which became a movement in its own right, was mostly a set of economic and moral practices preoccupied with the influences arising from the milieu and from the fruits of human capital: production and reproduction.[21] This is particularly evident when one considers the medical origin of Lamarckian eugenics. As the French historian of medicine Jacques Léonard emphasized, its medical roots are what made eugenics in France pre-Galtonian and even pre-Darwinian. It was Léonard who first identified eugenics, not as an abstract foreign theory, but as a practice performed by a specific social group: physicians. According to Léonard, rather than collecting genealogical charts and statistics as mainstream eugenicists such as anthropologists, demographers, and statisticians did, French eugenicists, mostly physicians, used medical knowledge to create law and policies.[22] With this as our backdrop, this book moves our understanding of eugenics forward by analyzing the international proliferation of Lamarckian eugenics in particular and its association with the utopian ideas that forecast both new perfect societies and perfect spaces, and the early-twentieth-century practices of urban planning, architecture, and landscape design.

Set in a region of the world virtually unexamined in the literature of eugenics, this book gave me the opportunity to delve deeply into the theories, dialogues, and practices of modernists in France and Latin America. Over the last decades, there have been some studies of eugenics in France, but Nancy Leys Stepan's 1991 book, *The Hour of Eugenics*, remains the only comprehensive examination of eugenics in the Latin American region.[23] By going beyond the still-prevailing Anglo–North American geographical focus of most literature on eugenics, my work contributes to twenty-five years of scholarship that posits eugenics as anything but a single homogeneous movement, implemented under the same set of goals and policies throughout the world.[24] The history of eugenics in Latin America shows that this movement was not always politically conservative and neo-Mendelian—both characteristics attributed to what has been known as mainstream eugenics. The reception of evolutionary ideas and the drive to make profound changes in the name of modernization made Latin American nations particularly receptive to the Lamarckian inheritance theory that postulates that structural changes in living beings were caused by adaptation to environmental conditions, which could be re-created and managed by humans.

However, it would be too simplistic to imagine that there was un-challenged acceptance of the profound impact of the environment on human evolution. In fact, the principle of the "inheritance of acquired characteristics" endorsed by Lamarck and accepted by the majority of scientists of the nineteenth century, including Darwin, was soon disputed.[25] In the first place, this theory was debated during the early 1890s by the German cytologist August Weismann, who proposed the autonomous germinal plasma theory, which argues that hereditary information is fixed and impermeable to the environment; and then through the rediscovery of hereditary laws by Gregor Mendel, according to which hereditary information reappears without changes in the following generation. In this manner, Mendelian genetics confirmed the inviolability of Weismann's plasma theory. From the moment in which Galton, in his attempt to create a science capable of breeding a better race, distinguished nature from nurture, he triggered a debate about how evolutionary changes transpired from generation to generation—a debate that surfaced throughout the twentieth century and continues to this day. Convinced that human attributes such as intelligence and talent run in families, Galton championed nature—genetics or inborn biological factors—over nurture—environmental influences, including social, political, and cultural circumstances. By so doing, Galton established a mutually exclusive dyad in which nature (heredity) was associated with science, and nurture (environment) with ideology. Yet in spite of the influence of Galton's theoretical canon, and the century-long effort of hereditarians and environmentalists alike to declare the end of the nature-nurture debate, this highly charged dispute never ceased. Thus, in France, Lamarckian theory surged again and again in the public arena as a way to argue for the transformative power of the environment. In fact, at the turn of the nineteenth century, a contingency of scientists worldwide, calling themselves neo-Lamarckians, extended Lamarck's ideas to global arenas, including the United States, where environmental reforms for the sake of race betterment were known as "euthenics."[26] This reliance on the power of the environment, in turn, gave efficacy to social ideologies "undergirding theories of mental development, race formation, racial and gender differences" and practices of architecture and urban planning and even theories of modern art.[27] Over the past two decades, Lamarckian ideas have reappeared worldwide as a result of new developments in biology, including global genomic research and the rise of epigenetics, which essentially posits that gene expression, outside of the genetic code itself, produces an environmentally driven transformation of individual traits, thus reinvigorating the nature-nurture dichotomy.[28]

This brings us to the main contribution of this book: an examination of Lamarckian eugenics' influence on the construction of the modern built environment, unveiling a hitherto underplayed collusion between aesthetics, science, and politics at the core of Latin

American architectural modernism. By adopting a transnational and interdisciplinary model of historical investigation, I identify in this work a crucial dialectic within the Lamarckian strain of eugenics that first developed in France within the realm of medical science and then crossed the Atlantic to ultimately instrumentalize architecture and urban planning as a means to engineer human life. Specifically, through my analysis of medical and architectural reports, blueprints, photographs, periodicals, and unpublished and published primary sources in scientific and architectural archives, I show how this strain of eugenics, embedded in medical discourses, was appropriated into the practices of French and Latin American social reformers, architects, and urban planners. This includes physicians and architect members of the Parisian Musée social; reformers and urban planners in Brazil and Argentina; and international figures such as the most celebrated modernist, the architect-artist-writer Le Corbusier, and the critically influential eugenicist and 1912 Nobel laureate in Physiology or Medicine, Alexis Carrel, whose central role in the propagation of eugenics in the name of nothing less than the "remaking" of humankind will become quite clear in the upcoming discussion.[29] How these discourses traveled across boundaries between disciplines and countries, how they were appropriated by widely divergent political agents with distinctive ideological agendas, and how they found their way into practice define the analytical model I designed to examine a form of eugenics in which science, aesthetics, and morality became almost indistinguishable.

THE MIGRATION OF FRANCE'S "SCIENTIFIC MODERNISM" INTO LATIN AMERICA

While investigating the complicity of medicine and architecture in Lamarckian eugenics, it is also important to trace the precise mechanisms that enabled France to have such a profound impact on the crafting of Latin American nations in the early twentieth century—particularly on the scientific modernization of Brazil and Argentina. French cultural influence in the construction of modern Latin American nations has been extensively analyzed in the history of urbanism. These studies recognize the primacy of French urbanism and humanism in Latin America from the last decades of the nineteenth century to World War II, the event that marked the beginning of North America's dominance in the region.[30] Some of these studies acknowledged originality in the implementation of Haussmannian models in Latin America, arguing, as Ángel Rama does in his seminal 1984 book, *La ciudad letrada* (*The Lettered City*), that these urban, surgical interventions were not simply copies of Second Empire Paris but a "genuine recreation" of Latin Americans' obsession with the French élan.[31] These urban interventions were seen by the elites as the means to eradicate their Spanish and Portuguese colonial past and reinvent their cities as progressive, independent megalopolises. However, the end of Latin America's Belle Époque, in which boulevards and Frenchified buildings redrew the urban fabric and the features of many Latin American cities, overlapped with a period of scientific discoveries, evolutionary theories, and medical concepts. These historic breakthroughs embody notions of physical space that Latin America put into practice in the construction of its modern nations. My book identifies the migration of these developments in France to noncolonial yet culturally related countries in Latin America, pinpointing the cross-pollination of scientific ideology and spatial practices fueling the clinical agenda of architectural modernism.[32] More specifically, uncovering material that has been largely unexamined by art and architectural historians, this interrogative model intertwines the history of science, urbanism, architecture, and landscape design with debates on race, gender, immigration, and nation in two Latin American countries, Brazil and Argentina, the most densely populated in the region.

Between the last decade of the nineteenth century and the mid-twentieth century, the process of industrialization and accelerated urbanization that took place in Brazil and Argentina provoked a population explosion that transformed bourgeois cities into real metropolises.[33] Yet the choice to explore these two specific countries was primarily a response to environmental and racial factors: first, during the turn of the nineteenth century, Brazil and Argentina were the main territories of environmental transformation, aided by the ideology of progress and the concomitant institutionalization of eugenics; second, more than half of the population of these two countries was of nonnative origin—African slaves in Brazil and European immigrants in Argentina.[34] By exploring the social, political, and aesthetic dynamics of the Brazilian and Argentinean quest to "un-underdevelop" themselves in their crafting of modernity, I show in this work that in both countries eugenics acted as a pervasive agent of modernity, dismantling not only the prevailing view that eugenics was essentially an Anglo-American movement tied to Mendelian genetics but also exclusively a reactionary one associated with Nazism and fascism. Brazil, a country that had received the world's largest slave population from colonial times to 1888, became a republic as late as 1889, only a year after the final abolition of slavery. During the period from 1889 to 1930, Brazil saw the most extraordinary physical transformation in its history. In fact, Rio de Janeiro alone faced dramatic human-made interventions into its natural landscape and urban fabric, including the complete demolition of a populated mountain; the redesign of its southern shoreline; and the creation of not only avenues, tunnels, and majestic parks but also lush tropical forests.[35] Argentina, a country that had acquired its independence in 1810, over a decade earlier than Brazil, received a net immigration of 3.5 million people between 1857 and 1930, meaning that about 60 percent of the total population increase during that time could be attributed to immigration.[36] During those decades, Argentina became the second-largest destination for European immigrants (second only to the United States) and one of the most urbanized countries in the world, with more than 80 percent of its population living in urban agglomerations.[37] As this book shows, these two Latin American nations offer a rich and diverse spectrum of social structures, economic development, racial ideologies, and territorial characteristics that expose the way Lamarckian eugenics fueled the search for progress through spatial politics in Latin America. Although these two countries had inexorable differences, during the first half of the twentieth century, both demonstrated an imperialistic attitude toward France rather than toward Portugal or Spain, their colonial nations. In fact, France became the most influential country in the region, culturally and scientifically. It was to France that Latin American physicians, biologists, architects, and artists went for their professional training. It was also to France that intellectuals and national leaders looked for inspiration and direction. French was the second language learned by intellectuals and scientists and a common language adopted for their publications.[38] In other words, France became a primary catalyst for scientific modernism in Latin America.

Although the exact origin remains a subject of debate, the term "Latin America" has largely been credited to a "pan-Latinist" movement that emerged within intellectual circles in Paris in the 1850s. The French economist and Saint-Simonian Michel Chevalier, a member of these circles and a close collaborator of Napoleon III, argued for a "Latin race" to justify France's political and economic offensive throughout Spanish and Portuguese America in the 1860s.[39] In his support of French expansionism, Chevalier differentiated the Latin nations of Europe (France, Belgium, Spain, Italy, and Portugal) from Europe's Germanic, Anglo-Saxon, and Slavic nations, visualizing the Latin population of the Americas as an extension of a Latin European family under France's leadership and in contrast to the Anglo-Saxon population of the new world. Thus was "Latin America" conceived as a geopolitical entity in mid-nineteenth-century transatlantic debates over the relationship between race and nation.[40] Other accounts, such as the one defended by the Uruguayan philosopher Arturo Ardao, argued that the concept of Latin America emerged even before France's intervention in Mexico in the 1860s. Ardao attributed the first use of the term to José María Torres Caicedo in a poem titled "Las dos Américas," published in 1857 in *El Correo de Ultramar*, a Parisian Spanish-language newspaper. Other Latin American intellectuals argued that the term was used for the first time by the Chilean politician Francisco Bilbao in a speech delivered also in Paris in June 1856, before the publication of Torres Caicedo's poem.[41] In any case, the accounts of both Torres Caicedo and Bilbao, who were preoccupied by the threat to Latin American sovereignty represented by US expansion of capitalist activities, marked a clear delineation between South America and North America, between the Latin race and the Saxon race, which included notions of Pan-Latin racial unity similar to those promulgated in France by Chevalier and his collaborators. In a quest to defeat Latin America's association with backwardness, fundamentally due to its tropical climate and native, African, and mestizo populations, the elites of the "Latin" countries in the Americas eagerly adopted this geopolitical construction for themselves. In spite of Latin America's racially differentiated countries and regions, the so-called Latin race that permeates these nations satisfied the elites' imperative to distinguish themselves as essentially European.[42] Clearly, the term "Latin America" emerged from racially motivated "ideas of progress and modernity" that were codified in spatial terms. Indeed, ever since the late 1890s, "race . . . [has] constructed space" and "space [has] constructed race."[43]

But what activated this disquieting symbiosis of space and race? How did the built environment become the arena for social engineering in Latin America? We cannot answer these questions without considering the powerful triad of modernism-modernization-modernity that framed this highly charged symbiosis. By *modernism*, I refer specifically to architectural modernism, the movement that employed space as power in its crafting of modernity, participating in a global strategy of social engineering, legitimized by the authority of science. *Modernization*, the process of economic and social change, assumes a universal model of development established by the West to which the rest of the nations are compared, thus dividing the globe into developed and underdeveloped nations, into "the West/modern and the Rest/nonmodern."[44] From this partitioning, *modernity* became a hegemonic discourse among those in power, and a desirable and ethical imperative to be reached and replicated by the rest of the world.[45]

Arguing for a reconsideration of our understanding of eugenics in this book, I place modernity outside conventional center-periphery models to recognize it as a product of multiple networks and transnational interconnections. Most importantly, this book shows that, given the complexities of modernism and modernization in the global world, we can no longer see just one side or the other, separating Europe from the Americas and North from South. For this reason, it becomes imperative to recognize modernity and its techno-cultural partner modernism as worldwide phenomena. Thus, this book contributes not only to the body of scholarship that analyzes the work of French architects and urban planners in Latin America, or Le Corbusier's international role; it also makes the case for resituating their oeuvre—along with their scientific and architectural Latin American counterparts—within a truly global context, as major components of a world culture that posits a new understanding of modernity and its often denied discontents.

ORGANIZATION OF THE BOOK

At the beginning of the twentieth century, the primacy of the medical sciences and the leadership of physicians in Latin America were not necessarily responses to the sanitary needs of the population, as they were in the case of France and other European countries. Instead, in Latin America, medicine became a hegemonic method to study and then reconfigure the national population. As previously emphasized, my work demonstrates how medicine also became a method for the reconfiguration of the physical environment. Although the term "social Darwinism" actually refers to the laissez-faire idea of not interfering with the "natural selection" process or the progression of disease, physicians in Latin America appropriated the term as a way to activate the most comprehensive evolutionary ideas that allowed them to reimagine society and the nation in biological terms.[46] In so doing, the city became a complex biological organism to be treated and healed by reformers, architects, and urban planners. To effectively examine how eugenics used physical space in its attempt to "normalize" Latin America's heterogeneous population, I have adopted a methodological approach through which the dynamics of modernity and eugenics are investigated in the fields of utopianism (chapter 1), urbanism (chapter 2), architecture and landscape design (chapter 3), and modernism itself (chapter 4). I hope this discipline-based approach will spark a new understanding of modernity as an elaborately conceived ethos of progress and rational order that was carried out through systematic spatialization.

From the early-twentieth-century Latin American utopian narratives, which intertwined eugenics and space, to the construction of supermodern Brasília in the late 1950s, this book shows how the built environment became the main "transmitter of modernism" in Brazil and Argentina.[47] To do so, I demonstrate how a yearning for progress mandated an agenda-driven delineation between civilization and wilderness, organization and chance, normal and abnormal, purity and contamination, and beauty and ugliness, as applied not just to nature and plant and animal species but to the human species as well.[48] Although modern architecture and urbanism have mostly been perceived as icons of progress and positive social change, it is crucial to understand that spatial production also became embedded in gender and race discrimination and class distinctions. Disclosing the stage on which Brazilian and Argentinean modernism emerged out of the complicity between aesthetics and ideology, and under state patronage, I ultimately demonstrate the empowering apparatus that placed physicians and architects among these countries' main technocrats and made beauty a critical measurement of progress.

Chapter 1 sets the stage for this story through a travelogue of Latin American utopian narratives that, at the turn of the century, portrayed perfect societies and perfect spaces, both achieved through the mechanism of eugenics. These societies and spaces were imagined not as futuristic fantasies but as plausible territories of transformation. Therefore, utopian texts, or what can be called early Latin American science fiction, morphed from pure fiction to concrete plans—from fantasy to social policy—engendering an intimate connection between utopia, eugenics, and the built environment. This chapter highlights how Latin American utopias, written mostly by physicians and published in scientific journals, emerged at the very intersection of the ideal as codified by the eugenics movement, with its focus on race, gender, nature, and urban space.

Chapter 2 examines the practices of physicians and architects who were members of the Musée social—that interdisciplinary institution founded in Paris in 1895 to study the social problems of modern France. Specifically, this chapter focuses on the interplay of three technocrats: the natalist Adolphe Pinard, who revitalized the concept of *puericulture*, a human analogue of agriculture for the "scientific cultivation" of the mother-child unit; the hygienist Louis

Landouzy, who, by focusing his attention on the "social diseases" of modernity—alcohol, syphilis, and tuberculosis—argued for the cultivation of the human species through his concept of *hominiculture*; and the architect Donat-Alfred Agache, who envisioned Rio de Janeiro, Brazil's capital city at the time, as a laboratory for social reform. Their combined work significantly influenced both French and Latin American eugenic discourses, but it was in Latin America where these discourses found their way into practice, and urbanism became both a eugenic technology and its ultimate aesthetic form.

Chapter 3 moves the inquiry to Argentina to examine the confluence of medicine, society, and milieu used to "normalize" a so-called feeble society in the name of constructing a modern nation. Deciphering the binary code of medicine and society under the spell of architecture and the city, it interrogates modern architecture's clinical agenda. It also balances the social history of the modern urban institutions that attempted to ameliorate the population of Buenos Aires with the architectures that were imagined alongside them as national clinical projects of healing and social reform. In this way, this chapter explores the means of imagining a network of buildings, parks, gardens, playgrounds, reformatories, schools, and even the family home—the apparatuses of health and reproduction—to reveal how this complex technological system regulated global flows of people, rationalized sexuality, and sought to purify reproduction in the new Latin world. Prescribed by physicians and executed by architects, these urban spaces—specifically, new medical and disciplinary *dispositifs* ultimately aiming to reconfigure the family and the nation—emerged out of prophylactic and pronatalist outlooks, as well as out of the belief that progress derives from the dualism of life and matter.

Chapter 4 explores the relationship between modernism and eugenics, chiefly through the influential work of Le Corbusier. Examining Le Corbusier's alignment with eugenics—from his formulation of universal type-needs to his Modulor and its normative human body—this last chapter reveals how architecture was made complicit in a genetically inspired program that mirrored eugenics' attempts to "improve" the human race. Between Le Corbusier's first trip to Brazil in 1929 and his second in 1936, his discourses were centered on the racial and sexual "other"—the primitive, nature, and death; but it was in Rio de Janeiro during the summer of 1936 that Le Corbusier clearly aligned himself with eugenics.[49] This chapter investigates a global moment in which Le Corbusier embraced eugenics' ideology as a viable doctrine wherein the built environment would be put to work in the so-called remaking of humankind.

Overall, this book is a transnational story that grapples with theories of modernity, modernism, and modernization, placing architecture and urbanism at the very center of eugenics' espousal of white superiority. What the French physicians and architects thought was going to be the pure and direct materialization of Lamarckian eugenics turned out to be much more of a negotiation between positivist ideologies and Latin America's different approaches to its racial and environmental reality. In my examination of the multiple protocols of institutional contexts, economies, technologies, politics, and sciences that shaped architectural modernism in Latin America, race and environment materialized as the primary devices used by technocrats and the state to breed a new society and its discrete forms of habitation. Yet, I have been asked far too many times by scholars and architects alike: Why do we need to talk about racism at a time when everyone was supposedly racist anyway? Why do we need to know about Le Corbusier's complicity with eugenics? And, in the end, what is the connection between eugenics and architecture? To the skeptics and to those who would like to preserve architecture as a pure techno-aesthetic artifact, I would say that in the first case, racism was and still is a main rationalization in the name of progress; we are not yet cognizant of how race is still the main driving force in the geopolitics of space. In this sense, race is a social construction that dangerously legitimizes the conviction that inequality is inevitable. This conviction has justified slavery, apartheid, genocide, and its current politically charged forms of segregation and racism. In the second case, Le Corbusier, the genius of modernism, was clearly influenced by theories of evolution and driven by an allegiance to the white race as a superior normative model that crafted not only *his* doctrine but also the global doctrine and global forms of high modernism. Le Corbusier's alliance with evolutionary theories, which fully materialized after his first trips to Latin America, led him to disclose a direct connection between race and environment, underscoring how much race had become an agent to construct space, and that space, in turn, constructs race. It is not by chance, then, that the built environment became the main "transmitter of modernism" in Latin America.[50]

So, this is a book about something society remains reluctant to discuss. It is a book that places at its very center the disturbing relationship between racial theories and the canonically embraced production of modernity that academics, curators, and architects today remain unwilling to discuss. It is a book about modernism's systematic exclusion of the disenfranchised—the native and black populations, the poor, the sick, the non-European immigrants, and other "undesirables"—in the name of progress and modernization. While the book recognizes that modernists were mostly well intended in their instrumentalization of space to improve human conditions, it reveals the actual power of the state and global capitalism in their striving to homogenize society through space. In other words, this is a book about how eugenics and architecture became intertwined to achieve the normalization, commoditization, and productivity of human beings and their environment.

PRACTICING UTOPIA

Eugenics and the Medicalization
of the Built Environment

FROM FICTION TO PRACTICE

A few months before his death, the British scientist Francis
Galton (1822–1911) turned to fiction to depict a utopian
state organized according to his view of heredity. Influenced by his cousin Charles Darwin's *On the Origin of
Species*, Galton was the first to propose that human populations could
be engineered and improved by selective breeding.[1] In his fictional
narrative, Galton, who had earlier coined the term "eugenics" from
the Greek *eugenēs*, meaning "well born," visualized his modern utopia
named Kantsaywhere.[2] At the power center of Kantsaywhere was the
Eugenic College, an institution that exercised absolute control over
the entire population.[3] Moved by the aim to evolve a "superior race of
men," the Eugenic College defined its main mission as the evaluation
and classification of citizens to identify those with optimum traits.
A medical examination was mandatory for every citizen to obtain a
"Pass certificate for 'Genetic' qualities." Certified physicians were sent
to the main entry posts to examine the arriving immigrants. Those who
passed the preliminary examination were certified as acceptable, with
"fitness in body and mind." Those who failed, considered "undesirable
as individuals and dangerous to the community," were required to
emigrate and were escorted to ships "to convey them back to whence
they came."[4] The cost of deportation and other incentives were offered
"on the condition of their never returning." If they refused to emigrate,
they were either segregated into labor colonies outside the city where

celibacy was mandatory or were allowed to stay under rigorous surveillance "so long as they propagated no children."[5] Conversely, those who passed the medical examination were entitled to compete in an "Honorable Examination" and then to be classified and rewarded.[6] Citizens equipped with the highest genetic qualifications were given financial incentives—farms, houses, hostels, and funds, all used "to encourage early marriages [and greater procreation] among the most highly diplomaed."[7] Galton's eugenic utopia characterized the mainline of the eugenics movement at the turn of the twentieth century with its primacy of nature over nurture. It seems that for Galton, Kantsaywhere represented a world ruled just by nature—genetics or inborn biological factors. There, nurture—external environmental factors or social, political, and cultural circumstances—was simply irrelevant.[8] For Galton, desirable qualities were only transmitted from generation to generation through biological inheritance. Galton was convinced that "race improvement could occur only when nature provided a distinct and heritable organic chance [biologists of the day termed it a sport] upon which selection, natural or eugenic, act [sic]."[9]

FIGURE 1.1.
La Rotonda, Immigrants Hotel, Buenos Aires Harbor. fs4 186, Colección Witcomb. Archivo General de la Nación Dpto. Doc. Fotográficos. Buenos Aires, Argentina.

FIGURE 1.2.
Immigrants from Italy on their way to Buenos Aires on the ocean liner Augustus (Navigazione Generale Italiana), 1939. MUNTREF-Museo de la Inmigración Collection.

FIGURE 1.3.
View of the Great Hall at Ellis Island, where millions of immigrants underwent medical inspection (1902–1913). These people have passed the first mental inspection. William Williams Collection, The Miriam and Ira D. Wallach Division of Art, Prints and Photographs: Photography Collection, The New York Public Library. http:// digitalcollections.nypl .org/items/510d47da -d778-a3d9-e040 -e00a18064a99.

Claiming objectivity, science—in the form of eugenics—became the main social and cultural determinant in Galton's fictional society of Kantsaywhere, where genes were everything.

Kantsaywhere was written as the journal of Professor I. Donoghue, a prosperous immigrant and the main voice of the story. According to him, that which is transmissible by heredity—the natural—was, in fact, the government's most pressing concern. As Donoghue explains,

"... what they are concerned with in one another are the natural, and therefore the only heritable characteristics." Then, he clarifies,

> We have heard much in political talk of the "prairie value" of land, that is to say, of its value when uncultivated, neither fenced nor drained, ploughed nor planted, only to be reached over the waste, and having neither houses nor farm buildings. Applying this idea to man, as if he were land, it is the "prairie value" of him that the Kantsaywhere people seek to ascertain.[10]

The supremacy of the "natural"—whether land or people—was undeniable in Galton's tale. In other words, it was only the "prairie value" of the inhabitants of this utopian society—people as a natural resource—that was significant. But what does this "naturalness" of the population imply if not that people, just like land, are merely technical objects of management and exploitation? Equating people with land, and seeing the population not as political subjects but as primary resources like petroleum, zinc, coal, or salt, is precisely one of the key strategies of modernization.[11]

Through the lens of late-nineteenth and early-twentieth-century Latin American utopian narratives—portraying perfect societies and perfect spaces achieved through the mechanism of eugenics—this chapter identifies an intimate connection between utopia, eugenics, and physical space, in which medical science and the built environment became critical instruments in the process of imagining, planning, and crafting Latin American modern nations and their cities. Tracing the mode in which utopian texts passed from pure fiction to concrete plans, this chapter explores how eugenics, a dominant ideology of progress and the very vehicle of its materialization, infiltrated the imagination and desires of Latin American utopian writers.[12] These writers, mostly physicians and science journalists, were actively participating in the construction of the social, legal, educational, and political structures of Latin America. Thus, they conceived their utopian narratives more as ideological products than as aesthetic ones; they were written in a descriptive manner, in most cases lacking a sophisticated plot, as if they were simply pragmatic plans to be implemented rather than literary expressions.[13] In this sense, these utopian texts written by physicians and science writers were inevitably as scientific as they were futuristic.[14]

It is not by chance that the first chapter of this book begins with a utopian text: Galton's *Kantsaywhere* is not only relevant to this study because it portrays a society organized around eugenics practices, or because these very practices are utopian in nature, but rather because, as implicit in the name ~~Kant-say-where~~, it is an evocation of both ideology and space.[15] As the French architectural historian Françoise Choay describes, architectural treatises and utopian texts represent critical precedents for the discourses of urbanism. From their origins, these two kinds of texts—as seen in Leon Battista Alberti's *De re aedificatoria* (1485) and Thomas More's *Utopia* (1516)—share a critical approach to an existing reality and a theoretical spatial model on which to build the future. Both represent similar mechanisms for the production of space: architectural treatises through the formulation of principles and rules, and utopian texts through the construction of a model.[16] Just as More's *Utopia* was a critique of sixteenth-century England, utopian texts came to life as critiques of an existing reality, offering an untenable model of society and a blueprint for the ideal space it would occupy.[17]

utopian lit

It is important to note that utopian texts proliferated, especially at the end of the eighteenth century, a period of great upheaval and change, and became hyperspatialized during the nineteenth century in concert with the major urban transformations taking place at the time.[18] Proposing a countersociety, utopian texts described new forms of space, in some cases so vividly that they seemed to embody a reality to come. Charles Fourier's *La Phalange* (1829), Étienne Cabet's *Voyage en Icarie* (1840), Robert Owen's *New Lanark* (1841), and Benjamin Ward Richardson's *Hygeia* (1876) are among the nineteenth-century utopias in which spatial organization is described in painstaking detail.[19] Nevertheless, it was not until the nineteenth century—in the shadow of the industrial era, when economy and efficiency became the ideal—that utopian texts reached a more sophisticated level of spatial description, reflecting a clear desire to shift from fiction to reality. In fact, the imagined spaces for ideal societies visualized by Fourier, Cabet, and Owen were constructed and replicated in different regions of the world for the materialization of self-contained societies. It seems inevitable, then, that at the turn of the twentieth century—a period coinciding with a decline in utopian literature and the birth of the utopian movement of eugenics—Latin American texts shared a paradoxical shift from the primacy of the ideal that characterized the utopian genre to the clear pragmatism implicit in the work of planners and reformers during the following decades.[20]

This chapter illuminates these very points of intersection between the ideal, as codified in utopian literature; the institutionalization of the eugenics movement; and the emergence of modern urbanism. It is important to emphasize that most of the Latin American utopian

I. Vol.   Frontifpice   *et 180 .*

Victorin prenant son vol .

narratives were of medical origin, published either in medical journals or in massively distributed periodicals. At the same time, while Latin American elites were trying to transform their countries into modern nations, the biological characteristics of the population became highly relevant economic factors that could be used to subject, manage, and optimize the productivity of their peoples.[21] Thus, eugenics as a form of science provided the means to institutionalize and legitimize a national transformation, using architecture and urban planning as economic and political technologies. At the onset of the twentieth century in Latin America, no complicity was more active than the one between social prophylaxis and urban transformation. At this juncture, eugenics and hygiene became practically one and the same. From Patagonia to the north of Mexico, physicians and science journalists imagined new Latin American capital cities as feasible medical

FIGURE 1.5.
Étienne Cabet, plan for the Icarian utopian city of Cheltenham, Missouri, USA, ca. 1848. Bibliothèque nationale de France, Gallica, http://gallica.bnf.fr.

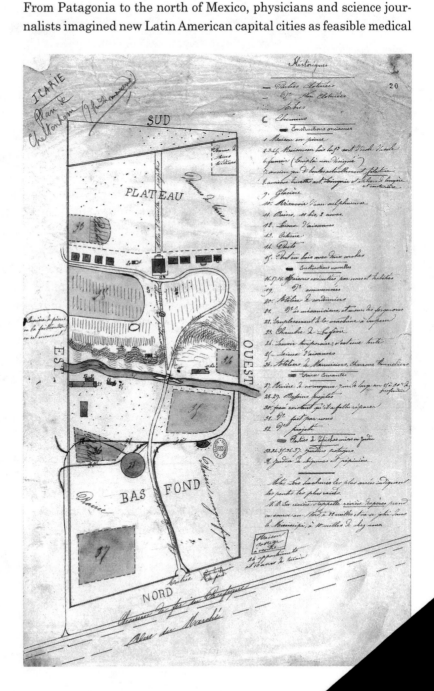

utopias. In some cases, these visions were conjoined with plans for the urban transformations of their territories. In other cases, they anticipated the responsibility of the state in public health policy and the role it would play in the modern construction of the built environment—both natural and architectural.[22] In fact, these utopias were written at a time when Latin American countries, in their quest to "un-underdevelop" themselves, embraced selective immigration and procreation, racial "whitening," and other segregationist programs in parallel with the process of defining their territorial boundaries and organizing their urban and rural spaces.[23]

BIO-UTOPIAS: THE MEDICALIZATION AND BEAUTIFICATION OF BODIES

In his 1959 essay "Medical Utopias," the microbiologist and environmentalist René J. Dubos argued that the study of diseases had greatly contributed to the science of human ecology, which understood individuals as part of the social body.[24] Positivism brought to Latin America a strong conviction that science would provide, along with progress, a world without disease.[25] In this context, there was no better science to embody this modern ideology than medicine, and there was no clearer target of analysis and intervention for this ideology than the city.[26]

The illusion of perfect health has manifested itself in different forms throughout history. At the end of the nineteenth century, scientists and pseudoscientists—hygienists and eugenicists—visualized and promised a utopian world. But their promises were, in fact, caught in a quagmire of clashing evidence and contradictions associated with a modern understanding of both nature and the human body. On the one hand, they believed that a healthy mind and body could only be achieved through a harmonic relationship between human beings and nature.[27] By associating disease with filth, pollution, and microbes, and even with the ugliness that proliferated in the industrial world, they claimed that health could simply be restored by bringing nature back to the urban masses in the form of pure air, pure water, and verdant natural environments.[28] On the other hand, they inevitably found themselves believing that there was nothing nurturing in Mother Nature, and that life was, in reality, a war against the forces of nature.[29] From the end of the eighteenth century, as the French physiologist Marie-François Xavier Bichat theorized, a new concept of the body emerged, where it was not seen as a hollow container but as a contingent of membranes with varying degrees of permeability and stability.[30] The body, according to Bichat, was exquisitely vulnerable to the relentless assaults of the outside environment. Life was, by this definition, "the ensemble of functions by which death is resisted."[31] In this sense, Lamarckian eugenicists were right in their conviction that body and environment critically impact one another. The process of survival—of keeping ourselves alive—is "reflexive and flexible, rather than fixed and confined," as was the common belief.[32] As already noted, this form of eugenics emphasized the convergence of two equally powerful forces for the so-called improvement of the human species: heredity and milieu. In their conception of modern societies and cities, Lamarckian eugenicists exercised a powerful function, bringing together body and environment as plausible territories of intervention and hope.[33]

It is in this context that modern architecture provided the illusion of order and stability. As such, it provided a barrier against the outside elements, a container for breeding healthy humans, and a semicontrolled petri dish in which experiments could be conducted at the scale of the urban population. Thus, a new complicity between architecture and medicine was born at the center of Lamarckian eugenics. Conceiving architecture as an influence just as powerful as nature, scientists and social reformers were convinced that architecture had the potential to become not only a stabilizing force but also a disciplinary and regulatory one for the human body. Health, considered "an expression of fitness to the various factors of the total environment," was based on the idea that fitness "is achieved through countless genotypic and phenotypic adaptations to these factors." However, any environmental change demands adaptation, and it is definitely this capacity for adaptation that allows us to maintain a state of fitness or not.[34]

The body-environment dynamic, so present in architectural contexts and discourses, comes to full force within the notion of milieu, wherein Lamarckian eugenics brings together organisms and their environments in a state of contingency. Despite understanding the dynamism of this relationship, this particular strain of eugenics was also trapped in a rigidity that, as Lewis Mumford states, afflicts all utopias.[35] Consequently, through the naturalization of the population—considering people not as political subjects but as natural resources—and the exploitation of the environment—with the conviction that the environment has the potential to change the human body—Lamarckian eugenics had the same ultimate goal as mainstream or Mendelian eugenics: the homogenization of the population. This led to a rigid and utopian notion of the human body as a stable, controllable, beautiful, racially and gender determined, and, of course, healthy entity, as Francis Galton aspired to realize in his bioengineering laboratory. Thus, it is not surprising that utopia is spatially imagined as the most dramatic finite space—an island—as we saw with More, and the perfect human body is imagined as a single phenotype with very particular features: those of the white man. More specifically, Latin American utopias emerged as a visualization of a better world in which both bodies and spaces were designed and managed through the forced complicity of architecture and medicine. And this visualization, based on eugenics' Lamarckian roots, integrated heredity and milieu and instrumentalized race, gender, and the environment as its primary tools.

GENDER, BEAUTY, AND REGENERATION

When Galton coined the term "eugenics" as "the science of improving inherited stock," he created the very scientific and ideological platform for producing the "ideal type" against which every human being would be judged and reimagined. One of the primary strategies for achieving this was the control of sex and reproduction. In the name of progress and modernization, this newly imagined body was harnessed as a productive apparatus by which life itself could be managed. As already noted, the human body, then, became an essential target for the implementation of new economic and moral practices that were intent on exploiting the fruits of human capital: production and reproduction.[36]

No utopian novel better represents this scientific and ideological platform than *Eugenia: Esbozo novelesco de costumbres futuras*, the novel written by the Cuban-born Mexican physician Eduardo Urzaiz in 1919.[37] The title of Urzaiz's novel comes from the name of one of the main characters, Eugenia, a young woman portrayed as the best example of her race.[38] Recruited to be an "Official Breeder of the Species," Eugenia is a member of an elite group selected by the central government of Villautopía, the capital city of the subconfederation of Central American countries in the year 2218. This imagined city was Urzaiz's re-creation of twenty-third-century Mérida, the capital of the state of Yucatán in Mexico, where he lived and worked as a physician and educator for practically his entire life.[39] With futuristic features, Villautopía appears as a modern city of white architecture that contrasts with the vibrant and sharp greens of the tropical landscape. Wide avenues lined with trees, tall buildings, and crowded moving sidewalks are overflown by aerobikes, space baskets, and other flying forms of transportation.[40] A pyramidal structure in neo-Mayan style is the Central Station of the city and the only reference to the indigenous

Because Eugenics policy aimed to result a homogenous population, the human body is a resource. "ideal type" of Thought sex and reproduction.

heritage of the region, which presumably had rid itself of all Indians and mestizos.[41] Against this backdrop, in a futurist society obsessed with the reproductive vitality of its citizens, Eugenia is handpicked to perform the most noble and rewarded job in the utopia: to birth ideal offspring.

The novel begins with another protagonist, Ernesto del Lazo, waking up in his modern home. Initiating his day with personal rituals, including "a brief session of vibratory automatic hydromassage," a "cold shower," and a moment of vanity contemplating with "intimate satisfaction" his image in the mirror, Ernesto is convinced that his "body was worthy of admiration." The references to Ernesto's beauty are classically Greek: his body has "the exact proportions, the perfect muscular relief, and the harmonic robustness of Doryphóros"—the statue by Polykleitos, which, 450 years before Christ, had become synonymous with the perfection of human proportions. Ernesto's face is similar to Hermes' face—as in the statue by Praxiteles of Athens—but even "more refined," with "that expression of intellectuality that human physiognomy had acquired after many centuries of civilization." Also, considering "the warm tonality of his healthy skin, uniform, silky, and clean of unnecessary hair," Ernesto, at twenty-three, is "a model worthy of Greek statuary."[42] It does not seem a coincidence that less than two years later, the Mexican evolutionist Alfonso L. Herrera announced that, through "science," humanity will be able to materialize a paradise on earth, in which the ideal of "beauty of form, intellect and virtue," will be "Hellenic."[43] In Urzaiz's words, Ernesto is "a good example of how the advances of hygiene had succeeded in the social engineering of a society that several centuries earlier . . . , we knew as rachitic, intoxicated, and weakly."[44] Unsurprisingly, Ernesto's perfect body is the codified result of environmental influences.

As the story continues, Ernesto is about to leave his home for his daily aerocycle ride around the city when he sees a letter addressed to him with a government stamp.[45] The official letter, dated March 2, 2218, and signed by Dr. Remigio Pérez Serrato, president of the Eugenics Bureau (Presidente del Bureau de Eugenética), announces that Ernesto, like Eugenia, has been selected for a year of reproductive service as another "Official Breeder of the Species" due to his "robustness, health, beauty, and other qualities."[46] Ernesto would have the responsibility to propagate the species, providing a certain number of healthy and perfect children to the confederation. Reproduction of the species is supervised by the state and regulated by science—from the initial moment of fertilization, artificial implantation, and delivery; to the process of raising and educating the children, "the products," in state-run "farm-nurseries" and state schools; up to the final moment in which they are allowed to form groups with other adults.

Ernesto lives with three friends and his lover Celiana, an intellectual woman who, in spite of her brilliance and her "disturbing and unique beauty," had been sterilized during her early youth after having been considered "incapable of engendering perfectly healthy and stable products." Due to her "excessive braininess" (cerebralidad excesiva) and an "insatiable and almost morbid thirst for knowledge"—traits usually associated with and only appreciated in men—Celiana was earlier diagnosed as abnormal.[47] In one of his celebrated talks, the president of the Bureau of Eugenics criticizes the fact that, in previous centuries, the human species had voluntarily renounced the process of natural selection that in other species had allowed "the triumph of the stronger or better adapted to the environment."[48] In this way, those who triumphed were "the most intelligent . . . , who were generally the less physically gifted, and, because of this, the species degenerated in a steady and outstanding way."[49] Celiana's "abnormality" is a testimony to the utopian view that intelligence in women was a threat to patriarchy and its control of procreation, a view that still permeates society to some degree today.

It is remarkable that Urzaiz's novel forecast the historical role that gender would soon play in the implementation of eugenics in Mexico. Urzaiz seems to have anticipated the growing support for eugenic sterilization, proposed two years later by Félix Palaviccini, one of the main organizers of the First National Children's Conference in 1921, where eugenics made its first appearance in Mexico.[50] Furthermore, Urzaiz also seems to have anticipated the confluence of Mendelian eugenics and Lamarckian ideas that led Mexican elites not only to legalize the sterilization of criminals in the state of Veracruz but to extend this policy to those affected by social diseases, genetically transmitted to the following generations in the form of so-called idiocy, perversion, and mental illness.[51] So, on the one hand, Mexican eugenicists were distressed about the degenerative effects of syphilis, tuberculosis, and alcoholism, which led to medical restrictions on the right to marry. Prenuptial registration and medical tests were required by law, and healthy marriages were promoted in eugenic campaigns. Yet, at the same time, these eugenicists formulated a new agenda by which gender would be instrumentalized as a means to racially transform society. This agenda was in keeping with postrevolutionary Mexico's move to recognize the rights of the native population and include them in the 1920s construction of the nation's new progressive identity.[52] But this move that, at first glance, appeared to be egalitarian was in fact driven by racial bias: in an attempt to assimilate the Indian population, the postrevolutionary government of General Álvaro Obregón adopted *mestizaje*—the racial mixing of Indian and European peoples—as a means to rescue the Indians from their own "underdevelopment."[53] As José Vasconcelos, the new Secretary of Public Education, put it, "the Indian offered a good bridge for racial mixing" through which a new universal race, a "cosmic race," would emerge.[54] In Vasconcelos' utopian vision, the "naturally superior" white race would merge with the "modernized," ameliorated darker races. He even argued that this cosmic race would emerge through a "spiritually driven aesthetic eugenics" that would make the black race entirely disappear; Vasconcelos claimed that no one would mate with those deemed "fundamentally recessive and undeserving, for that reason, of perpetuation."[55]

In a highly publicized manifestation of these eugenicists' zeal, an actual racial beauty contest to honor Mexico's beguiling indigenous women was promoted by Palaviccini, the newly appointed Minister of Foreign Affairs, in his popular newspaper *El Universal*. Although the contest, known as "La India Bonita" (The Beautiful Indian), was apparently conceived as entertainment for the newspaper's bourgeois audience, it was in fact a tool in the construction of Mexico's sexual politics.[56] As the art historian Adriana Zavala observes, the India Bonita beauty contest articulated two discourses: one that dignified Mexico's "suffering race" by exalting not only the physical attributes of Indian women but also their "pre-modern feminine virtue," and another that redirected male sexual attention to the body of indigenous women.[57] These two obviously opposing narratives had a single-minded goal: to promote the procreative femininity of Mexico's female indigenous population among the white and mestizo male population. In this way, the contest "provided an ideal opportunity to reinscribe the status quo, by *gendering*" the Indian race as feminine, arguing that out of the conflation of "pure Indian femininity and pure white masculinity a new ideal hybrid Mexican would be created." In point of fact, this contest that "effectively gendered race and raced gender"[58] revealed how beauty and gender were intertwined in the state celebration of racial hybridity.

The instrumentalization of this double-edged sword of gender and beauty in the implementation of eugenics was, in fact, prefigured in Urzaiz's work. As a bizarre evocation of "intersexuality" in a utopian society in which human reproduction was controlled by the state, the male body was now endowed with the ability to give birth. As hormonal therapies artificially prepared men to become "selfless

incubators of future humanity," the female body was thus stripped
of what had been considered its most profound and noble function:
gestation.[59] This brings us to question why Celiana—a woman made
unable to reproduce, and not Eugenia, the woman designated as an
official gestator—was selected to be on the cover of some editions of
Urzaiz's novel. Depicted as an eroticized, androgynous figure with
distinct masculine features, smoking a cigarette and resting her arm
on a black skull, Celiana embodies not only the opposite of the aesthetically perfect model to which eugenics aspired but also the gender

ambiguity construed as an aberration, as one of the most feared and censured "evils" of humanity.[60] At the same time, this image of Celiana on the cover of *Eugenia* is in contrast to the image of her portrayed in the narrative as a jealous lover, inflamed by anger and passion—those atavistic feelings ascribed mainly to women. Thus, both images, the sexually undefined and the merely feminine, are considered despicable in a "*machista*" tradition like the one that still prevails in Latin American society. However, what emerges from this dual representation is that Celiana's cross-gender embodiment demonstrates the ubiquitous assumption that intelligence, professional independence, and motherhood are incompatible with one another, and that biological differentiation is not really wholly based on nature, but on a system of representations by which gender, as well as race, is a socioscientific construction.[61] Eugenics in Latin America played a critical role in the construction of racial and gender differences, both crafted as biological and social facts of an empirical nature but permeated by issues of class and identity.[62]

In an uncanny way, Urzaiz's *Eugenia* predicted the Lamarckian nature of Mexican eugenics and its critical connection to the creation of a new patriarchal order for the control of women, their sexuality and reproductive rights, and the promotion of child welfare in the postrevolutionary period.[63] In this new order, eugenicists in Mexico chose the female body, the structure of the family, and children as their main objects of clinical intervention. As Michel Foucault said in his seminal work on sexuality, in an attempt to reduce sexuality to its reproductive function, to its heterosexual adult manifestation and matrimonial legitimation, the eugenics movement institutionalized mechanisms of power that led to the hysterization of women's bodies, the pedagogization of children's sex, the socialization of procreative behavior, and the psychiatrization of pleasure.[64] Just like the subconfederation of Central American countries imagined by Urzaiz, the patriarchal structure of the state would replace the traditional patriarchal structure of the family.

RACE, BEAUTY, AND DEGENERATION

Another provocative utopian text, *O presidente negro ou O choque das raças: Romance americano do ano 2228* (The black president or Racial clashes: American romance in the year 2228), written in 1926 by the influential Brazilian journalist José Bento Monteiro Lobato, focuses on race as the main target of national transformation. Considered a weak novel but an extraordinary document of the historical and cultural context of its production, this book portrays an imagined society in the United States that clearly differentiates the United States—with its ability to separate the presumably "superior" race from the "inferior" races—and Brazil—where the mixture of races was unavoidable. Criticizing Brazilian miscegenation as an "unfortunate" solution that degrades all races, Miss Jane, the daughter of the scientist-inventor of a machine that envisions the future, describes her admiration for what she considers the ultimate US triumph: the political and spatial segregation of races and the consequent preservation of their purity. She is convinced that the only way to save Brazil from degeneration is to divide the country into two distinct regions: the southern temperate zone, where most of the people are white European immigrants, creating the "Great Republic of Paraná" with Argentina, Uruguay, and Paraguay; and the rest of the country, a tropical republic where its people "would suffer the terrible mistake of the mixture of races."[65] In point of fact, what Miss Jane really observes is the confluence of racial determinism and environmental determinism, both of which emerged at the end of the nineteenth century in Latin American utopian eugenics.

In the fictionalized United States imagined by Monteiro Lobato, the Ministry of Artificial Selection (Ministério de Seleção Artificial) was responsible for carrying out the extermination of all newborn children with birth defects and the sterilization of not only blacks but also of other "undesirable" individuals, such as "the deaf and dumb, the crippled, the insane, the lepers, the hysterics, the natural born criminals, . . . the swindlers, the corruptors of young women, the prostitutes and a whole legion of physically and morally ill individuals who created all sorts of disturbances in human society."[66] Following these eugenics policies, the United States in the year 2228 had become a country where blacks no longer have dark skin, after being whitened through a scientific process that destroyed their pigmentation. Yet, they still have curly hair or what Monteiro Lobato calls "cabello carapinha," commonly called "bad hair."[67] In this society in which the standard of beauty for blacks is represented by the white race, a product is invented called Raios Ômega (Ômega Rays) with the ability to permanently straighten curly hair. In this eugenic fantasy, blacks are seen hurrying to receive this beauty treatment, and for a period of three months and in only three applications, all the blacks of the United States are subjected to this "second camouflage."[68] Hidden from the public is the fact that this new product had been developed not simply as a normalizing agent but also as a perniciously conceived political tool to sabotage the recent triumph of Jim Roy,

the first black president of Monteiro Lobato's United ~~States~~. In addition to straightening "bad hair" in pursuit of the white ~~standard~~
of beauty, the Ômega Rays product had a secondary but irrev~~ocable~~
consequence: sterilization.

On the night preceding the first black president's inauguration,
the defeated white candidate shockingly reveals to the new president
that his race has, in fact, been finally and effectively exterminated.
With extreme coldness, he states: "Your race is dead, Jim, . . . the
Ômega Rays . . . had a double virtue . . . while straightening people's
hair it sterilizes them."[69] In this way, blacks' desire to adopt white
beauty standards seals their own extinction. Monteiro Lobato tells
us that this peculiar triumph occurred as a result of a division within
the white vote into "Male Party" and "Female Party."[70] But the newly
elected black president dies, presumably from grief upon hearing
this revelation, and the female party's candidate is also politically
annihilated; she gives up her aspirations, marries the male party's
candidate, who takes over the presidency while his wife simply becomes his ally and aide. In this way, eugenics policy exposes its true
sinister character. The already-counterfeit democratic process totally
implodes: the white candidate not only eliminates his opponent but
also annihilates the black race and female power.

In contrast to the underlying ideology of Monteiro Lobato's novel,
in which there was no solution but the extinction of the black race,
during the first decades of the twentieth century Brazilians turned to
miscegenation not as menace or as cause of degeneration but as the
vehicle of transformation. In this view, race was not defined by heredity alone but by other factors as well; the Brazilian elites accepted
"white superiority," although not "white supremacy," seeing miscegenation precisely as the mechanism for "wiping out the black" and for
the consequential "whitening" of the population.[71] Improvement of the
environment would bring improvements to the race; the white man
would no longer suffer a degenerative process due to the simple fact of
living in tropical territories; the black man would disappear through
miscegenation as the result of the prevalence of the supposedly superior white race; modernization would advance society. In alignment
with this racist ideology of progress, and fully aware of the escalation
of biomedical science in Brazil, Monteiro Lobato had created an entire
body of work based on his new faith in the social-engineering capacity
of science and the environment. In his 1918 nonfiction book, *Problema
vital*, published by none other than the São Paulo Eugenics Society
and the Pro-Sanitation League of Brazil, Monteiro Lobato illustrates
Brazil's crisis of sanitation.[72] Struck by scientists' statistical proof

devastation caused by malnutrition, malaria, hookworm, and tropical diseases, he cites the resulting data of two scientists eugenicists, Belisário Penna and Arthur Neiva, carrying out ons for the Fiocruz Institute in the interior of the country.[73] Em- ng Lamarckian theories of race improvement, Monteiro Lobato d hope for his famous 1914 fictional character, Jeca Tatu, who was ginally portrayed as the very embodiment of Brazilian backward- ness and degeneration precisely because of his "inferior" mixed race. In *Problema vital*, Monteiro Lobato had changed his mind about the origin and immutability of his character's degeneracy. By including a short story titled "Jeca Tatu: A ressurreição," his famous character is "resurrected" by science, becoming a healthy, prosperous, and re- spected farmer—the very embodiment of Brazilian progress. In an ex- altation of the crucial role of science through the lens of Lamarckian eugenics, Monteiro Lobato proudly announces: "Jeca Tatu is made, not born."[74] In other words, in this account, social and environmental diseases, rather than mixed race, are the reasons behind Brazilian backwardness.[75] Even so, still clinging to the superiority of the white race, just a year after publishing *Problema vital*, Monteiro Lobato wrote to the Brazilian writer Alberto Rangel: "The world is for those who can, and the Brazilian—coming from the Portuguese, the Negro and I don't know what else—*can't . . .*"[76] As the historian Dain Borges observes, "part of racial thinking in Brazil reflected the general medi- calization of social thought that began when early-nineteenth-century physicians called for hygienic reforms within upper-class families to protect children from hereditary or environmental contamination."[77] Thus, by the onset of the twentieth century, the medicalization of physical space had been institutionalized, consolidating the complic- ity that the eugenics movement was about to establish between the built environment and the formation and prefiguration of the modern society that would inhabit it.

ECO-UTOPIAS: HYGIENE, SOCIAL HYGIENE, AND THE CITY

This medicalization of both bodies and spaces had the resounding effect of setting in place a normalizing and normative goal in which racial, gender, and environmental determinism, along with an entire system of exclusion shielded by science, contributed to canonizing elitist fantasies as if they were empirical facts. Of course, driving this goal was the steam engine of Lamarckian eugenics, propelling the simultaneous construction of a white heterosexual society as the "nor- mal" and desirable one and of a healthy and modern environment that would contribute to this "normalization."[78] Influenced by the power of medical science and the instrumentalization of nature—everything from the sun to the wind and the trees—in the reimagining of society, hygienic and eugenic practices became complicit in the process of constructing Latin American modern nations. In Argentina, the nation was, in fact, seen as a sick organism, and reformers—including social scientists, architects, and urban planners—were tantamount to physicians who would have the responsibility of diagnosis and treatment.[79] It makes sense, then, that many utopian narratives in Argentina visualized a city in which nature and space were conceived as a unified clinical apparatus of health and reproduction.

One such utopian narrative by Achilles Sioen, a French journalist living in Argentina, imagined Buenos Aires as a sanitary utopia in which urban hygiene was the technology used to sanitize and moralize a "degenerate" society. In his utopia, a new practice of intervention was implemented that "began in the city's public spaces" and then extended to individual bodies, "especially the bodies of the poor."[80] Sioen's utopia, titled *Buenos Aires en el año 2080: Historia verosímil* (Buenos Aires in the year 2080: A believable history), read more like an urban plan for the actual construction of a metropolis, free of disease and vice, than a literary re-creation of an ideal society. As its title announces, Sioen's novel represents a possible and credible history. Celebrating the connection between nature's bounty and science's achievements, Sioen visualized a sort of eco-medical utopia in which the sun was a source of life and energy, water a cleaning agent, the trees hygienic and moralizing resources, and medicine the successful science par excellence that made possible a world without disease. In Sioen's capital city, tree-lined avenues—usually used to commemorate patriots and national heroes—would celebrate science and progress. In Sioen's urban plan, a new metropolitan park, the city's "green lung," was the primary surgical maneuver whose purpose was to improve the very "respiration of the city."[81] So the city imagined by Sioen in 1879 was more than a representation of contemporary Haussmannian urbanism, with its wide avenues built to facilitate the circulation of people and goods and to emphasize civic urban axes and monumental spaces. It forecast the image of a city built on a different form of hygiene called *social hygiene*. Initially conceived as the "art of knowing" the influences that came from the milieu, social hygiene converged in a single vision three illnesses— tuberculosis, syphilis, and alcoholism—perceived as direct vehicles of the much-feared process of species degeneration.[82] And it is precisely through this convergence that social hygiene (and its etiology) was defined, associating the origin of each illness with the behavior of its victims. To combat these environmentally derived "social" and "moral" illnesses, which would affect not only the individual but also his or her descendants, toward the end of the nineteenth century, social hygiene became a focused economic science concerned with the twin fruits of human capital: production (*travail*) and reproduction.[83] In fact, as previously noted, the pronatalist Justin Sicard de Plauzoles, following the ideas of two prominent French physicians, Adolphe Pinard and Louis Landouzy, would define social hygiene in the following terms:

> Social hygiene is an economic science, having human capital as its purpose, its production and reproduction (eugenics and puericulture), its conservation (hygiene, medicine, and preventive assistance), its utilization (professional and physical education), and its output (scientific organization of work).[84]

FIGURE 1.7.
Benito Carrasco, Municipal baths and pier, Paseo Balneario La Costanera del Sur, Buenos Aires, 1918–1925. Photograph by Enrique Broszeit and Juan Bautista Borra, ca. 1925. Courtesy of the Colección Familia Borra, "El Puerto de Buenos Aires."

In other words, this economic science controlled the production and reproduction of human capital through eugenics and puericulture; its conservation through hygiene, medicine, and hominiculture; and its augmentation through professional and physical education for the sake of increasing productivity. Thus, social hygiene, whose domain extended beyond the individual sick body to the collective social body, assumed the liberal idea of *prévoyance* as its fundamental principle. Understood as "the moral imperative to use foresight" as a valid and efficient method to eliminate poverty, *prévoyance*, with its prophylactic nature, was deployed for the preservation and planning of society, the optimization of its output, and the provision of sanitary conditions in public spaces.[85]

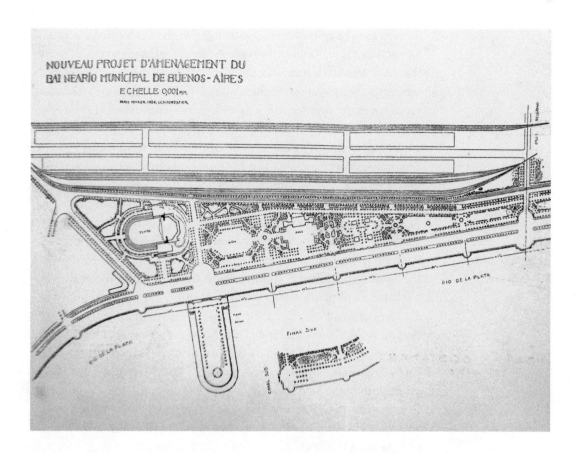

FIGURE 1.8.
Jean-Claude Nicolas Forestier, new development project for the municipal baths of Buenos Aires, Paseo Balneario La Costanera del Sur, 1925. Published in Comisión de Estética Edilicia, Proyecto orgánico para la urbanización del municipio: El plano regulador y de reforma de la capital federal. *(Buenos Aires: Talleres Peuser, 1925).*

Considering fresh air, green spaces, and water as particularly healthy elements, Sioen imagined a city that anticipated the most outstanding features of Buenos Aires' turn-of-the-century urban plans, in which the construction of green, sanitizing, aesthetic, and pedagogical entities defined the city's urban fabric and its supposedly democratic public spaces. Of these, the project for a metropolitan park, presented to the municipality by Juan de Cominges in 1882, and the series of gardens and promenades, later to be designed by the Argentine agronomy engineer Benito Carrasco and by the French landscape architects Eugène Courtois, Carlos Thays, Joseph Antoine Bouvard, and Jean-Claude Nicolas Forestier, are clear materializations of Sioen's vision.[86] The overlap is unsurprising when one considers that Forestier was an active member of the Parisian Musée social, the interdisciplinary institution that played a crucial role in French social reform and in the simultaneous urban transformation of Latin American and Mediterranean cities. Forestier was also a member of the Urban and Rural Hygiene Section of this French institution along with Landouzy, the physician who first recognized tuberculosis as a social disease and who is known for defining "hominiculture" as a form of social hygiene in the battle against the tuberculosis-syphilis-alcoholism triad. Indeed, Forestier was the architect who designed the 1924 Master Urban Plan for Buenos Aires, which displayed an innovative and systematic health and welfare structure, including parks, gardens, and waterfronts within the urban fabric of the Argentinean capital city.[87]

Yet the engineering capacity of hygiene, and then social hygiene, was never more evident than in the Argentinean physician Emilio Coni's utopia, "La ciudad argentina ideal o del porvenir" (The ideal Argentinean city or the city to come). Published in a medical journal in 1919, this mini-novel portrays a modern Buenos Aires based on scientific discoveries in Europe, especially in France, and the social hygiene movement implemented in Argentina at the beginning of the twentieth century.[88] In fact, it was through Coni's interest in the installation of potable water systems, sewage treatment, and other sanitary infrastructure in the city that he became focused on the organization of institutions devoted to the preservation, moralization, and social welfare of the population, as demonstrated in his 1887 book, *Progrès de l'hygiène dans la République Argentine*, and in his practice during the following decades (as discussed in chapter 3).[89] Echoing his own interests and medical practice, Coni's utopian city was conceived as a worker's model city in which the middle class and those at the margins of modernization (mostly of migratory and Creole origin) would be relocated from the *conventillos*, their so-called unsanitary tenements, to standardized and hygienic districts. In them, every worker's home became a wellspring of health, a sanitary preventive unit, and part of a net of prophylactic institutions whose real purpose was the "physical and moral amelioration of the race" under the homogenizing project of eugenics.[90]

In Coni's Buenos Aires, the protection of pregnant women and infants became a priority. Thus, a series of medical *dispositifs* were built, including maternity wards, gynecological and nursing dispensaries, shelters for single mothers and their children, neighborhood day-care centers, maternal asylums for orphans and schools, and colonies for weak and disabled children.[91] Even though Coni emphasized the importance of incorporating medical *dispositifs* and drugstores in the factories, as well as the construction of workshop asylums for the vagrants and nighttime shelters for the homeless, his primary concern was social prophylaxis for women and children, and with it the prevention units for what Argentineans called the "science of the moment": puericulture.[92] In most of Latin America, puericulture—a sort of faith-science revitalized in France by Pinard as a human analogue to agriculture for the scientific nurturing of the mother-child unit—was transformed into a Lamarckian eugenic modality.[93] Revealing the influence of French medicine in Argentinean medical circles, puericulture was at the center of debates in the early decades of the twentieth century and was even established as a mandatory course in public and private schools.[94] In a country as vast as Argentina, Coni's texts emphasized the relevance of reproduction over production. Following the slogan "Governing is populating," successfully proclaimed by Juan Bautista Alberdi in the mid-nineteenth century, the pro-natalist stance of Lamarckian eugenics underlined the practice of puericulture as one of the most accessible routes to perfect the human species.[95] In this manner, in Coni's utopia, sustained regeneration through prophylaxis and philanthropy became the main strategy.

Thus, in Sioen's and Coni's texts, which can be classified as medical utopias, health is "more than normality; in simple terms, it is normativity"; it represents "the possibility of tolerating infractions of the habitual norm and instituting new norms in new situations."[96] Given this clinical agenda, the relationship between the organism and its environment became the modern nation-states' main target of transformation. At first glance, these utopias seem to be superimposed over the structure of the Haussmannian city, imported to Argentina, with its primacy of the circulation of commodities, people, cars, clean air, and sunlight; its urban parks, gardens, and plazas as both aesthetic instruments and hygienic entities; its connecting series of monuments and views; its modern sewer and water systems; and its creation of a modern face for the city. However, these utopias imagined the city as the result of a project that attempted something far more comprehensive: bringing "both norms and forms into a common frame that would produce a healthy, efficient, and productive social order."[97] In contrast to the Paris of Haussmann, and in concert with the authors' own historical contexts, these utopian texts visualized the city of Buenos Aires not only as a political, economic, and technical object but mainly as a social and biological entity. It is this attempt, as Paul Rabinow observes in his celebrated book *French Modern: Norms and Forms of the Social Environment*, that defines the modern mind-set of urban intervention.

These Latin American utopian texts, in which the hygienic and eugenic ideals share a dominant place, suggest an intriguing relationship between utopia, eugenics, and the city. But what kind of city are these utopias imagining? What kind of society is eugenics imagining? What kind of utopia is eugenics? Utopia and eugenics embody the will to construct a moral blueprint for the "improvement" of both society and the city. A key challenge here is to scrutinize the ideology under-pinning the moral blueprint that became the instrument through which utopias materialize through science, with a moral and corrective aim: to transform a depraved society into a "virtuous" one. More than in any other latitude, Latin American utopian texts empowered the environment as a plausible scenario in which the transformation of the body was deemed instrumental to the titanic march toward progress.[98] So, if the end of the nineteenth century saw the exhaustion of the utopian genre in literature, it also witnessed the subsequent appropriation of utopia's structures by a new "comprehensive model," one which, established at the beginning of the twentieth century, unites "spatial, social, and scientific elements."[99] The name for this new model, as we shall presently see, is urbanism.

CHAPTER 2

PARIS GOES WEST

From the Musée Social to an "Ailing Paradise"

World's Fairs have always been showcases for the products of nations' progress, manifested in grandiose monuments, machines, technological and scientific breakthrough exhibitions, and even in disturbing displays of those "other" people and cultures to justify racial stereotyping and the discriminatory practice of differentiating between the civilized and the savage. With the advent of the "social question" in France—referring to the social implications of industrialization that became the country's main domestic challenge at the turn of the nineteenth century—the 1889 World's Fair was more than a stage for the Eiffel Tower and the extraordinary Gallery of Machines.[1] It was, in fact, the launching ground for a new form of hygiene—social hygiene—which, focusing on people not as isolated entities but as interrelated agents of infection and contamination, would fervently attempt to ameliorate both the human race and its physical milieu. In a country that had had advanced public health and urban hygiene for a whole century, it was difficult to distinguish the boundaries between these practices and what was developing as a social hygiene crusade. It is important to remember that *urban hygiene*, as it was envisioned by Georges-Eugène Haussmann, was essentially a surgical transformation and regulation of the city of Paris that viewed the city as an economic-technical object but not yet as a social one; in contrast, *social hygiene* went beyond the health of the city and its population to encompass a new method for not only preserving the human race but achieving its "constant improvement, to its perfection."[2] As I demonstrate in this chapter, this method developed into a movement that eventually manifested itself as the revolutionary science known as eugenics—again, the social and biological movement that sought the "improvement" of the human race. In fact, the 1889 World's Fair and its Social Economy Exhibition was where the fundamental ideas—ideals and fears—embedded in the redefinition of the "social question" laid the groundwork for the new type of eugenics first developed in France and then institutionalized in Latin America. This event also led to the formation of the Musée social, a conservative institution aimed at conjoining social change with what was branded as modern urbanism—that new comprehensive discipline devoted to diagnosing and treating the social, spatial, and scientific "body" of the city. This chapter traces the socio-spatial concerns and postulations of France, from the Social Economy Exhibition at the 1889 World's Fair, to the inner workings of the Musée social, to its prominent members' medical campaigns and urban practices in Latin America.

OPTIMISM AND ITS DEGENERATIVE AFTERMATH

Among the antecedents of our story, the Exposition Universelle Internationale de 1889, the World's Fair held in Paris from May to November of 1889, is seminal. This exhibition, the greatest fair of the nineteenth century, which simultaneously celebrated the achievements of the industrial era and the centennial of the French Revolution, exposed the Third Republic's position regarding the "social question" for the first time—the bourgeoisie's haunting interrogation of a new form of poverty associated with the advent of industrialization, the crisis of philanthropic reform within the new liberal economy, and the impact of urban growth.[3] The message, however, was not totally clear. On the one hand, the fair represented a celebration of progress, national pride, and the commencement of a new modern era. On the other hand, it revealed the problems caused by industrialization, a kind of anxiety over a lost social order, and the emergence of the so-called dangerous classes or the new poor—a segment of society that was seen as an urban human mass in which violence, criminality, diseases, and insurrection could materialize at any time.[4] During the months that preceded its inauguration, and during the period when this exhibition was at the core of Parisian life, newspapers, various other periodicals, and even the *Bulletin officiel de l'exposition universelle de 1889*, the official publication of the 1889 World's Fair, reflected this dilemma, showing both the triumphs of modern society and the

FIGURE 2.1.
Construction of the Eiffel Tower, Paris, 1888. © Roger-Viollet, The Image Works.

FIGURE 2.2.
Interior view of the Gallery of Machines (by the architect Ferdinand Dutert and the engineer Victor Contamin), Exposition Universelle Internationale de 1889, Paris. Library of Congress Prints and Photographs Division, Washington, DC.

social fears that lay behind them. Their pages were filled with articles on public assistance, health and education, the care of infants, and even criminal anthropology. It was no coincidence that simultaneous with the World's Fair, Paris was also the stage for several related scientific and sociological conferences where this social fear was at the center of debate.[5]

FIGURE 2.3.
Cover image of the
Bulletin officiel de
l'exposition universelle
de 1889, *no. 148,*
September 14, 1889.
Bibliothèque des Arts
Décoratifs, Paris.

FIGURE 2.4.
Charles Garnier,
dwellings of tribal
peoples of Africa, North
America, and the Arctic
regions in the History
of Habitation Exhibit,
Exposition Universelle
Internationale de 1889,
Paris, France. Library
of Congress Prints and
Photographs Division,
Washington, DC.

An article about one of these conferences, the Criminal Anthropology Conference, published in the *Bulletin officiel*, clearly manifested the fear of degeneration that haunted French society. The article highlighted the opposition of Léonce Manouvrier, a French physician and anthropologist who later would greatly influence Latin American medical science, to the idea promoted by the famed Italian physician Cesare Lombroso that criminality was a biologically determined condition. Manouvrier was convinced that transforming the milieu was a way to transform the human being, revealing French scholars' commitment to Lamarckian theories. According to the article, Manouvrier dismissed Lombroso's "born criminal" thesis by claiming that Lombroso failed to understand the complexities of the problem when he did not consider other factors such as race, gender, social class, and, even more importantly, the conditions of the milieu in producing criminality. Manouvrier even proposed uniting, under the term "anthropotechnology" (*anthropotechnie*), all the disciplines that had as their main goal the elevation of the human condition: "medicine, hygiene, morality, education, law, and politics."[6] It was clear that the influence of French thinkers established the worldview, which still persists today, that the "social environment plays the most important role, in the long run, in shaping the actions and nature of the criminal."[7] This Lamarckian view, which underscores the primacy of the environment as a transformative social agent, was prevalent in French intellectual and medical circles and was hotly debated at many of the congresses and events that accompanied the 1889 World's Fair.

Although the main goal of the World's Fair was to portray a victorious and positive image of the French Third Republic, which at the time still faced numerous political and social challenges, the fair actually displayed both the achievements and the tribulations of a modern republican society. Even the floor plan for the exhibition attempted to re-create the Arc de Triomphe to symbolize the pride of France.[8] The symbolic arc was formed by the two main platforms of the exhibition, the Champ de Mars and the Esplanade des Invalides, connected by the Quai d'Orsay. However, the division between these two main platforms clearly revealed the contradictions faced by France as a modern republic. At the center of the Champ de Mars, the Eiffel Tower reached for the sky as a new symbol of the republic; and the Galerie des Machines, in its no less extraordinary iron structure, celebrated the triumph of industrialization with a spectacular display featuring a conglomeration of machinery. On the other side of the exhibition, at the Esplanade des Invalides, a series of buildings, performances, and exhibits revealed a very different and complex image regarding progress.[9] This image was reflected in the stylistic palaces representing the French colonies, re-creations of African villages, and the first extensive exposition of colonized people, including over four hundred Indochinese, Tahitians, and Senegalese.[10]

Interestingly, the Social Economy Exhibition—the section of the World's Fair devoted to the "social question"—was sited just in front of these representations. It is notable that this exhibition, a tribute to social peace presenting the social technologies that could be used to reduce social conflict, was placed right next to the French Ministry of War. It is also revealing that the exhibition was located next to the Agriculture Fair—a showroom for what the state could achieve with the help of the private sector, namely, the organization,

FIGURE 2.6.
G. Traiponi, engraving,
"Une rue au Cairo."
Cover, L'Exposition
de Paris, *no. 10, May*
1889. University of
Glasgow Library,
Special Collections.

FIGURE 2.7.
Photos of indigenous
women from South Africa
at the Jardin zoologique
d'acclimatation, Paris;
Album "Hottentots"
presented at the 1889
World's Fair, Paris.
Vénus hottentotes au
Jardin d'Acclimatation
à Paris. *Photograph by*
Pierre Petit, 1888. Photo
© PVDE/Bridgeman
Images.

rationalization, and standardization of "a social hieroglyph into a legible and administratively more convenient format"—mirroring in the human realm what scientific forestry and agriculture were doing to the natural world.[11] Finally, the Social Economy Exhibition's location next to the Hygiene Pavilion, the state-sponsored display devoted to France's progress in health, is significant for the way it appropriated the scientific inquiry and authority of its neighbor. By 1889, under the light of Pasteur's bacteriological revolution, hygiene had acquired an indisputable scientific status, and the Social Economy Exhibition announced the emergence of a new science: the science of society.[12]

The Social Economy Exhibition embraced concerns about the ramifications of industrialization, assuming a critical position toward the liberal tradition and pointing to the moral and human aspects of industrial development. However, this exhibition was undoubtedly pro-industrial: it was conceived not as a critique of industrialization, portraying the working class as the forgotten stratum of French society, but as a warning about the social complexities that had to be faced by the republic.[13] In the same spirit that the colonial palaces and representations of Arab and African communities were portrayed as colonized societies proud to be part of the French grandeur, the Social Economy Exhibition opened with the "cité sociale," a working village in which proud workers were portrayed in their model houses, wearing

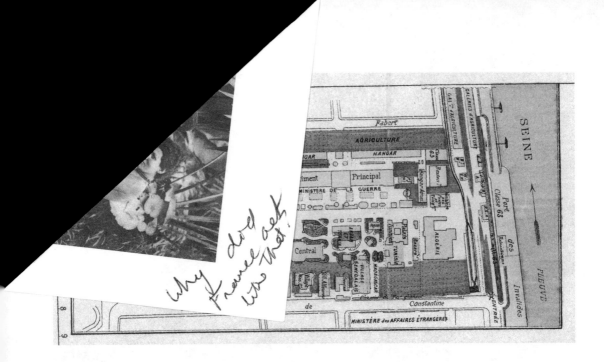

why did France do that!

FIGURE 2.8.
*Layout, Esplanade des
Invalides, 1889 World's
Fair, Paris. Département
des Estampes et de la
photographie, Biblio-
thèque nationale de
France, Paris; Gallica,
http://gallica.bnf.fr.*

their uniforms, and accompanied most essentially by their families.[14] Rather than the filth and darkness that characterized popular representations of industrial spaces and workers' slums at the time, the Social Economy Exhibition showcased the hygienic houses of orderly workers, low-cost cafeterias, day-care centers, dispensaries, and other social and economic organizations promoted by a new generation of industrialists.[15] As part of these displays, an exhibition hall, the Galerie de l'économie sociale, presented documents on industrial reform and social welfare. In the end, the exhibitions at the Esplanade des Invalides reveal a clear link between colonization and industrialization—the basis for the emergence of the utopian ideology of progress. In fact, it would not be inaccurate to say that discussions generated by these exhibitions "set the stage for the rise of the modern welfare state in France" and, with it, the major components of French eugenics.[16]

As part of its redefinition of the "social question," the Social Economy Exhibition turned its attention from the industrial world to society at large. One of its fifteen sections was devoted to a new concept of hygiene—social hygiene.[17] As noted in chapter 1, social hygiene was considered an economic science concerned with the outputs of human capital: production (*travail*) and reproduction.[18] The first to define social hygiene was the criminologist Alexandre Lacassagne, who, in 1876, saw it as an "art of knowing" the influences that come from the milieu; then, in 1902, the Pasteurian Émile Duclaux emphasized the broader theoretical dimension of the term in which illnesses were not seen as physical maladies but as social repercussions.[19] At the core of both definitions was an emphasis on the agency of the social

50 *EUGENICS IN THE GARDEN*

milieu and the notion that social hygiene, differing privée" (in which hygiene was seen as an individual mor governs the collective, not the individual, body. Thus, as late-nineteenth-century redrawing of boundaries between the and private spheres, social hygiene became an important aspect workers' lives and also of the greater social body and its milieu.

Even before eugenics became part of public policy, the Social Hygiene Section of the Social Economic Exhibition emphasized eugenics' main obsessions: the ravaging effects of modern social diseases; the "amelioration" of the infant, the child, and the adolescent; and the reimagining of the city as one means of eradicating degeneration.[20] Echoing these concerns, three of the fifteen sections that constituted the Social Economy Exhibition—Section XI: Workers' Housing; Section XII: Workers' Clubs, Recreation, and Play; and Section XIII: Social Hygiene—clearly considered architecture an influential element and one of the main instruments for improving the lives of the workers and their descendants. These sections emphasized the moral and physical results of improving spatial conditions for the workers, from the private space of their houses to the public space of their recreational and health centers—sport clubs, gardens, gymnasiums, temperance cafés, refectories, and lavatories.

In a guide to this 1889 Social Economy Exhibition, published in the journal *La Réforme sociale*, the engineer Émile Cheysson highlighted a main distinction between this exhibition and the one on hygiene in the 1867 World's Fair. A follower of the French social scientist and sociologist Frédéric Le Play, Cheysson argued that the emphasis shifted from one exhibition to the other, from the idea of assistance—merely helping and healing the individual injured body—to the liberal idea of *prévoyance* as the method for eliminating poverty and improving society's welfare.[21] Furthermore, if *assistance* was conceived as therapeutic and private, *prévoyance* was conceived as a broad-scale preventive measure for social planning. Seen as a progressive science, social hygiene was in fact reactionary in the sense that it "attempted to restore a previous status quo or reverse negative trends."[22] In its attempt to go beyond the health of the individual, social hygiene sought to overcome biological degeneration—the greatest fear haunting French society. Perceived as the culprits of degeneration, three major health problems—alcoholism, tuberculosis, and venereal disease—were grouped together to become known as "social plagues" or "moral diseases." With this clear threefold target, fears of degeneration thus provoked the implementation of social hygiene and the institutionalization of eugenics.

his same Social Economy Exhibition, Cheysson launched the
r a "social museum" that would represent and render appealing
ial technologies proposed to a wider public by the LePlayists,
rs of Le Play, whose essential objective was to assume a more
role in the construction of the French welfare system. This idea
permanent exhibition would later materialize as the "Experimen-
al Museum of the World" known as the Musée social.[23] So, in 1895,
the exhibition's previously nomadic collection of documents found
its permanent place at this institution, a kind of early think tank in
which an interdisciplinary group of professionals would address the
social problems of the times through a scientific mode of intervention.
From the start, the Musée social was conceived as a new kind of
museum that echoed the classical conception of *museion*, an institution going beyond the traditional museological functions of collecting,
classifying, preserving, and displaying to assume a more civic and
pedagogical role. In other words, this initiative refashioned the idea of
a museum: instead of isolating objects by their traditional functions,
it displayed them in relationship to their social and cultural circumstances.[24] Thus, the Musée social—a living museum of research and
practice—would host a permanent exhibition of social economy and a
library in its main facility in Paris' Seventh Arrondissement, and also
sponsor research by interdisciplinary professionals whose investigations of social questions went beyond the industrial world and the
boundaries of the French territory and its colonies. This new group
of social technocrats had considerable influence over French law and
discourse, but its main impact was actually on the French colonies and
on the non-French periphery in emergent Latin American nations.

PROFESSIONALIZING EUGENICS

Two of the most seminal figures of the Musée social, the physicians
Adolphe Pinard and Louis Landouzy, extended the ongoing social
discourse from the human body—both individual and collective—to
physical space. Pinard, while trying to unveil the causes of declining
fertility in France, developed the concept of puericulture—a kind of
human analogue to agriculture—for the "scientific cultivation" of the
mother-child unit.[25] In order to face the apparent depopulation of the
nation, Pinard, who was influenced by the morally driven analysis
of protosociologists such as Le Play, added a Lamarckian notion of
heredity to the moral exhortation of the value of raising children, in
this way connecting the well-being of the child to the mother's health,
the health of previous generations, and environmental influences.

Puericulture bound together pro-family and pro-natalist outlooks, which emphasized the traditional role of women in the family—women *in reproduction*—under the auspices of medicine, presented as an apolitical and empirical form of knowledge. In puericulture, the functions of morality and science were interchangeable.[26] While Pinard focused on the mother-child unit, his colleague Louis Landouzy, who was likewise influenced by Lamarckian ideas of heredity, argued for the cultivation of the human species across entire life spans. Landouzy focused on what he saw as social environmental poisons: alcohol, tuberculosis, and syphilis, the earlier-mentioned "social plagues." To define the battle against them, Landouzy coined the term "hominiculture." Influenced by Pinard and Landouzy, the hygienist and eugenicist Justin Sicard de Plauzoles evoked puericulture by naming three main components of social hygiene: the production and reproduction of human capital through eugenics; the conservation of this capital through hygiene and medicine; and the further development of this capital through professional and physical education.[27] Thus, as we shall see, puericulture paved the way for both the planning of the family and the planning of the city. For Sicard de Plauzoles, social hygiene provided the first opportunity to forecast the convergence of hygienics and eugenics in France. In this sense, these two apparently different movements—hygienics, acting to conserve the health of the body and to transform the milieu, and eugenics, acting to ameliorate human heredity—had converged to the point of fusion. The hygienists' goal—improving housing, education, public space, and health—was shared by both hygienists and eugenicists to the point that professionals in each field were listed among the members of both organizations. What brought these two groups together was a concern over the influences of the environment on the individual and social body.

Considered "the strong arm of the Musée social," the Alliance d'hygiène sociale—a coalition of public health groups that emerged in 1904 as the first organization of social hygiene—turned space into a key instrument for combating social diseases in "the preservation of the race, its improvement, and its perfection."[28] This was the first time that a group of physicians and architects had joined forces "to introduce a new way of conceiving and promoting collective action as a medical, moral, and social means of prevention."[29] Among the names of the Musée social's reformers were the most prominent architects and urban planners in France at the beginning of the century, such as Eugène Hénard and Adolphe Augustin Rey, making the urban fabric the main focus of collective action. Influenced by the poet and intellectual Gustave Kahn, the architects of the Musée social were ready to participate in a coalition driven by medicine that incorporated medical methodologies into the urban question. While Kahn in his 1901 book, *L'Esthétique de la rue*, had prophesied that "hygiene is God, the physicians are its prophets, and the architect follows their prescriptions," a few years later, the architects at the Musée social, however, were ready to take the lead.[30] Connecting beauty directly to health via the details of the street, Kahn's social critique created a concept of aesthetics with economic, hygienic, administrative, financial, commercial, and social questions at its core. Kahn's influence is clear in Robert de Souza's 1913 book, *Nice, capitale d'hiver*, and in Donat-Alfred Agache, J. Marcel Auburtin, and Édouard Redont's 1915 book, *Comment reconstruire nos cités détruites*, where they all voiced their conviction that hygiene and aesthetics were the main responsibilities of urban design. Taking up this call, Le Corbusier clearly saw himself as god, prophet, and technician—Kahn's medico-aesthetic trio—which he repeatedly claimed from the 1920s to the 1940s, as discussed in chapter 4.

With planning now as France's most powerful tool for resolving its social problems, in 1908 the Alliance d'hygiène sociale inspired the creation of a new section of the Musée social devoted to urban and rural hygiene, later called Section d'hygiène urbaine et rurale et de prévoyance sociale. A shift toward the social function of architecture, with a focus on the larger urban fabric rather than on individual buildings, characterized the work of its members, differentiating them from the more aesthetic-oriented traditions of the Beaux-Arts school. Three years later, the Musée social's faith in the ability of urban planning to combat social concerns was reaffirmed at the 1911 Congrès d'hygiène sociale in Roubaix. There, at Roubaix City Hall, architecture, urbanism, and landscape design became critically linked with a new urgency to sanitize houses and neighborhoods, working facilities, open spaces, parks, and playgrounds. Under the direction of Jules Siegfried, the president of the Musée social, the conference opened with a clear manifestation of its medical-spatial agenda: "the study of all questions relating to the health improvement of spaces."[31] The conference's program covered "topics ranging 'from the insalubrious city (Ville-Taudis),' where all forms of contagion, of misery and death are developed, 'to the garden city (Cité Jardin),' where the race gets fortified, where air and sun guarantee health and life."[32] Relevant members of the Musée social, such as the social engineer Georges Benoît-Lévy and the architect Agache, lectured on the importance of the "garden city." Even Georges Risler, who would later be president of both the Musée social and its Alliance de hygiène social, advocated

FIGURE 2.9.
*Cover for Georges
Benoît-Lévy's book,* La
cité jardin *(Paris: Henri
Jouve, 1904). Courtesy
of HathiTrust.*

FIGURE 2.10.
*Ebenezer Howard's
diagram "The Three
Magnets," translated and
published in Georges
Benoît-Lévy,* La cité
jardin *(Paris: Henri
Jouve, 1904). Courtesy
of HathiTrust.*

FIGURE 2.11.
*Ebenezer Howard's
diagram "The Three
Magnets," originally
published in 1898 in* To-
morrow: A Peaceful Path
to Real Reform *(London:
Swan Sonnenschein,
1898), and reprinted in
his celebrated 1902 book,*
Garden Cities of To-
morrow *(London: Swan
Sonnenschein, 1902).
Courtesy of HathiTrust.*

for the garden city as the right environment in which to breed communities of disciplined, family-oriented, hygienic, and preemptive workers. In the first session of the conference, Benoît-Lévy claimed that the "garden city" was the "social hygiene city par excellence" and even argued that the world's social history of the twentieth century was inscribed in the very subtitle of the conference: "De la ville-taudis à la cité-jardin."[33] And Agache highlighted the significance of healthy housing in the development of the "human plant," emphasizing the interdependence of physical hygiene and moral hygiene.[34] In fact, the so-called garden city, a new urban model of decentralization conceived to combat both the ill health of modern metropolises and the abandonment of rural territories, was an early synthesis of what Lamarckian eugenics would soon bring together: the complicity of medicine, morality, and architecture.[35]

After the creation of the new section on urban and rural hygiene, physicians and architects joined the Musée social in even greater numbers. A new official commitment to planning and urban development thus arose at the core of the Musée social with the work of Hénard, Augustin Rey, and Agache as well as other prominent architects, including Louis Bonnier, André Bérard, Jean-Claude Nicolas Forestier, Marcel Poëte, Léon Jaussely, Maurice Rotival, and Henri Prost, among others. In 1911, when Landouzy became the vice president of this section, it included ninety-eight members—almost a third of the total membership of the Musée social.[36] In 1913, this group, which took credit for conceiving the practice of modern urbanism, created the first professional association in France devoted to its

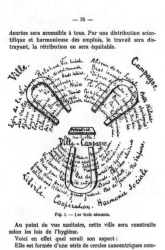

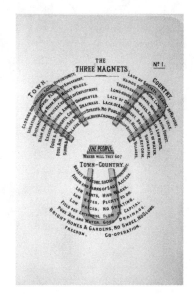

development, the Société française des urbanistes. With its fervent embrace of medicine as an emissary of progress, Latin America was identified as a perfect laboratory for this new generation of innovative reformers.[37] Within a few years, the architect members of the Musée social designed urban projects for Latin American cities, including master plans by Bérard for Guayaquil (1913), by Forestier for Buenos Aires (1924) and Havana (1925–1930), by Agache for Rio

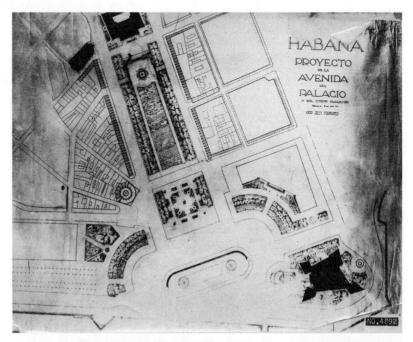

FIGURE 2.12.
Jean-Claude Nicolas Forestier, project for the Avenida del Palacio y del Nuevo Malecón, Havana Master Plan, *Secretaría de Obras Públicas, Havana, 1925–1930. Fonds Forestier and Fonds Leveau (150 Ifa-149 Ifa), SIAF/Cité de l'architecture et du patrimoine/Archives d'architecture du XXe siècle, Paris.*

FIGURE 2.13.
Jean-Claude Nicolas Forestier, project for the Avenida del Palacio y del Nuevo Malecón, Havana Master Plan, *Secretaría de Obras Públicas, Havana, 1925–1930. Fonds Forestier and Fonds Leveau (150 Ifa-149 Ifa), SIAF/Cité de l'architecture et du patrimoine/Archives d'architecture du XXe siècle, Paris.*

FIGURE 2.14.
Jean-Claude Nicolas Forestier, photograph, Antonio Maceo Park, Havana, Secretaría de Obras Públicas, Havana, 1928. Fonds Forestier and Fonds Leveau (150 Ifa-149 Ifa), SIAF/Cité de l'architecture et du patrimoine/Archives d'architecture du XXe siècle, Paris.

de Janeiro (1929), and by Rotival for Caracas (1935).[38] Most of these projects used science, morality, and aesthetics to legitimize a race-centered modernist agenda in which urbanism was recruited as a racial-class technology that allowed governments to segregate entire communities, constructing what the scholar Bruno Carvalho called "an environment of inequality."[39] So it is to Latin America that we now turn, specifically to Brazil's capital city during the early 1920s, when eugenics and hygienic ideas decimated an entire populated mountain, leaving in its wake the tabula rasa upon which Agache conceived his Rio master plan.

RAZING THE MOUNTAIN

In the early 1920s, a highly dramatic event took place in Rio de Janeiro. The battle against bubonic plague, yellow fever, and other tropical diseases had led to radical sanitary and urban reform that reached its climax with the sensational demolition of an entire populated mountain located at the center of the Brazilian capital.[40] This mountain, Morro do Castelo, was not just an ordinary mountain; it was the original site where the colonial city, with its historical buildings and underground infrastructure, was established in 1567.[41] In spite of its historical value, after Mayor Francisco Pereira Passos' urban reforms of 1902–1906 that expelled thousands of inhabitants

city, the Morro do Castelo stood in downtown
refuge housing the poor.[42] By the early 1920s,
almost 600 residential buildings that had been
Pereira Passos' *bota-abaixo* (shut-down) strategy,
Morro do Castelo destroyed another 408 buildings,
other 4,200 low-income residents to even less favorable
ons in the surrounding hills and on the outskirts of the
of these demolished buildings were collective housing
called *cortiços* (literally beehives)—the precarious tene-
uses that hosted the poor in overcrowded and unhygienic
ons.[44] According to the city's authorities, the Morro do Castelo
a "montanha de estrume" (a mountain of manure) that, together
n its "undesirable" inhabitants, needed to be removed from the
city center.[45] This led to the segregation of the southern part of the
city (the seafront neighborhoods) for the upper classes, the relega-
tion of the industrial north and the periphery for the poor, and the
emergence of communities known as favelas in the city's hills.[46] Due
to these urban reforms, from 1906 to 1920, a vastly uneven growth
distribution marked Rio's fate: its "population grew by 4 percent in
the areas with the most extensive renovations, while in the other
areas of the Federal District, where few or none of these improvements had taken place, the population increased by 61 percent" and in
the suburbs by 96 percent.[47] This did not happen without resistance;
many Morro do Castelo inhabitants refused to leave the center of the
city where the sources of work were located, moving to nearby hills
such as the Morro do Pinto and Morro de Santo Antônio, and to Santa
Teresa and the areas of Gamboa and Espírito Santo.[48] Although the
migration of poor people to the city's hills slowly began at the end of
the nineteenth century, it was not until "the era of the demolitions"
that the favelas, as urban slums, proliferated.[49] So the demolition of
the Morro do Castelo was the climactic moment in which science—in
the form of eugenics—justified both the radical transformation of the
built environment and an almost two-decades-long marginalization
of the disenfranchised, mostly blacks and mulattos, from the center
of the Brazilian capital.

The idea of eliminating this mountain was not new. As far back as
1798, a medical report had argued for the mountain's demolition on
the grounds that it was an enormous barrier that blocked the circulation of air from the sea and consequently facilitated the proliferation
of diseases.[50] But it was not until the 1920s that aesthetic and moral
reasons were added to sanitary ones, and the mountain came to be
seen as the very negation of modernity itself, a reservoir of vice and

FIGURE 2.15.
Augusto Malta, demolition of the Morro do Castelo, Rio de Janeiro, October 9, 1922. Image record 007A5P3F10-36, Augusto Malta/ Instituto Moreira Salles Collection.

FIGURE 2.16.
Augusto Malta, demolition of the Morro do Castelo, Rio de Janeiro, August 30, 1922. Image record 014AM005017, Augusto Malta/ Instituto Moreira Salles Collection.

diseases, a place of a "marginal" population—mostly poor blacks, prostitutes, and former slaves—who, according to the elites, invaded the center of the city "with their embarrassing practices of superstition and misery."[51] At that time, medicine had become the principal tool used by the state to study and then reconfigure its national population. It was only at this point, when hygiene became social hygiene, and hydraulic technologies had reached a more innovative level of development, that the implosion of the Morro do Castelo was possible. The engineer and industrialist Carlos Sampaio (1861–1930), the mayor of the city from 1920 to 1922, diverted $20 million allocated for the upgrading and electrification of the deteriorating main artery that connected the suburbs to downtown Rio to pay for the demolition of the mountain and the bulldozing of the central esplanade.[52] Moreover, Sampaio raised substantial funds from public and private sources to pay for the upgrading of fashionable southern neighborhoods and to engineer major urban and environmental transformations in the zone, including the flattening and sanitizing of the Rodrigo de Freitas lagoon and its urban border, the conclusion of the Avenida Beira Mar connecting downtown Rio with the Botafogo neighborhood, and the reconstruction of the Avenida Atlântica along the Copacabana waterfront.[53] In his attempt to move forward with the reforms initiated by Pereira Passos, Sampaio brought back to the forefront the "urban question" and its social implications. So it was not a coincidence that the demolition of the Morro do Castelo was executed almost simultaneously with new mandates that privileged European immigration and banned people of color. One such mandate was the "white only" decree (No. 4247) of 1921, which literally prohibited the immigration of blacks to Brazil.[54] In this way, the demolition of the Morro do Castelo, in progress that year, contributed not only to the overwhelming class disparity but also to a similar racial disparity between the low number of new "white" inhabitants moving into the urban developments in the south, and the "colored" inhabitants displaced to the north, with its inadequate services and poor sanitation.[55] As part of this whitening agenda, Sampaio was convinced that the once-valued mountain, now contaminated, had to be eliminated. As he victoriously stated:

> The celebrated mountain, historic due to the fact that the city of Rio de Janeiro was founded there, sacred due to the existence of a convent and two churches, legendary and enchanted due to the subterranean galleries in which it was said were gold and precious stone treasures, for more than a century challenged the physicians that recommended its demolition in order to ameliorate the poor hygienic conditions of the city, as well as the engineers who saw in such an action an important technical challenge and a lucrative operation.[56]

A few lines later, Sampaio pointed out not only the hygienic, technological, and economic justification for the mountain's demolition but also its aesthetic one:

. . . because it was a barrier to ventilation . . . and produced, due to its nonaesthetic and nauseating aspect, a bad impression on travelers, who, upon entering the splendid Rio de Janeiro Bay, had the same sensation as seeing a rotten front tooth in a beautiful mouth.[57]

FIGURE 2.19.
Poster for the Centennial Commemoration Exhibition of the Independence of Brazil in Rio de Janeiro, September 7, 1922, to March 31, 1923. Lithograph by Carlos Oswald, 1923. Archivo Nacional, http://www .exposicoesvirtuais .arquivonacional.gov .br/pt-br/exposicoes /60-4-rio-do-morro-ao -mar/283-a-exposicao -internacional-de-1922 -memoria-e-civilizacao.

So this dramatic demolition—which generated an extensive territory that, two years later, would be occupied by the 1922 Centennial Exhibition commemorating the one hundredth anniversary of Brazil's independence—represented the first and most radical action in the construction of a new national image, free of backward associations and racial exoticism.[58] The 815,000 square meters of flat land that resulted from the demolition of the mountain and the new esplanade landfill reclaimed from the sea was rapidly occupied by splendid eclectic pavilions, gardens, and public spaces, and even a hydroplane port built to provide a modern and glorious entrance to the city that was called "the port of Brazil." With this action that displaced thousands of "undesirable" inhabitants and eliminated Rio de Janeiro's original urban nucleus, the reformers' strategic vision of "changing the city to change the society" was emphatically proclaimed.[59]

Conceived as the modern and successful face of a country that, nearing the end of its First Republic (1889–1930), still faced serious political and economic crises, the 1922 Centennial Exhibition was placed over the void left by the erased mountain and its colonial center.[60] Most of the pavilions designed for the site were built in the neocolonial style—a style selected by the organizers to represent their new modern country in the centennial anniversary of its independence. One must ask: What about this style of architecture appealed to the exhibition's planners? First, it paradoxically offered the possibility of something new through the reformulation of its own old European forms. Second, it was a style that, by borrowing from colonial precedents, was believed to compensate for the colonial architectural heritage destroyed with the razing of the mountain.[61] Clearly, for the establishment in Rio, no other style could both evoke a new modern Brazilian identity and retain the country's deep European roots. And the Centennial Exhibition was the perfect showcase for this style

that architects themselves justified even from an evolutionary point of view. According to Fernando Nereo de Sampaio, the vice president of the Brazilian Institute of Architects at the time, architecture was the very "definition of an idea, . . . the synthesis of a social movement, the moral, material and intellectual state of a civilization."[62] In fact, following Lamarckian theories, Nereo de Sampaio compared the propagation of architectural styles with the propagation of new natural species—both of which he considered products of "heredity

FIGURE 2.22.
Advertisement, "Fabrica de Calçado Souto," published in O Livro de Ouro: Comemorativo do centenário da independência do Brasil e da Exposição Internacional do Rio de Janeiro *(Rio de Janeiro: Edição do Annuario do Brasil, 1923). Instituto Histórico e Geográfico Brasileiro, Rio de Janeiro.*

and [environmental] adaptation."[63] For Nereo de Sampaio, it was precisely through the influences arising from the milieu that those characteristics, passed on from generation to generation, could be modified, creating new forms linked to a specific period and society.[64] Other architects at the time, including Morales de los Rios Filho, followed these Lamarckian ideas to argue that by responding to heredity and environmental adaptation, architectural styles are the consequences "of a historic tradition, social and ecological exigencies, aesthetic sensibilities, racial or economic necessities, religious devotion, political transformation, the discovery of new materials, wars, invasions, migrations and customs."[65] Although not one of these architects ever directly referenced Lamarck or eugenics, they were actually using an architectural style as a way to express the main tenets of Lamarckian eugenics and also to announce a new era of architecture, permeated by ideological assumptions that undoubtedly declared their modernist agenda of social engineering.[66] In the end, for the Brazilian technocrats and elites, "modernity [was] equated with whiteness."[67]

O Livro de Ouro, the more than five-hundred-page catalogue for the Centennial Exhibition, was explicit when it described the exhibition as an "expression of the constructive energy of a new race," one that was able to triumph in the "battle between man, mountain, and ocean."[68] The exhibition itself represented a literal "triumph" over the territory—promoting itself as a tabula rasa, a new territory cleansed of its history and its unwanted inhabitants.[69] It is striking that even the catalogue speaks of a desire to totally eliminate all traces of African and indigenous components of Brazilian culture.[70] Exploring the imagery displayed throughout the catalogue provides a powerful demonstration of a new alliance between beauty, health, tropicality, and modernization adopted by the Brazilian elites to represent themselves and their new nation. In most publicity materials for companies and products, white men, women, and children of classic Greco-Roman appearance, wearing white robes and crowns, are arranged against a transplanted European-looking hill and gardens to frame the architecture and machinery of modern factories.[71] Here, the ideal of beauty and virtue is represented as "Hellenic."[72] These representations of white Mediterranean people grew out of a conviction that Brazilians would one day be "transformed into pure Greeks."[73]

Just as human beings are portrayed here as icons of the ideal, so too were natural monuments, released from their tropical fatality, politicized as new icons of collective identity and moralized as elements of transformation directly linked to the reimagining of the body. In several advertisements, the *Livro de Ouro* exalts the natural monuments of Rio de Janeiro, particularly those that were human-made or human-dominated. In fact, an advertisement for a medication portrays the Pão de Açúcar, a prominent mountain that rose up from the water at the entrance of the bay, as one of the Seven Wonders of the World, comparing it to monuments such as the Eiffel

FIGURE 2.23.
Advertisement, "O Contratosse e as sete maravilhas do mundo," published in O Livro de Ouro: Comemorativo do centenário da independência do Brasil e da Exposição Internacional do Rio de Janeiro *(Rio de Janeiro: Edição do Annuario do Brasil, 1923). Instituto Histórico e Geográfico Brasileiro, Rio de Janeiro.*

FIGURE 2.24.
Pão de Açúcar and the funicular, ca. 1912. Post card, n.d. Collection of the author.

FIGURE 2.25.
S. H. Holland, photograph of the construction of the Christ the Redeemer statue at the peak of the Corcovado Mountain, with view of Pão de Açúcar, Rio de Janeiro, Brazil, ca. 1931. Image record 013RJ009013. S. H. Holland/Brascan Cem Anos no Brasil Collection/ Instituto Moreira Salles.

Tower, the Statue of Liberty, and the Hanging Gardens of Babylon.[74] The advertisement exalts the mountain because of its beauty and history but especially because of its new funicular, the third cable car built in the world, which facilitated access to the peak. The exhibition catalogue also celebrates the Corcovado, the extraordinary mountain at the center of the Tijuca Forest, the world's largest human-made urban rainforest located at the very center of the city, which would be crowned a few years later with a monumental 40-meter-tall statue of Christ the Redeemer.[75] In fact, the stone foundation was laid at the peak of the mountain on April 04, 1922.[76] In razing the Morro do Castelo while transforming two other mountains within the city into sites of pure aesthetic pleasure, tropical nature—now monumentalized—is portrayed as a site of the interplay between the body, labor, and technology. In the end, the exhibition was conceived as a self-portrait of a modern nation—a nation that was able to undertake a self-remaking process, changing its milieu to change its population.

On another level, the exhibition itself represented a triumph of control over nature and over illness itself. Organized as main attractions of the fair behind the neocolonial façades of the exhibition's pavilions, two particular museums isolated the so-called social diseases presumably eradicated with the demolition of the mountain and the displacement of its supposedly "degenerate" inhabitants: tuberculosis and syphilis.[77] Thus, the demolition, part of the reform called "regeneration," reveals not only Brazilian elites' faith in their slow but steady march toward "whitening" the population but also their new fear of the pariahs of modern times: alcoholics, syphilitics, prostitutes, and sexual deviants. It was not by accident that most of the population eradicated by the reform was black—the same people that the Brazilian writer Lima Barreto had identified as those "non-invited to the party."[78] For Brazilian elites, medical science represented the medium through which modernity could be achieved and the rationalization by which their actions could be legitimized.

In his article in the *Livro de Ouro*, the well-known Brazilian physician and eugenicist Antônio Austregésilo cites one hundred years of Brazilian achievements in medicine, biology, and hygiene. H[e] emphasizes the primacy of medical sciences by stating that "na[tion] with primitive medicine cannot be great; without doubt, it is[ ] and biological experimentation that determine the sci[entif]ity of developed nations."[79] He exalts Oswaldo Cruz['s] eradication of yellow fever from the cities; Carlos [ ] against venereal diseases, leprosy, tuberculosi[s] Moreira's and Franco da Rocha's assistan[ce] various other policies adopted by the National Department of Public Health spanning from domestic hygiene to food control.[80] Austregésilo was convinced that "the Brazilian medical spirit was always a *satellite* of the French spirit." Although Brazilians were aware of medical advances produced in Germany, Italy, England, and the United States of America, he argues that it was to France that they turned for knowledge and orientation.[81] Clearly, a fear of the degeneration of their population provoked the French to shift their attention from infectious to genetic diseases, and to become preoccupied with a new series of medical classifications and new measurements for fitness. This new threat immediately assaulted the Brazilian establishment. Various articles published in the *Livro de Ouro* emphasize the "urgent protection of the fittest" and the need to extend social hygiene from the schools of medicine to general education in each elementary and high school throughout the country. In other words, the articles emphasize the importance of hygiene education, not only in medical circles but, most critically, in the education of "all men and women who will be fathers and mothers."[82] The ideas behind these articles and the numerous advertisements throughout the *Livro de Ouro* demonstrate the Brazilian elites' determination to merge hygienics and eugenics, materialized as the French science-faith known as puericulture.[83]

As at the 1889 World's Fair in Paris, the 1922 Centennial Exhibition in Rio also included several international scientific conferences.[84] Among them, the First Brazilian Congress for the Protection of Infants (Primeiro Congresso Brasileiro de Proteção à Infância), organized by the recently created Department of Infancy in Brazil, was an agent for France's transformation of puericulture into a neo-Lamarckian form of eugenics.[85] Revealing the influence of French medicine on Brazilian medical circles, the debates at the Congress focused on the importance of puericulture—a term revitalized by Pinard as "the research plication of all knowledge relative to the reproduc- and improvement of the human species."[86] Echoing physicians were convinced that "a child was the in equilibrium: heredity and milieu," and that con- ture in the Brazilian context was considered "one ble ways of conserving and perfecting the human vas a neo-Lamarckian; he believed in the heredi- f acquired characteristics. From this notion, two lerived. On the one hand, children—considered a olitical resource—and their mothers were treated arded as a "collective political economy." On the ment became the plausible stage for apparently

FIGURE 2.26.
Interview with the Bra-
zilian eugenicist Renato
Kehl, "A Puericultura
Pre-Conceptional," ca.
1940. Departamento de
Arquivo e Documentação,
Casa Oswaldo Cruz/
Fiocruz—Fundação
Oswaldo Cruz, Funds
Renato Kehl (Box 3),
Rio de Janeiro.

contradictory goals: the preservation of a country's national image and the transformation of its inhabitants, giving particular attention to urban planning and to the transformation of the milieu in which reproduction, maternity, and child rearing all occurred simultaneously. These two elements—heredity and milieu—were crucial for the transformation of puericulture into eugenics. In France, puericulture and its goal of producing healthy children rather than eliminating defectives had inaugurated a movement that sounded so benign and lovable that it soon attracted supporters from all sides of the political spectrum as well as interest abroad. By the time it was adopted in Brazil, where it morphed into its official form as the French Eugenics Society, puericulture had been tainted by the racial prejudice that characterized mainstream eugenics.[88] What is unmistakable about the way eugenics reverberated in Brazil was that it presented itself far beyond the structures of racial bias, seeping into the realms of science and aesthetics, becoming an "aesthetic-biological movement concerned with beauty and ugliness, purity and contamination, as represented in race."[89] It was at this very point in Brazil that the built environment, considered both the main carrier of vice and disease as well as the "main transmitter of modernism," became the ultimate technology of Lamarckian eugenics.[90]

AGACHE'S *LABORATOIRE* IN RIO DE JANEIRO

It was not by chance that, in 1926, four years after the commemorations of the independence of Brazil and its related scientific conferences, a group of physicians and architects met to discuss an urban plan that would determine the fate of the Morro do Castelo's esplanade, temporarily occupied by the exhibition's pavilions.[91] Alleging hygienic and eugenic factors, it was also not a coincidence that this group, led by the influential Rotary Club of Rio with members that included the engineer Armando de Godoy and the physicians José Mariano Filho and João Augusto de Mattos Pimenta, proposed for this urban transformation the name of two architects who were members of the Parisian Musée social: Jaussely and Agache.[92] It was, in fact, Mariano Filho, the physician and art critic—the most vehement proponent of neocolonial architecture in Brazil—who emphatically supported the candidacy of Agache.[93] Why did such an ardent promoter of a style inspired by Brazil's colonial past become the main advocate for the appointment of a French architect? It is clear that this appointment was an expression of a country that had preferred European over Brazilian designers and that, since the time of the Portuguese Empire, had brought a constellation of French artists and architects to the country.[94] But it is telling that Mariano Filho proposed an architect from the Beaux-Arts tradition even though he was the main promoter of a style based on the incorporation of elements from a national tradition—one that emerged as a response to the "destructive cosmopolitanism" that its backers believed would disfigure the "face" of Brazilian cities.[95] The choice of Agache arose amid the cultural and political tensions of the 1920s between the "conservative" modernists—who argued for a modernity based on the languages of the country's colonial heritage or on the languages of nineteenth-century Europe—and the vanguard modernists of the Semana de Arte Moderna (Week of Modern Art) in São Paulo—who wanted to represent modern Brazil as a stylized mixture of the foreign, the indigenous, and the African.[96] In a context in which the state supported a style that was in a sense antimodernist, pro-Iberian, and at the same time "white" as an emblem of progress and modernity, the inscription of the new Morro do Castelo esplanade with European forms was a contradictory act.[97] First, the esplanade's tabula rasa that supposedly would bring forth a modern urban center was filled with neocolonial pavilions, and then it was reimagined with Agache's Beaux-Arts forms. What is clear here is that inviting Agache to formulate an urban plan in a European vernacular identified by the elites as their own expressed a visual ideology of "whiteness" that was the common denominator of both the neocolonial and the Beaux-Arts styles.[98] Of course, these elites—politicians, reformers, intellectuals, and physicians—were not a homogeneous group, but they seemed to agree on the normative élan they wanted for their cities. Even Mário de Andrade, one of the main protagonists of the Semana de Arte Moderna, was also an open supporter of Mariano Filho's ideas and the promotion of the style he called "maternal architecture."[99] In fact, in 1928, in a series of articles published in *Diário Nacional*, Andrade recognized and celebrated the role of the architects working for the "normalization" of the neocolonial as a Brazilian national style.[100] In many ways, these "modern" attitudes sought to homogenize the city and, with it, its population, and then proclaim the esplanade a political and economic altar to power, infused with European forms.

Agache arrived in Rio on June 25, 1927, and a few days later delivered his first lecture, "What Is Urbanism?" (O que é o urbanismo?). He began his lecture by introducing himself as the physician who, having a medical case on his hands, had to produce a diagnosis for the pathological condition of the sick city—Rio de Janeiro—that, due to its impetuous growth, needed to ⸍reated:

> I want you to see me as a kin⸍   ⸍een consulted and
> who is more than pleased to ⸍   ⸍d to be able
> to make use of it in his con⸍   ⸍hmit-
> ted for examination. I say
> rioca [referring to Rio ⸍
> But do not be afraid,
> is curable, because ⸍

For Agache this ⸍
800,000 in 1906 ⸍
result of a lacⱶ
urgently reqⱶ

Madem⸍
rioca"

EUGENICS IN THE GARDEN

the rapid development of her circulation, is now ailing. Her breathing, her circulation, and her digestive system soon will be threatened. What to do? A physician needs to prescribe a severe regimen, a model of progress and discipline, and urgently provide her with a regulatory plan that allows her to blossom favorably.[102]

To control the city's growth, Agache proposed a "discipline" that years earlier he had helped create with his colleagues at the Musée social in Paris, defined as "a science and an art" but overall as a "social philosophy."[103] According to Agache, to whom the term "urbanism" was attributed, urbanism embodied the "rules" for the "amelioration" of the city—it was, in his own words, "the renovation, the expansion, and the beautification of a city, accomplished by a methodological study of *human geography* and *urban topography* without disregarding financial solutions."[104] Underlying this statement is an interesting assumption: that both land and people can be codified and controlled. In any case, Agache's definition of urbanism highlighted the difference between the "modern" urbanism born at the Musée social and the urban transformation undertaken earlier by Haussmann and imported to Rio de Janeiro by Mayor Francisco Pereira Passos to inaugurate the century. This distinction is apparent in modern urbanism's emphasis on social welfare, the primacy of the socioeconomic aspects of urban planning that displaced preoccupations with circulation and hygiene, which drove Haussmann's interventions.[105] In the search for moral and economic progress, this move from circulation to social welfare, from hygiene to eugenics, was conceived as part of a new interdisciplinary and transnational mission undertaken by the architect members of the Musée social. They found in medicine a rationale and a methodology for their practices, and in the Latin American nations, culturally dependent on France, the perfect site for their experiments and for the promotion of the new "science" of urbanism—complicit with social engineering.

In November of 1927, Agache received a commission to develop the first comprehensive master plan for Rio de Janeiro. After studying the city and its problems for two years, Agache and his team produced a complete diagnosis of Rio, elaborating on the various short- and long-term projects that should be executed for its "expansion, amelioration, and beautification." In 1930, Agache's master plan was completed. Although the plan included the expected blueprints and photographs urban areas to be surgically altered as well as each building's also included more than three hundred pages of text de- otion of his main goal: social ideology. Beyond the possibility of an immediate execution of his plan, Agache sought to indoctrinate the people of Rio in the "cause" of urbanism. From his very first lecture in Rio, he warned his audience that it "is necessary that the sick patient be the first to desire her cure." In no uncertain terms, Agache was referring once again to Rio as a young female while describing his role as a "positivist missionary" who was there in a "conquest" to indoctrinate "the maximum number of adherents to the cause of urbanism," the social doctrine that would ensure the city's cure.[106]

In his master plan, following his historical account of the development of the city, Agache produced two documents that would allow him to convey his plans to radically transform the city center by demolishing two mountains: a current aerial photograph of Rio to produce what he called "plan photo-topographique," and his "plan schématique." Agache used both documents to identify the nearly razed Morro do Castelo, whose demolition produced a new infill of land that included an area that Agache called Ponta do Calabouço.[107] Through these documents, he also identified the still existing Morro

FIGURE 2.27.
Donat-Alfred Agache, "Plan Schématique" published in Agache, A cidade do Rio de Janeiro, remodelação, extensão e embeleza- mento, 1927–1930 *(Paris: Foyer Brésilien, 1930).*

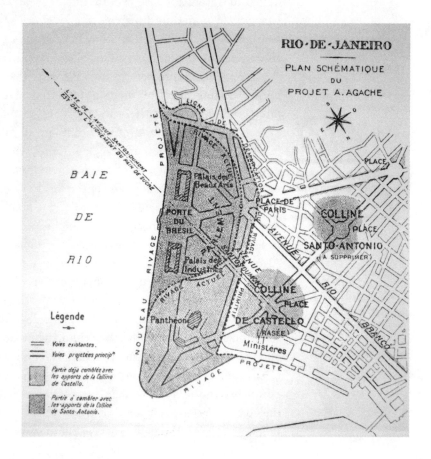

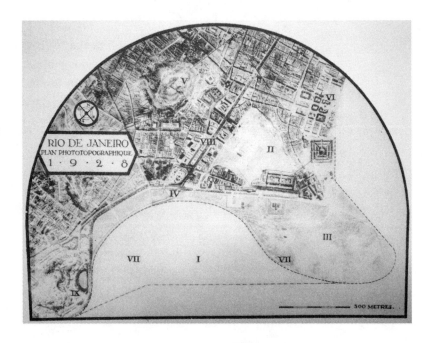

de Santo Antônio, whose eventual demolition would also produce a
new infill of land, thus drawing a more rectilinear border from the waterfront of the Glória neighborhood to Agache's Ponta do Calabouço.
In the schematic plan, Agache marked an axis from the epicenter of
the former mountain, now Castelo Plaza, to the Pão de Açúcar, Rio's
natural landmark at the other side of the bay.[108] Advocating the demolition of the Morro do Castelo and the Morro de Santo Antônio, Agache
argued that the administrative and financial area of the city found
itself trapped between these two mountains, with the only circulatory
road being the Avenida Rio Branco, the main axis of Pereira Passos'
urban intervention. The razing of the Morro de Santo Antônio would
add another 200,000 square meters of flat land on the other side of
Rio Branco Avenue, and about 650,000 square meters of land filled
in to rectify the border of the Glória and Flamengo neighborhoods.[109]
Also, the elimination of this mountain would eradicate the crowded
and inefficient conditions of the streets and houses of the colonial
city, replacing them with parks and majestic avenues. Clearly for
Agache, as for his promoter, João Augusto de Mattos Pimenta, urban
intervention in Rio meant more than the demolition of mountains
and the creation of new urban esplanades; it meant the identification
of the "unhealthy" areas to be clinically removed from the "healthy"
new urban fabric. The push for the mountains' demolition, which had
fueled the elites' agenda for almost a decade, was without doubt a prelude to eugenics, the new "science" that, as would soon be described

FIGURE 2.29.
*Donat-Alfred Agache,
green urban areas and
reservoirs (Map/detail),
published in Agache,* A
cidade do Rio de Janeiro,
remodelação, extensão
e embelezamento,
1927–1930 *(Paris: Foyer
Brésilien, 1930).*

FIGURE 2.30.
*Donat-Alfred Agache,
business center and
Castelo Square in Rio
de Janeiro, published in
Agache,* A cidade do Rio
de Janeiro, remodelação,
extensão e embeleza-
mento, 1927–1930 *(Paris:
Foyer Brésilien, 1930).*

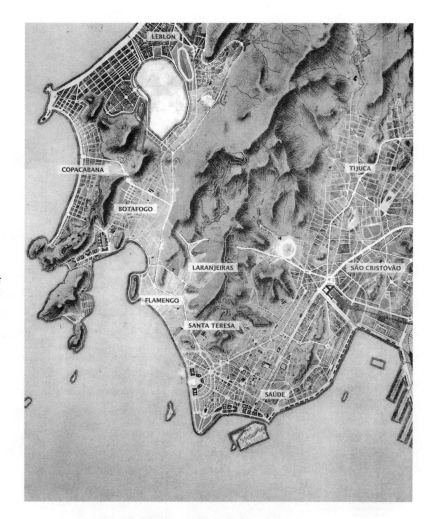

at the inaugural session of the First Brazilian Congress of Eugenics in Rio, "guaranteed the efficiency and the perfection of the race."[110] Thus, when Agache supported the demolition of the two mountains by saying this was the only way to create an aesthetically pleasing, functional, and prolific downtown urban area, he was actually championing architecture as the only means capable of improving the health and beauty of the city and its population.

Agache argued that "those territories recovered from nature due to human tenacity will allow us to offer two essential functional ele-

FIGURE 2.31.
Donat-Alfred Agache, Ponta do Calabouço, or city's social area, published in Agache, A cidade do Rio de Janeiro, remodelação, extensão e embelezamento, 1927–1930 *(Paris: Foyer Brésilien, 1930).*

FIGURE 2.32.
Donat-Alfred Agache, gardens in Ponta do Calabouço, published in Agache, A cidade do Rio de Janeiro, remodelação, extensão e embelezamento, 1927–1930 *(Paris: Foyer Brésilien, 1930).*

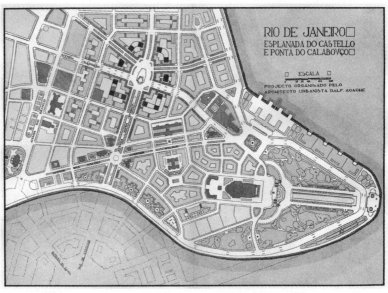

ments to the city: the government center and the financial center . . . representing urban economy in harmony with the modern needs of progress."[111] In a further delineation of the central area of the city, Agache organized three main functional elements: the business center, the "city's social" center, and Rio's "command post." In the area that was once occupied by the Morro do Castelo, Agache visualized the "Castelo" business center—an architectural complex of identical skyscrapers that represented the "economic forces associated with the social ideals of our epoch."[112] As the architectural historian David Underwood observes, "for Agache, this meant the creation of good urbanistic ensembles that subordinated undisciplined individuals and single buildings to a disciplined and uniform total environment that could satisfy modern 'social and economic exigencies' in a 'logical and regular' fashion."[113] These series of skyscrapers that emerged from a solid platform of horizontal buildings, hosting shopping arcades, parking facilities, and other public services, surrounded a colossal plaza crowned at its center with an almost cartoonish miniature monument to commemorate the place and the founder of the city: a monument that resembled a ruin, one fragment of those buildings dislodged from the hill on which the city was founded. At Ponta do Calabouço, a kind of isthmus reclaimed from the sea, Agache visualized cultivated nature, a kind of "tropical Versailles," a French formal garden with a reflecting pool surrounded by a succession of glorious palm trees and gazebos marking an axis between the magnificent views of the bay and a monumental building, a pantheon for national heroes. Agache saw this area of gardens and promenades as the perfect setting for

FIGURE 2.33.
J. Carlos's cartoon, "Negócio da China," published in Careta, *August 27, 1921.*

FIGURE 2.34.
J. Carlos's cartoon, "Os extremos se tocam," published in Careta, *August 27, 1921.*

the location of foreign embassies—a tropical land that was cultivated and healed for the enjoyment of European tourists, which, as a result of Agache's transformation, would make Rio "among all the tropical regions, the one in which the white man can most easily adapt."[114]

Notably, there was no accommodation for the poor—mostly blacks—in Agache's plan, including those people who would be displaced after the Morro de Santo Antônio was demolished. In a talk given at the Rotary Club on November 12, 1926, Mattos Pimenta anticipated Agache's plan:

> Nevertheless, to outline the plan, even before its adoption, it is relevant to put an immediate stop, to raise a prophylactic barrier against the overwhelming infestation of the beautiful mountains of Rio de Janeiro by the plague of the "favelas" [the slums]—the leprosy of aesthetics that emerged on the hillside . . . and was spread everywhere, filling in dirt and misery. [The slums] do not constitute purely a ruthless crime against aesthetics; they are particularly a serious threat to peace and public health.[115]

This racist and classist view, equating the black race and poor people with what Mattos Pimenta called the "leprosy" of favelas, was also evident in Mariano Filho's ideology. He suggests that when blacks isolate themselves in the favelas, away from white civilization, "violent impulses [arise] from the unconscious." In his own words, the "return to primitive life enables blacks to satisfy their racial tendencies, their fetishistic practices, their dances and the macumba." As the Brazilian scholar Joel Outtes observes, if the favelas provoked criminality and immorality, then, according to technocrats of the time, architecture had the power to fix it.[116] In a dramatic way, the demolition of the Morro de Santo Antônio—which would produce the esplanade for the construction of Agache's command post or "the entrance to Brazil"—was in fact a repressive project that was intended to provide order to a "feeble" society. This civic center, which Agache said would be the ideal space for the carnival parade so beloved by Brazilians, was presented in his drawings as a highly formal ceremonial space in which the multitudes, rather than dancing, were shown in army formation, in geometrical molded squares, as if they were part of the surrounding architecture. It seems that in his need to map people as if they were spatial components, Agache materialized what he called "anthropogeography," a term that Le Corbusier would also use in his 1936 talks in Rio and in his 1942 book, *La Maison des hommes* (*The Home of Man*), as a way to collapse his concept of urban topography

FIGURE 2.35.
*Donat-Alfred Agache,
downtown aerial
perspective of Rio de
Janeiro, including the
Command Post and the
Castelo Business Center,
published in Agache,* A
cidade do Rio de Janeiro,
remodelação, extensão
e embelezamento,
1927–1930 *(Paris: Foyer
Brésilien, 1930).*

FIGURE 2.36.
*Donat-Alfred Agache,
Command Post (the
entrance to Brazil),
published in Agache,* A
cidade do Rio de Janeiro,
remodelação, extensão
e embelezamento,
1927–1930 *(Paris: Foyer
Brésilien, 1930).*

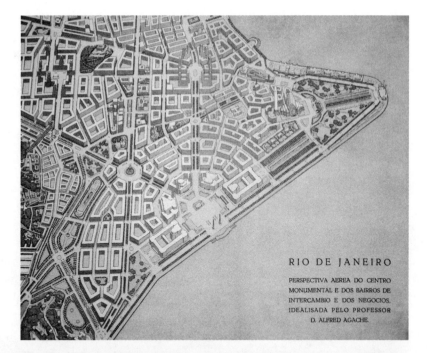

into his notion of human geography—a topic for in-depth discussion in chapter 4.

As Agache was finishing his master plan for Brazil's capital city in 1929, Le Corbusier was making his first trip to Latin America, and at the same time, the First Brazilian Congress of Eugenics was opening in Rio with an important statement that brought architecture to the center of the social and biological movement of eugenics. At the inaugural session, the physician and anthropologist Edgard Roquette-Pinto addressed an audience of physicians preoccupied with the question of how a country as vast as Brazil could best increase, and even improve, its population. To accomplish this, Roquette-Pinto exalted "eugenia" as the new science that, together with medicine and hygiene, would guarantee the efficiency and perfection of the race.[117]

According to him, eugenics integrated heredity and environment as its primary tools: "It is critical to emphasize that the influence [on our race] does not stem from the natural environment but rather from the artificial environment, created by man."[118] With these words, Roquette-Pinto underscored a positivist agenda that was at the very core of the eugenics movement in Latin America: the crucial role of the built environment in the "amelioration" of "the biological patrimony" of the region's diverse population.[119]

A few months earlier, this same eugenics stance was embraced by Lúcio Costa—the architect best known for his extraordinary modernist plans for the country's new modern capital, Brasília.[120] In a 1928 article, he publicly declared:

> I am pessimistic about . . . architecture and urbanism in general. All architecture is a question of race. When our nation is that exotic thing that we see on the streets, our architecture will inevitably be an exotic thing. It is not those half dozen who travel and dress on Rue de la Paix, but that anonymous crowd that takes trains from Central [Station] and Leopoldina, people with sickly faces who shame us everywhere. What can we expect from people like this? Everything is a function of race. If the breed is good, and the government is good, the architecture will be good. Talk, discuss, gesticulate: our basic problem is selective immigration; the rest is secondary—it will change on its own.[121]

It is clear that these sentiments represent a racist eugenics policy—one that has essentially gone unmentioned in the urban literature of Rio and that was almost absent from Costa's own historiography. Just as the neocolonial style, appropriated in Brazil as the emblem of progress and modernity, was nothing less than the embodiment of "whiteness," so too was Agache's intention for Rio—manifested in his lectures, exhibitions, and even the texts that accompany his Beaux-Arts urban master plan—a bold expression of the historically overlooked interplay between social engineering and architecture. Yet it is undeniable that underlying these architectural styles and urban strategies are the evolutionary theories that were first internalized by influential modernists and then instrumentalized in their practices: from the demolition of the Morro do Castelo, to the construction of the centennial's neocolonial pavilions, to Agache's urban laboratory, and finally to the functionalist utopian canons of Lúcio Costa and Le Corbusier.

It seems inevitable, then, that at almost the same time in 1930, Getúlio Vargas was taking steps to authorize the creation of the

FIGURE 2.37.
Lúcio Costa, Oscar Niemeyer, Jorge Moreira, Affonso Eduardo Reidy, Roberto Burle Marx, Carlos Leão, and Le Corbusier, Ministry of Health and Education, Rio de Janeiro, 1936–1942. GC Foto 496, No. 46. Collection Gustavo Capanema, Centro de Pesquisa e Documentação de História Contemporânea do Brasil, FUNDAÇÃO GETULIO VARGAS— CPDOC, São Paulo.

Ministry of Health and Education to house the offices of culture, labor relations, industry, education, and health care—all under the roof of one federal institution that would, from that moment on, consolidate the eugenicist policies already in practice. It is also significant that a few years later, at the epicenter of Agache's transformation in Rio—the esplanade that remained after the Morro do Castelo was demolished—a modernist building for this new ministry would be constructed.[122] This ministry, which was in charge of implementing Brazil's eugenics agenda, is the same one that invited Le Corbusier to be the key adviser to Costa and his design team.[123] As we shall see in chapter 4, this new building for the Ministry of Health and Education, the most celebrated icon of Brazilian architectural modernism, aesthetically referenced the eugenics movement's strategy to control nature by incorporating, for example, a cellular panel on the building's façade—the so-called *brise-soleil*—that functions as both an environmental device and a decorative element associated with tropical climates and primitive cultures.[124] It is telling that this decorative "tattoo" undermined the unadorned aesthetics that characterized the International Style, which was founded on an evolutionary stance that equates cultural progress with the "extinction" of ornamentation—just as "primitive races were dying out through a biological process of selection."[125] Although the heart of this story is discussed in chapter 4, it is important to note here that it was in Rio de Janeiro that Le Corbusier first articulated his eugenics stance during his 1936 talks; and just a few years later, he would consolidate his position by going so far as to claim that the built environment was a critical antidote to the body's degeneration, arguing that "the degeneration of the house, the degeneration of the family, are one."[126] It is evident, then, that Costa's eugenics syllogism of breed begetting good government begetting good architecture would also work in reverse: as Le Corbusier envisioned it, architecture was poised to become an innovative tool for social engineering, an optimum medium for "the rebirth of the human body."[127]

CHAPTER 3

MACHINES FOR MODERN LIFE

The Apparatuses of Health and Reproduction

Deciphering the binary code of medicine and society under the spell of architecture, in this chapter I interrogate a central but disregarded project of modern architecture—its clinical agenda—which traveled on the back of medical science and Lamarckian eugenics, inserting itself into the urban fabric of early-twentieth-century Latin America.[1] Although this clinical project was central to modernism at large, this chapter focuses on Argentina, a country that, in its obsession with the struggle between "civilization and barbarism," placed hygiene at the center of its modernization quest.[2] I illuminate both the social history of the modern institutions that attempted to ameliorate the health of the nation and the architectures that were simultaneously created as medical instruments—as national projects of healing and social reform. In other words, by exploring the means of imagining a network of buildings, parks, gardens, playgrounds, reformatories, schools, and even the family home—the apparatuses of health and reproduction—I reveal how this complex technological system regulated global flows of people, rationalized sexuality, and sought to purify reproduction in the new Latin world.

Prescribed by physicians and executed by architects, these spaces became tangible extensions of the eugenic concept of puericulture, which, as previously discussed, focuses on the mother-child unit and the reproduction and improvement of the human species; and of the concept of hominiculture, which focuses on the entire span of individual human life with particular emphasis on the consequences of the so-called social diseases—syphilis, alcoholism, and tuberculosis.[3] Tracing the roots of degeneration theories from France to Latin America at the turn of the century, I examine the confluence of medicine, society, and milieu used to "normalize" a so-called feeble society in the name of constructing a modern nation. In doing so, I postulate a cross-section of ideas about health and disease, nation and citizenship, productivity and modernity through an examination of new *dispositifs* of human perfectibility, those spaces, regulations, and ideologies expressly created to permeate the city, with the ultimate aim of reconfiguring the family and the nation.[4] With the term *dispositif*, I refer to the apparatus "that has in some way the capacity to capture, orient, determine, intercept, model, control, or secure the gestures, behaviors, opinions, or discourses of living beings," as it was defined by Giorgio Agamben. *Dispositifs*, as Agamben points out, include traditional institutions in which discipline and power are clearly exercised—such as prisons, insane asylums, schools, and factories—but also applies to anything that manages us in certain ways that may not be apparent, including language, culture, and even food.[5]

Before it was imported to Latin America, the fear of *dégénérescence*—a "self-reproducing force" transmitted from generation to generation that drags the individual body and society itself down to decay and final extinction—was, without a doubt, the main obsession of late-nineteenth-century France.[6] Following the Lamarckian idea of "inherited characteristics," individual pathologies were both a symptom of degeneracy and a cause of continued decline.[7] Theories of degeneration became the most dominant explanation for the causes and consequences of the so-called social diseases affecting the French nation at the time—alcoholism, tuberculosis, venereal diseases, and also "the incapacity (or unwillingness) to procreate."[8] As previously noted, it was at the end of the nineteenth century that the social hygiene movement in France addressed for the first time in a single vision these three health problems, which until then had been seen as separate. It was precisely this convergence that characterized the social hygiene movement and its concept of biological regeneration. In this sense, neo-Lamarckian ideas provided the platform for the emergence of social hygiene.

A major voice of this "progressive pathology" was the well-known French writer Émile Zola, who, writing under the impetus of science, devoted his entire series *Les Rougon-Macquart* (1871–1893) to the powerful interaction between pathology, society, and space. Echoing the positivist physiologist Claude Bernard's work on the influence of the physical environment on the development of human lives, Zola argued:

> Man cannot be separated from his milieu . . . [he] is completed by his clothing, his house, his city, and his province; . . . [we cannot] refer to one single phenomenon of his brain or heart without searching for its causes and consequences in the milieu.[9]

By portraying a degenerate family across successive bloodlines, the twenty novels that comprise the series *Les Rougon-Macquart* would set out to reveal how the dual question of heredity and milieu determines the continuity of mankind.[10] Zola wanted to show in a single family "the play of race modified by the milieu."[11] He extended the characteristics of individual degeneration to the entire body of the nation at a time when medicine, the science that had become a constitutive component of the very idea of society, had spread into new social spaces. These new spaces went beyond the traditional hospital to pervade the city at large and the domestic space of the home, ultimately permeating society and its cell, the family. What is so remarkable about his system is that Zola, the writer, actually assumed two other personas—that of the physician making diagnoses of disease

FIGURE 3.1.
Émile Zola, genealogy of the main characters in Les Rougon-Macquart. *Preparatory dossier for* Le Docteur Pascal, *1893. Manuscrits, NAF 10.290, f. 121 and NAF 10.290, f. 185 (color). Bibliothèque nationale de France, Gallica, http://gallica.bnf.fr.*

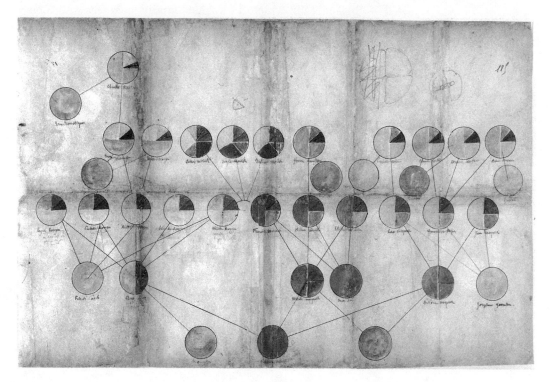

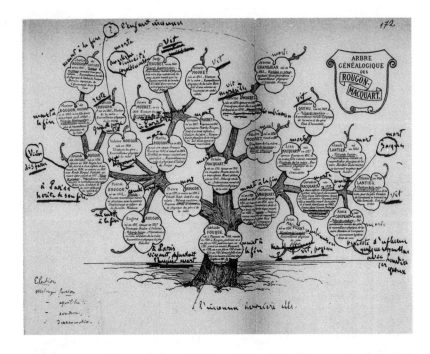

and degeneration, and that of the architect drafting more than 150
plans and sketches as the materialization of the very antidote—the
built environment—to society's ills.[12] These unique graphics include
Zola's fictional hereditary diagrams and genealogical family trees as
well as the spaces in which the various family members were imagined to have lived—spaces that were thought to be both the cause of
and the cure for degeneration.[13] He portrayed a family—a social cell
on the spectrum between the individual and the collective—tainted
by diseases caused by environmental factors in order to demonstrate
how degeneration permeated society and how space itself had become
the spark that reshaped society.[14]

In his diagnosis of France during the Second Empire, Zola moves
from portraying the entropic decline of a nation to affirming life as
an organizing force that overcomes entropy.[15] Influenced by scientific
ideas circulating at the time, in particular by Prosper Lucas' notion of
heredity and Claude Bernard's conviction about the centrality of the
physical environment to the development of organisms, Zola's work
reveals his positivist faith in order and science as a medium to arrest
the steady progress of decay.[16] The subtitle of his *Rougon-Macquart*
series, *A Natural and Social History of a Family under the Second
Empire*, suggests his epistemic agenda, aiming to demonstrate how
human nature is determined by heredity—the natural—and by the
environment—the social. In a sense, this is tantamount to Zola depicting the built physical environment as a technology of eugenics.

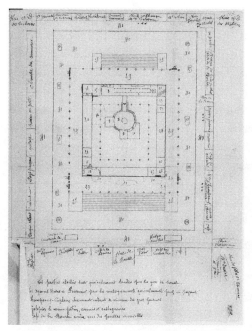

FIGURE 3.3.
Émile Zola, plan for "La Bourse." Preparatory dossier for L'Argent, *1891. Manuscrits, NAF 10.269, f. 137. Bibliothèque nationale de France, Gallica, http://gallica.bnf.fr.*

FIGURES 3.4–3.5.
Émile Zola, Les Halles Food Market (Pavilion 3 and Pavilion 5) and its surroundings. Preparatory dossier for Le Ventre de Paris, *1893. Manuscrits, NAF 10.338, f. 267 and NAF 10.338, f. 135. Bibliothèque nationale de France. Gallica. http://gallica.bnf.fr.*

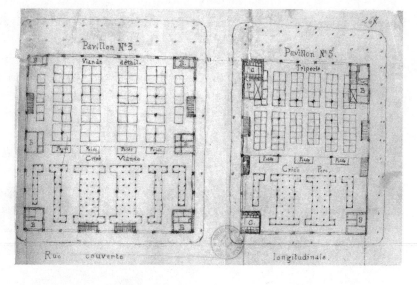

More specifically, from the first novel, *La Fortune des Rougon,* which recounts the origins of the Rougon-Macquart family, to the last novel, *Le Docteur Pascal,* which presents the pro-natalist solution to the decay of the family and society, Zola offers a remarkable portrait of the ravages of alcoholism, syphilis, sexual depravity, prostitution, corruption, and insanity.[17] Analyzing the legal union between the mentally ill Dide and a local peasant (the Rougon side), along with Dide's adulterous union with a drunken poacher (the Macquart side), Zola dissects the way the family's capital was inherited as genes, and how alcoholism was transmuted into forms of perversion, venereal diseases, and homicidal madness. But what represents an extraordinary passport to my study is Zola's creative system, which integrates architectural plans, a sort of geometry, an element of order in which Zola inserts a world of social disorder—a floundering market, disease, corruption, and crime—through the personas of the speculator, the alcoholic, the syphilitic, the murderer, and the anarchist. Seeing his own work as a scientific document, Zola invented preparatory hereditary diagrams as a rationale for the genealogical trees appearing in some of his novels to show, for instance, the birth of a criminal in *La Bête humaine*, and the hereditary trends and ills used to reconstruct the genetic history of the entire Rougon-Macquart family in *Le Docteur Pascal*. Zola also presented and re-presented the urban plans of the communities and neighborhoods that he imagined to have shaped his characters, noting the names and the layout of streets and sidewalks; and the architectural plans of the buildings, including the worker house in *L'Assommoir*,[18] the miner house in *Germinal*,[19] the cabaret and the prostitute's cabinet in *Nana*,[20] the wagon train in *La Bête humaine*,[21] the bourgeois apartment and garden in *La Curée* and in *Pot-Bouille*,[22] and the modern food market pavilions that nourished Paris in *Le Ventre de Paris*. In fact, in this latter novel, Zola describes the neighborhood of Les Halles in detail, where the characters spend hours wandering through the food market pavilions, painstakingly naming the streets and even the location of goods, as well as the architectonic characteristics of each one of the pavilions—those modern iron and glass halls designed by the architect Victor Baltard. Clearly,

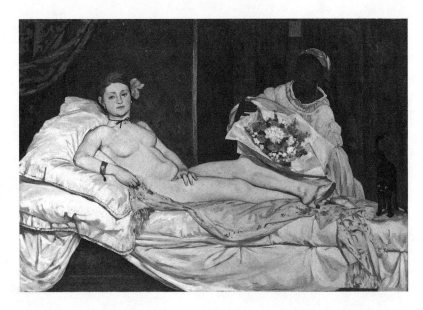

FIGURE 3.6.
Edouard Manet (1832–1883), Olympia, *1863. Oil on canvas, 130.5 × 190.0 cm. RF644. Photo: Patrice Schmidt. Musée d'Orsay, Paris, France. © RMN-Grand Palais / Art Resource, NY.*

Zola's intention was to meticulously materialize the very order—the built environment—that had the capacity to restore health and well-being to a steadily declining citizenry.

Thus, in a highly tangible way, the *Rougon-Macquart* series constitutes a quasi-medical diagnosis of a national process of degeneration that haunted French society, offering a Third Republic retrospective view of Second Empire France. In the same way, *Fécondité*, Zola's next book, was conceived as the repository of a medical technology, presenting the Third Republic's conviction that France's low birthrate—the lowest in Europe—was due to the progressive and pathological weakness of the population, and that the most successful way to confront degeneration was through the generation of healthy children.[23] *Fécondité*'s glorification of family and fertility, its optimistic belief in a pro-natalist solution, took the form of a utopia that embodied France's faith in Lamarckian eugenics—later masquerading in Latin America as an ideology of progress and civilization. Thus, the extraordinary influence of Zola's naturalism on Latin American literature and culture is not surprising.[24] So it was that Argentine naturalists, some of them medically trained novelists, not only used references to biological theories but also adopted medical discourses, which provided epistemological assumptions about sexuality, gender, race, and disease, to legitimize their prejudices and state supervision of any possible threat to the family and the nation. As the Argentine scholar Gabriela Nouzeilles has observed: "Literary naturalism was a reflection upon the conditions necessary to obtain, through eugenic experimentation, the national family—the strong race that would make possible a perfect society." In other words, as Nouzeilles argues, "naturalism, nationalism and medicine complemented each other" in Argentina.[25]

BUENOS AIRES: A PORTRAIT OF A PATHOGENIC MODERN CITY

In 1910, the year of the centennial celebration of Argentina's independence, Buenos Aires was perceived as a postcard of a civilized European city. Illustrious visitors exalted the similarities between Buenos Aires and the most celebrated cities in the world, impressed by its gardens and boulevards, its palaces and monuments. "In architecture it is the South American Paris; in commerce, the South American New York. . . . It was constructed with an extravagance worthy of an ancient Roman emperor," argued H. R. Wallace in his report for *The Journal of Education*.[26] Georges Clemenceau, the French physician and statesman who was prime minister of France in the early twentieth century, describes the Buenos Aires of the centennial as "a large European city, giving everywhere an impression of hasty growth, but foreshadowing, too, in its prodigious progress, the capital of a continent."[27] He compares the Avenida de Mayo with London's world-famous Oxford Street, Palermo Park with the Parisian Bois de Boulogne, and the supermodern industrial buildings along the Riachuelo—grain elevators, meat lockers, and packing plants—with Chicago's magnificent industrial facilities. Amazed by the French cultural influence on local elites, he exalted the hygiene of the city and its health centers, the "Latinity" of its mixed population, and Argentineans' social ideals, their pro-natalist ideology—celebrating that even rich Argentineans "take pleasure in having large families."[28]

However, the city—its ornamented palaces, theaters, clubs, gardens, and the pavilions extolling the centennial—masked the fear and anxiety of degeneration that haunted Argentine society. By the time of these celebrations, at least half the Argentine population was of foreign descent, and immigration, which initially was seen as a vehicle to modernization, had become a threat to the health and stability of the nation. Far from being the strong and civilized white immigrants expected from northern European countries, the actual new inhabitants of Argentina were what the writer Leopoldo Lugones would call "the ultramarine plebeians"—mostly illiterate southern Europeans and also "undesirables" from Eastern Europe, Asia, and the Middle East. According to Argentine power brokers, these groups were dangerous, either because they were thought to carry biological and "social" diseases or because of their poverty, supposedly "criminal" propensities, and subversive revolutionary ideas. Marking the years surrounding the centennial celebrations, fear of these modern masses, coupled with the growing urgency to control the unrest provoked by their demands and even their very presence in the city, triggered a need to reverse the social decay of the masses, ultimately justifying the social-engineering policies implemented thereafter. In fact, during the months prior to the centennial, the city became the stage for workers' riots, social protests, and violence. President José Figueroa Alcorta declared a state of emergency to guarantee that celebration of the nation would pass without political and social upheaval. However, immediately after, on the night of June 26, 1910, a bomb exploded at Teatro Colón in Buenos Aires, instigating a wave of reactionary attacks against immigrants and state repression and immigrant deportation.[29]

The boom in the country's agricultural exports, the consequential expansion of the city, and the institutionalization of democracy had created a new eclectic elite and urban geography in Buenos Aires. Wealthy and politically influential families tied to agricultural networks; merchants from the provinces whose modest incomes were transformed into fortunes; successful politicians, professionals, and technocrats—all joined the traditional upper class as part of an oligarchy that transformed the colonial city into a showcase for European architectural styles.[30] The economic growth of the last decades of the nineteenth and the first decades of the twentieth centuries, and the resulting upward social mobility, had also created the largest middle class in Latin America—whose new working sector's demands for better wages and living conditions sparked reactionary reverberations among elite conservatives and right-wing militants, as well as state repression, immigrant deportation, and patriarchal misanthropy.

Out of this turmoil came a strengthening of opposition against the conservative government by leftist factions, which, in 1916, led to the election of the first populist president, Hipólito Yrigoyen.[31] Over the next decade, tensions continued to build, escalating by 1930 into the first military coup d'état in Argentine history, to the extent that the euphoria of democracy and social progress was now culminating in the powerful menace of authoritarianism, emblazoned by xenophobic and racist policies. The tumultuous political and social conflicts during these decades thus engendered a system of population control that reached its most fascistic expression in the 1930s.

Within this population that the elites feared and attempted to control were immigrants, once welcomed and celebrated, as well as "uncultured" rural people, workers, and, of course, the anarchists.[32] Influenced by evolutionary theories, José María Ramos Mejía, the physician and politician who was one of the first interpreters of European scientific ideas in Argentina, considered this modern urban "crowd" a colony of misfits endangering the "quality" of Argentina's national population. Echoing Gustave Le Bon's 1895 book *The Crowd* (*Psychologie des foules*), Ramos Mejía conceived Argentine society as a collective organism that requires cultivation. As he argues:

> When I was studying the admirable progression adopted by nature as it slowly developed organic types (from our modest Silurian ancestor, to the primitive fish, right up to man), it seemed reasonable to me that in the formation of this society something analogous must have happened. That at a certain stage in its development the first embryo, the immigrant, must have given the social order something like the anatomical structure of fish, later that of amphibians, and finally that of mammals. By that I mean that the immigrant would have followed a similar series of transformations in perfecting his intellectual and moral development.[33]

According to Ramos Mejía, who directed the National Department of Public Health during the last decade of the nineteenth century, the immigrant's amelioration was only possible through medical science and spatial order, as he explains:

> When he [the immigrant] first begins to walk on our land, he is, in part, the vigorous protoplasm of the new race. We must convince ourselves that this unpolished peasant does not *feel* as we, the Creole elite. . . . But the *environment* works marvels on the moldable submissiveness of his almost virgin brain.[34]

As in France, degeneration in Argentina was conceived as a biologically and environmentally based national disorder that could only be
remedied through medicalization.[35] Ramos Mejía criticized the opti-
mism that embraced the large masses of immigrants, but he was still
able to visualize a future Argentine race evolving from the prophylaxis of those modern crowds—a selective intervention that sought to
discriminate and eliminate the so-called unpalatable characteristics
of this new heterogeneous population.[36] To do this, he not only conceptualized a systematic apparatus for identifying degenerate immigrants that effectively weeded out those he considered inherently
pathological; but he also called for the reengineering of those without
criminal propensities who, with the help of science, could be re-bred
into the nation.[37] Insisting that the "biology of the crowd" should be
under surveillance, Ramos Mejía's ideology infiltrated the mind-set
of the government, including right-wing vigilantes who took control
of the city as an immediate response to the precentennial riots and
protests, orchestrating a nationalist movement fueled by xenophobia,
anti-Semitism, and class and gender prejudices.

It was clear that the Buenos Aires elites sought a medical diagnosis
for their city. They were convinced that the heterogeneous foreign
population, an inevitable consequence of modernization, could indeed
be saved by science. Influenced by Lamarckian ideas, these elites
also believed in the shaping power of the environment. Lamarck's
widely accepted theories of heredity—which explained how improvements to the individual's health could be passed to future generations—introduced an environmentalist dynamic into racial thinking.
To combat degeneration, social hygiene—making medicine the core
of the nation's reform movement—replaced the hygienic practices
that had made urban infrastructure the core of the state's activities.
Comtean positivism contributed to the medicalization of the urban
fabric: invested in a kind of objective and unquestionable authority,
science—and its promise of progress, discipline, and morality—permeated the conceptualization of physical space, no longer as the
receptor of hygienic policies but as the very technology of Lamarckian eugenics. As a result, space, natural and architectural, became a
major constituent in the transformation of modern medicine into an
agent of the normative.

Thus, during the year that followed the centennial celebrations, the
physicians José Penna and Horacio Madero finished and circulated
what can arguably be called the first portrait of a modern pathogenic
city. In their two-volume report, *La administración sanitaria y Asistencia Pública de la Ciudad de Buenos Aires*, innumerable urban

maps, architectural blueprints, operative diagrams, and data graphics deploy the binary code of medicine and society through the scrutiny and instrumentalization of space. In these documents, disease appears to have been reenvisioned as a relationship spawned by the intimate and idiosyncratic confluence of society and space. Although the report goes back to colonial times in its aim to narrate the history of health administration in Buenos Aires, its main focus was on the last two decades of the nineteenth century and the first decade of the twentieth century, when the system of power relations that Foucault identifies as "bio-technico-political—now known as welfare—was set in place as state policy.[38] In fact, the report focuses on the years in which these

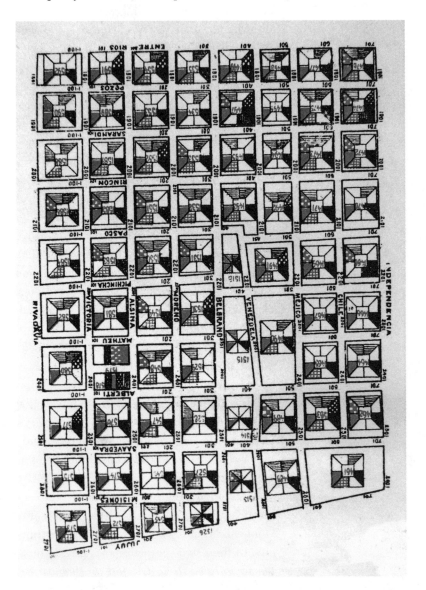

FIGURE 3.8.
Map of distribution of diseases affecting Buenos Aires. Center of the city, Section X. Included in José Penna and Horacio Madero's study, La administración sanitaria y Asistencia Pública de la Ciudad de Buenos Aires *(Buenos Aires: Kraft, 1910).*

FIGURE 3.9.
Legend detail (top) and map (bottom) of distribution of diseases affecting Buenos Aires. South of the city, Section III. Included in José Penna and Horacio Madero's study, La administración sanitaria y Asistencia Pública de la Ciudad de Buenos Aires *(Buenos Aires: Kraft, 1910).*

SECCIÓN III

Limites—Al Norte, calle de Garay; al Sud, el Riachuelo; al Este, Avenida Montes de Oca, Pinzón, Garibaldi y Paseo Colón; al Oeste, Entre Ríos y Velez Sarsfield.

practices of social control, implemented in the name of life, health, and the social well-being of the population, were institutionalized by the creation of the National Department of Hygiene and the municipal Department of Welfare, just after the federalization of the capital in 1880.[39] This latter institution, then under the direction of Penna and Madero, appointed itself the custodian of the "anatomo-politics" of the

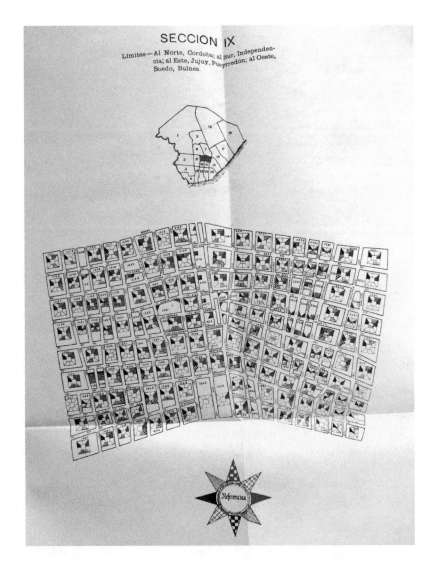

human body, seeking to optimize and integrate human beings into an efficient system of production and progress.[40]

In their report, Penna and Madero delineate a neighborhood-by-neighborhood distribution of the main diseases affecting Buenos Aires' population at the beginning of the twentieth century through a series of twenty detailed urban maps. Represented on each block with a specified black or red pattern, each disease is identified in a star-shaped index located at the bottom-right corner of each map. A number in red shows the total number of inhabitants affected by the identified disease, and a chart that accompanies the map offers detailed information about the relationship between each specific disease and the number of people affected, block by block, neighborhood by neighborhood. The eight diseases identified in these maps were those associated with the social implications of Buenos Aires' rapid urban and demographic growth and with the lack of personal and public hygiene, contagious through the environment. Among them were typhoid fever, a bacterial illness transmitted by ingesting food or water contaminated with feces; puerperal or childbed fever, associated with a lack of hygiene and appropriate physical conditions during delivery; and contagious diseases such as smallpox, measles, scarlet fever, and diphtheria, all of which remained a significant cause of death even after Louis Pasteur's discovery of vaccination and pasteurization. With the exception of tuberculosis, which was considered a "disease of excess" in Buenos Aires due to its association with hypersexuality, alcohol, and neurasthenia, all of these diseases identified on the maps were primarily childhood diseases that urgently needed to be controlled for the amelioration of the Argentinean race.[41]

Embodying the French nineteenth-century conception of milieu as a relational system that brings together space and society in a state of contingency, Penna and Madero's maps of Buenos Aires in fact display what the great cholera epidemic of 1832 in Paris demonstrated: that disease, social class, and environment were intimately interconnected.[42] Upon close inspection, the maps representing the poorest neighborhoods of the city, those southern districts located along the Riachuelo, inadvertently show, in almost every single block, the ravaging impact of disease on the poor and working classes, whereas the maps representing the upper-class neighborhoods, the northern districts that surround the Palermo parks and the palaces and pavilions that celebrated the centennial, appear almost untouched. Thus, these maps stand as documentation for the undeniably well-fortified connection between hygiene, society, and space in the construction of unequal modern Buenos Aires.

At the beginning of the twentieth century, hygiene—a dominant Latin concern that was transformed into a modern reform movement of global proportions—emerged from the intersection of science, society, architecture, and government.[43] In *The Pasteurization of France*, Bruno Latour defines hygiene as a program of reform for the reconstitution and reorganization of human life.[44] Latour argues that, within hygiene's ambition for reorganizing society itself, there was "a mixture of urbanism, consumer protection, ecology (as we would say nowadays), defense of the environment, and moralization."[45] According to him, no cause could be ruled out, including bacteria, space, air, water, and, of course, human behavior. In fact, hygienists, understanding hygiene as a complex "ensemble of knowledge, doctrines, and practices," were convinced that these diseases were so rampant that they needed to act upon every source at once.[46] The ideology of hygiene, its contagiousness, led reformers like Penna and Madero to become instant authorities on space and human organization. It is striking that in their report, hygiene had clearly shifted its focus from the city's sewage and drainage systems, its humidity and ventilation, to social hygiene, or what they called prophylactic hygiene, and its related associations to urban morbidity and mortality. Although they recognized that there was still a great deal to do to bring sewers and clean water to all of the city's districts, their report characterized the city as a medicalizable object and medicine as an instance of social control, identifying priority areas of medicalization, attaining new medico-administrative knowledge, and prescribing therapeutic agents to serve the social economy of the city.

Not only did Penna and Madero portray a city infected with diseases, pinpointing districts where diseases were prevalent, but in their report they also created and graphically represented conceptual models that defined the structure and functionality of some of the mechanisms implemented in the city to combat contagia. For instance, they included a network diagram to delineate the interdependent components that participate in the process of disinfecting family homes by marking new preventative apparatuses that were distributed throughout the city—the sanitary stations of disinfection.[47] The diagram illustrates an unmistakable clinical purification system within the urban space. Notable components of this system include the central office, the sanitary station of disinfection, and the family home—and its main actors: the main sanitary inspector (the physician); the *cuadrillas*, or disinfection teams; the cars to transport contaminated goods from the family home to the station; and the cars

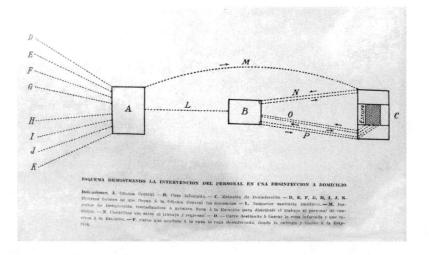

FIGURE 3.11.
Network diagram of disinfection of family homes. Included in José Penna and Horacio Madero's study, La administración sanitaria y Asistencia Pública de la Ciudad de Buenos Aires *(Buenos Aires: Kraft, 1910).*

FIGURE 3.12.

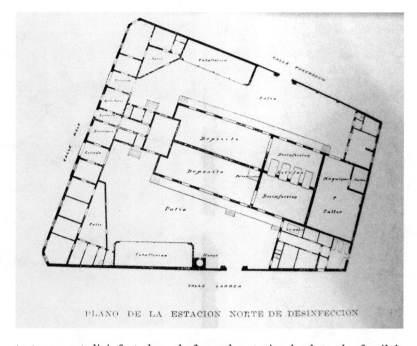

PLANO DE LA ESTACION NORTE DE DESINFECCION

to transport disinfected goods from the station back to the family's domestic space. An entire chapter of their report is devoted to these sanitary stations of disinfection.[48] A schematic map shows their distribution in five delimited areas of the city, identified as Flores, Belgrano, South, North, and Boca; and a specific station's architectural plan clearly represents the clinical process that regularly occurred behind its façades. A long wall, into which the gas ovens of disinfection are embedded, divides the building into a symmetric mirroring plan of discriminated spaces. One side of the wall is designated as contaminated; there is a patio on which the cars transporting infected clothes and household articles parked to be delivered for treatment, with storage areas and a room to hold the infected goods. The other side of the wall is designated as antiseptic, where there is another patio with the same kind of spaces, in this case organized for the reception, storage, and loading of the disinfected goods, now to be redistributed. The only space with access to both areas is the control room, located at the extreme of the dividing wall, allowing simultaneous control of both the contaminated and the antiseptic sections of the sanitary station. To avoid contamination, cars enter and leave the station through independent gates. According to Penna and Madero, when they wrote their report, new sanitary stations of disinfection in Flores, Belgrano, and Boca had recently been opened, with the South and North stations completing the five stations that the city counted in 1910.[49] In the same chapter of the report, they announce another

FIGURE 3.13.
Disinfection Station,
Contaminated Section.
Included in José Penna
and Horacio Madero's
study, La administración
sanitaria y Asistencia
Pública de la Ciudad de
Buenos Aires *(Buenos*
Aires: Kraft, 1910).

ESTACION DE DESINFECCION DE FLORES
(parte sucia)

mechanism for supporting their disinfection scheme—the *garitas de desinfección*, or chambers of disinfection. Provided with fumigation machines of Marot gas and ventilation tubes, these essentially cubic chambers (approximately 13 ft. long by 10 ft. wide by 11 ft. high) were designed to be large enough for all contents within cars and ambulances to be flushed clean of contamination. Constructed of iron with zinc hermetic façades, the chambers were to function automatically, minimizing human labor and, in their portability, facilitating their transportation to critical areas of need.[50]

In this way, identifying the city's priority areas of medicalization was tantamount to drawing a direct correlation between disease, people, and space, making it possible to exercise medical control over larger segments of the population through the installation of therapeutic agents in their own backyards. By instrumentalizing these agents throughout the city, including the sanitary stations and chambers of disinfection described in the Penna and Madero report, the city administration developed structures of "medico-administrative knowledge" to record and control not only people's health and disease but their very "conditions of life, housing and habits."[51] With this burgeoning scheme to target people and their dwellings, a new *dispositif* called *casillero sanitario*, modeled after the Parisian *casier sanitaire*, became a strategy of inventory and housing surveillance, established "to see into the obscure corners of the capital's pathologies," particularly into the housing of the poor and the working class.[52] Evoking the traditional "*cordon sanitaire*," which refers to the process of confining disease to a particular area, the *casier sanitaire* indicated the need to classify and compartmentalize, to understand the disease in its own locus, analyzing it statistically, etiologically, and geographically. Forms and charts were used to collect information about individual houses and also about industries and small businesses that potentially were used as family homes. Among the forms, the *carpeta de casa* (house folder) was an official document designed by the municipal government to record relevant information: house location, its date of construction, number of bedrooms, number of inhabitants, sanitary systems (type of sewage, if any, water sources, physical and sanitary conditions of bathrooms and kitchens), and any occurrence of contagious diseases or treatments for household infection. A gridded area on the form was included for any drawings of the houses' architectural plans to visualize the distribution of spaces thought or suspected to be unhygienic or nefarious.[53] Thus, the *casillero sanitario* in Buenos Aires, like that in Paris, "envisioned the constant surveillance of all lodgings, informed by both medical and social knowledge, backed by the authority of the state and the possibility of official intervention."[54] In other words, the domestic space had now been integrated into the dominant etiology of disease.

Thus a prior preoccupation with treating epidemic diseases—bubonic fever, cholera, and yellow fever—was now displaced by a preoccupation with treating outcast perpetrators of social diseases—alcoholics, syphilitics, prostitutes, tuberculars, sexual deviants, and the mentally ill—and protecting the newly valued entity of the mother-child unit. Both constituted the twin targets of modern reform. In fact, Argentina's obsession with modernization spawned hyperintense scrutiny of all forms of productivity, including that of the land, the livestock, and, of course, the people. Out of this came a proliferation of medical reports, such as that by Penna and Madero, that included whole chapters on the control of syphilis, tuberculosis, and insanity, along with rabies and other diseases of animal origin. Part of this mission was an urgency to control those of society's activities that often resulted in corruption, contamination, and a lack of production. The growing convergence of two usually separate movements—hygienics and eugenics—was driven by a scientifically supported mission to engineer both land and resources. Both were part of that new form of hygiene, social hygiene, which, as previously noted, turned its attention to both society at large and its milieu, focusing on the products of human capital: production and reproduction.[55] Without limiting the scope of hygienist ambitions, urban and rural spaces were to be brought under the control of reform. It is not a simple coincidence that the Penna and Madero report included a chapter on the meat industry, arguing for hygienic facilities and veterinary control that eluded the eyes of society, "bearing out a unified ideology of purification, medicalization, aestheticization and productivity."[56] The hygiene movement even called for the eradication of the blood and stench produced by the meat industry from the city's streets and waterways, in parallel to industrialists' call for more productive land in the Pampas.[57] In fact, in the last decades of the nineteenth century, during the governments of Domingo F. Sarmiento, Nicolás Avellaneda, and Julio Argentino Roca, three simultaneous movements of people and animals radically changed Buenos Aires and the surrounding Pampas. First, the military operation known as the Conquest of the Desert displaced and killed thousands of native peoples along with the so-called racially inferior gauchos. Second, following a call to think of populations in agricultural terms, politicians, scientists, and technocrats prepared the city for the import of a new, more industrious European population. Third, laws were implemented to prohibit unhygienic meat-processing operations within city limits and to transfer incoming undesirable immigrants to both the countryside and the meatpacking district in the south in an attempt to eliminate all living bodies thought to carry pestilence and disease, both physical and ideological.[58]

Through these lenses of medicalization and productivity, the state reframed society as an organism and social scientists as physicians diagnosing pathologies and implementing technologies, while using architecture as one of the key tools to normalize society and maximize its productivity. In the same way as the nineteenth-century Romantic view of women as emotional, neurotic, and hysterical (and thus unproductive) was replaced by a positivist vision of them as procreators and nurturers, so the traditional notion of architecture as a superior art form, romanticized for its aesthetics, was replaced by its essential modern manifestation—its clinical agenda of transforming human beings. This idea that medicine was bound to the concept of milieu, that society itself was conceived in medical terms and visualized as an organic form, was the impetus for medical eugenics. The individual body was no longer the only repository of health and disease. The collective body, which included more than organisms, was the new territory for this complex duality. Medicine became a "matter of assemblages," an overlapping landscape of spaces, bodies, and techniques.[59] As Michel Foucault observed, this individual and collective body became amenable to profitable use due to the need to integrate the population into the apparatus of production, a relevant economic factor since the end of the eighteenth century.[60] Thus, it had become imperative to organize a state apparatus that would ensure the population's subjugation or, as Foucault called it, "subjection" in relation to the population's optimal productivity.[61]

INSTITUTIONALIZING EUGENICS IN ARGENTINA

The threat to Argentinean modernity, represented in the nineteenth century by the Indians of the southern Pampas and northern Patagonia, had expanded in the early twentieth century to the so-called degenerated hybrids and, most importantly, to "undesirable" immigrants: on the one hand, the mestizos, mulattos, and *zambos* (of mixed African and Amerindian origin), and, on the other, the Jews, Asians, and Middle Easterners. As early as 1890, even before the institutionalization of eugenics in Argentina, Francis Galton's school of biometrics and identification processes had found a perfect laboratory in La Plata, Buenos Aires' neighboring city. It is interesting to note that in Argentina, the development of the "science of identification" to detect the "criminal," the "inferior," and the "abnormal" originated in La Plata—a planned city conceived as a "metaphor for order" in which "the regularity of its forms would determine its inhabitants' civilized behavior."[62] Initially adopted as a mechanism for criminal detection, this identification system was transformed by the head of the statistical bureau of the city police, Juan Vucetich, into a comprehensive system of demographic control that placed "the entire population under the vigilant eye of the authorities."[63] Vucetich sought to create a system capable of identifying criminals, and in so doing, he defined the limits of normalcy as a way of measuring and regulating social deviance.[64] To do so, he studied and compared the two most important systems of identification adopted worldwide at the time: Galton's "pictorial statistics" and Alphonse Bertillon's "verbal portrait" (*portrait parlé*).[65] Bertillon, a French police official in Paris, had invented the first modern system of criminal identification by combining the precision of photographic portraiture, anthropometric description, and statistics on a single fiche, then organizing the information into a comprehensive filing system.[66] Galton, the English statistician, anthropologist, evolutionary theorist, and founder of eugenics, invented a method of "composite portraiture" in which he attempted to consolidate into a single visual document the iconography of a biologically determined criminal "type."[67] These two systems of identification were both built on the notion of the "average

man" (*l'homme moyen*) conceived by Adolphe Quetelet, the sociologist
who first introduced statistical reasoning into the social sciences. As
a quantitative social mechanism, Quetelet's "average man" constituted "an ideal, not only of social health, but of social stability and
of beauty"—a model that revealed all deviations from the "normal."[68]
Following Quetelet's statistical and aesthetic rating system, Bertillon
and Galton combined visual representation—photography in particular—and social statistics into their own systems of identification.
Through the ordering and sorting of human nature, the science of
society, the new discipline of sociology, became a normative science.[69]
Conceiving the human body as a measurable "type," Quetelet also
provided the means for architects to think of space as something that
could be defined statistically, extending the idea of normalization
from the body to such social constructions as the family—and the very
spaces that housed them.[70]

In the same way as Bertillon promoted his system of identification
within the recidivist debate that had grown out of the French agricultural crisis of the 1880s, causing a massive urban influx of peasants
and a subsequent fear of idleness, Vucetich developed his system
when Argentina entered the severe sovereign debt crisis of the early
1890s. The Argentine agro-export model, whose success was based on
supplying agricultural goods to the industrial world, was hit by the
outbreak of a short but devastating financial crash—interestingly
called the "crisis of progress"—that marked the end of a decade of
large capital flowing into Argentina and the beginning of an economic
downturn that left thousands of new immigrants without jobs.[71] As a
consequence, a myriad of social pathologies—prostitution, vagrancy,
anarchism, diseases, criminality—were identified among the poor
and working classes by academic and professional elites who thought
that these people should be identified, subjected to scientific analysis,
"quarantined physically and politically from the 'true' Argentina," and
disciplined, if they were diagnosed as recuperable.[72] In Argentina as
in France, the fear of these masses fused "the vagabond, the anarchist
and [the] recidivist into a single composite figure of social menace,"
a figure that required classification and then isolation or reform to
bring them in line with the statistical norm.[73] It is precisely in the
context of this crisis that Vucetich came across Galton's research
on the scientific use of dactyloscopic analysis, or the analysis of fingerprints, and decided to incorporate it into his own system.[74] By
September of 1891, Vucetich had created the world's earliest criminal
identification system using dactyloscopy, making "fingerprint patterns a practical means of indexing a large criminal identification

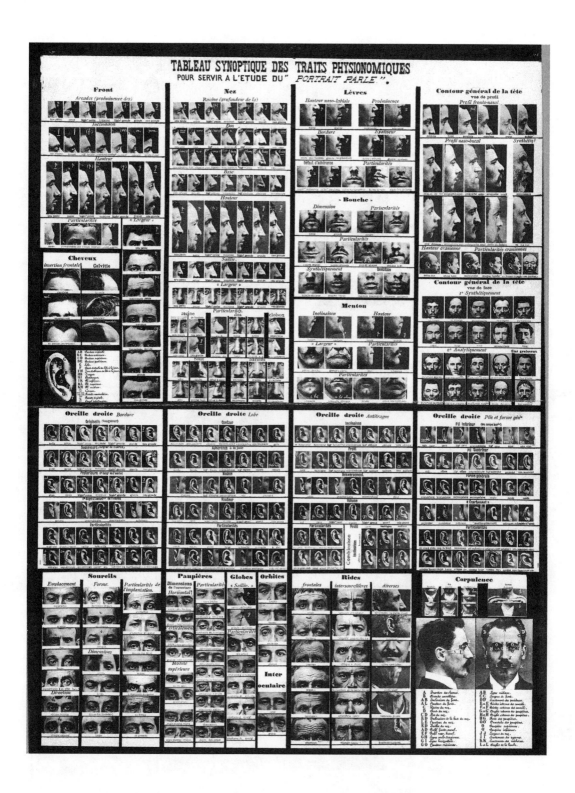

file, much in the way that anthropometric measurements indexed Bertillon files."[75] This sophisticated archival system for collecting visual and statistical information about human bodies in Argentina announced a new mind-set that would divide the human population into "biotypes" to be engineered into biological resources. Including

FIGURE 3.15.

Francis Galton, "Specimens of Composite Portraiture," 1883. Included in Francis Galton, from Inquiries into the Human Faculty and Its Development *(London: Dent and Sons, 1907).*

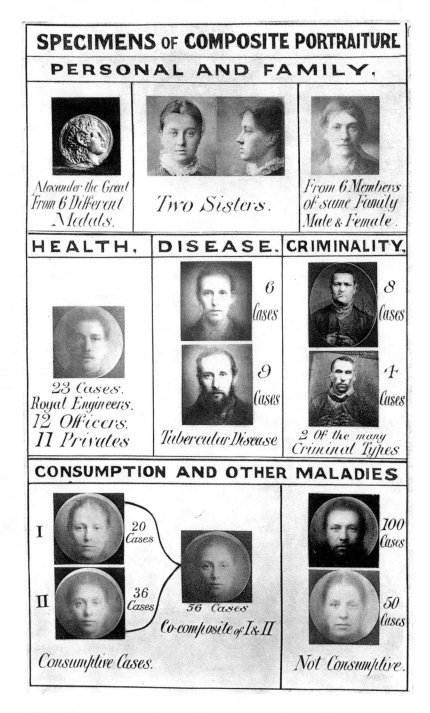

anatomical, physiological, and psychological traits, this new science of human classification, known as biotypology, was created to ensure the understanding and "efficient development of the biotypes of the nation, since each biotype was believed to show distinctive functional aptitudes, psychic pathologies, and susceptibilities to illness and crime."[76] It is quite extraordinary how notions such as "type" and "typology" were borrowed and adopted by architects from the fields of criminology, anthropology, and sociology without acknowledging and critically analyzing their origins.[77] Furthermore, architecture's participation in the control of life and goods in the world's biopolitical economy continues to go unnoticed. It is indeed significant how long it has taken for art and architecture historians to trace the historical and crucial role played by the fields of criminology and anthropology in the history of both photography and architecture.

During the following decades, the classification, study, and possible engineering of the "biotypes" of Argentineans brought together a group of reformers interested not only in immigration control but also in maternity, heredity, and children's health. These programs would be built on the conviction of the superiority of the white man—the ideology that prevailed during the extermination of Argentina's native population—which paved the way for the emergence of both biotypology and eugenics. Without acknowledging preconquest traditions, as was done in Mexico and the Andean regions, and disregarding the nation's nomadic native population and the few remaining who originated from Africa, Argentine elites identified themselves with Europeans.[78] Since the mid-nineteenth century, as noted, Argentine governments had attempted to increase immigration from northern European countries through advertising and promotion. But at the beginning of the twentieth century, the vast majority of "imported" people were from the southern European Latin countries, or from the "least desirable" regions of Eastern Europe and the Middle East. According to some national physicians and scientists, all of these groups were dangerous, either because they brought diseases, including social problems such as poverty or crime, or subversive revolutionary ideas. Nearly declaring a state of emergency, in 1910, a new law, the Law of Social Defense, gave the government the right to expel any immigrant posing a possible threat to the nation. In fact, this xenophobic law was an amplification of the Law of Residence of 1902, which permitted the national government to expel foreigners who "compromised national security or disturbed executive order," which meant that any immigrant trying to form a labor union or organize a protest could be deported.[79] These two laws were reactions against any form of popular organization, including those of labor unions and anarchists. In a country where immigrants comprised the majority of workers, having received almost 6 million between 1871 and 1914, eugenics found in the control of immigration, and in the problems produced by its accelerated urbanization, its first raison d'être, and in the Museo Social Argentino its first promoter.[80]

Inspired by the Parisian Musée social, the Museo Social Argentino was founded in 1911 in the aftermath of the centennial celebration, with the double mission of studying "the social and economic problems of the country" and "advertising Argentina throughout the world."[81] This new institution, "one of the most emblematic and influential organizations of national liberalism," emerged as an independent agent—a mediator between the state, the academy, and the agro-industrial world—charged with analyzing and facing up to the social challenges of Argentina's modernization.[82] The Museo Social de Buenos Aires (eventually named the Museo Social Argentino) was sponsored by a multifarious constellation of local institutions, including the Argentine Science Society (Sociedad Científica Argentina), the Progress Club (Club del Progreso), the Society for the Protection of Infants (Sociedad Protectora de la Infancia), the Fine Arts Academy (Academia de Bellas Artes), the Regional Public Health Directorate (Dirección General de Salubridad de la Provincia de Buenos Aires), the Central Society of Architects (Sociedad Central de Arquitectos), and the National University of Buenos Aires (Universidad Nacional de Buenos Aires), along with a heterogeneous group of individuals, among them the lawyers Leopoldo Maupas and Rodolfo Rivarola, the engineers Santiago Barabino and Nicolás Besio Moreno, the agronomists and ranchers Emilio Frers and Miguel Casares, the physicians Julio Iribarne and Gregorio Aráoz Alfaro, the feminists Elvira Rawson de Dellepiane and Elvira V. López, the sociologist Agustín Álvarez, the museologist Carlos Zuberbühler, and the criminalist Vucetich.[83] Tomás Amadeo, a member of the Argentine Science Society, had encountered the Parisian Musée social in 1905 when he went to Paris on an official mission to research French agricultural cooperatives and creditors, and to inform Europeans of employment and living opportunities in Argentina.[84] As noted in chapter 2, in 1908, when planning became a powerful tool for resolving France's social problems, the Musée social created a section devoted to urban and rural hygiene, after which physicians and architects joined in greater numbers. This became a source of inspiration for Argentina's leaders, who were worried about the social consequences of the capital city's radical transformation, the subsequent abandonment of the countryside, and the objectionable immigrants moving there.[85] For these leaders, the rural domain became the perfect platform for realizing their dream of modernizing the country and its capital city.[86] Thus, in the case of the Museo Social Argentino, "the identity of the institution was marked by a certain regard toward Buenos Aires that attempted to define its problems and visualize its solutions from an outside perspective, with its focus on colonization and agricultural development."[87] It became evident to the new Argentine institution that the city and its spaces could become effective tools for the resolution of social problems, as was the case for the Parisian Musée social, for which the "urban question" had become a crucial response to the "social question."

Yet, the first advance of the Museo Social Argentino was to turn to the more profitable development of the countryside and the consolidation of its productive cell—the peasant family.[88] To accomplish this, the institution sought to repopulate the countryside with the right "type" of immigrants, lobbying to deny access to the "inferior races"—the "black and yellow races" and the Jews—on the grounds of racist and xenophobic considerations, such as that there was "no other race that stems from Europe as degenerated as the Jews."[89] The famous slogan "to govern is to populate," attributed to the highly influential politician Juan Bautista Alberdi, was rephrased as "to govern is to populate" but selectively.[90] In the explanatory first pages of his book *Bases y puntos de partida para la organización política de la República Argentina*, Alberdi claimed: "Each European who comes to our shores brings more civilization in his habits, which will later be passed on to our inhabitants, than many books of philosophy. . . . A hard-working man is the most edifying catechism . . ." Thinking of people as agricultural crops, Alberdi continues, "Let us bring living pieces of these qualities . . . and let us plant them here."[91] In fact, immediately after World War I, the Museo Social Argentino surveyed renowned personalities about the future of immigration in modern Argentina. Their responses were published in a special 1919 offprint issue included in the museum's official bulletin.[92] More than forty politicians and intellectuals responded to questions such as: "What class of immigrants is most needed? What methods should be adopted to attract and retain such immigrants? What class of immigrant do you consider undesirable? How may the undesirables be prevented from entering? What is the maximum number that the country can conveniently receive and retain yearly?"[93] According to findings of the report, most of the respondents voted for reinforcing the existing mechanism of immigration control, restricting the immigration of "exotic races," and limiting immigration to a total of nearly 300,000 per year.[94] Some viewed the illiterate population from agricultural regions as desirable, but not the Russian urban population, whose socialist ideas and conversion of workers into "revolutionary workers" represented a potentially serious threat to order.[95] Based on statistics, the report also claims that the exodus of immigrants between 1914 and 1918 had more to do with local economic factors and immigrant conditions in Argentina than with the war. Consequently, the report argued for the promulgation of agrarian legislation that might improve immigrants' lives in the countryside, allowing them to become Argentinean citizens and landowners.[96] In this way, the countryside was chosen to be the ideal territory that would receive the selected immigrants and act as the testing ground for the Museo Social Argentino's pragmatic project: the "agricultural home" (*hogar agrícola*), a concrete entity whose primary social function was to stop the depopulation of the rural areas.[97] Healthy Europeans were persuaded to colonize the countryside, where programs for women were implemented to guarantee the preservation of the social order, with "the ultimate aim of converting women to a regenerative factor of rural life."[98] Thus, in Argentina, a fertile territory for the implementation of eugenics was sown through pastoralization and population control—the biopolitical management of land and resources, natural and human.

Throughout the entire development of eugenics in Argentina, eugenicists claimed that "the amelioration of the human race depended on heredity and the environment."[99] Even though this Lamarckian principle was not commonly endorsed beyond the Latin world, eugenics in Argentina was passionately embedded in the country's long tradition of regarding the environment as a primary force in the construction of modernity, with immigration and medicalization as its principal regenerative agents. Its history moved from production to reproduction, from the countryside to the city, and from the environment to the human body and its sexuality. During the first two decades of the twentieth century, Argentinean eugenics was associated with psychiatric and criminological circles and with the initiatives of left-wing professionals and anarchist groups interested in sanitation and procreation—hygiene and reproductive health.[100] Then, in 1918, the Argentine Eugenics Society, the first eugenics institution in Argentina, was founded with a particular emphasis on the social environment's nocive influences on reproduction and heredity.[101] But the Argentine Eugenics Society had a very short life. Its mission was promptly adopted in the 1920s, first, by the Argentine League of Social Prophylaxis, which claimed to have found inspiration in Adolphe Pinard and Louis Landouzy's call for the control of social diseases and the improvement of the quality and quantity of newborns; and then, in the 1930s, by the Argentine Association of Biotypology, Eugenics, and Social Medicine, whose link to the Italian science of biotypology marked a definitive shift from the left to the right with conservative and fascist overtones.[102] From the moment eugenics was institutionalized in Argentina in 1918, to the moment in which it reached academic status in 1957, the Museo Social Argentino was on the front lines of the biopolitical battle that attempted to achieve eugenics' ultimate aim: the construction of a perfect race. Even after the ravaging effects of the Nazi holocaust during the Third Reich that marked the end of most eugenics institutions worldwide, the Museo Social Argentino created a university that opened its doors in 1957 with two academic tracks, one of them devoted entirely to eugenics.[103] From its founding, the Museo Social Argentino was invested in the programs that characterized eugenics in Argentina: the determination of the "type" of desirable immigrants, the medicalization of its population and its surroundings, extending the idea of normalization from the body to such social constructions as the family and to the very spaces that housed them.[104]

THE ARCHITECTURES OF PUERICULTURE AND HOMINICULTURE

To activate eugenics' sweeping agenda, a network of reformative institutions was instrumentalized throughout the first half of the twentieth century to transform society by transforming the family, its idealized nucleus, into an agent of medicalization, and to transform the space of the city into a medicalizable object. Out of this conjunction of people and architecture new medical *dispositifs* emerged throughout Buenos Aires and other cities, shaping a heterogeneous ensemble of architectural forms, regulations, and ideology—or, as previously mentioned, as "anything that has in some way the capacity to capture, orient, determine, intercept, model, control, or secure the gestures, behaviors, opinions, or discourses of living beings."[105] In other words, *dispositifs* were not precisely such public institutions as prisons and schools, where power is clearly exercised, but constellations of entities in which human activities and beliefs are formulated, monitored, and disciplined.[106] With the *dispositif* of human perfectibility functioning to create apparatuses of health and reproduction, germs and genes were identified as objective causes of disease and degeneration, thus becoming targets of scientific reform. At the same time, physical space, more than a vehicle for germs, became a vehicle for Lamarck's

FIGURE 3.16.

Plan, "A Hygienic City, La Plata, Capital of the Province of Buenos Aires." Published in Emilio R. Coni, Progrès de l'hygiène dans la République Argentine *(Paris: Ballière et Fils, 1887).*

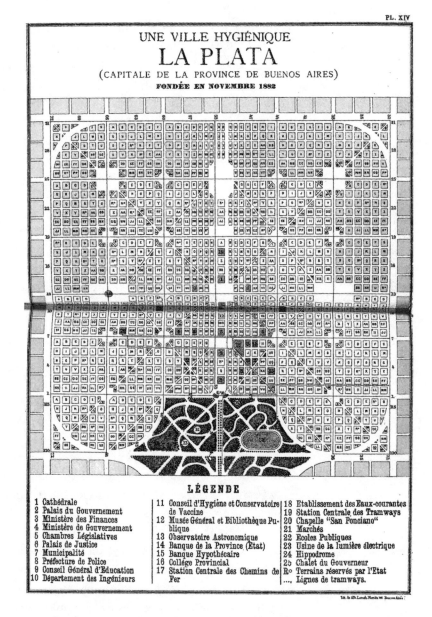

UNE VILLE HYGIÉNIQUE

LA PLATA

(CAPITALE DE LA PROVINCE DE BUENOS AIRES)

FONDÉE EN NOVEMBRE 1882

LÉGENDE

1 Cathédrale	11 Conseil d'Hygiène et Conservatoire de Vaccine	18 Etablissement des Eaux-courantes
2 Palais du Gouvernement		19 Station Centrale des Tramways
3 Ministère des Finances	12 Musée Général et Bibliothèque Publique	20 Chapelle "San Ponciano"
4 Ministère de Gouvernement		21 Marchés
5 Chambres Législatives	13 Observatoire Astronomique	22 Ecoles Publiques
6 Palais de Justice	14 Banque de la Province (État)	23 Usine de la lumière électrique
7 Municipalité	15 Banque Hypothécaire	24 Hippodrome
8 Préfecture de Police	16 Collége Provincial	25 Chalet du Gouverneur
9 Conseil Général d'Éducation	17 Station Centrale des Chemins de Fer	R° Terrains réservés par l'Etat
10 Département des Ingénieurs		..., Lignes de tramways.

hereditary "acquired characteristics" and a critical instrument in the launching of modern medicine. It was at this juncture, when both pathology and space emerged as a fused object of analysis and intervention, that the foundation of modern medicine was laid down. In other words, the beginning of society, viewed as a "historical/natural whole," marked the beginning of "society as a target of state intervention" and Lamarckian eugenics.[107]

Looking back at the late-nineteenth-century launching of this agenda, it is clear that medical, civic, and legal authorities began to urge the Argentine government to take more concrete steps to regenerate society. Thus two main public health organizations were established: the National Department of Hygiene (Departamento Nacional de Higiene) in 1880 and the municipal Department of Public Welfare (Departamento de Asistencia Pública) in 1881.[108] The purpose of the National Department of Hygiene was to control the practice of medicine and pharmacology; monitor the hygienic deficiencies of the capital city and its ports; and regulate prostitutes, the destitute, and orphans. This work was complemented by the new Department of Public Welfare in Buenos Aires, which would be devoted to the organization of Buenos Aires' diverse medical facilities, including hospitals, asylums, and dispensaries—new clinics that would proliferate throughout the city as part of the larger health care apparatus—a machine for modern life.[109] Inspired by its French counterpart, this department was created by José María Ramos Mejía, the main hygienist and one of the founders of the Argentine Medical Circle, and by Emilio Coni, the physician who, as we recall from his utopian vision in chapter 1, was obsessed from his earliest days with the interactive relationship between space and society.[110] "We began by studying human beings' hygiene in their childhood, followed by that of their diet, their housing, as well as the crowds and the surrounding air," Coni wrote in the preface of his 1887 book, *Progrès de l'hygiène dans la République Argentine* (Progress of hygiene in the Argentine Republic).[111] In this book, presented for the first time in Vienna at the 1887 International Congress of Hygiene and Demography, Coni identifies the importance of creating a diverse range of health institutions to benefit different segments of the population, particularly children, in addition to the importance of cleaning up the water system, establishing a new network of urban sewers, analyzing the locations of markets and slaughterhouses, prisons and cemeteries—all of them relevant elements in what he called the "remediation of cities."[112] To show the progress of sanitation in Argentina, Coni includes architectural plans of public buildings, from military institutions to schools to hospitals to specialized asylums for the insane, the deaf, the blind, and the orphan. He also includes urban plans showing sewers, water supplies, and the effects of cholera in 1886–1887 Buenos Aires, and the urban plan and detailed description of La Plata, the new capital of the province of Buenos Aires, which he called the City of Health. Even a detailed plan of the State Laboratory, an institution equipped with the most advanced scientific instruments to analyze the quality of any article of public consumption, was included together with plans for the new national penitentiary as a panopticon type of prison and for a garden-city worker village, both built in Buenos Aires.[113]

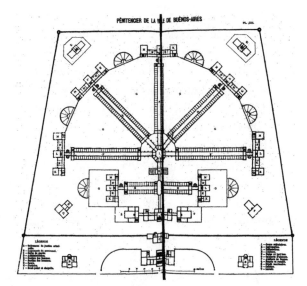

FIGURE 3.17.
*Plan of Buenos Aires'
penitentiary. Published
in Emilio R. Coni,*
Progrès de l'hygiène
dans la République
Argentine *(Paris:
Ballière et Fils, 1887).*

FIGURE 3.18.
*Plan of Buenos Aires'
Municipal Workers City.
Published in Emilio
R. Coni,* Progrès de
l'hygiène dans la Répub-
lique Argentine *(Paris:
Ballière et Fils, 1887).*

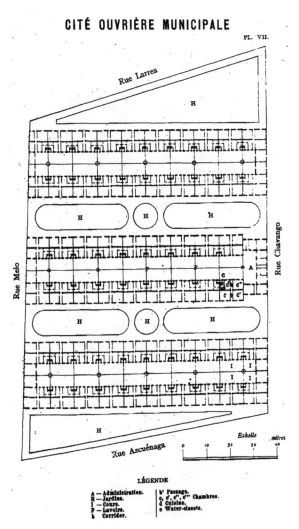

Another early report, a 1911 study by Juan E. Milich on the evolution of medicine and hygiene in Argentina, presents a picture of the early development of the Department of Public Welfare's health institutions built throughout the city.[114] In the process of conceiving these institutions, architecture was becoming an extraordinary tool that brought with it the possibility of purifying society in Buenos Aires. Among the early modern institutions named in Milich's study were the Doctor Cosme Argerich Hospital (1897) in the south of the city and its syphilitic dispensary for prostitutes working in the area of La Boca; the Tornu Sanatorium (1904), a hospital for treating tuberculosis in the northwest part of the city with a large colored-glass solarium;[115] the Torcuato de Alvear Hospital (1909), a large medical complex in the west of the city, conceived as the most important sanitarium in South America and designed as a restorative park by Penna himself along with the French landscape architect Joseph Antoine Bouvard;[116] the Casas de Socorro, "miniature hospitals" located in strategic areas of the city for emergencies; and a nursing school, a central house for first aid, and other satellite facilities in the neighborhoods of San Carlos, Nueva Pompeya, Las Heras, Santa Lucía, and Villa Devoto. As constituents of a larger apparatus, this variety of medical institutions gave form to the *dispositif* of perfectibility, penetrating the urban fabric as a means of remedying the reformer's obsession with those feeble members of society. Proliferating throughout the city were health dispensaries, human regenerative gardens, open schools, "colonies for weak children," day-care wards for newborns, maternal-child health and education centers, birthing institutions, and "eugenic homes."[117]

With their recruitment mission, these apparatuses of health and reproduction became the main prophylactic measures used to register and identify the "unproductive" and to optimize the "productive," understanding the family as its fertile territory and the mother-child unit as its main instrument. To legitimize and activate this goal, puericulture—calling for the improvement of the quality and quantity of newborns—and hominiculture—calling for the improvement of the entire spectrum of the human enterprise—became operational methods of social normalization. As discussed in chapter 2, these ideological practices allowed their creators in Paris, the Musée social's physicians Adolphe Pinard and Louis Landouzy, to extend the social discourse from the human body to physical space, paving the way for planning—both the planning of the family and the planning of the city. Thus was architecture instrumentalized as a clinical device in the agenda of ameliorating and perfecting the population. So, when Pinard, influenced by Lamarckian ideas of heredity, first set his aim on the scientific cultivation of the mother-child unit, he went beyond the territory of the child's body to the mother's body, her health, the health of previous generations, and the environment. Meanwhile, Landouzy aimed for the scientific cultivation of the entire life span of the human species by identifying diseases he saw as social and environmental poisons—alcohol, tuberculosis, and syphilis. Specifically, in Argentina, government leaders, physicians, hygienists, and feminists were convinced that the best way to defend national progress was through the expansion of institutions specially designed for improving children's health and modernizing education to identify degenerate children, as well as potential delinquents, while reeducating women to make them better nurturers and wives. They also aimed to control the spread of social diseases through the clinical identification of alcoholics, syphilitics, and TB carriers while targeting the poor and other politically threatening groups. In this way, puericulture, the "science of the moment," as it was called by the Argentine physician Genaro Sisto, and its partner hominiculture became the engines of change, spawning new clinical facilities serving the strategy of human improvement.[118]

Advocacy for puericulture took center stage in most international congresses organized in Buenos Aires during the first decades of the twentieth century—from the First International Feminine Congress held during the centennial celebrations of 1910, in which physicians and feminists addressed maternal and child care and the advancement of social prophylaxis, to the First American Congress of the Child of 1916, where the state was first portrayed as responsible for the protection of women and children.[119] Thus, in this congress, papers presented by distinguished physicians and intellectuals called for both private and public efforts to offer "adequate care to mothers and children, not in the spirit of charity, as had been customary in the first decade of the century, but as a civic service to the nation."[120] Puericulture continued gaining popularity and support during the following decades, despite increasing numbers of women in the work force. Members of the Museo Social Argentino, including well-known physicians and social reformers such as Elvira Freimann, José Ingenieros, and Carlos Octavio Bunge, called for modern education for both children and women, the passage of legislation to protect them and regulate their labor, and the expansion of special institutions for the mother-child dyad.[121] They even required the inclusion of puericulture in girls' curriculums in public and private schools across the nation, and they pushed for the establishment of national institutions to educate women on how to become better mothers.[122] Through these lenses, children were seen as "biological-political resources of the nation, and the state was regarded as having an obligation to regulate their health."[123] In the same way, a woman's role was seen, in its most traditional conception, as a simple reproductive force. So, puericulture shaped a powerful mind-set for scientific motherhood that kept "women in reproduction, healthily rearing their children according to modern medical principles for the good of the country."[124] Many eugenic policies were centered on women; their lives and bodies were subjected to the control of the state and to the surveillance of the entire population. Puericulture, invested with the authority of science, played a crucial role in the construction of gender differences, reinforcing society's sense of entitlement over the purification of women's sexuality and the control of their bodies and reproductive rights, which still persists today. Historians of science such as Jacques Léonard claim that Lamarckian eugenics, with its puericultural roots almost untouched by Mendelian genetics, was in fact "pure hygienism" with all the fault aimed at negative environmental influences, ignoring gender implications. More recent studies such as Nancy Leys Stepan's book *The Hour of Eugenics* point to the ways in which this so-called pure environmental determinacy was acted out on the bodies of heretofore invisible women, politicizing gender differences under the cloak of science in a way that undermined them.[125] In the same way that urban strategies in Brazil swept away the poor, mostly blacks, from the cities' desirable areas in the name of progress, the use of architecture in Argentina to infiltrate the city with institutions devoted to the care of women and children "for their own good" confined women to a singular role within a constraining apparatus designed to shape the population—and control them.

Just as facilities for the health improvement of mothers and children were interconnected to create a more efficient eugenics apparatus, the dispensaries created to attend specific social diseases served complementary purposes, together forming a system of interrelated institutions for the improvement of the population, illustrated below. For instance, although a specific type of dispensary was designated for each social disease, alcoholism—believed to be susceptible to tuberculosis—was treated in ad hoc dispensaries dedicated to both, preventing tuberculosis and providing platforms for anti-alcohol campaigns.[126] Regenerative gardens were built throughout the city as institutionalized spaces for children's recovery and recreation, but also for adults' physical and moral cultivation. Beyond aesthetic and respiratory functions, these gardens were designed to provide "productive leisure" (*loisir productif*), according to the very ideals of the efficiency and productivity of eugenics.[127] Parks and playgrounds within gardens were also used to house "weak" children—those at risk of becoming unproductive. For mothers and their infants, other types of dispensaries were established, including lactation dispensaries (*dispensarios de lactantes*) for the distribution of breast milk, maternal cafeterias (*cantinas maternales*) for the nourishment of mothers, and children's kitchens in the most populous neighborhoods. Open schools, inspired by the French architectural typology *école de plein air*, functioned more as clinics than schools, more as gardens than buildings; and although they were initially established for the recovery of "weak" children, they also included a mechanism for identifying "abnormals." As economo-politico agents, day-care wards for newborns were established in workplaces to guarantee the ultimate efficiency of working mothers. And, finally, as an essential part of this machinery, homes were reconceived as incubators for developing perfect citizens. Once regarded as the unit that would reinvigorate the countryside, the *hogar agrícola* in the city became the *casa eugénica*: thus, the advent of modern medicine, which had already transformed existing hospitals from charity shelters into "curing machines," now began reconfiguring the house of the working family, the institutions of the family, and the city itself.

RESTORATIVE GARDENS FOR PRODUCTIVE CITIZENS

For the city of Buenos Aires, there was no more prolific urban apparatus conceived in the service of healthcare and social reform than the parks and plazas designed during the end of the nineteenth century and the first decades of the twentieth century. And for the Argentine elites, there were no more attractive designers and technocrats to imagine these spaces than the French landscape architects and urbanists trained under the influence of the new "green" Paris, the city created with its hygienic and moralizing public parks by Napoleon III, Baron Haussmann, and Adolphe Alphand.[128] Without a doubt, Paris was the first source of inspiration for modern Buenos Aires, which led to Domingo Sarmiento's desire to transform Buenos Aires into a civilized "French and mercantile" city.[129] Sarmiento's obsession with "civilizing the barbarians" (*civilizar la barbarie*), as clearly manifested in his famous 1845 book *Facundo: Or, Civilization and Barbarism (Facundo, ó Civilización y barbarie)*, was at the core of his motivation to create a grand public park and the first neighborhood gardens for the capital city.[130] It was clear that the public garden concept itself, which the nineteenth-century urbanistic revolution started to materialize in the different cardinal points of Paris, emerged as part of a new way of thinking about the city.[131] To create a grand metropolitan park, Sarmiento counted on the support of the hygienists of the moment, such as the physician Eduardo Wilde, who argued for the creation of urban parks to "send surges of oxygen to the city, to regenerate our blood," because "every city needs, as an essential hygienic element, the proximity of a neighborhood jungle, a forest, a plain—that is, sites with trees."[132] But Sarmiento imagined something more. Also inspired by North American cemetery design, the Frederick Law Olmsted parks in Boston, and Central Park in New York, Sarmiento visualized a metropolitan park for Buenos Aires as a planning instrument and as a technical device to control the territory.[133] For him, a grand park should be a genuine "technical laboratory," offering not only oxygen and recreation with its open spaces, greenhouses, and plant nurseries but artificial pasturelands, facilities for agriculture and industrial exhibitions, areas for experimentation and technological innovations in agriculture, and even a training field for topographers and military engineers.[134] In other words, as Adrián Gorelik argues in his seminal book *La grilla y el parque* (The grid and the park), the park emerges as a "medium for a restoration: a restoration of a degraded city, of a segmented society; a regeneration of deviant conducts, of nature and memory."[135] Sarmiento imagined the park in the 1870s as a modern "typology" capable of embracing "civilization's values," capable of "burying in its cultivated green 'the last sprout of ancient barbarism.'"[136] At once, the park became a modern apparatus that, as a *dispositif*, was capable of formulating and monitoring human productivity.

Yet from Sarmiento's time to more than five decades later, Argentine governments believed that the French were best suited to imagine green devices. The French landscape architects and urbanists Édouard André (1840–1911), Eugène Courtois (1843–1914), Charles (Carlos) Thays (1849–1934), Joseph Antoine Bouvard (1840–1920), and Jean-Claude Nicolas Forestier (1861–1930) came to Buenos Aires to design the new green civilized city.[137] Initially, the projects imagined for late-nineteenth-century Buenos Aires were conceived in the Alphand tradition following the hygienic mentality of the time—as works of art, as aesthetic entities that do not pretend to simply imitate nature but to offer healthy environments. But this discourse promptly turned into a social hygiene program. Architects, physicians, government authorities, and utopian writers advocated the construction of green spaces that would serve as "lungs for the city."[138] In fact, former president Nicolás Avellaneda believed that the city's green spaces were necessary to "soften, improve, purify, and ennoble the sentiment of the multitudes."[139] For example, in 1902, at the inauguration of Parque de los Patricios, Mayor Adolfo Bullrich addressed the young men from the Correctional Prison who built the park, telling them that their "instincts and perversions" would be replaced with more desirable productive habits through the civilizing virtues of parks.[140] According to Bullrich, these prisoners, now "converted into useful citizens for the country and the family," were the first beneficiaries of Patricios Park.[141] In this way, this southern area of the city, once the site of animal slaughter and processing, became one of life and regeneration.[142] Soon after, green spaces were used as a way to gentrify the most unsavory neighborhoods, thus adding a social and economic function to the aesthetic and environmental one. As the Argentinean agronomic engineer Benito Carrasco states:

> In 1914, being the director of "Paseos Públicos" [Municipal Director-ate for Parks and Walks], . . . I understood . . . that it was time to complement the decorative and respiratory function that parks and gardens had assertively performed, according to the inspiration given by the nineteenth-century school, with other [functions] that, without abandoning that concept, would . . . fulfill the necessities and require-ments . . . imposed by the growing of human agglomerations. . . . To achieve this goal, I decided not only to improve the aesthetic aspect . . . [but to introduce] . . . those elements whose effect would contribute to orienting our public promenades toward more emphatic social action . . . this was the concept that motivated the implementation . . . of large floral pots, children's playgrounds with their sandboxes, gymnasiums, courts of basketball, tennis . . ."[143]

Thus, plazas and parks were no longer conceived as representa-tions of the pastoral aimed at the bourgeois mise-en-scène; rather, they were seen in the context of the demographics of the city, as clinics for healing, controlling, and producing citizens.[144] They were designed to provide the *"loisir productif"* according to the ideals of efficiency and productivity that eugenics proclaimed. Nevertheless, modern gardens as social and economic constructs were a preoccupation not only for Carrasco but also for Forestier, the French architect mem-ber of the Parisian Musée social, who in 1923 would be invited to collaborate in the development of a comprehensive master plan for Buenos Aires.[145] As early as 1906, in an article by Forestier published in *Revista Municipal*, he proposed the concept of the "neighborhood garden," not for the beautification or hygienic integrity of the neigh-borhood itself but for its power to "save children from bad influences and criminal associations."[146] As the French architectural historian Françoise Choay observes, Forestier's desire "to articulate, through history, the social, economic, and aesthetic problems of the city" intensified as a result of his connection to the Parisian Musée social.[147] In Forestier's own words, "The garden today should be attached to the industrial building and to the castle, to the most modest home and to the most splendid one."[148] Following the ideas of Georges Benoît-Lévy, his colleague at the Musée social, Forestier stated that "cities can no longer be different than city-gardens."[149] Clearly, he believed that they were the perfect laboratories to reconceptualize gardens "for health, for charity, for beauty" (Por la Salud—Por la Bondad—Por la Belleza).[150] In line with Forestier's ideas, and aware of Buenos Aires' radical expansion, Carrasco insisted on the need to transform existing parks and to create new gardens as true civic centers to be located in expanded areas of the city. In a 1908 article published a few months after an article by Forestier appeared in the same popular magazine, *Caras y Caretas*, Carrasco visualized Buenos Aires as a centerless city.[151] In his article "La ciudad del porvenir" (The city of the future), he argues for the city's radical transformation through land acquisition and transformative interventions that occur away from the city center, where the colonial grid dissipates into wide avenues and new tree-lined boulevards—making Buenos Aires "the real city, the grandiose city of the near future, the city that will make America [the continent] and the race proud . . ."[152] According to Carrasco, the transformation of new open spaces into parks and gardens would be "the radical remedy to the disease."[153] The nearly simultaneous visions of the modern city and its open spaces that Forestier and Carrasco presented in Buenos Aires were aligned with the ideology that generated the creation of a new Section on Urban and Rural Hygiene of the Musée social in Paris that same year, which became the stage on which physicians and architects began to play out the mutual transformation of space and society.

In complicity, then, the physicians and architects of this new section joined forces to regenerate society through the technification of space. Seeking popular and official support for their plans, they displayed twelve thousand posters at Metro stations and throughout Paris just before the 1908 municipal elections, showing the locations of nine urban parks on the city's periphery designed to provide light, fresh air, and space for the cultivation of the human body. To reinforce the value of urban planning as a crucial social hygiene instrument, the Musée social organized a workshop with Eugène Hénard himself, the architect behind the plan for the nine city parks promoted on

FIGURE 3.19.

*Poster designed by
the Musée social's
Section of Urban and
Rural Hygiene for the
municipal elections of
1908, Paris. CEDIAS-
Musée social, Paris.*

the posters, as well as a large-scale public meeting at the Sorbonne devoted to "Les Espaces libres à Paris."[154] There, important leaders presented their ideas to an audience of 1,500, including Georges Risler, the industrialist president of the Musée social's new section, and its vice president Louis Landouzy, the physician who had coined the term "hominiculture." Lecturing at the Sorbonne, they explained the need for healthy housing to combat tuberculosis based on Landouzy's report on tuberculosis-infected dwellings in Paris; outlined ecological and preservationist concerns; and insisted on transforming the land occupied by the military's fortifications into public parks for the working class in the service of fighting social diseases to revitalize "its force and its virility."[155] The interventions also had nationalist and eugenics undercurrents, nationalizing physical exercise as a critical means of preserving and improving the French race at a time when France's falling birthrate was attributed to physical degeneration.[156] It was then clear that the idea of a park-garden system as a social and economic construct was at the core of the emerging discipline of modern urbanism, and it was at the Parisian Musée social that physical space found its ultimate expression: as a social technology.[157]

This ideology promoted modern urbanism, with its social and environmental orientation and its attention to city expansion and *espaces vertes*, as the most efficient way to combat public health problems.[158] The need "to balance aesthetic considerations with the scientific collection of social, hygienic, and economic data" was at the center of debate about whether the role of the leading architects and urbanists at the Musée social's hygiene section was that of an "artist" or of a "sanitary engineer."[159] For Forestier, the answer was clear. In the introductory pages of his 1920 book, *Jardins, carnet de plans et de dessins*, he argues that "the garden, today, is more than a work of art or luxury; it responds to new needs; it has a beneficial social role; it must be duplicated everywhere."[160] Affirming that "many people, prisoners of their cities, were incapable of finding the healthy condition of agricultural life," Forestier asks: "Is not gardening a refined version of agriculture?" For him, "the garden was the only entity capable of providing repose and acting as a preventative measure against mental and physical diseases." In other words, only the garden was singularly capable of simultaneously providing "health, hygiene, and aesthetics."[161] By the 1920s, three lines of action arising from these ideas were identified by Risler as priorities for the section's members. First, to review and reinforce the law of 1919 (Loi Cornudet) that required all cities with more than ten thousand inhabitants to develop plans for extending, ordering, and beautifying, based on hygienic, functional, and aesthetic considerations. Second, to more vigorously combat venereal diseases, and third, to focus more attention on problems associated with low birthrate, or what they called "the question of natality."[162] What initially had seemed to be only a matter of land acquisition and city expansion became a matter of social control, or the "management of *la matière sociale*."[163] And it was Forestier who was credited by Jules Siegfried, one of the Musée social's founders, for this very ideology of social control initially fueling the creation of the Museo Social's urban and rural hygiene section.[164] Thus, it is not surprising that by 1923, when Forestier was invited by Carlos Noël to participate in the design of the city's master plan, he reimagined Buenos Aires beyond its administrative limits, as one continuous social agglomeration that included its potential for growth through a system of parks and gardens.

This comprehensive plan, titled *Proyecto orgánico para la urbanización del municipio*, represented the first attempt to extend efforts to address all the problems of the capital city, including the social and scientific needs of the city's peripheral districts. The *Proyecto orgánico*, "the first local document that tried to adopt the points of view of 'modern urbanism,'" was based on a variety of diagnostic studies and previous projects that attempted to balance the discrepancies between Buenos Aires' urban structure and the needs of its population that had skyrocketed during the last decades.[165] Within the construct of this master plan, it is clear that it was Forestier's mission to draw upon the Musée social's ideology, instrumentalizing urban planning as "the first principle of social hygiene" in his effort to create green spaces that would "improve" the population as well as the physical attributes of the city.[166] Particular attention to open spaces and their potential therapeutic use as parks and gardens was thus driven by the conviction that planning was "of primordial importance to the physical development of our race and its moral and intellectual elevation."[167] Forestier joined the Comisión de Estética Edilicia, an ad hoc committee in charge of developing the *Proyecto orgánico*, with the aim of creating a system of parks and gardens that comprised all green spaces scattered throughout the city, including the territories along the river.[168] Considering existing plans, in particular those developed under the direction of Thays and Carrasco, Forestier visualized 2,500 hectares of landscaped space through the creation of various "types"

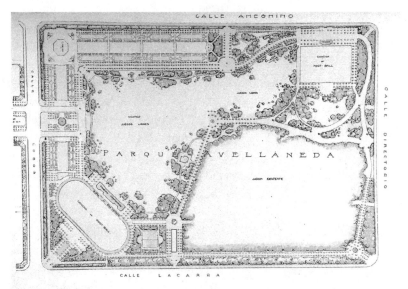

FIGURE 3.20.
Jean-Claude Nicolas Forestier, Parque Avellaneda. Published in Comisión de Estética Edilicia, Proyecto orgánico para la urbanización del municipio: El plano regulador y de reforma de la capital federal, 1925 *(Buenos Aires: Talleres Peuser, 1925).*

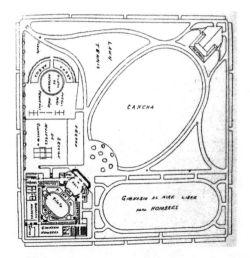
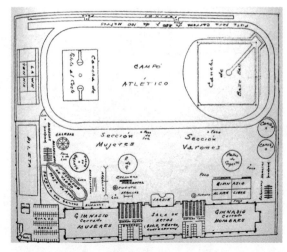

FIGURES 3.21–3.22.
Ernesto Nelson,
architectural sketches
of playgrounds and
civic centers. Published
in Boletín del Museo
Social Argentino
(Buenos Aires: Museo
Social Argentino, 1913).

of green spaces.[169] These green spaces were organized within a system that included metropolitan parks linking the city with the region and preserving natural reserves such as Tigre Delta to the north; urban parks to be located in the most diverse areas of the city, including in landfill territories along the river that were transformed into La Costanera park; private gardens to increase the percentage of green areas in the city; commons and tree-lined boulevards, park-cemeteries, and plant nurseries. In addition, Forestier designed playgrounds for children away from the streets, circumscribed by plantings, and under surveillance by women rather than men; municipal playing fields (371 indoors and 25 outdoors) designed according to the size of the population and the types of sporting activities; and gardens for the workers, a direct response to the mayor's requirements and to Forestier's sense that gardens should be located not only in elegant neighborhoods but also in the most humble ones, near both the workers' houses and their workplaces.[170]

In keeping with Forestier's approach, the *Proyecto orgánico* emphasized the need to develop a "Parque-Bosque," a large forest-park to be located on 660 hectares of land in Flores, a southern neighborhood of Buenos Aires, an area seen as "a substandard and unsanitary zone, calling for an intelligent and service-oriented vision."[171] In the same neighborhood, Forestier also designed a new plan for Parque Avellaneda, used as a public park since 1914. Following a diagonal axis that linked two soccer fields, partially framed by a series of geometrical gardens organized in an L-shaped composition, Forestier's plan curiously resembles the architectural plans of two parks described in 1913 by the Argentine educator Ernesto Nelson in an extensive and well-illustrated article published in the bulletin of the Museo Social

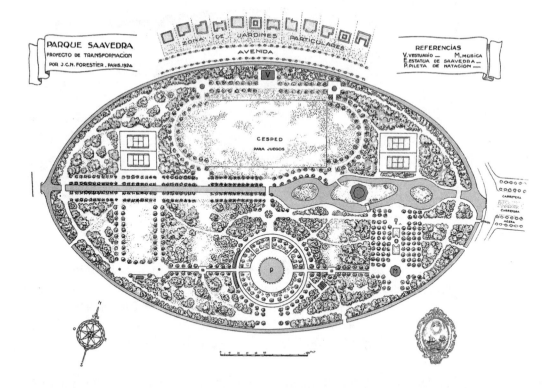

FIGURE 3.23.
Jean-Claude Nicolas Forestier, Parque Saavedra. Published in Comisión de Estética Edilicia, Proyecto orgánico para la urbanización del municipio: El plano regulador y de reforma de la capital federal, 1925 *(Buenos Aires: Talleres Peuser, 1925).*

Argentino.[172] The sketches of the two parks described by Nelson show quadrangular layouts, one organized along a diagonal axis with the main entrance located at one of its corners, and the other organized along a central horizontal axis, but both partially framed by an L-shaped composition that included sports facilities as well as gardens and playgrounds.[173] The parks described by Nelson seem to have anticipated Forestier's architectural proposal for Parque Avellaneda while also following the Musée social's social-engineering agenda—with its nationalist and eugenics overtones—presented in its effort to preserve green spaces and instrumentalize sport and playground facilities for the health of city inhabitants and the preservation of the French "race."[174] Nelson was convinced that children's playgrounds were "preventives of crime" in a city in which most of the reported criminals between 1902 and 1911 were young. He saw the playground as a complement to the schools' educational mission and thought they "should be located in those areas of the city in which youth delinquency is more frequent, [because] the influence of those institutions does not go beyond ten blocks."[175] Arguing in favor of the social benefits of playing and exercising, he criticized overprotective parents who, by not allowing their kids to join these collective activities, would engender a "mariconado," crudely put, a "fag."[176] Forestier's system also included projects for smaller parks and gardens such as the project for Parque de los Irlandeses next to the Orphanage for Irish Children, surrounded by gardens and equipped with tennis courts, running and walking tracks, and a central field for playing.[177] As Forestier himself reiterated, his long-standing preoccupation with designing neighborhood parks arose from his belief in the regenerative power of green space.[178]

Yet it was "the conquest of the river"—a project that sought to optimize the relationship between the city and the river—that was Forestier's main emphasis. Following the committee's guidelines, he designed a waterfront avenue-park that would include panoramic promenades, public beaches, sport facilities, residential neighborhoods, a theater, an aquarium, a hotel, a ballroom, and a concert hall—all contributing to a green system that could provide healthy

FIGURE 3.24.
Jean-Claude Nicolas Forestier, Jardín de los Irlandeses. Published in Comisión de Estética Edilicia, Proyecto orgánico para la urbanización del municipio: El plano regulador y de reforma de la capital federal, 1925 *(Buenos Aires: Talleres Peuser, 1925).*

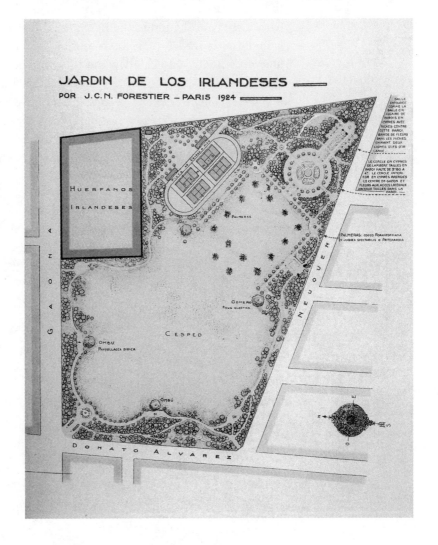

recreation to Buenos Aires' citizens and consolidate the center and periphery into one metropolitan agglomeration through the modern notion of public space.[179] This river avenue-park, the Avenida Costanera, was set within the city limits, but he designed it in such a way that in the future it could be extended along the coast to Tigre and along the new perimetral boulevard that would circumvent the city.[180] In fact, this focus on the simultaneous growth of the city and its population defined Forestier's ideological thrust—he believed that the park system was capable of regenerating not only the integrity of the city but also that of its people. At one point, in a report on his work in Buenos Aires to the Musée social in Paris, he revealed his frustration that the city officials did not grasp the importance of designing the system of open spaces with the inevitable growth of the city in mind.[181] With regret, Forestier says, "It would have been necessary to complement these projects, which could only be slowly applied, with a study of the industrial neighborhoods that stand outside the boundaries of the city . . . but the limits of my mission and the available documents did not allow me to go further."[182] His frustration seems to forecast his growing sense that landscape architecture, as a key component of urban planning, had a restorative influence on urban dwellers as well as a reformative power on those segments of the population occupying the outskirts of the city, namely, the workers and the poor. In fact, in 1928, Forestier accepted the presidency of the

FIGURE 3.25.
Jean-Claude Nicolas Forestier, plan for Avenida Costanera. Published in Comisión de Estética Edilicia, Proyecto orgánico para la urbanización del municipio: El plano regulador y de reforma de la capital federal, 1925 *(Buenos Aires: Talleres Peuser, 1925). IFA Centre d'archives d'architecture du XXe siècle (Cité de l'architecture et du patrimoine, Institut Français d'Architecture IFA), Fonds Forestier-Leveau, Paris.*

FIGURE 3.26.
*Jean-Claude Nicolas
Forestier, plan for
Avenida Costanera.
Published in Comisión
de Estética Edilicia,*
Proyecto orgánico para
la urbanización del
municipio: El plano
regulador y de reforma
de la capital federal,
1925 *(Buenos Aires:
Talleres Peuser, 1925).*

Urban League, later named the Urban and Rural League for Environmental Planning of French Life, an association he founded with Jean Giraudoux, the influential playwright who envisioned urban planning vis-à-vis a process of improving the French population.[183] Considering France a country invaded by refugees and "undesirable" immigrants, Giraudoux advocated strict immigration policies to avoid what he called the "continuous infiltration of barbarians," those people who "could corrupt a [valuable] race." He also promoted firm policies "concerning the physical well-being of French citizens, calling for active participation in sports" and comprehensive campaigns against social diseases.[184] Giraudoux's ideas were welcomed by Forestier and also by other renowned architects, including Le Corbusier, who clearly aligned himself so much with Giraudoux that he told his mother, "We are the left and right hands of a single body."[185] Thus, although Forestier never identified himself as a eugenicist, his ideology, which was intimately compatible with Giraudoux's, created a modern social hygiene apparatus that contributed to the growing acceptance of the utopian project of eugenics.

SCHOOLS FOR REGENERATING "WEAK" CHILDREN

Parks and plazas were also considered the perfect platforms for other modern apparatuses of health and social reform. In 1884, with the promulgation of the General Common Education Law 1420 under President Julio Argentino Roca, the National Council of Education

began playing an exceptional role in the formation of the modern Argentinean state—instrumentalizing architecture itself as a primary vehicle for remaking every aspect of human life, including the social, political, cultural, and physiological well-being of the population.[186] By 1909, the National Council of Education decided to establish the first two "Schools for Weak Children" (Escuelas de Niños Débiles) in Parque Olivera and Parque Lezama, both in the southern neighborhoods of Buenos Aires.[187] The neo-Lamarckian and puericulturist orientation influenced Argentinean leaders to see these new medical-educational institutions as instruments to combat the physical, psychological, and cognitive weaknesses manifested in some children. It was believed that "weak" (or "at risk") children, the products of their progenitors' alcoholism, tuberculosis, and syphilis—heredity—combined with malnutrition, lack of hygiene, and the substandard or inadequate conditions of their homes—milieu—could be regenerated through medicalized therapeutic spaces.[188] In 1910, Ramos Mejía, president of the National Council of Education at the time, created a committee to formulate the guidelines that would prescribe every aspect of the functioning of these schools: from admission criteria for children and medical inspection procedures to their diets, physical therapy, and educational programs.[189] From September to May, in three-month cycles, these schools received children recruited from the "normal" public schools in the city, who, after being evaluated by a medical academic committee (Cuerpo Médico Escolar), were identified as "weak" or backward.[190]

In these outdoor schools at the center of major public parks, children received their academic curricula under shady trees; gardening and agriculture lessons in flower beds, pergolas, and vegetable patches designed for their training; curative sunbathing, physical exercises, and directed games on well-kept lawns; shower baths and nutritious meals in orderly hygienic facilities.[191] From dawn to dusk, these children were taught in a healthy environment and under the vigilant eye of both teachers and physicians.[192] A medical examination was conducted every fifteen days to evaluate each child, monitoring important data such as "weight, thoracic capacity, muscular strength, biacromial and thoracic diameters, visual and auditory alertness and acuity . . . and improvement in intelligence."[193] These were conceived as regenerative schools. Their aim was to ameliorate the mental, moral, and physical conditions of children perceived to be defective; their status was recorded every day, and "as soon as the child [was] pronounced *normal*," he or she was required to leave and go back to their regular schools.[194] A 1912 study written by the Argentine physician Hamilton Cassinelli argues that these schools were for children who had the capacity to be "easily perfectible," in other words, for children whom "the regular school finds not normal enough and the hospital finds not sick enough."[195] The study specifies that these schools were not "for the idiots and imbeciles impossible to educate [who] have their schools in asylums"; not for "the deaf-mutes and the blind [who] have their special institutions"; and not for "the parasites, vicious and delinquent, [who] also have their place in the Reformatory Marcos Paz."[196] Yet, to select the children who were appropriate for these regenerative institutions from their regular schools, the guidelines established a process similar to the one implemented by Vucetich for the identification of criminals: "taking frontal and profile photos of each child . . . as well as their fingerprints . . . together with a report regarding their character, intelligence, and attitude."[197] Offering fresh air, sunlight, and a sense of freedom and welfare for future citizens of the new world, these schools masked a system of

FIGURES 3.28–3.29.
"Types of Physically Weak Children" (Tipos de Niños Débiles Físicos). Photos included in the clinico-anthropological report for Schools "Nicanor Olivera" and "Parque Lezama." Published in Hamilton Cassinelli, "Contribución al estudio de los niños débiles y retardados en edad escolar," PhD diss., Universidad de Buenos Aires, Facultad de Ciencias Médicas, 1912.

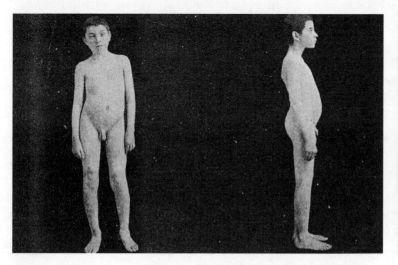
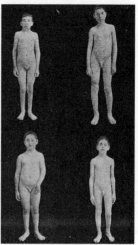

surveillance and control over children's health and education that was inserting itself into larger eugenic aspirations—as *dispositifs* for the improvement of the "biological capital" of the nation.[198]

The motivation for the creation of the Escuelas de Niños Débiles in Argentina is strikingly discernible when one considers the motivation behind its direct antecessor, the Écoles de Plein Air in France—a new "type" of institution, formulated as a spatial strategy for child saving that would become instrumental in the national process of racial regeneration.[199] A hybrid between sanitarium, school, and garden to rehabilitate pretubercular and deficient children, "the open-air school was [simply thought of as] the school of regeneration."[200] Responding to the fear of depopulation and degeneration that haunted French society during the Third Republic, the open-air school emerged as a new therapeutic and medicalized space fostered by physicians and architects alike in which nature and architecture actively participated in the social-engineering process of national construction. In 1912, the French architect and Musée social member Augustin Rey delivered a talk titled "L'École de l'avenir" (The School of the Future) at the International Conference on Demography and Hygiene in Washington, DC.[201] In his talk, Rey called for a new "type" of school building capable of bolstering children's health, recognizing the power of architecture "to exert a profound influence on the overall development of the race." The open-air school, Rey argued, "should therefore be like a nursery where the young plant develops and strengthens and not where it atrophies."[202]

So, for Rey, as it was for physicians and educators in Argentina, the open-air school was the modern "greenhouse" for a better race.[203] Although the open-air schools began functioning in makeshift spaces as part of urban parks and gardens, their appeal as a potential eugenic health apparatus attracted architects, whose early visions condensed the clinical agenda that modern architecture would come to embody.[204] Open and flexible classrooms with large-scale sliding windows or glass folding walls faced patios and gardens; roof terraces, balconies, and sheltered areas for gardening and relaxation accompanied clean and modern facilities for children's hygiene and medical examination. These elements were then incorporated into the architectural design of schools and working-class homes with the conviction that fresh air and sunlight would contribute to the generation of a healthier proletariat, and thus to the productivity and economic health of the nation. Years before the inauguration of the first two open-air schools in Buenos Aires, Emilio Coni had begun a campaign for their implementation in Argentina.[205] For years, Coni called for the creation of

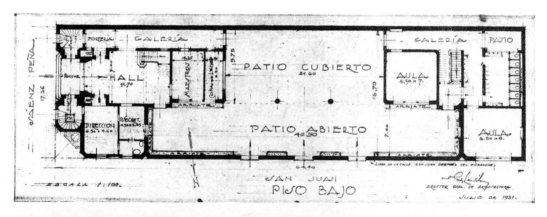

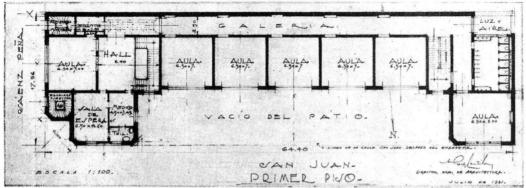

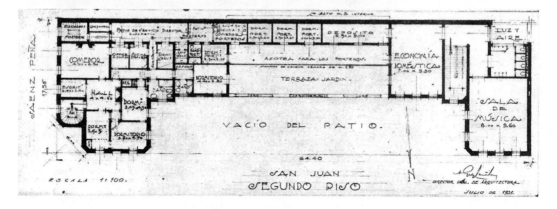

FIGURES 3.30–3.32.
Plans School Ricardo Gutiérrez, Constitución, 1931. Published in the Revista Arquitectura, *1935. Courtesy of the Sociedad Central de Arquitectos.*

more open-air schools as a complement to the positive results he had achieved while leading the Argentine Anti-Tuberculosis League. In its first four years, the league created "two 500-bed hospitals, two 300-bed sanitariums, and twelve dispensaries," plus ambulatory programs of sanitation and disinfection in schools and family homes.[206] Many physicians and educators joined Coni in his campaign, publishing books and articles and delivering lectures in scientific and popular magazines and other outlets.[207] In 1917, Coni continued his public campaign, asking the National Council of Education to "multiply" the

FIGURES 3.33–3.34.
*Sunbathing and helio-
therapy at the Solarium,
n.d., Mar del Plata.
Published in Samuel
Madrid Páez,* Sociedad
de Beneficiencia de la
Capital: Su misión y
sus obras, 1823–1923
*(Buenos Aires: Sociedad
de Beneficiencia de la
Capital, 1923).*

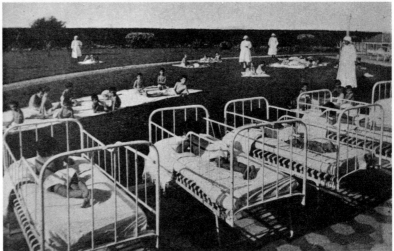

existing open-air schools.[208] But in 1921, after celebrating the opening
of a third open-air school in Parque Chacabuco, Coni lamented that
this "type" of school was not yet disseminated enough throughout
Argentina.[209]

Yet, it would not be until the late 1920s that Argentina's interest
in open-air schools took a more eugenic and architectural turn. The
government was convinced that this "type" of school represented "the
most efficient formula to preserve infancy through the simultaneous course of hygiene as well as physical, intellectual, and moral
education under medical control."[210] Architects joined educators and
physicians in their call to do something to reverse the debilitating
conditions in which children were growing up, "crowded in sties and
conventillos, [or slum dwellings, which were] the principal source
of tuberculosis, alcoholism, and all moral vices."[211] "What could we

expect from a child that was born and raised in such an environment?" asked Benito Carrasco.[212] Clearly, because of a growing fear that an unsanitary environment could spawn a generation of defective children, a new architectural model of health for neighborhood schools emerged, inspired by the open-air model. This new prototype, which would house children for over ten hours a day, replaced the traditional central courtyard with patios and gardens open to the street, literally inverting the architectural layout so that what was a central patio within a school became a school within nature. This move followed the French architect Adolphe Augustin Rey's criticism of continuing to build interior patios as the main source of light and ventilation in buildings; for him, these interior patios were potential incubators for tuberculosis.[213] In fact, the National Educational Council's publication that celebrated the fiftieth anniversary of Law 1420 highlighted Rey's conviction that "we cannot talk seriously of ventilation and illumination in the interior of rooms until this reform [of the traditional interior courtyard] is a fact."[214] Materializing this new architectural typology, a new school opened in 1933 in the working-class neighborhood of Parque Chas.[215] There, all classrooms were opened along the "external façades," with large 18.70 by 7.55 foot windows that "virtually imply that . . . students receive their lessons 'al aire libre.'"[216] Other urban schools, located on constricted lots, committed entire façades to the circulation of fresh air and sunlight. Crafted in metal and glass, these external walls could be positioned such that, "when opened entirely, the student would be placed in the open air."[217] By 1935, the General Directorate of Architecture, an arm of the National Council of Education, had built twelve such urban schools in which surrounding green space had replaced traditional interior patios.[218] Three more schools for "weak" children were also opened in addition to the others in Parque Lezama, Parque Olivera, and Parque Chacabuco.[219] All of these schools were equipped with their own sanitary pavilion, doctor's office, and shower basins—facilities that "hygiene and pedagogy considered indispensable."[220] Although the neighborhood schools based on the open-air model were designated for "regular" children, they were conceived as part of a larger educational and health network paired with the "colonies for weak children" that were developed outside of the city.[221] In 1936, the National Council of Education established one such permanent colony in the mountains of Tandil, and in 1937, another by the sea, in Mar del Plata, for the treatment of weak and TB-carrying children. These colonies carried forward the mission that the Solarium and the Asilo Marítimo, then under the direction of the Sociedad de Beneficiencia de la Capital, had assumed in Mar del Plata to rehabilitate children, mostly poor children transferred from Buenos Aires hospitals.[222] Evidently, the creation of many different "types" of open-air institutions for children was part of the eugenic strategy to improve the "biotypes" of the Argentine population. Physicians, educators, and architects had chosen to implement a new educational-medical topology as a means to classify and normalize the population—children in particular. It is not by chance that even the celebrated writer Leopoldo Lugones would say about Ramos Mejía and his first open-air schools that "his brilliant and productive intelligence laid the foundation for the most efficient monument within the educational system [precisely] because it attempts to 'improve' the race."[223]

SPACES OF QUARANTINE AND REPRODUCTION FOR WOMEN

The sustenance of the family and the procreation of healthy children have always been understood as the key responsibilities of women. Even in modern developed countries, women were usually confined to the domestic sphere, and those women who did not want to procreate or cooperate with their husbands' demands were considered barbaric or immoral or were diagnosed with maternal phobias.[224] In modern Argentina, where women were often idealized as mothers or bestialized as sexual objects, the state felt entitled to remove "ill" women from public spaces, segregating them in enclosed places, hiding them as much as possible, and trapping them in asylums, never to step outside the state's surveillance. According to the French historian of medicine Alain Corbin, it was precisely the need to control women's sexuality outside the home that led to the legalization and regulation of prostitution.[225] Legal in Argentina between 1875 and 1934, prostitution was medically controlled by the state primarily to protect the clients, not the prostitutes themselves. In Argentina, as in France, prostitutes were considered the incarnation of social diseases, such as syphilis and tuberculosis, and the incarnation of vice itself—justifying the national development of a comprehensive system of control.[226] Called the "French system," Argentina's strategy for the regulation of prostitution, which was based on the creation of an "enclosed milieu," invisible to society but transparent to the authorities, would become the incarnation of eugenics itself—and its main target: the mother-child unit and the spaces designed to engineer them.

The morally justified starting point for this engineering agenda was the regulation and spatialization of prostitution. A system of the quasi-incarceration of prostitutes was thus conceived. This system was compartmentalized into four different enclosed spaces, all functioning together. First, as the gateway of the system, the sanitary dispensary (*dispensario de salubridad*) was developed for the registration and medical examination of prostitutes. Second, those found to be sick were sent to a syphilis asylum (*el sifilocomio*) for isolation and treatment.[227] Third, prostitutes considered fit to work were then confined to prostitution houses or bordellos, which were either camouflaged or banished to specific areas of the city. And fourth, hermetically sealed carriages were designed as the only permissible means of transportation of prostitutes from one place to another.[228] Thus, prostitutes were an important component of urban pathology. As such, they were virtual prisoners, treated as confessed criminals to the point that they were not allowed to leave their bordellos without authorization—unless they were married. Suspected of carrying degenerative diseases, these "medically dangerous" women were removed from the visible urban dynamics. As Benjamin Dupont, a French hygienist living at the time in Buenos Aires, said, these so-called medically dangerous women "should be repressed and subject to surveillance because . . . [prostitution] endangers public health by propagating contagious diseases. For this reason every prostitute should be suspected a priori of being ill."[229]

In fact, as evident even in Penna and Madero's 1911 report, the identification and isolation of prostitutes represented the starting point for modern public health programs in Buenos Aires.[230] For instance, as early as 1888, the first dispensary especially designed to target and treat syphilis and other venereal diseases was established in the city, and eventually propagated in particular neighborhoods, including the upper-middle-class neighborhood of Recoleta. Of course, to combat these diseases, the main targets of intervention were again women, not men.[231] What is remarkable here is that the architecture of this dispensary and its location, as described in detail in Penna and Madero's study, mimics the hermetic properties of a system designed not only to combat sexually transmitted diseases but also to make sure that targeted women were removed from decent society. As the report specified: "The building was constructed along the perimeter of [municipal] land, reserving an empty space of 310 square meters for parking the carriages that bring the registered prostitutes for examination: [the carriages] access through the front door on Larrea Street and exit the building through the back door on Barrientos Street."[232] In this way, the prostitutes were hidden from sight by being directly transferred to an area inside the building, "saving the neighbors from the disturbances that would take place if [transfer] occurred in the street"—considered an imperative, given its paradoxical location in one of the most fashionable districts of the city.[233] The report itself exalts the dispensary's specially customized architectural features, its succession of spaces and clinical activities: "a registration hall, a waiting and distribution hall, a cabinet for examination, a consultation room, [another] cabinet for examination, a laboratory for micrographic services, the offices of the director and the secretary, office of statistics, sterilization room, changing room, a kitchen, a latrine, and a dark room."[234] Thus, architecture can be seen as the handmaiden of health reform. In the same way, the houses of prostitutes were spatially masterminded within this system of control: as a one-story house with only one door for access, no attractive colors on the exterior façades, no publicity or identification of its function, few open windows, and with prescribed dimensions that correspond to specific conditions for "hygienic and moralistic reasons," having as its primary purpose the shielding of society from such a source of degeneration.[235] Zones of tolerance were clearly demarcated to prevent prostitution from appearing in other public spaces.[236] But it is interesting to note that syphilis, highlighted in its own chapter in Penna and Madero's study, was not visible on the same report's urban pathology maps—as if the diagnosis of syphilis, assigned only to women, had to be hidden along with them.

Of course prostitutes were not the only women considered medically and morally dangerous: women outside the domestic sphere, particularly lower-class workers such as servants and nurses, were also suspect. These women's sexual freedom, rather than the potential disease, was perceived as the real threat to public health, whereas men who participated in keeping the disease alive were not under surveillance at all. Thus, although not as widely enforced as the prostitution ordinance, a public health law was passed calling for the mandatory registration of domestic female servants and nurses.[237] It is remarkable that the prostitute's house, designed to be easily monitored by the authorities, became a paradigm for the conception of the ideal lower-class house in Buenos Aires.[238] Apprehension about women working outside their homes was linked to the very idea of the preservation of the family and the nation. Women, valued only in their "natural" reproductive role rather than in the productive labor sphere, represented a national menace.[239] The family, as the basic unit of society, forms a critical link to national identity in most modern nations, but it has been argued that the family was used as the main mechanism for marginalizing individuals and depriving them, women in particular, of civil rights.[240] In early modern Argentina, the politics of social control of female prostitutes and lower-class female workers was based on the social construction of gender and class, family and nation. In fact, as early as 1871, a civil code explicitly stated that the role of women was to marry and bear children. With such an intense focus on reproduction, the mechanism for building a healthy nation— and a healthy home—was in the hands of science, circumscribed by moral principles. In this way, a healthy home was understood not only as a hygienic house but as an entire "apparatus of the interior," able to shore up the social construction of the family, in which matrimonial alliance, sex, reproduction, and education were thought to be part of the national mechanism to rebuild the nation's stock—producing and cultivating healthy citizens.[241]

The house—the locus of the family, especially in relation to the working-class family—acquired a prescriptive function: as a seminal embodiment of the *dispositif* shaping the process of civilization that had the family as its object. Convinced that "the health and prosperity of a population is based on the welfare of family life," the young architect Carlos María Della Paolera, speaking at the Museo Social Argentino's first housing conference in 1920, stated that the family house should be organized in a very particular way that included "separate bedrooms for the parents and children, and as many bedrooms as necessary to split the children by gender."[242] Another participant at the conference, the physician Wenceslao Tello, argued that the Argentinean house should be institutionalized as a school for learning the conventions of family life, a school where the main principles of the modern nation were being taught.[243] In this way, maternity became politicized, children became the most valuable resource of the nation, and women became a natural resource but only within the family.[244] These ideas suggest that the family milieu contributes to the moralization and medicalization of the individual, and that heredity makes sex—its alliances, diseases, and productivity—an issue of "biological responsibility." This responsibility required the organization of a national project for managing sexuality at its active legal site—the family house—where Foucault says "sex and its fertility had to be administered."[245] From its first years of activity with the implementation of its project for the creation of the "agricultural home," the regular publication of articles on the family and housing for the rural and urban working classes, and the organization of the Housing Congress in 1920, the Museo Social Argentino showed that the family and the administration of its locus and activities were among the primary means to control the population. Recognizing that the "house problem" was crucial to governmentality and social order, in 1915 the Argentine state created the National Council of Low-Cost Houses (Consejo Nacional de Casas Baratas).[246] Before 1920, the conceptualization of the house and even its physical manifestation had been in the domain of physicians, social reformers, and politicians, not architects. So, it was not a surprise that when architects got involved in housing issues, they followed certain moral and scientific precepts—spatial compartmentalization, sanitation, ventilation, and illumination—established by the medical and social sciences.[247] As the Argentine architectural historians Anahi Ballent and Jorge Francisco Liernur stated, "The house was considered an instrument of social reform, capable of transforming habits and behaviors."[248]

Yet, it was not until the 1930s that the family home, like schools, became clearly eugenic. The popular magazine *Viva Cien Años*, published every other week between 1934 and 1949 with the support of the most important health institutions in the country, invaded Argentineans' homes with an array of eugenic values.[249] Considered the first South American health magazine, *Viva Cien Años* promoted common responsibilities for a collective health that included sports and physical education, sex education and puericulture, and the comfort and hygiene of the habitat.[250] The articles visualized the Argentinean family within an urban network of apparatuses of health and reproduction that was capable of offering welfare to its inhabitants while balancing the quantity and quality of the national stock. As noted previously, in addition to the family house itself, this network included infant milk depots, newborn crib chambers, health dispensaries, puericulture institutes, and, of course, the open-air schools—-all of which were part of a system of social engineering.

As a primary component of this medicalized system, projects of domestic architecture—what the architect Jorge Kálnay would call the "eugenic house" (*la vivienda eugénica*)—were conceived as a way to restore the organic link between humankind, space, and nature through a declared war on disease, degeneration, and infertility.[251] For Kálnay, architecture was tantamount to urbanism: "A house in the countryside that is not linked to nature, 'that has not planted its roots in it,' does not deserve to be called architecture; neither does the urban house, no matter how decorated its façade, dignify the environment or blend in with it."[252] Central to this discourse was a correlation he identified between what he called "*urbanología*" and the so-called science of man, sociology—equating *urbanología* with "applied sociology" and urbanization with "social technique."[253] In 1935, at the First Argentine Congress of Urbanism, Kálnay argued: "Statistics related to police, hygiene, and the economy of the nation reveal that [rates of] crime, accidents, and mortality; decreases in natality; and [levels of] misery are directly linked to how populations are housed in unhealthy communal houses and in neighborhoods without green spaces for the normal development of children."[254] Architecture and landscape design were thus instrumentalized to rehabilitate the body, improving its health and procreative capacity. In the same way as nature was used to rehabilitate children in schools, essential features of early sanatorium design were used to rehabilitate families in their homes by, for example, adding terraces and solariums, furnished with reclining couches that mimicked the chaise lounges used by TB carriers during their heliotherapy.[255] Five years later, a conviction that the "bad house" was the cause of high mortality drove the First

FIGURE 3.35.
Leo Fontan, Poster of the French National Campaign against Syphilis. Ministry of Public Health, France, 1920s. Archives Départemental des Bouches-du-Rhône, Marseille.

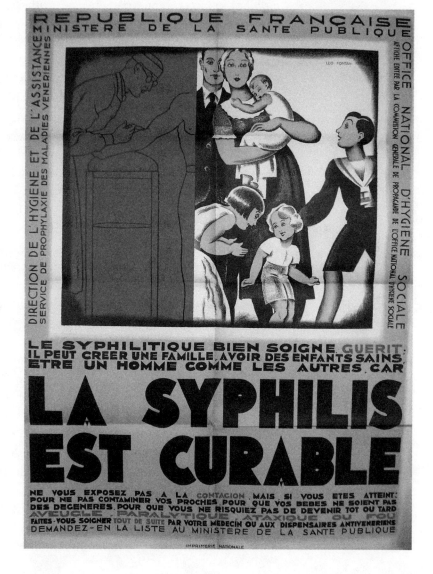

Congress on Population, organized by the Museo Social Argentino, to pass various motions to regulate the family home.[256] Among the many debates within this conference, Pinard and Landouzy's theories of puericulture and hominiculture were endorsed as the way to ensure the preservation and amelioration of Argentine society.[257] Gender as well as space was important to eugenics because it was through sexual reproduction that acquired characteristics were transmitted.[258] Patriarchal values, supported by men and also by women on the right and left side of the political spectrum, confined women to a reproductive-maternal role.[259] The Argentine jurist and eugenicist Carlos Bernaldo de Quirós, president of one of the panels, advocated "the eugenic constitution of the family" and for this he declared that in order to protect women as potential mothers, "it is convenient to limit, even more, women's work outside their homes."[260] Adopting the resolution that "the eugenic constitution of the family must be guaranteed," the congress considered that "eugenic legislation of matrimony was obligatory to prohibit marriage to any person with a chronic, contagious, or hereditary disease." All persons would then be required to provide a prenuptial health certificate before marriage.[261]

Thus, during the first half of the twentieth century, all state and institutional efforts to manage the family and its domestic space had been motivated by the ideologies of progress and modernity. The family, as the cell of the nation, had been conceived as a productive and reproductive unit, with a key economic function. In fact, a medical social tradition that was essentially eugenics based had targeted the family as the primary and natural embodiment of the collective moral order and, in consequence, as "the repository of the maladies of the nation and the hope of its transformation."[262] A powerful 1920s poster for a national campaign against syphilis, produced by the French National Office of Social Hygiene and designed by the well-known illustrator Leo Fontan, was emblematic of the critical role of women within the family and the future of the nation.[263] Above the poster's title, "Syphilis Is Curable," is a dual image. On the left, a simple silhouette, drawn on a red background, depicts a medical scene: a physician vaccinating a male patient whose arm, the only part of his body seen as complete, rests on an examination table at the center of the monocolor image. On the right, a colorful illustration on a white background depicts a pleasant bourgeois family scene: a woman holding a baby comfortably sleeping in her arms, surrounded by her happy and healthy children, with her husband standing in the background. The text above and below the title is emphatic: a well-treated syphilitic could be cured, could create a family and have healthy children. This text encourages prevention so that science could play its role and the syphilitic man would not necessarily produce a degenerate child. In the end, as the binary image of this poster so graphically illustrates, the solution to degeneration and the construction of a healthy nation was both medical and moral—a duality embodied in every single one of the apparatuses of health and reproduction: from the restorative garden, to the regenerative school, and, of course, to the eugenic home.

CHAPTER 4

PICTURING EVOLUTION

Le Corbusier and the Remaking of Man

In the history of modern architecture, no one has received more attention than the architect, artist, and writer Le Corbusier. Since the 1920s, hundreds of books and films have been filled with discussions about his work; courses and curricula have been dedicated to his legacy; and details about his sketches, writings, and projects continue to appear on the pages of today's architectural journals, books, exhibitions, and reviews.[1] It would seem that there is little left to say about this modernist icon. Yet out of this great proliferation of analyses—and even though Le Corbusier himself was quite outspoken about his allegiance to this ideology—almost no one has acknowledged his unmistakable complicity with eugenics.[2] From the early 1930s, he endorsed the French science-faith of *puériculture*, which promoted policies to improve the quality of newborns and to manage "defective" infants.[3] Le Corbusier himself merged puericulture and eugenics when, in an article published in 1931 in the neo-syndicalist journal *Plans*, he called for the establishment of special nurseries directly connected to every single dwelling, "run by qualified nurses and supervised by doctors: [to provide] security-selection-scientific child rearing—puericulture."[4] A year later, in an unpublished article, "Aménagement d'une journée équilibrée," Le Corbusier once again advocated for the rubric "eugenisme-puériculture," titling the fourth section of his article with that word pair.[5] His advocacy for the connection between eugenics and puericulture continued for the next decade. As we will see, by the early 1940s, Le Corbusier was absolutely convinced that, as he said: "Eugenics, puericulture will ensure a well-bred race."[6] Within this context, Le Corbusier came to believe not only that there was an intimate connection between architecture, health, and the perfection of the human race but that he had been chosen as the primary agent to materialize this coalescence. Drawing on Le Corbusier's archives in France and Brazil detailing his collaborations, and giving preference to his intellectual life as he portrayed it in his writings, sketches, and speeches produced between the 1920s and 1940s, what follows is a significant history of Le Corbusier's ideological trajectory—one that is not at all quiescent, but rather shows him to be willfully eager to implicate architecture in the "perfecting" and "whitening" of the human race.

In fact, Lamarckian eugenics was at the epicenter of Le Corbusier's ideology. As neo-Lamarckian discourses, first articulated in France, crossed the ocean and then became intertwined with modernist discourses in early-twentieth-century Latin America, Le Corbusier fervently positioned himself at the center of a complicity between aesthetics, medical science, and the construction of the built environment. Eugenicists in France argued that if the consequences of degenerative influences could be inherited, the population could easily be "improved" precisely by controlling those influences. Moving from Paris to Rio de Janeiro and back, this story thus begins in the early 1920s in France, on the heels of the country's obsession with human degeneration. This "self-reproducing force," which was considered "not the effect but the cause of crime, destitution and disease," was used to characterize other races as inferior to the white race and to stigmatize individuals' clinical pathologies.[7] In this chapter I trace the formation of a high-modernist ideology that was formulated and delivered by no one more influential than Le Corbusier, aimed not only at a new form of living but at a new form of man. While this goal may seem benign, without understanding the Lamarckian nature of the eugenics movement in France and Latin America, and the prevalence of neo-Lamarckian ideas in Le Corbusier's own work, the racial and eugenic underpinnings embedded in his projects and statements have gone unnoticed despite their centrality.

ORTHOPEDICS: MODERNISM AND NORMATIVITY

With their eyes trained on the perception of order, and aiming to bring the rigor of the hard sciences to art, the architect Le Corbusier, the painter Amédée Ozenfant, and the poet Paul Dermée founded a magazine in 1920 titled *L'Esprit nouveau*.[8] Defining art as if it were science,

these editors identified in both fields a dependence on numbers, constants, and invariants and a shared aim to bring order to the world.
It was with the inception of this publication that Charles-Édouard
Jeanneret, now known as Le Corbusier, underwent the transformation of his own name in a process of objectifying himself, as if this
new name would provide order, which he called "the most elevated of
human needs."[9] As the result of a scientific process, he aligned himself
with his own definition of art and invented a persona with its own
"protective shell."[10]

Years later, in 1925, for the International Exhibition of Modern
Industrial and Decorative Arts in Paris, Le Corbusier presented a pavilion also called L'Esprit Nouveau. Made of industrial and replicable
materials, Le Corbusier's pavilion was conceived as a monument to
standardization.[11] It was a standard unit—an ideal cell for living—in
which every element was industrially produced. Representing an uncanny tie between the decorative arts and evolution, the pavilion was a
maison-outil, equipped with modern appliances, furniture, and works
of art but also imbued with what Michel Foucault calls "regimes of
practices" or "programs of conduct," those instruments of governance
that "normatize" daily life, from the division of space to the regulation
of sexuality.[12] With remarkable relevance to our discussion, Foucault
understood normalization as a practice of standardization, which, as
"one of the great instruments of power," is both repressive and productive: it "imposes homogeneity" that is actually responsible for making
the "individual."[13] One could describe the domestic habitat as a place
"saturated by different, overlapping forms of institutions (ownership,

sexuality, kinship, family, lineage, technics, servitude, repression, civilization, privacy, intimacy)" that transform this habitat into a piece of "equipment"—an "economic device" inserted into systems of production.[14] In this sense, by being a standard unit, Le Corbusier's pavilion seems to have exemplified Francis Galton's definition of the "normal" as both "statistically most common and socially preferable; it is the average and also an ideal."[15]

Thus, more than merely an architectural contribution to the exhibition, the L'Esprit Nouveau Pavilion allowed Le Corbusier to synthesize the normalizing agenda of modernity.[16] This synthesis of the arts and sciences was captured in a series of books that collected articles he published since the 1920s in *L'Esprit nouveau* magazine. These four volumes covered architecture in *Vers une architecture* (1923), urban planning in *Urbanisme* (1925), painting in *La Peinture moderne* (1925), and decorative arts in *L'Art décoratif d'aujourd'hui* (1925).[17] It was in the latter publication that Le Corbusier, inspired by Hermann Muthesius' interest in evolutionary object types, introduced his new concepts of "type-needs" and "type-objects" to articulate a program that proposes science as a norm in which rationality is put

FIGURES 4.2–4.3.
Le Corbusier, "type-needs, type-objects" (besoins-types, meubles-types), pages from L'art décoratif d'aujourd'hui *(Paris: Éditions Crès, 1925). © FLC/ ADAGP, Paris / Artists Rights Society (ARS), New York 2017.*

1925
EXPO.
ARTS. DÉCO.

6

Rechercher l'échelle humaine, la fonction humaine, c'est définir des besoins humains.
Ces besoins sont types. Nous avons tous besoin de compléter nos capacités naturelles par des éléments de renfort.
Les objets-membres humains sont des objets-types répondant à des besoins-types.
L'art décoratif est un terme inconnu et inexact par lequel on représente l'ensemble des objets-membres humains. Ceux-ci répondent avec une certaine exactitude à des besoins d'ordre nettement objectif. Besoins-types, fonctions-types, donc objets-types, meubles-types.
L'objet-membre humain est un serviteur docile. Un bon serviteur est discret et s'efface pour laisser son maître libre.
L'art décoratif est de l'outillage, du bel outillage.

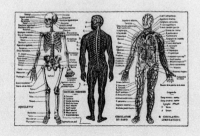

BESOINS-TYPES
MEUBLES-TYPES

C'est ici que l'on quitte les royaumes angoissants de la fantaisie et de l'incongru, et que l'on peut reprendre possession d'un code aux articles rassurants. Le poète déchoit, c'est vrai; il chute

to work.[18] Aware of Muthesius' view that, of all the arts, architecture was the one that tends most naturally toward a type, Le Corbusier began to standardize furniture and everyday objects—what he understood as the decorative arts—in response to a single human type, living in standardized housing. As Muthesius had put it in 1914 at the Werkbund Congress in Cologne, "It is characteristic of architecture to press toward standard types."[19] Following Muthesius' argument, Le Corbusier imagined a standardized body with standardized needs, which he called "type-needs." His "type-objects" were those pieces of furniture and decorative objects organized around that standardized human body, serving that body almost invisibly as, in his own words, "a docile servant . . . discreet and self-effacing."[20]

Articulating this normative body-object relationship in *The Decorative Arts of Today*, Le Corbusier begins with a discourse on scale. "To search for human scale, for human function, [he writes,] is to define human needs." Furthermore, he states: "These needs are type, that is to say they are the same for all of us; we all need means of supplementing our natural capabilities, since nature is indifferent, inhuman (extra-human), and inclement; we are born naked and with insufficient armour."[21] Creating a single human typology at a particular scale, Le Corbusier draws furniture and everyday objects into the service of man. Within this discourse, Le Corbusier introduces what he calls an "orthopedic" relationship between furnishings, objects, and the human.[22] Just as the term "orthopedics" is traditionally defined as the branch of medicine attending to the correction of injuries or disorders of the skeletal system, Le Corbusier's terminology clearly signals a clinical, medical shift in man's relation to the arts—architecture and the decorative arts in particular. In this way, Le Corbusier instrumentalized the twin concepts of "type-needs" and "type-objects," redefining man's relationship to the decorative arts from one of aesthetics to one of normativity, and in the process recasting the decorative arts as essential tools for the medical correction of human beings rather than as mere surplus objects of pleasure and wealth. Perhaps Le Corbusier, like other architectural modernists, was unaware of the biological origin of the concept of typology, popularized within the field of architecture during the nineteenth century. However, it is evident that "the introduction of the term *typology* put into circulation, unbeknownst to architects, ideas whose origins were actually to be found in nineteenth-century ethnography and criminology."[23] In fact, Muthesius had clearly articulated the normative agenda of the term, which in his words "spurns the abnormal and seeks the normal."[24]

Of course, Le Corbusier is not alone in theorizing a relationship directed toward mankind's improvement through contact with the environment. Through this discussion of "type-needs" and "type-objects," Le Corbusier's writing leans close to a much older theory of influence, formulated by the eighteenth-century French physician and anatomist Marie-François Xavier Bichat. At a time before microscopes, Bichat discovered the tissue structure of organs and, in 1799, submitted his now famous definition of life as the "ensemble of functions by which death is resisted."[25] This ensemble, made up of layer upon layer of varying permeabilities, gave new shape to theories of the body wherein the body is variably shielded and made vulnerable to the workings of the outside world through its layered yet permeable membranes. Made up of *vegetable functions*—digestion, circulation, respiration, and secretion—and *animal functions*—the cerebral, nervous, and musculoskeletal systems—Bichat's theorized body moved away from the hollow-vessel formulation that predated him to be understood as a layered entity under constant attack from without. Thus, the vegetable functions only provided a rough sketch of a body, which still had to be clothed. Drawing on the double entendre built into the French word *habit*, alternately implying a link to daily clothing (as opposed to seasonal fashion, or *la mode*) and to the repetition of daily actions (as we understand the word in English), Bichat proposed that it is daily *habit* that, first, protects the body from its surroundings, and second, refines the animal over and above the vegetable core of man, through the alignment of moral practices and a protectively shaping environment.[26] Le Corbusier's desire to bring orthopedic correction to mankind through the decorative arts resonates almost too well with Bichat's focus on everyday habits. As if he were literally following Bichat, Le Corbusier pursued a line of study that at once praised and sought to master the influence of the environment on the constitution of the human being, aligning with the claim by Georges Canguilhem that the body is only quasi natural due to its profound responsiveness and vulnerability to its life conditions.[27] By recognizing that the "living being and its environment are not normal," and that "it is their relationship that makes them such," Canguilhem inadvertently gave Le Corbusier the rationale he needed to go beyond designing functional spaces, to instead create the physical conditions that were necessary to engineer modern life.

It cannot be understated that the seductive nature of environmental adaptation theories for architects, medical practitioners, and reformers of the twentieth century comes to light in this history of Le Corbusier's normative projects. Jean-Baptiste Lamarck's work on the effects of the milieu on a given organism, coupled with Charles

Darwin's theory of natural selection and Herbert Spencer's work on the impact of climate on individuals, added up to a trendy and timely amalgamation of research and social theory that began seeping into medicine, environmental sciences, politics, and the arts.[28] Adolf Loos' writings are exemplary of this collusion. Merging the disavowal of architectural ornament with human evolution, Adolf Loos' evolutionary ideas, as expressed in his famous essay "Ornament and Crime" (Ornament und Verbrechen), sprang from a blind and problematic melding of architecture with the social and biological sciences, informing criminology and ethnography.[29] It is in "Ornament and Crime" that Loos, as Christina Cogdell argues, "not only offers a contemporary layman's solid understanding of Lamarckian theory and its theoretical extensions, but demonstrates his application of these ideas toward creating a stripped-down aesthetics of modern architecture and design."[30] Loos was forthright in his belief that "as culture progresses, [it] frees one object after another from ornamentation . . . [And furthermore,] . . . just as conquered primitive races were dying out through a biological process of selection, ornament was facing extinction."[31] He shared this errant evolutionary stance with Le Corbusier, who also stated in *The Decorative Art of Today*: "We can see decorative art in its decline, and observe that the almost

hysterical rush in recent years towards quasi-orgiastic decoration is no more than the final spasm of an already foreseeable death."[32]

Highlighting the supposedly environmental malleability of nature through a misguided account of the evolutionary theories of the time, particularly Darwin's theories of change, Robert Mallet-Stevens and the brothers Jan and Joël Martel give body to this misreading in the bold form of a modern garden made out of concrete trees. In their contribution to the 1925 International Exhibition in Paris—the same exhibition for which Le Corbusier designed his monument to human standardization, his L'Esprit Nouveau Pavilion—Mallet-Stevens and the Martel brothers' garden exemplifies two obsessions at the center of modernity: an attempt to control nature and the threat of impending death. Jean-Claude Nicolas Forestier, a member of the Parisian Musée social, who at the time was in charge of the urban master plan for Buenos Aires and directed all the parks and gardens projects for this exhibition, recounts their garden project:

> Four tall trees were required for this small garden, and we could not plant them in June; furthermore, their shapes and sizes needed to be strictly identical. . . . With audacity, Mr. Mallet-Stevens resorted to reinforced cement. . . . A puerile copy of nature, like that of artificial flowers, was to be avoided. . . . The design frankly expressed the material's characteristics while its overall perception was that of a tree. . . . It is rather difficult to comprehend the extent of ingenuousness and art that is required to complete such a work.[33]

This "ingenuousness," this move to replace unpredictable, seasonally restricted, nonidentical living trees with concrete and thus formable, identical, white, implacable, and undying replications, foreshadows what architecture could and would do for Lamarckian eugenics. In other words, modernists assumed a new kind of power that allowed them to believe that they could harness nature and, along with it, human life itself. The use of concrete, a human-made material used as early as the Roman Empire and with the capacity to be shaped into

FIGURES 4.6–4.7.
Le Corbusier, terraced garden at the L'Esprit Nouveau Pavilion, International Exhibition of Modern Industrial and Decorative Arts, Paris, 1925. Fondation Le Corbusier, Paris, FLC L2 (8) I-19. © FLC/ ADAGP, Paris/Artists Rights Society (ARS), New York 2017.

SECRETARIA DE OBRAS PUBLICAS
NEGOCIADO DE CALLES Y PARQUES   NO. 2543.
PLAZA DE LA CONFRATERNIDAD, ARBOL DE DICHO NOMBRE.   MAY. 19. 1928

FIGURE 4.8.
Jean-Claude Nicolas Forestier, Árbol de la Fraternidad Americana, Havana, Cuba, 1928. Collection Forestier-Leveau 150. SIAF/Cité de l'architecture et du patrimoine/Archives d'architecture du XXe siècle, Paris.

any form desired, was appropriated in the 1925 Paris exhibition as a statement of universality and malleability. Celebrating nature and at the same time modifying it, Forestier championed the way nature and artifice meet in the concrete-green garden of Mallet-Stevens and the Martels. All the modernist gardens at the exhibition were designed as complements to architecture, as extensions of interior living spaces and decorations, as products of both industry and craft, and as nature objectified.[34] Even the artificially conceived "wild" landscape that Le Corbusier created for the L'Esprit Nouveau Pavilion, and that Forestier described as a garden "without any apparent order," fueled the nature-nurture debate that highlights modernism's obsession to instrumentalize nature. A single tree at the center of the pavilion appears to be both protected and constrained by a simple, bare opening in the roof of the terrace; its horizontal windows and the opening of the terrace itself act as screens that frame and fix nature, creating the illusion of both performance and control.[35]

At the same time that Forestier was fostering the nature-nurture connection in the gardens of the Parisian exhibition and in Buenos

Aires' urban fabric, he was also in the process of undertaking a major commission in Havana, Cuba, to which he traveled a month later.[36] It is compelling to observe that among the urban interventions aimed at the modernization of the city was a scheme in which nature was revealed not only "as the referential and legitimating ground of the city" but also as a manageable element that architecture and planning were capable of exploiting.[37] In this way, Forestier's interventions emphasized Havana's natural settings, its topography, its lush tropical vegetation, and the ocean splashing along its zigzagging shore while at the same time making the case for architecturizing nature, for monumentalizing it. So it was that, next to the colossal Capitolio Nacional, at the center of Forestier's new Plaza de la Fraternidad, a symbolic ceiba tree was planted to celebrate the emergence of Cuba into the international community of modern American nations. This event carries the weight of history due to its association with the founding of Havana in 1519 and with the inauguration of the republic in 1902.[38] However, in its modern setting, the living ceiba tree, also associated with the *arbor infelix*—the *picota* for the punishment of slaves during colonial times—was confined by an elaborately decorated wrought-iron fence.[39] Here, surrounded by orderly palm trees, elevated on a circular platform, and protected by this magnificent ornamental grille, the "poor ceiba"—evoking the city, the nation, and its international integration—became the incarnation of the social history of the country and its normative and disciplinary apparatus in service of modernization. Forestier's tree prefigures a tree that Le Corbusier would develop in the early 1940s to champion the modern ideology of eugenics. In each case, a tree comes to represent the powerful collusion of nature, society, and the state, uncovering the orthopedic function that the built environment—as an extension of state power—played in the "improvement" of the natural, humans included.

BUILT BIOLOGY

Between Le Corbusier's first trip to Latin America in 1929 and his second in 1936, his discourses were centered on the racial and sexual other, the primitive, nature, and death.[40] A fear of degeneration had haunted French society for decades, and a sense of impending death inhabited modernity. During these years, the social and political power of architecture became the focus of Le Corbusier's investigations. He was convinced that technology was a medium for "the rebirth of the human body" rather than an end in itself, and that architecture was an innovative tool for social engineering.[41] Le

Corbusier envisioned architecture as an antidote to degeneration, and Brazil as the perfect territory for this mission, with its significant black and mulatto population, its tropical landscape, and the chance for him to practice utopia.

In 1936, while preparing his series of talks in Rio de Janeiro, Le Corbusier, in a cardboard sketch, brought together the image of a man and a series of words connecting three seemingly unrelated topics: nature, architecture, and eugenics.[42] Written at the top of his notes was the word "Castello," followed by the name "Lúcio Costa," the phrases "pedro aller police" and "Castello coûts clichés," and the name "Carlos Porto." There was also a reminder to himself, "Acheter livre Carrel," to buy the book by Alexis Carrel, the French Nobel Prize–winning

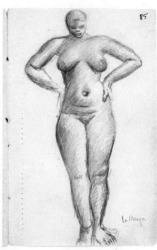

FIGURES 4.9–4.11.
Le Corbusier, sketches made in Rio de Janeiro, 1929. Fondation Le Corbusier, Paris, FLC Carnet B4—276 and 287.© FLC/ ADAGP, Paris/Artists Rights Society (ARS), New York 2017.

physician who had just published his 1935 international bestseller, *Man, the Unknown*, a loud call for white supremacy and the implementation of eugenics.[43] The sketch places the name of the demolished mountain at the center of Rio de Janeiro, Morro do Castelo (the history of which is analyzed in chapter 2), with the names of modern Brazilian architects, the celebrated French eugenicist, and the representation of the simple man who became the object of transformation for Carrel, Le Corbusier, and Brazil's government.[44]

What made Le Corbusier think of Carrel while thinking of Rio de Janeiro? Was Carrel's theory of "the salvation of the white race" at

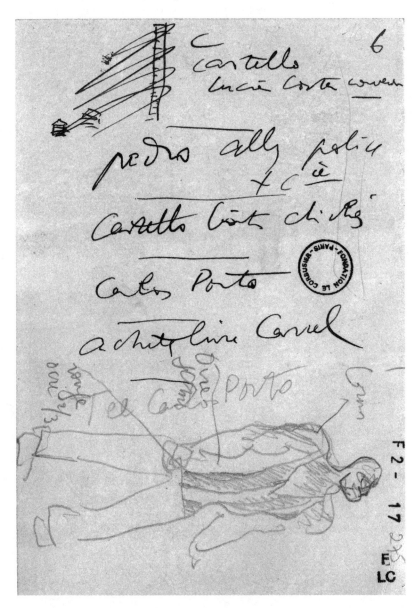

Rio and its enchanted offshore view! From the houses, no one sees it. There is no more land to build upon. Find communications? Open up new ways? Where?
There are nearly a dozen bays, closed, isolated. If you walk through the maze of streets, you rapidly lose all sense of the whole. Take a plane and you will see, and you will understand, and you will decide.

This sketch, done in the plane: an idea is born.

Here a city planner of the classical school has once again proposed courtyards and corridor-streets.

the core of Le Corbusier's ideas on landscape, urban planning, and architecture at the time? It is not a mere coincidence that "Castelo," the site of one of the greatest eugenic laboratories in Latin America, is the first word that appears on the cardboard. It was the pulverized mountain from which thousands of inhabitants, mostly black and poor, were displaced in the early 1920s. It was the esplanade remaining after this devastation that became the stage for the 1922 international exhibition, with its neocolonial pavilions and its image of white Brazil. It was also the name of the epicenter of Rio's master urban plan conceived by the Musée social member Alfred-Donat Agache as a medical intervention for the city, to promote discipline and control over a modern tropical metropolis cleansed of diseases and "undesirables."[45] And finally, it was also the name of the new building for the Ministry of Health and Education, the institution that would be in charge of developing and enforcing Brazil's eugenic policies under Getúlio Vargas' new authoritarian regime.[46] The building—for which Lúcio Costa was leader of the design team and for which Le Corbusier was invited as a design consultant—would be located on this very site where Castelo Mountain once stood. Lúcio Costa, the architect best known for designing Brasília, was the main advocate for selective immigration, seeing it as the only vehicle to achieve good government and good architecture. As was stated in chapter 2, a few years before planning the design for the Ministry of Health and Education building, Lúcio Costa publicly tied together architecture and race, declaring that he was pessimistic about architecture and urbanism in general, since "architecture is a question of race." While the Brazilian population continued to be that racially mixed crowd with "sickly faces" that he observed in Rio's streets, architecture would mirror it. "Everything is a function of race. If the breed is good, and the government is good, the architecture will be good."[47] Linking the dramatic transformation of the urban territory of Rio with Lúcio Costa's words and Carrel's vision for the remaking of society, Le Corbusier distilled and concretized, on one piece of cardboard, the most basic and accepted rationale for modernity: *change the environment, change the man.* For Le Corbusier, Costa's eugenic syllogism of breed begetting good government begetting good architecture also worked in reverse.[48] This association between the human body, the state, and the built environment would become the trigger point for much of Le Corbusier's thinking over the next several years. But it was in Rio during that summer of 1936 that Le Corbusier publicly aligned with Carrel's eugenic ideology, establishing a direct connection between Carrel's ideas and his own.

On July 31, 1936, Le Corbusier began his six talks at the National Institute of Music in Rio de Janeiro by addressing the means by which the remaking of man was to take place: through the collusion of the state and "the technician."[49] By celebrating the work of Rio's mayor Francisco Pereira Passos, "the *prestidigitateur de Rio*," Le Corbusier acknowledged the importance of civic authorities' *grandeur de vue*, but at the same time he emphatically underscored the crucial role played by the technician: "the one who observes phenomena; who analyzes and synthesizes; who recognizes the laws of this world; who discovers new aspects of the continual mutability of life; who imagines new combinations, and applies them on behalf of man."[50] Apparently, for Le Corbusier, this position, which he regarded as powerful and techno-social, was reserved for the architect, who, like a laboratory scientist, he put in the position of providing diagnosis and treatment. In collaboration with the civic authorities, the architect was called upon to assume the crucial role of remaking society by optimizing and controlling technology. In other words, he was convinced that the architect was that "technician," or technocrat, who had the power and the duty to launch "a veritable revolution" by creating "the essential equipment of a mechanistic civilization."[51] As he said to his audience:

> Today, populations have arrived at a grave hour, at a time of great enterprise, the hour of "great works" throughout the world. . . . I have

the occasion to evoke this term, "mechanistic civilization," and sometimes to show that, in fact, this is not a normal evolutionary trend but a veritable revolution, a revolution introduced by mechanization after a hundred years and which has the effect of projecting us from habits and traditions into a new era.[52]

Less than a year earlier, Le Corbusier had published an essay in *L'Architecture d'aujourd'hui* titled "L'autorité devant les tâches contemporaines," in which—by recalling his 1925 inquiry "architecture or revolution?"—Le Corbusier elaborates on the revolutionary role architects were called to undertake. In his own words, commonly, "revolution means to break something and to place oneself on the top of the debris; [and] architecture means to put in order, to conceive, to organize, to build."[53] But, as he notes, architects' investigations call for the establishment of a "new architecture" as the embodiment of a "new civilization" that formulates a new, nonexclusive axiom: "revolution *and* architecture."[54] By deliberating on the role authority should play in society, Le Corbusier argues for a new revolutionary authority that must be entrusted to the architect—an authority that will not only master "the technological elements" but also the social, economic, and political phenomena. In his view, authority is no longer understood as a "static regulator that holds everything in equilibrium" but rather an agile one that moves according to the times—the kind of authority that is capable of looking ahead and seeing clearly, because "the hour of clairvoyance has arrived."[55] He believed so strongly in this revolutionary form of authority that he named the Congrès internationaux d'architecture moderne (CIAM), the organization he helped found in 1928, as the institution where architects "will find a precious form of authority," that is, the main "guidelines for the urbanization of the 'civilisation machiniste.'"[56]

Drawing on the key metaphor of a tree that he systematically details in many of his 1930s publications, Le Corbusier constructs a direct link between what may be understood as *archi-tecture* and *agri-culture*: for him, architects should act "in a permanent cycle of the analytic and the synthetic . . . constantly reexamining origins, sowing seeds to make trees grow straight." As he states, "Tree makers . . . that is our role . . . we architects." In saying this, Le Corbusier not only pronounces the architect a technician but also a gardener with the "meticulous, persistent, and courageous job" of cultivating the "harmonic and continuous cycle" of trees with their "profound roots, trunk, well-multiplied branches, well-attached leaves . . . [and, of course, their products:] flowers, fruits, grains." The architect, "the

FIGURE 4.14.
Le Corbusier, tree draw-
ing featured in Table of
Contents of The Radiant
City, *1935. Originally*
published as La Ville
Radieuse *(Boulogne-*
sur-Seine: Éditions
de L'Architecture
d'aujourd'hui, 1935).

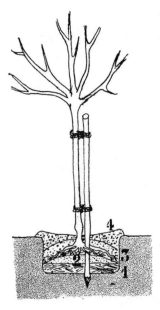

To plant a tree well: 1. good earth and basic manure
2. a covering of fine soil
3. very fine vegetable earth
4. subsoil and fertilizer

man of authority with this tree, will make forests."[57] It is significant
that the opening pages of his 1935 book, *La Ville Radieuse* (*The Radi-*
ant City), describe in detail how to plant and grow a tree, essentially
implying that nature and nurture are conjoined—intimating that the
seed, the "good earth," and the sun are as important as the addition
of fine soil, manure, fertilizer, and the wooden structure drawn by
Le Corbusier that makes the tree grow straight.[58] Cultivating the
landscape and structuring the growth of the tree through this simple
artificial device, Le Corbusier uses this centrally placed image as an
emblem of his book's doctrine, evoking the disciplinary power of architecture and the correctional techniques that architecture is capable
of imposing on humans.[59]

This vision of an architectural revolution that places the architect
in the crucial position of a techno-social authority was at the center of
his opening remarks in Rio de Janeiro. He began by stating that the
series of talks he was inaugurating on that day were not going to focus
simply on architecture and urbanism, as his talks six years earlier in
Buenos Aires had. Citing what he characterized as the new demands
of a new civilization, in this series of talks Le Corbusier argues for a
révolution architecturale capable of formulating new solutions for a
complete renewal of a country, not only of its cities and towns but of
its suburbs and countryside—a renewal that he called *l'urbanisme*
totale.[60] According to Le Corbusier, the conditions for the materialization of the "second era of the machine civilization" were all set. He
states that architects now have "the tools and the technical means"

to renew themselves, to transform themselves in order "to achieve that new society furnished with the necessary instruments for its life and its vitality."[61] He then argues that the machine should stop being viewed simply as an object of efficiency and productivity and more as a means to recover that very vitality of life. To do this, Le Corbusier proclaims that we need to control the machine as "our own creature," because "the slavery of the first machine era has ceased," and now the machine—rather than enslaving us—"will liberate us, will imbue us with its benefits, will offer us its abundance."[62]

It is within this context, as part of his own introduction to the Rio talks, that Le Corbusier first makes reference to Carrel's book, *Man, the Unknown*. Just as Carrel argued that man is not the nineteenth-century *homo oeconomicus*, who "must ceaselessly consume manufactured products in order that the machines, of which he is made a slave, may be kept at work," Le Corbusier points out that man, in order to be transformed, must be seen in all his complexity.[63] In fact, he argues that the "rebirth of the human body," a body that is not only a physical entity but also a moral and spiritual one, can only occur through a new environment, an environment that, as "a living organism," becomes an integral extension of man's needs—what Le Corbusier called a biological unit.[64] Le Corbusier clearly identifies himself with Carrel and even muses about the possibility of materializing Carrel's ideas in his own work. Evoking his book, that doctrinaire compendium advocating the implementation of eugenic measures and practices for "the remaking of man," Le Corbusier comments to his audience:

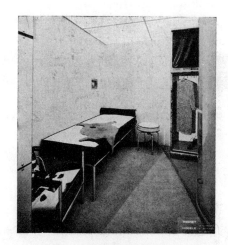

9. THE BIOLOGICAL UNIT: THE CELL

OF 14 M² PER OCCUPANT

(1930 – BRUSSELS CONGRESS)

DEDICATED TO THE INTERNATIONAL CONGRESSES FOR MODERN ARCHITECTURE

The various sketch-plans relating to this problem were published as a whole in "PLANS" 1931: 1. bachelor apartment; 2. apartment for two persons; 3. and 3a. idem; 4. and 4a. couple and 1 or 2 children; 5. a couple and 2, 3, or 4 children; 6. a couple and 3, 4, 5, or 6 children; 7. a couple and 5, 6, 7, 8, 9 or 10 children. This work was carried out in collaboration with Charlotte Perriand.

FIGURE 4.15.
Le Corbusier, "The Biological Unit: The Cell," in The Radiant City, *1935. Originally published as* La Ville Radieuse *(Boulogne-sur-Seine: Éditions de L'Architecture d'aujourd'hui, 1935).*

Plon, an editor who published my book [*When the Cathedrals Were White*] in North America, welcomes at this time the success of his latest book: *Man, the Unknown* by Dr. Carrel. "Write," he told me, "a book that will be an echo of that one." I will do it with pleasure: the man and his shell, in other words, the habitus in which a man is obliged to pass a great portion of his life. It [the dwelling] must be completed and equipped with the essential joys, which can be defined as psycho-physiological. They must be added to the technical possibilities that are not provided by current means.[65]

This appears to be the very first time Le Corbusier made public reference to Carrel. In all likelihood the architectural audience in Brazil did not know who this physician was that Le Corbusier was inspired to emulate. However, it was clear that the Nobel Prize winner's manifesto for "the remaking of man," which Le Corbusier was reading during those days in Rio, legitimized his own ideas, becoming a main source of inspiration for the techno-social doctrine and architectural canons that made Le Corbusier the most famous modernist on earth.

The initial impetus for this inspiration was Carrel's view that the science of the material world (i.e., mechanics, chemistry, and physics) had advanced more rapidly than the science of living beings (i.e., physiology, psychology, and sociology), especially the science of the "human individual." Carrel's outrage at the lack of knowledge we have of ourselves and the consequences of this ignorance in a modern world—built "according to the chance of scientific discoveries . . . without regard to the laws of our body and soul"—became a cry for the emergence of a new science: "the science of man."[66] This was a plea for a more comprehensive discipline capable of apprehending the human being's indivisibility and extreme complexity, including, as Carrel argued, "his essential needs . . . the characteristics of his mind and organs, his relation with the environment . . . the spiritual, the intellectual, and the physiological." This was a science "capable of giving birth to a technique for the construction of society," which he believed would give man the power to renovate it, a "mastery over life and over himself."[67] Another physician and hygienist, Pierre Winter, who was Le Corbusier's friend and collaborator in *L'Esprit nouveau* and in the neo-syndicalist journals *Plans* and *L'Homme réel*, had already made this cry in his 1934 article, "Pour une science de l'homme" (For the science of man). Winter understood the science of man as modern medicine, "a sort of large biology applied to the life of individuals and groups."[68] But Carrel felt that there was "no method capable of apprehending him [the human being] simultaneously in his entirety, his parts, and his relations with the outer world."[69] Although he recognized that physiology and medicine have been the most efficient sciences to teach us about ourselves, Carrel argued that these sciences have been incapable of explaining "man's affective and moral form, his inner life, his character, his esthetic and religious needs, the common substratum of organic and psychological activities, the intimate relations of the individual and his mental and spiritual environment."[70] Thus, these sciences, Carrel maintained, have been incapable of "improving the intellectual and moral quality of populations." In order to combat the dangers that modern life brings to race, nation, and individuals, he argued that this "new science [of man] must progress by a double effort of analysis and synthesis," which, according to Carrel, was the only way to apprehend the human being in all his complexity.[71] It is Carrel's method of "analysis and synthesis," purportedly required to remake man and society, that, interestingly, Le Corbusier attributed to the practice of architecture and illustrated in his tree metaphor the same year that Carrel published his book.[72]

Although since the 1920s, Le Corbusier had begun to think of architecture in biological and even eugenic terms, it is evident that he found in Carrel's 1935 call for this "science of man" a revolutionary opportunity for architecture. Even though Carrel advocated sterilization, euthanasia, and even the use of gas chambers to eliminate the "unfit," his position regarding evolution admittedly shifted from time to time, from Lamarckism to Darwinism and back. His relationship to evolutionary theories was complicated by his fervent Catholicism on the one hand and his attraction to neo-Lamarckianism on the other. In the end, Carrel, whose ideas on evolution were closer to those of French biologists of his time, was convinced that "the primary factors of evolution are the environment and the *genre de vie*. The secondary factor is natural selection, mutation."[73] Clearly, Le Corbusier's agenda was validated by the primacy of the environment in Carrel's ideology, wherein man's physical and psychological traits could be modified. So when he announced to his audience that he was going to write "a book that will be an echo" of Carrel's *Man, the Unknown*, Le Corbusier celebrated the social-engineering power of architecture, its capacity to actually implement Carrel's agenda. "The man and his shell" (as Le Corbusier described the topic of his forthcoming book) was certainly a call for a more "human-centered second machine age" in which the human habitat would be conceived as a functional-rational-biological apparatus, equipped with its necessary "psycho-physiological" attributes.[74] In this inaugural talk, Le Corbusier made no less than six references to the term *psycho-physiologique* (the physiological basis for psychological processes), at times referring to architecture, at times to nature, at other times to man himself—making an ideological and biological link between all three. His first reference to this term was when he qualified the desirable characteristics that architecture should provide humanity, stating that the habitat "must be completed and equipped with the essential joys, which can be defined as psycho-physiological."[75] Then, while visually illustrating his ideas on a large sheet of paper, he once again uses the term. With words that evoke nothing less than the narrative voice in Genesis, Le Corbusier proceeds: "To start, I design a man . . .", and then "I design a sun . . . and to finish I design the trees, the benevolent companions of man . . . and thus, I establish the fundamental basis for man's psycho-physiological sensations."[76] Here, he applies the term to man's capacity to perceive what he considered "the most profound needs of human nature: sun, sky, space, and trees."[77] But a few seconds later he again uses this same term to characterize the motive that he believes "must sit at the core of urbanism," suggesting that these "profound needs" are not simply needs but also clinical instruments in the remaking of man.[78] With this agenda, he reaffirms the human being as "a psycho-physiological entity," extremely vulnerable to life conditions—reinforcing what he regards as an imperative interplay between body, nature, and habitat. By drawing the trajectory of the sun, he introduces the role of time, suggesting that there is a universal system that rules our lives: "Here is the sun that rises and follows its course, here the horizon; it disappears and it is night. Then a new sun rises and it is a new day . . . [therefore] I realize a crucial thing: the 24 hours of solar time is the measure of all our actions."[79] Le Corbusier understood, as the Lamarckians did, that the inevitable influences of nature (i.e., the 24-hour cycle of the earth's rotation, our internal circadian rhythm, and the natural environment) create and modify living beings, and that these influences can also be manageable. He visualizes architecture as a technology capable of taking on nature's role, while also managing nature's life-changing forces.[80] It is not surprising that when Le Corbusier uses the term "psycho-physiological" for the last time, at the very end of his lecture, he portrays architecture and city planning as suprainfluential entities, the only ones capable of repairing society.[81]

During the succeeding lectures, Le Corbusier followed Carrel's rationale for technology and modern society, which states that scientific knowledge has radically transformed the human habitat and the very mode of life. Carrel had enumerated some of these transformations in "The Need of a Better Knowledge of Man," the first chapter of *Man,*

FIGURE 4.16.
Le Corbusier, Sketch Lecture: "Revolução Arquitetural e Urbanismo," 1936. Wax pencil on paper glued on canvas. Collection Museu Nacional de Belas Artes / IBRAM / MinC (n°. 010 / 2017). Photographer: Jaime Acioli.

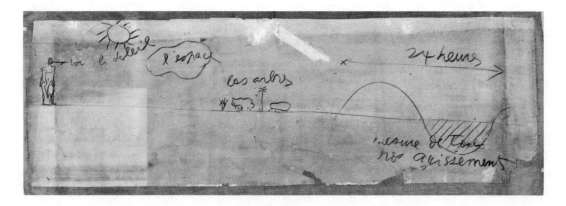

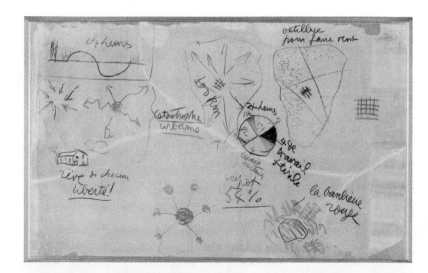

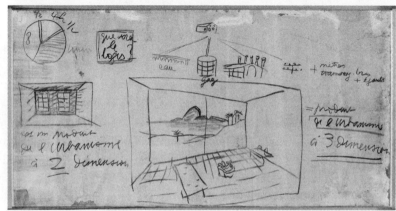

the Unknown: the built environment replaced the natural domain; industrialization triggered the exodus of a large part of the population,
provoking them to move beyond the city center; rapid communications—modern trains, automobiles, airplanes, and telephones—modified the relations between men and nations worldwide; machines—
including elevators and mechanical stairs—decreased the intensity
of human effort; medicine and hygiene—especially after Pasteur's
discoveries and doctrines—eliminated infectious diseases, increased
the quantity of human beings, and extended their life span.[82] All
these changes transformed modern life and the way human beings
spend their 24-hour solar cycle. In his second talk in Rio, Le Corbusier
points to this very issue, arguing that the way human beings are
spending their solar cycle has "begun to be extremely dangerous."[83]
In a specific diagram at the center of a large drawing, Le Corbusier
describes a typical 24-hour cycle, consisting of eight hours of sleep;
eight hours of productive work; over four hours of "sterile work," or

work that, according to Le Corbusier, is essentially meaningless, which includes time for transportation to and from work; and what remains is roughly four hours of evening leisure. "During the last forty years, [Le Corbusier explains,] men escaped from center cities as [if] escaping from a plague. . . . The nineteenth-century cities chained man's freedom, and man searched for it somewhere else . . . [which generated] an urban catastrophe." As a consequence, "men have built huge cities and . . . this [was] a waste of time"—a waste of time circulating from one place to another; a waste of energy working to keep the machines at work.[84]

Influenced by important social reforms occurring in France at the time of his Rio talks—reforms by which the new Front Populaire government had reduced the working week to forty hours and prescribed twelve days of paid vacation time for workers for the first time—Le Corbusier pinpoints an emergency: the need to instrumentalize leisure time as part of the productive mechanism of modern life.[85] So when he began his series of lectures in Rio, Le Corbusier was convinced that "from the nineteenth century to today, the machine has placed man in the service of techniques; [and] it was time to think about how to place the techniques in the service of man."[86] He stated that "mechanization will lead to leisure time" and that this was not a "lightweight promise" but "the most serious problem of contemporary sociology." And, of course, a moral call would follow: "[We need] to prepare people to use leisure in the same way that we need to prepare people to defend the territory or to adapt to the consequences of science."[87] As Carrel himself had argued in his book, "Certain forms of modern life lead directly to degeneration. . . . In the poor as well as in the rich, leisure engenders degeneration."[88]

For Le Corbusier, leisure, the new player of modern times, had to be regulated and disciplined. He addresses the dichotomy between technocracy and humanity's biological, moral, and spiritual nature in *The Radiant City*. In this book, Le Corbusier had already pointed out that "the leisure time made available by the machine era will suddenly emerge as a social danger: an imminent threat." And he noted that "the necessity for transforming this still vague notion of 'leisure time' as quickly as possible into a disciplined function is therefore immediately evident."[89] But it was in his third talk in Rio, which he devoted to this topic of leisure—"the veritable occupation of mechanistic civilization"—that Le Corbusier envisioned a better and paradoxically more productive life due to a new conception of urbanism in which "rather than eight hours of work a day [just] six or even four hours of work" are preferable. Thus, he prescribes a new

FIGURE 4.19.
Le Corbusier, urban plans for Montevideo and São Paulo, 1929. Fondation Le Corbusier, Paris, FLC 30301. © FLC/ADAGP, Paris/ Artists Rights Society (ARS), New York 2017.

24-hour cycle: "eight hours of sleep, [with] the time of transportation significantly reduced . . . four hours of efficient work, and this huge portion . . . of leisure activities . . . divided into two categories: the one that concerns the body and the one that concerns the spirit."[90]

In terms of the body, Le Corbusier tells his audience that he believes that in the modern city, sports have to be implemented not as a spectacle, as previously performed in huge stadiums and coliseums, but as a daily activity, as the scientific training of the body for productivity. In line with the idea of the beach, which had been promoted by physicians since the eighteenth century as a healthy and wholesome environment for the body and the spirit, Le Corbusier shows his drawings for a new form of living in which man can essentially have a "beach" next to his house. Le Corbusier argues that the creation of an urban "beach" to play "real sports" for "half an hour . . . run, swim, take a sunbath . . ." will bring all the benefits of nature and body culture into the city, making it clear that it is the architect alone who can provide the necessary instruments for leisure time education. Notably, in saying this, he makes an unexpected connection between his vision for the *Radiant City* and the geographic region where this new urban canon came to life. Using a sermon-like vernacular, he tells his audience:

> And now I will show you, in just one design, how I keep my promise of conceiving cities capable of giving their inhabitants the necessary elements to occupy and host leisure activities, of a physical and spiritual order. I have baptized this the Radiant City, a term that was born accidentally when I came back from my first study trip to South America [in 1929]. It was in Buenos Aires, in Montevideo, in São Paulo, [and] in Rio where the great ideas of urbanism came to me.[91]

When Le Corbusier refers to his "great ideas of urbanism," he brings together two social spheres that are commonly segregated, both spatially and temporally: work and leisure.[92] These two themes, together with housing and transportation, were at the center of Le Corbusier and Pierre Jeanneret's Temps Nouveaux pavilion for the

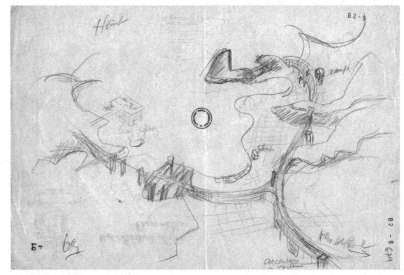

Third Republic's last major cultural event—the 1937 International Exhibition of the Arts and Techniques of Modern Life in Paris. With the support of the CIAM and in line with the spirit of the Front Populaire's leftist programs, the pavilion was not promoting the arts and techniques, as the title of the exhibition had announced, but rather social transformation. In contrast to the 1925 L'Esprit Nouveau Pavilion, the 1937 pavilion was not an architectural model but a suspended large canvas container that recalled several of Jeanneret's projects: the experimental canvas vacation bungalows that he conceived as part of the leisure-time policies for the new Ministère des Loisirs; the series of canvas pavilions commissioned for the traditional Communist Party's Fête de l'Humanité; and the giant canvas roof cover for the Center for Popular Festivities, a 100,000-person multipurpose stadium.[93] Without question, the pavilion's architecture was Jeanneret's contribution, transformed into a mobile container for Le Corbusier's new reform manifesto. Le Corbusier saw the pavilion as the "table of contents" for an open book that would travel around France, preparing the population for architecture's redemptive power.[94] And extending his ideas beyond architecture, he claimed that the critical contingencies of urbanism were "region, race, culture, topography, and climate."[95] More than an opportunistic response to the triumph of the Front Populaire and its leftist programs, this reform manifesto was Le Corbusier's synthesis of an agenda that touted the economic

FIGURES 4.22–4.24.
Le Corbusier and Pierre Jeanneret, Temps Nouveaux Pavilion, interior views and main façade, canvas. Exposition Internationale des Arts et Techniques de la Vie Moderne, Paris, 1937. © 2017 Artists Rights Society (ARS), New York/ADAGP, Paris.

le 31 Août 1932
E1 12 158
F2 13   F2 3

ÎLE SAINT·GILDAS
PENVENAN
(CÔTES·DU·NORD)

Cher Monsieur,

Je viens d'avoir le plaisir de recevoir votre lettre de Liège. La nouvelle que vous me communiquez est malheureusement absolument fausse. Le colonel Lindbergh ignore même l'existence de l'île Milliau. En outre, il est très satisfait de l'hospitalité que lui offre l'Angleterre, et n'en cherche aucune autre.

Je ne vous ai pas écrit encore au sujet des deux ouvrages que vous avez eu l'amabilité de m'envoyer. Je suis occupé à les lire. Et ils contiennent une telle richesse d'idées qu'il est impossible d'en prendre connaissance de façon rapide. On se trouve comme au milieu d'une forêt d'arbres magnifiques appartenant aux essences les plus diverses

Il me faut encore quelque temps pour faire l'inventaire de ce monde dans lequel vous évoluez avec tant d'aisance - Pour moi, qui dois le considérer, non pas dans sa valeur intrinsèque, mais dans ses relations avec les propriétés de l'être humain, et son pouvoir d'adaptation, la tâche est difficile. Le problème de l'habitat, et du mode de vie, est d'importance fondamental

Je vous suis reconnaissant de m'avoir fait part, en m'envoyant vos livres, du trésor d'idées qui se meuvent en vous.

Croyez bien, cher Monsieur, à mes meilleurs sentiments

Alexis Carrel

F
LC

and social interplay between the well-being of the city and the countryside on the one hand, and the amelioration of the environment and
the human body on the other.

During this talk in Rio, and others that followed, Le Corbusier was
not simply communicating the main tenants of his Temps Nouveaux
Pavilion; he was also working out what was to become *La Maison des
hommes* (*The Home of Man*), the book that would echo Carrel's project
for the remaking of society. This work, coauthored with the engineer
and future Vichy collaborator François de Pierrefeu, took a more
dogmatic tone than even his Rio talks, drawing a direct line between
the state, man, and the built environment.[96] It is crucial to note that
in the time between his 1936 lectures in Rio and the publication of
this book in 1942, Le Corbusier had begun an intellectual alliance
with Carrel that directly influenced his own ideological stance. At
some point during the summer of 1937, Le Corbusier sent his books
to Carrel—not as an act of cordiality or as publicity for his work, but
rather as a way to initiate an intellectual exchange. In doing so, Le
Corbusier was seeking the opinion of the man who had written the
most influential and popular theory of eugenics and who would also
become his collaborator and mentor during the Vichy regime. Carrel
responded to him in a four-page letter during the summer of that
year, stating that he needed more time to reflect on the richness of
Le Corbusier's ideas. Carrel explained that "to consider not just its
intrinsic value but its relationship to the properties of human beings,
and with their power of adaptation, the task is difficult. The problem
of the habitat, of the way of living, is of fundamental importance."[97]

By September 1939, Le Corbusier retreated to Vézelay, a small
village in Burgundy, to work on his new book, *The Four Routes*, organized around the four transportation systems: highway, railroad,
water, and air. The program for this book was similar to the pro-
natalist book *Pleins pouvoirs*, published by Jean Giraudoux that
same year, advocating large-scale public works that would give "the
[French] citizen faith in the omnipotence of his race."[98] Giraudoux was
Le Corbusier's collaborator at *Plans* and at the time the Minister of
Information and Propaganda under Édouard Daladier's government,
which abolished the forty-hour work week and decreed the "Family
Code," a most significant piece of legislation for racial regeneration.[99]
The code's measures included a series of economic incentives for
women to remain at home and procreate; emblematic of the times, its
racialist pro-natalism was not criticized but rather lauded by all sides
of the political spectrum, from the far right to the communists. While
in Vézelay, Le Corbusier wrote a letter to his mother and brother in

which he restates his position that leisure must be instrumental-ized in order to avoid degeneration, as stated by Carrel in *Man, the Unknown*.[100] As Le Corbusier writes:

> A good nap leads to collapse. Doctor Carrel, whom I saw last Thursday, told me as much: comfort annihilates the human race. There must be struggles. So do not take life's difficulties (whatever they may be) as catastrophes but rather as good hygiene. It's what makes life possible. For, if the contrary point of view prevails, everything seems merely a disaster. We have philosophized with Carrel down to the last is-sue—the search for what is best for mankind—and we are in perfect agreement: the power to create, to intervene, to act is our lifeblood; otherwise, deterioration. Carrel will work with us.[101]

By "us," Le Corbusier refers to himself, Giraudoux, Pierrefeu, and the physician Pierre Winter, who were the founding members of the new Committee on Preparatory Studies of Urbanism (Comité d'Études Préparatoires d'Urbanisme; CEPU), which would be the organization "to establish juridically and legally the status of urbanism in France and in the colonies," during the last months of the Third Republic, just before Paris's occupation by the Nazis in June 1940.[102] The alignment with both Carrel and Giraudoux represents a more radical position than Le Corbusier had taken just a few years earlier, now troubled by what they called "the continuous infiltration of barbarism" through the influx of immigrants with the potential to degenerate France's population.[103]

PICTURING EVOLUTION

In the history of eugenics and architecture, the image of a tree has been a consistent icon of both heredity and milieu—from the tra-ditional representation of family genealogy to the modern emblem of the doctrine Le Corbusier began to visualize in the 1920s. But it was not until 1942 that he drew a tree for *The Home of Man* to syn-thesize and symbolize his social doctrine.[104] With this tree, which directly recalls Darwin's evolutionary Tree of Life—the arbor vitae by which, in 1837, Darwin illustrated the interconnectedness of or-ganisms in his theory of evolution—Le Corbusier graphically depicts the interconnectedness between the state, the family, and the built environment.[105] While he clearly labels the trunk as the French state, it is the root system itself that graphically represents the modern ideology of progress championed by eugenics: the left root as "man"

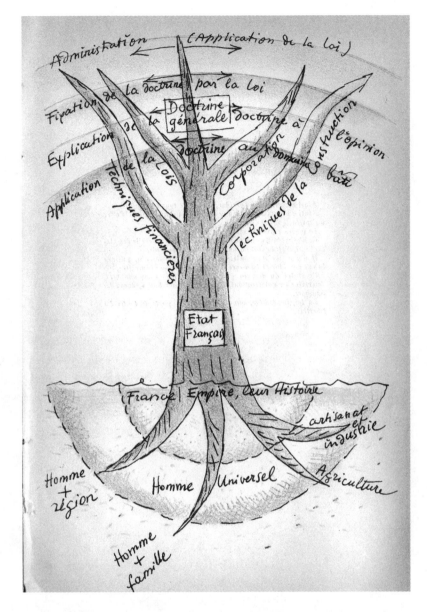

FIGURE 4.26.
Le Corbusier, The Tree of the Built Domain, *published in Le Corbusier and François de Pierrefeu,* La Maison des hommes, *1942. Fondation Le Corbusier, Paris. © FLC/ADAGP, Paris/ Artists Rights Society (ARS), New York 2017.*

and his "region," the environment; the middle root as "man" and his "family," the social structure; and the right root, splitting into two, with "agriculture" on one side, and "craft and industry" on the other. Together, these three roots respectively link milieu, reproduction, and production at the base of the built domain, creating a graphic synthesis of the interconnectedness of man, nature, and family, all held together by the state and its executive tool: the built environment. With this tree, Le Corbusier placed himself within the company of evolutionists, inserting a powerful orthopedic function whereby the stability of the family, the French nation, and its empire depended on the stability of the physical environment. This is the image that Le Corbusier chose for an article introducing his new book, *The Home of Man*, which he had announced in 1936 in Brazil as the book that would parallel Carrel's 1935 controversial book, *Man, the Unknown*.[106]

In the first chapter of *The Home of Man*, titled "The Time to Build," Le Corbusier and coauthor de Pierrefeu begin: "It is over twenty years since, from every rostrum in France, the most authoritative voices raised the cry: 'We must build new houses, the future of our race depends on how it is housed.'" Notably, their book starts with a stated connection between race and architecture. They continue, claiming the redeeming power of the built domain "to create the necessary transformation of home life, or to infuse into it order, fecundity."[107] It is these infusions of Lamarckian ideas that Le Corbusier's tree roots invoke as the critical instruments of the utopian project of eugenics. In the tone of a manifesto, the chapter continues to emphasize how the remaking of life is completely dependent on how human beings are housed, whether in domestic dwellings, the workplace, the city at large, the countryside, or the wider metropole.

Clearly, Le Corbusier and de Pierrefeu sought to materialize Carrel's eugenics doctrine by formulating "another conception of human progress" by which we can "remake this world according to the laws of life and the knowledge of [the] body."[108] Analyzing France's perceived degeneration of the population at the time, from Paris to the countryside, they convey an allegiance to a eugenic theory that moves beyond the body to encompass the built environment. In doing so, they enumerate the main obstacles to progress that Lamarckian eugenics would alleviate:

> In Paris only:
>
> Two hundred thousand persons live in houses classified as unfit for human habitation.
>
> Ten thousand families, of four or more, live in one single room.
>
> In Lyons, Marseilles, Nantes, etc., a proportionate number of such slums can be counted; whence sterility, promiscuousness and other blights rampant in our homes. One Frenchman or woman dies of tuberculosis every five minutes.
>
> Lack of buildings, lack of pre-natal care, crèches, nurseries. Lack of town-planning, absence of green spaces, playgrounds, swimming pools.

They further condemn small towns and villages for their "prevalent unhealthiness" and "incredible proportion of all-but-ruined or ill-kept houses," continuing:

In the countryside:

Elementary hygiene far too much ignored . . .

Lack of "youth centers" of playgrounds, stimulating the community spirit. Lack also of public halls and of communal amusements.

Whence boredom, fields neglected, wasteland. Futile political squabbles in cafés instead of spontaneous happiness, instead of intellectual or moral exercise.

In addition to itemizing the disparate conditions of poverty, overcrowding, promiscuity, and the so-called social diseases, they conclude by voicing what had become a national concern: the French population's incapacity or unwillingness to procreate.

In the country as a whole:

53 per cent. of the households are childless;

23 per cent. have only one child;

20 per cent. have two.

Quite obviously the remaining 4 per cent. are unable to maintain our birthrate.

So much for the social aspect; the economic seems not a whit better.[109]

This detailed analysis of degeneration in France was voiced with theoretical, almost visionary emphasis by Le Corbusier just a few months earlier, in a 1941 radio broadcast in which he restated an idea he used to close the pages of his book *Destin de Paris*: "The house problem . . . is the key to both the family's regeneration and the spirit's regeneration, the key to the nation's regeneration."[110] Identifying the built environment as both the cause of and the cure for degeneration, he tells his listeners that "the degeneration of the house, the degeneration of the family, are one." And extending this idea to the countryside, he says, "The degeneration of the peasant's home, the abandonment of the land, are also one."[111] Here Le Corbusier not only echoes the tenets of Lamarckian eugenics and Lúcio Costa's eugenic syllogism of breed begetting good government begetting good architecture, but he also prefigures the main agenda of *The Home of Man*.

In the first pages of *The Home of Man*, the authors call for a "genuine political doctrine" translated into "built language," which they claim will "alone [be] capable of inspiring and sustaining a long-view scheme" embodied in a *master plan*.[112] The master plan was understood as a rational tool for development—a comprehensive blueprint that integrates the multiple protocols of production, economy, technology, geography, and politics through physical and nonphysical actions.

For over a decade, Le Corbusier had looked for opportunities to assume the role of the "techno-social" international expert, a tradition initiated by Musée social technocrats who, working for France and other states, produced master plans for cities and villages in the Latin world. In fact, throughout the book, Le Corbusier and de Pierrefeu argue for the institutionalization of an "authentic doctrine of human dwelling" that would integrate Western traditions with the new conditions introduced by mechanization, not only in France and its colonies but also beyond its borders, especially in Latin America, which was particularly susceptible to French influence.[113] Convinced that this doctrine needed to "succeed for the good of humanity," they are even more emphatic a few pages later: "because one's home, one's working place (not forgetting their reciprocal influences) do not merely act as shells for the life of individuals and society; they go deeper, reach within this life, impregnate, colour it by a thousand various approaches, some of which we deem sentimental, others rational."[114] In other words, there is an outcry here that this doctrine—which sees the human body (and the anatomo-politics of its productivity) as well as the built environment as powerful mechanisms of control—should be adopted and managed by the state.

It is interesting that this entire discussion is built on "the necessary transformation of home life" to unequivocally stabilize the family, using heredity and the environment as the primary tools. This stability undergirds the authors' belief that "family continuity, and therefore the stability of the human race, depends on physical stability of environment and occupation."[115] Arguing that "change" is an agent of individual and family disintegration, whether this is a change of place or social status, Le Corbusier and de Pierrefeu call for the privileging of stability in harmony with geographical constants, over and against change, which they believe has been misconceived as the basis of life. They describe architecture and urban planning—"a wisely progressive technique"—as tools to achieve "stability in space" and "stability of occupation," thus offering a spatial and social structure to secure a kind of harmonious "human concentration."[116] In this crusade for stability, Le Corbusier calls on puericulture, which he understood as equivalent to eugenics. In his 1930 "Commentaires relatifs à Moscou et à la 'Ville Verte'" (Commentaries relative to Moscow and the "Green City"), Le Corbusier clearly established a direct link between the two when he said, "Puericulture: breeding, the constitution of a healthy race."[117] Then, as aforementioned, in 1931, in *Plans*, he once again defines and champions puericulture, calling for the establishment of designated medical spaces connected to the family home to provide "security-selection-puericulture [scientific child rearing]."[118] A year later, Le Corbusier once again advocates for the rubric "eugenisme-puériculture," using it as a subtitle within a section on child raising and education.[119] And a few years later, in an article published in the journal *Volonté*, Le Corbusier calls for the creation of a "solid and beautiful race, a healthy [race]," for the "institutionalization of health medicine (Dr. Peter Winter), to save infants, to raise them, to train the youth, to awake the social mass, to animate, to restore civility."[120] It is not surprising that by the early 1940s, when Le Corbusier began collaborating with the Vichy regime, he was convinced that "eugenics, puericulture will ensure a well-bred race."[121] In this sense, Le Corbusier, inspired first by Winter and then by Carrel, visualized an opportunity for architecture to materialize Carrel's eugenic doctrine, this new "conception of human progress" to "remake this world according to the laws of life [and] the knowledge of [the] body."[122]

Two years before the publication of *The Home of Man*, Le Corbusier established himself in one of the hotels where Maréchal Pétain set up the Vichy regime in the spa town of Vichy, in the so-called Free Zone of France. Driven by his persistent efforts to work with Pétain's government, Le Corbusier made Vichy his base of operations. During the following two years, Le Corbusier's faith in both the goals of the Vichy regime and his own potential to contribute to them were curbed only by frustrations with the regime's lack of interest in urban progress. He was undaunted by the atrocities perpetrated by the regime with which he was eager to collaborate.[123] In fact, Le Corbusier was at the same time happy to find a government that was embracing ideas that he had been developing on his own since the 1930s. He himself had identified these ideas as the base of his core doctrine, first articulated in *Précisions sur un état présent de l'architecture et de l'urbanisme* (1930), the book he wrote about his first travels to South America in 1929; rearticulated in *The Radiant City* (1935); and in the books he wrote in the 1940s: *Destin de Paris* (1941), *Sur les quatres routes* (1941), *La Maison des hommes* (1942), *L'urbanisme des trois établissements humains* (1945), *Propos d'urbanisme* (1946), and *Manière de penser l'urbanisme* (1946). This doctrine aimed not only at a new form of living but at a new form of man.[124] To this end, Le Corbusier's doctrine depended on firm control over nature through the standardization of living and the creation of a universalized and normative human being, in order to deploy a system of secularized salvation—the quasi religion of urbanism. It is important to note that Le Corbusier began to articulate the elements of this doctrine in 1930, immediately after his first trip to South America, but it was not until

1936, after he came back from his second trip and established a relationship with Alexis Carrel, that he was able to solidify his doctrine.

At that time, no one was more influential to Le Corbusier than Carrel. In 1942, both became active members of Vichy's Committee for the Study of Habitation and the Urbanism of Paris.[125] Carrel, who was simultaneously in the process of creating a new foundation, congratulated Le Corbusier on the publication of his books in a postcard, dated February 19, 1942. In it, Carrel acknowledges the critical importance of architecture's role in remediating human problems. As he writes, "I attach, as you know, very great importance to the influence of the milieu on the human being." And he cautions that given the current social and political challenges, the two of them "must investigate them, very deeply, before offering indispensable remedies."[126] Cementing their relationship even further, in 1943, Le Corbusier accepted Carrel's invitation to become a "technician of value" for the French Foundation for the Study of Human Problems, known as the Carrel Foundation, whose main purpose was studying the most appropriate measures "to improve the psychological, mental, and social conditions of the population."[127] With its research aims targeting the social hygiene of the population and the physical hygiene of industry, the foundation's scientific work was undertaken by six departments: population biology, child and adolescent biology, biotypology, biosociology, work, production and rural economy. However, the most critical components of this research were the investigation of the causes of low birthrates and the promulgation of eugenic measures that would encourage the birth of "hereditarily gifted children."[128] Yet, in spite of being one of

FIGURE 4.28.
Le Corbusier, adaptation of Lúcio Costa's sketch for the Ministry of Health and Education in Rio de Janeiro, published in Le Corbusier, Oeuvre complète 1934–1938 (Zurich: Éditions Girsberger, 1953). Fondation Le Corbusier, Paris. © FLC/ ADAGP, Paris/Artists Rights Society (ARS), New York 2017.

FIGURE 4.29.
Le Corbusier, first project for the Ministry of Health and Education on Rio de Janeiro's waterfront. Fundação Getúlio Vargas—CP-DOC, Collection Gustavo Capanema, Rio de Janeiro. Document: Série F, 34.10.19, II-30. This perspective was included in Le Corbusier's report to Gustavo Capanema, Rio de Janeiro, August 10, 1936. Fondation Le Corbusier, Paris. © FLC/ ADAGP, Paris/Artists Rights Society (ARS), New York 2017.

the key proponents of this agenda in 1943, when the Allies arrived at Normandy and it became clear that Vichy would be on the losing side, Le Corbusier immediately resigned from Carrel's projects—although his enthusiasm for Carrel and his ideology never waned.

VISUALIZING THE TROPICS/THE REMAKING OF MAN

In his *Oeuvre complète 1934–1938*, Le Corbusier included a sketch of the Rio de Janeiro Ministry of Health and Education building, rising above one of the urban blocks Agache had proposed in his master plan for the esplanade, where Rio's Morro do Castelo had once stood. The sketch of the building that would later become the symbol of

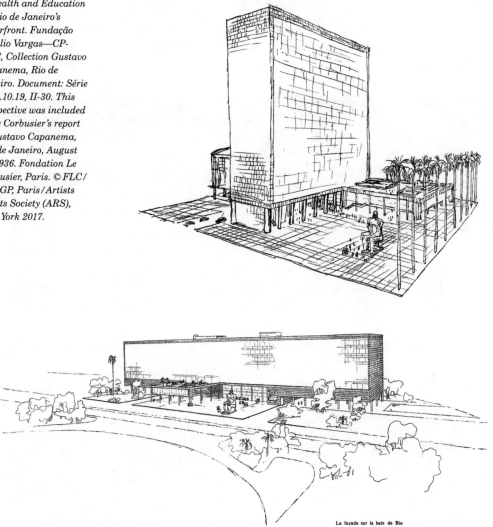

La façade sur la baie de Rio

Brazilian modernism shows an open courtyard surrounded by *pilotis* and orderly tropical palms, and, at its center, a colossal sculpture of a seated man with a strong, well-defined body and a tiny head.[129] The gargantuan man is reminiscent of both Le Corbusier's drawings of African Brazilians made during his first trip to Rio in 1929, and the drawing of the man in his 1936 sketch in which he reminded himself to buy Carrel's book, the one that argues for the eugenic amelioration of the population "through both selective breeding and selective eradication."[130] Minister Gustavo Capanema had commissioned both the building that would host the state institution he called the Ministry of Man, which in his own words was destined to "prepare, compose, and perfect the Brazilian man," and the sculpture he wanted to embody the ideal "Brazilian man" that the state itself was directed to produce.[131] Following Costa and Le Corbusier's suggestion, Capanema asked the Brazilian artist Celso Antônio to produce a 12-meter-high granite statue that would represent that ideal man at the entrance of the Ministry building.[132] Personally invested in finding a tangible image for the ideal Brazilian genotype, Capanema pondered, "How will the body of the Brazilian man be, of the future Brazilian man, not the vulgar man or the inferior man but the best exemplar of the race? How will his head be? His color? The shape of his face? His physiognomy?"[133]

For Capanema, this sculptural representation would not simply be a work of art but rather a scientific tool to establish the Brazilian type—"the ideal figure that would be legitimate to imagine as representative of the future Brazilian human being."[134] To achieve this goal, Capanema turned to science. First, he sounded out Francisco José de Oliveira Vianna, one of the main voices of the "whitening" thesis, which argued that by mixing blacks and mulattos with whites, darker skin and "black" features would be "filtered," and the white

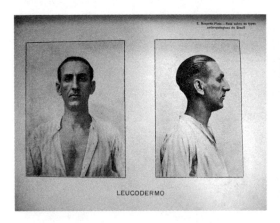

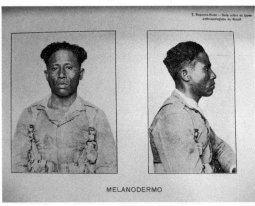

LEUCODERMO

MELANODERMO

race (considered by Vianna to be the superior race) would become dominant.[135] Capanema also consulted with other recognized scientists, including Juvenil da Rocha Vaz, Álvaro Fróes da Fonseca, and Edgard Roquette-Pinto, the eugenicist who, at the opening of the First Brazilian Congress of Eugenics, argued for the instrumentalization of architecture—the human-made environment—in the process of ameliorating human beings. These scientists' responses to Capanema's questions were extensively argued and supported by their own "scientific" studies, which indicated that, in spite of their differing views, the representation of the Brazilian man should basically be a white man. For the sculpture, Roquette-Pinto proposed the adoption of one of the "Leucodermos," an anthropological term he used to classify the predominant type of "whites" in Brazil. He suggested a white man with dark enough skin to look Mediterranean, "the white that would more easily 'acclimate' to Brazil."[136] According to Roquette-Pinto, the Leucodermo was the racial type toward which the "morphological evolution" of the Brazilian population was marching.[137] Similarly, Rocha Vaz, supporting biotypology in Brazil, argued for representing the morphological characteristics of "the white type [who, according to Rocha Vaz, was] the most common type in Brazil," the type that presents the following morphological characteristics: "height 1.66 to 1.70 meters, weight 60 to 65 kilograms, straight hair, dark eyes," and so on.[138]

However, Celso Antônio, the sculptor who was finally commissioned for the project, didn't want to design a figure like the one described by the scientists. The artist argued that as there was no pure Aryan type in Brazil, the Brazilian man should be modeled "as the one he observed from the Amazon to Rio Grande do Sul." But Capanema, "disgusted by the mestizo of rough feature . . . that was taking shape in [Celso Antônio's] atelier," invalidated the agreement with Antônio.[139] He explained that since Antônio had refused to submit his work for the consideration of the committee of national specialists deemed capable by Capanema of evaluating the proper "correspondence between the project [the statue] and the racial Brazilian type fixed" by the scientists, Capanema was obliged to declare the agreement null and void.[140] In January of 1938, the Ministry of Health and Education considered launching a competition, juried by the physician and eugenicist Roquette-Pinto and cultural representatives, to select a new artist for the design of the statue. Yet, almost immediately, the idea for a competition was discarded, and, in spite of other artists being considered, including Ernesto de Fiori and Victor Brecheret, the statue was never built. Nonetheless, the pressure to define the ideal

FIGURE 4.32-4.33.
Maquette of the Ministry of Health and Education with model for the sculpture by Celso Antônio, Rio de Janeiro, 1936–1942. GC Foto 494, No. 3 and No. 7, Collection Gustavo Capanema, Centro de Pesquisa e Documentação de História Contemporânea do Brasil, FUNDAÇÃO GETULIO VARGAS— CPDOC, São Paulo.

"Brazilian man" remained a primary agenda of the regime. However, the building itself, which seemed to have been created to transform a simple man into the Brazilian man, became the very embodiment of modernity.

For Le Corbusier, the 1940s began in the shadow of the incredible success of Brazilian architecture. Despite Le Corbusier's now-looming legacy, during those years more international attention was given to Lúcio Costa, Oscar Niemeyer, and other Brazilian modernists than to Le Corbusier. The decade began with the enormous success of the Brazilian modernist pavilion for the 1939 World's Fair in New York.[141] Designed by Costa and Niemeyer to represent Brazil as both a modern nation and a tropical yet progressive one, the pavilion announced that "modernism and *brasilidade* [i.e., a distinctive sense of Brazilian-ness, directly linked to its tropicality] were synonymous."[142] Conveying two conditions typically seen as opposites, "tomorrowness *and* otherness," this acclaimed building immediately became a showpiece of Brazilian modernism, provoking the interest of New York's Museum of Modern Art (MOMA) and of specialized magazines.[143] Its popularity continued, in fact, throughout the decade. In January 1943, MOMA opened *Brazil Builds*, an exhibition devoted to Brazilian architecture, occupying the entire main hall and ground floor of the museum.[144] The exhibition was so successful that it was featured during the following years at museums and other institutions in the United States, Mexico, and Canada. By the end of the decade, in 1949, the prestigious École des Beaux-Arts in Paris opened a new exhibit to celebrate Brazilian architecture. At all these events, the *pilotis*, the open ground, the roof-garden, the garden-city, and the *brise-soleil*—the environmental device used to shield a building from

FIGURE 4.34–4.35.
Sculpture by Ernesto di Fiori, GC Foto 501, No. 6 and No. 8. Collection Gustavo Capanema, Centro de Pesquisa e Documentação de História Contemporânea do Brasil, FUNDAÇÃO GETULIO VARGAS—CPDOC, São Paulo.

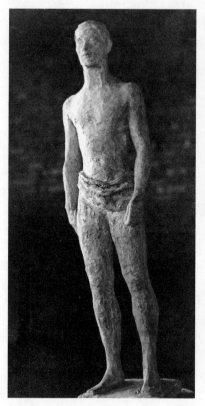

intense sunlight—all became part of what was recognized as Brazilian architectural vocabulary. At this point, Le Corbusier, who had been actively, and unsuccessfully, pursuing a Brazilian commission for years, became frustrated and angry at seeing what he considered his ideas on display as Brazilian inventions. Denouncing the "nationalization" of his thoughts, Le Corbusier had clearly developed a sense of himself as a one-of-a-kind thinker and form-giver whose ideas he believed had been stolen.[145] In other words, he felt that he alone laid claim to this architectural vocabulary.

There is also a larger implication to this story. As far back as the late 1920s, Le Corbusier traveled for the first time to the Americas and visualized new plans for Rio de Janeiro, São Paulo, Montevideo, and Buenos Aires from both the sea, "adopting the perspective of a modern-day Christopher Columbus," and the air, adopting the perspective that aviation introduced—the "bird's-eye view" from which "nature lay exposed to be exploited for the benefit of mankind."[146] For him, as airplanes flew over forests, savannahs, rivers, mountains, and seas, and the world map was criss-crossed by national and international air routes, the world shrank. His flight to Moscow in 1928 and his flights over Argentina and Brazil in 1929 offered Le Corbusier a new perception of the world, one in which "the spherical mass of the earth was without borders."[147] The aerial view that Le Corbusier praised in several of his books, from *Précisions . . .* (1930) to *Sur les quatres routes* (1941), reveals the "simplifying fiction" of what James C. Scott called "high-modernist optics."[148] This lens, through which Le Corbusier was now afforded a strategic view, gave credence to his desire to use architecture and urban planning to remake man and his environment. At the same time, Le Corbusier was drawn to evolutionary theories and ideas widely circulating at the time, when fears of barbarism, primitivity, degeneration, and chaos dominated modernist discourses. Thus, the larger implication of this story points to the multiplicity of networks and transnational interconnections that crafted modernity. This takes us back to a particular moment: the summer of 1936 that Le Corbusier spent in Brazil. During that time, he was reading Carrel's *Man, the Unknown*, which contributed to the formulation of his own doctrine, later materialized in his 1942 book, *The Home of Man*. At the time, he also participated in the creation of the building for the Ministry of Health and Education that would implement Brazilian eugenic policies, and he witnessed a debate over the statue that was to embody the future whiter Brazilian man to be located at the building's entrance. So the very ideas Le Corbusier claimed as his own in 1949 had actually been made tangible through

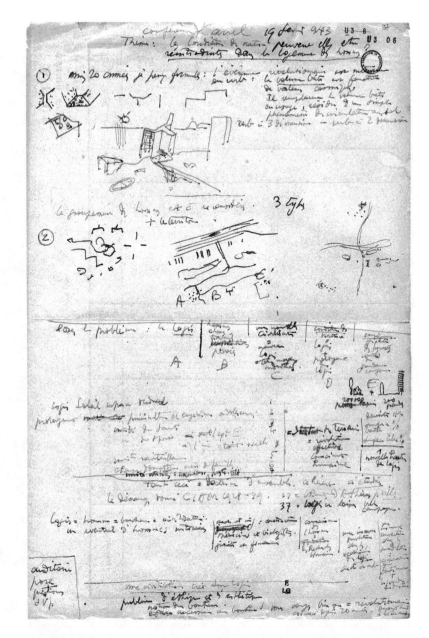

his interactions with other modernists in France and beyond—and of course through his interactions with Carrel. Through all of these exchanges, Le Corbusier was able to transform ideology into architectural canon—from the standard living cell to his own formulation of the ideal man.

By 1943, while the world was celebrating Brazilian architecture, Le Corbusier was in France, examining some of his most fundamental design ideas. For over seven years, Le Corbusier had found Alexis Carrel's work of immense interest. So, on one particular day in February,

FIGURE 4.37–4.39.
Le Corbusier, Unité
d'habitation *in Marseille,
1945–1952 (the roof-
terrace and its nursery
school, gymnasium, and
solarium). Photos by
Rene Burri, 1959. © René
Burri / Magnum Photos.*

he sought out the ideas he had found so provocative by attending a
lecture by Carrel. Immediately, Carrel's eugenic ideas triggered his
own long-held vision of a clinically inspired human habitat, where
all human needs can be met in a single domestic tower. At the top of
his notes, Le Corbusier writes what is either his own question or the
theme of Carrel's lecture: "Can the condition of nature be reintroduced
in the housing of men?" Further down in his notes, after showing
how urban circulation patterns had changed, Le Corbusier lists from
1 to 7 the structural organization of his idealized "vertical garden-city"
(*cite-jardin verticale*). Starting at the top of this vertical structure,
he conceptualizes numbers 1 and 2 as the roof-garden terrace—a
solarium-like place dedicated to physical health and exercise—and as

a place for puericulture, a medico-educational dispensary for the care of infants.[149] Then, he lists the floors with standardized housing units, and a level in between for communal services, and, at the bottom, an open floor that separates the building from the ground, inviting people to freely circulate the grounds as in a public park. Under all these numbered elements is a line, which seems to indicate that Le Corbusier is now summarizing. The result is his doctrine, or "*tout ceci = doctrine.*" It seems clear that by listening to Carrel, Le Corbusier is considering a final structure for an architectural model, or ideal type: his "vertical garden-city" with its solarium, kindergarten, and gymnasium at the top; its service street with restaurants, food shops, and other services at the center; and its columns rising up from the ground, all hallmarks of the building Le Corbusier would later design for war-torn Marseille.[150] This 337-apartment building, the Unité d'habitation in Marseille, replicated by both Le Corbusier himself and many others around the world, embodies his doctrine, which he translates into an equation: "logis = men = happiness = civilization." As Le Corbusier states in the last lines of his hand-written notes, "a civilization creates its own housing, problems of ethics and aesthetics, notions of happiness, and access to happiness."[151] The construction of this building became the strategic showcase for Le Corbusier's doctrine, which included the standardization and modularity embodied

FIGURE 4.40.
Le Corbusier in the "Atelier 35 S," with a lithograph of his Modulor on the left. Paris, 1959. © René Burri / Magnum Photos.

by his new canon—a proportional system for regulating space and thus edifying human life. This proportional system, which Le Corbusier cast in concrete on the façade of his "vertical garden-city" in Marseille, became known as the "Modulor."

The Modulor—a term Le Corbusier invented from the word *module* and the notion of the golden section—came to life in 1946 as a way to epitomize the fruits of his research on proportions. Although this work began in the 1920s, it was not until the 1940s that it was codified under the influence of the Commissariat à la normalisation, the committee of the Order of Architects advocating policies of standardization.[152] It was during this period, as a result of the Vichy regime's agenda of normalization, that Le Corbusier consolidated his comprehensive proportional system. Developed with the collaboration of other architects, art historians, and consultants, among them, of course, Carrel, the Modulor established ideal statistical measurements of the human body intended to dictate the proportion of buildings and their components but also the proportions of nature: "a tree, a forest, a lake, a hill, peaks on the horizon, clouds and so forth."[153] The Modulor, the scale to bridge both the metric and Anglo-Saxon systems, was designed to center all aspects of architecture around a particular human model. Based on a man of 6 feet, with a raised arm, Le Corbusier's Modulor was an antidote to disorder, an organizational scheme that breathed regularity and, ultimately, normativity into each of his buildings. But the overly large hands and feet and relatively small head of the Modulor, so emblematic of primitivism in modern art, seem to contradict Le Corbusier's modernist canon. Yet, in fact, this depiction of a towering white man, whose hands, feet, and head evoke the very primeval features he observed in those "exotic" beings in Brazil, is intentionally a direct reference to Le Corbusier's faith in the extraordinary social-engineering capacity of the built environment. Cast in concrete in many of his buildings, at Le Corbusier's bidding, the Modulor became a map to his own history and involvement with evolutionary theories; a record of his pursuit of order, normativity, and purity; and an enduring global symbol of architecture's past complicities with Lamarckian eugenics.

EPILOGUE

As a young child growing up in Mérida, a university city in the Venezuelan Andes, I spent hours after school in my mother's human embryology laboratory at the Universidad de los Andes School of Medicine, where she was a research scientist. Her laboratory was my earliest playground, filled with microscopes, test tubes, incubators, and glass beakers and flasks containing human eggs and embryos in different states of evolution. Although these were deemed defective, having enlarged or undersized heads (hydrocephalus and anencephaly), a single eye, tumors, clubfeet, conjoined bodies, and cleft palates, somehow I saw these embryos as the variations we find in nature rather than freakish abnormalities. At the same time, school puzzled me with a completely different perspective. In a mandatory class for girls called Puericultura for the preparation of maternal duties, part of the secondary school curricula in Venezuela until at least the 1980s, I was instructed in the "science" of the mother-child unit, from prenatal care to late infancy. Although I didn't know it at the time, of course, this was my first introduction to the homogenizing utopian project of eugenics—a contagious movement, as I would later come to understand, that, among other things, equated modernity with normativity.

Now, decades later, I look back and I am stunned by the impulse of those educators driven to mold our young minds in a manner that pathologized difference, made whiteness a virtue, and turned us against the very "otherness" that I had first encountered in my mother's laboratory. The teaching of social hygiene was compulsory in all secondary schools, emphasizing the duties and pride of mothering, polarizing gender roles, and institutionalizing eugenics and its attempt to produce a "better" race, fortifying along the way modernity's normalizing project. As late as the 1980s, during my last years of high school, the French science-faith of puericulture remained a central part of the curricula in many other Latin American countries, and eugenics, in spite of its association with the atrocities of Nazism, was still a career track in the Universidad del Museo Social Argentino in Buenos Aires.[1] Modernizing the nation-state, civilizing the population, and ameliorating race were part of the ideology of progress that still permeated daily life in Latin American cities during the last decades of the twentieth century. So why should we be surprised by its reemergence now? In fact, the story of power, race, and space at the core of this book continues right up to the present moment. The potential misuse of the genomic revolution, the popularization of genetic screening such as DNA sequencing available to anyone who wants to know their racial and ethnic ancestry, and the return of conservative thinking that reinforces a belief in racial and gender differentiation make the story of *Eugenics in the Garden* disturbingly relevant today. Eugenics, which in the early twentieth century was used to justify the exclusion of Africans, Asians, and even immigrants from southern and eastern Europe in an attempt to normalize a patriarchal society, ideally white and heterosexual, is now reactivated, and with it, racism and segregation have once again been officially legitimized.

From its inception in the late nineteenth century, genetics was entangled with evolutionary theories and their social and political interpretations; and today, genetics, vulnerable again to being usurped by those harboring racist agendas, reinforces assumptions about race as a genetically meaningful means of categorizing human beings. Urban planners and architects are also at risk of reinforcing the same assumptions by seeing progress as attainable through spatial segregation, gentrification, and its racial and class stratification.[2] Looking back, we must recall the entanglement of biological Darwinism and what became known as "social Darwinism"—the unfortunate term coined by Herbert Spencer to commandeer evolutionary ideas in order to activate a new social canon by which human beings, like animals and plants, were understood as competitive entities in a struggle for existence. Known as the most popular nonfiction writer of his time, Spencer developed key concepts that applied Darwin's evolutionary theories of natural selection to humans, which resulted in the infamous doctrine of the "survival of the fittest."[3] Although science today is mostly a territory of progressive thinking, and contemporary scientists separate themselves from these elitist assumptions, the risk of misusing new scientific knowledge in the implementation of white nationalism and its perverse discrimination and racialization is back to center stage. On the other extreme of the nature-nurture debate, the environment—the nongenetic factor at the center of Lamarckian eugenics—reemerges as the "missing piece of the puzzle" of how to improve human health and achieve social progress.[4] Once disempowered in the nature-nurture debate in which heredity equals science and environment equals ideology, the environment is now revalued and conceptualized in various ways, from the cell itself as the environment of the gene to the neighborhood in which we live. During the last few years, postgenomic research has argued for the study of the gene-environment interaction as "a necessary corrective to the . . . Human Genome Project's 'genocentric' view of human health and illness."[5] At the center of this research is the pressing need to investigate the role of the environment in modifying "the processes and outcomes of gene action."[6] Underlying this need is the conviction that investigating the interaction between genes and the environment will help us understand and improve human health for all, regardless of race, class, and gender. Research in epigenetics, which essentially posits that changes in the environment can change gene expression, "promises new ways of understanding how racial and socioeconomic differences—as manifest in differences in sociomaterial environments—become embedded biologically."[7] In fact, recent investigations suggest that the causes of some diseases like cancer are far less due to genetic factors (10–30 percent) than to the environment, which makes the latter a major territory of investigation.[8] Of course, here the environment is broadly understood as the complex "complement of the genome," which includes those internal environments inside the body, such as metabolism, and those external ones, such as air pollution, social norms, and the design of buildings and streets. A better understanding of the environment is therefore critical to a better understanding of the genetic-environmental interaction that could lead to far less extreme health and human disparities.

Architectural research is thus called upon now to shed more light on the crucial role played by the built environment in promoting, advertently or not, health disparities and social inequality. Cities from Buenos Aires to Chicago and from Rio de Janeiro to Paris are differentiated along socioeconomic and racial lines. Although many of the federal and local policies that created race-based housing segregation have been officially abolished worldwide, segregation persists in different forms and in many cases is provoked and consolidated not only by governments but by architects as well. Our built environment has too often been designed to exclude poor people and people of color by various means: by creating highways that separate poor and black neighborhoods from wealthy and white ones, and from the so-called noble areas of city centers; building walls to seclude entire neighborhoods; eliminating sidewalks in government zones and in luxury residential areas to avoid the circulation of "undesirable" people; and instrumentalizing nature by delineating vacant greenbelts and natural reserves to cloister entire cities away from poor satellite neighborhoods and shantytowns. In Latin America, no other city materializes this ideology of exclusion better than Brasília, the supermodern capital city created ex nihilo in the hinterlands of Brazil, conceived right from the start as hermetically sealed, not only from change but also from those living on its margins.[9] But there are, of course, countless examples all over the world resulting from multiple and divergent national and transnational ideas and practices that must be understood at local, national, regional, and global scales so that architecture can go beyond cultural and economic specificities to reveal its truer, wider frame of knowledge. These different lenses allow us to see what we are really doing to ourselves, our land, and our communities. At this point, we are still ignoring the inherent regulatory nature of architecture, which, along with urban planning, continues to subscribe to social and racial segregation.[10] So in this story of eugenics and architecture, the metaphor of a garden is apt: we value order, systemization, and beautification over encouraging the organic growth of vegetation and cultivating a diverse species.[11] In this way, architectural modernism has also acted deliberately as well as unknowingly as a techno-social authority. A more comprehensive understanding of all the different facets of life that architecture shapes and is shaped by would help us rescue the built environment from its historic complicity with social engineering.

NOTES

INTRODUCTION

1. "There is only one way to represent truly the surface of the Earth. Curves are to be translated in curves; a sphere or fragment of a sphere must be reproduced by another sphere or fragment of sphere. Therefore are we really astonished that public attention and the special care of geographers are so little attracted towards this logical mode of geographical work." Reclus, "A Great Globe," 402.

2. Ibid., 404–405.

3. Scott, *Seeing Like a State*, 342–357.

4. By "developing" world, I refer to the regions that later, in the early post–World War II neocolonial division of the world, were identified under the rubric "Third World." As is well known, in 1952, the French demographer and anticolonial thinker Alfred Sauvy coined the terms "First World" to refer to the bloc of democratic-industrial countries; "Second World" to refer to the Eastern European bloc of the communist-socialist countries; and "Third World" to refer to the poor and "underdeveloped" remaining countries of Asia, Africa, and Latin America.

5. Jean-Baptiste Pierre Antoine de Monet, Chevalier de Lamarck (1744–1829), was the very first naturalist to propose a comprehensive theory of evolution. His mentor Georges-Louis Leclerc, Comte de Buffon (1707–1788), introduced the idea that life may not be fixed, but undergoes processes of change, but it was Lamarck who, in his 1809 book *Philosophie zoologique*, presented a revolutionary theory of evolution in which he argued that species change over time into new and more complex species. See Lamarck, *Philosophie zoologique*, and Burkhardt, *Spirit of the System*.

6. I am here calling it science because at that time eugenics was adopted as pure empirical knowledge. During the first half of the twentieth century, the main support for eugenics in France and Latin America came from the field of medicine.

7. Louis Bonnier, who had worked as general inspector of the World's Fair of 1889, was a member of various medical and architectural organizations, including the Société de médecine publique et de génie sanitaire, Société des amants de la nature, and the Conseil supérieur d'hygiène publique de France. Bonnier was a cofounder of the École supérieure d'art public in 1917, which became the École des hautes études urbaines in 1919, and the Institut d'urbanisme de l'Université de Paris in 1924. He was also cofounder with Marcel Poëte of the École des hautes études urbaines' journal, *La Vie urbaine*. He published numerous articles on health and urban themes, including articles on tuberculosis written with Poëte or with the physician Paul Juillerat, both members of the Musée social.

8. Marey's techniques also inspired an entire generation of avant-garde artists. The Italian artist Giacomo Balla, one of the founding members of futurism, visiting the 1900 World's Fair, had the opportunity to see Marey's chronophotographs displayed at the Palace of Optics. Marey's work served as a model for Balla's futurism.

9. Welter, *Biopolis*, 191. In the 1850s, Wallace had written two seminal papers on evolution by natural selection as a result of his studies on the origin of the species developed during his years of explorations in the Malay Archipelago and the Amazon. These papers pushed Darwin to complete his work that he had been developing in secret for years. I refer to Wallace's "On the Law Which Has Regulated the Introduction of New Species" and "On the Tendency of Varieties to Depart Indefinitely from the Original Type." For an account on the relationship between Darwin's and Wallace's work, see Brackman, *A Delicate Arrangement*, and the extraordinary synthesis that Nancy Leys Stepan articulates in her book *Picturing Tropical Nature*.

10. Lamarck argued that when environments change, organisms have to change in order to survive. Perhaps his most well-known example of this influence is that of the giraffe, who in order to reach the acacia tree's leaves, its favorite food source, triggered a bodily transformation of its neck, a gradual change that was inherited by the following generations. The neck continued stretching over time, in a similarly induced reversal to the way organs get smaller and atrophy over time when they are not used.

11. Galton, "Eugenics." This definition was first read before the British Sociological Society of London on May 16, 1904.

12. Stepan, *The Hour of Eugenics*, 40. According to the scientific historian Nancy Stepan, "Of all the branches of science cultivated in Latin America, medicine was the most institutionally advanced and professionalized. Medical schools had been among the first scientifically oriented institutions to be established in Latin America. Throughout the nineteenth century, medical education, along with law, served as Latin American equivalents of, or substitutes for, the liberal arts degree." Ibid., 41–42.

13. Latin America offers a prominent example of the influence of positivism. Perhaps its most tangible expression could be seen in Brazil, where the positivist motto "Ordem e Progresso" (Order and Progress), inspired by Auguste Comte's motto "L'amour pour principe et l'ordre pour base; le progrès pour but" (Love as a principle and order as the basis; progress as the goal), marked its origin as a republic. The motto is portrayed in Brazil's current national flag, which in 1889 replaced the flag of the Empire of Brazil (1822–1889).

14. See Clark, "Emergence and Transformation of Positivism"; Nachman, "Positivism, Modernization, and the Middle Class in Brazil"; and Burns, *A History of Brazil*.

15. Although the term "biopolitics" seems to have first been coined in 1916 by the Swede Rudolf Kjellén (1864–1922) as part of his organicist conception of the state as life-form and in connection to the term "geopolitics," biopolitical thought has mostly been a Latin-European modern preoccupation. It was Michel Foucault who, in 1976, revitalized the concept of biopolitics in the first volume of *The History of Sexuality* and in his lectures at the Collège de France, *"Society Must Be Defended."* In these works, Foucault puts forward the concept of biopolitics as a form of deconstruction of sovereignty, as he defined it: "the power to 'make' live and 'let' die." Foucault, *"Society Must Be Defended,"* 241. For Foucault, biopolitics is a new "technology of power," which, Cary Wolfe argues, "applies to bodies and what they do rather than to lands and what they produce." Wolfe, "Life." For Kjellén's and Foucault's first approaches to biopolitics, see Kjellén, *Staten som livsform*; Foucault, *The History of Sexuality* and *"Society Must Be Defended."*

16. In fact, the notion of "milieu" was initially introduced by Sir Isaac Newton in the field of physics, but the term defined as "material space where bodies move" first appeared in the mid-eighteenth century in the famous *Encyclopédie* by Denis Diderot and Jean le Rond d'Alembert.

17. It was Lamarck who would import the notion of milieu from the field of physics to the emerging field of biology. Canguilhem, *Knowledge of Life*.

18. Biopower is defined by Michel Foucault as "the set of mechanisms through which the basic biological features of the human species became the object of a political strategy, of a general strategy of power, or, in other words, how, starting from the eighteenth century, modern Western societies took on board the fundamental biological fact that human beings are a species." Foucault, *Security, Territory, Population*, 1.

19. Esposito, *Bios*, 9.

20. Ibid., 15.

21. The French natalist Justin Sicard de Plauzoles defined it thus: "Social Hygiene is an economic science, having human capital as its object, its production and reproduction (eugenics and puericulture), its conservation (hygiene, medicine and preventive assistance), its utilization (professional and physical education) and its output (scientific organization of work)." Sicard de Plauzoles, quoted in Jacques Donzelot, *La Police des familles*, 178. All translations to English are mine unless otherwise indicated.

22. In 1982, in a letter to Anne Carol, Léonard stated: "Eugenics in France did not start in 1912 [the date of the First International Congress on Eugenics held in London], eugenics was an ancient preoccupation, older than Darwinism's introduction in France." Continuing the work of Léonard,

Carol observes that it is "the connection between eugenics and medicine" that makes French eugenics original. See Jacques Léonard, quoted in Carol, "Les médecins français et l'eugénisme," 43. See also Carol, *Histoire de l'eugénisme en France*, 364.

23. Although Lamarckian eugenics was adopted in various countries on both sides of the Atlantic, including France, Belgium, Argentina, and Brazil, the history of eugenics has practically been devoted to Mendelian eugenics; histories that trace how Lamarckian eugenics became involved in the construction of modernity in these countries is still very limited. On French eugenics, in addition to Anne Carol's work, see Schneider, *Quality and Quantity*; and, of course, Jacques Léonard's "Les origines et les conséquences de l'eugénique en France" and "Eugénisme et Darwinisme."

24. It is surprising that even Germany, a country whose eugenics movement has been commonly associated with the racial policies of the Third Reich, was practically absent from the historiography of the movement from the 1920s until the late 1980s. Among the most relevant studies of eugenics beyond England and the United States are several salient examples, which include Adams, *The Wellborn Science*; Broberg and Roll-Hansen, *Eugenics and the Welfare State*; and McLaren, *Our Own Master Race*. On eugenics in Germany, see Holmes, *A Bibliography of Eugenics*; Aly, Chroust, and Pross, *Cleansing the Fatherland*.

25. Long before, even as far back as the work of Hippocrates and Aristotle over two thousand years ago, this same notion of the "inheritance of acquired characteristics" was widely recognized in scientific circles. Darwin himself developed his own theory of "inheritance of acquired characteristics" called Pangenesis (from the Greek *pan*, meaning whole, and "genesis," meaning birth). According to Darwin, this theory implies that every part of the organism reproduces itself and contributes to the formation of the entire organism. In fact, medical scientists in France saw Lamarck as Darwin's harbinger, unjustly eclipsed by him. In this sense, as Charles Richet, winner of the Nobel Prize in Medicine in 1913, aptly observes, Lamarckism was "the transforming influence that comes from the milieu," and Darwinism was the "hereditary transmission of this resulting transformation." Richet, *La sélection humaine*, 37. For Darwin's Pangenesis, see his last chapter, "Provisional Hypothesis of Pangenesis," in *The Variation of Animals and Plants under Domestication*.

26. The term "euthenics" was used by neo-Lamarckian reformers in the United States to convey their belief that external factors such as education and the environment improved human functioning and well-being. In the case of Latin America, I only use the term "Lamarckian" or "Lamarckianism," without the prefix "neo-," because of the steady reception of Lamarck's theories that justified the environment as a critical agent of social engineering. For a historical survey of Lamarckian ideas and their impact today, see Gissis and Jablonka, *Transformations of Lamarckism*.

27. Cogdell, *Eugenic Design*, 16–17. Cogdell's book, *Eugenic Design*, is the only work I know that has examined eugenics in the context of modernist creativity.

28. Research on molecular biology has shown that the genome is responsive to the environment and that its information can be transmitted to the following generations through ways other than DNA. Jablonka and Lamb, *Epigenetic Inheritance and Evolution*, 26.

29. Alexis Carrel, a Nobel Prize winner, was best known for his book *Man, the Unknown*, a worldwide best-seller in the 1930s that widely disseminated eugenics ideology.

30. In the introduction and first chapter of his book *Planning Latin America's Capital Cities, 1850–1950*, Arturo Almandoz offers a remarkable genealogy of postcolonial Latin American cities' urban historiography. See also Violich, *Cities of Latin America*; Hardoy and Morse, *Repensando la ciudad de América Latina*; Gutiérrez, "Modelos e imaginarios europeos en urbanismo americano, 1900–1950"; and Novick, "Foreign Hires."

31. Rama, *The Lettered City*; originally published in Spanish as *La ciudad letrada*.

32. Besides Rabinow's *French Modern*, three other books on French urbanism in France's colonies are relevant to this study: Wright, *The Politics of Design in French Colonial Urbanism*; Cohen and Eleb, *Casablanca, mythes et figures d'une aventure urbaine*; and Cohen, *Algiers*.

33. São Paulo passed from 240,000 inhabitants in 1900 to 1,326,000 in 1940 and 7,750,000 in 1970; Rio de Janeiro went from 650,000 in 1895 to 1,800,000 in 1940 and 6,700,000 in 1970; and Buenos Aires passed from 661,205 in 1895 to over 1,500,000 in 1914 and almost 3,000,000 million in 1970. As the Argentine historian José Luis Romero argues, "In 1900, only ten [Latin American] cities had more than one hundred thousand inhabitants; but by 1940 the population in four of these cities—Buenos Aires, Mexico City, Rio de Janeiro and São Paulo—had reached more than 1 million residents. Buenos Aires, which reached 2.1 million, was among the most populated cities in the world." In fact, in the 2006 World Almanac, these four cities appeared among the twenty most populated cities of the world. Romero, *Latinoamérica*, 327–328. Most figures are taken from Romero's book and from Morse, Conniff, and Weibel, *The Urban Development of Latin America, 1750–1920*, 1–21.

34. By 1810, Brazil had received over 2.5 million Africans—one-third of the Atlantic slave trade at the time. By 1825, people of African origin already represented half of Brazil's inhabitants, and according to the national census of 1872, blacks and mulattos already represented 55 percent of the entire population of the nation. In the case of Argentina, between 1871 and 1914 the country experienced a significant population increase caused by immigration. Argentina received over 6 million immigrants, with almost half staying permanently. While the majority of immigrants were of Latin European origin, Italians (46 percent) and Spanish (32 percent), thousands of people came from other European countries, as well as from Syria and Lebanon. So the effect of immigration on the demographics of Argentina was greater than in any other country in the Western Hemisphere. Thus, while Brazil's population was mostly an Afro-European mix, Argentina's population instead became more distinctly European. Most of these figures are taken from Skidmore and Smith, *Modern Latin America*; Lattes and Sautu, "Inmigración," 2–3; and Rock, *Argentina 1516–1987*.

35. Lise Fernanda Sedrez, "'The Bay of All Beauties,'" 62–110. See also Sophia Beal, *Brazil Under Construction*, 23–53, and Cavalcanti's essays "Moderno e brasileiro" and "When Brazil Was Modern."

36. Skidmore and Smith, *Modern Latin America*, 72.

37. Lattes and Sautu, "Inmigración," 2–3.

38. Stepan, *The Hours of Eugenics*, 72–79.

39. As part of Napoleon III's expansion of the French Empire, in late 1861 France invaded Mexico, which was then under the presidency of Benito Juárez, a lawyer of modest Indian origin. This invasion took place under the leadership of the Austrian archduke Ferdinand Maximilian von Habsburg, known as Maximilian I, with the initial support of the United Kingdom, Spain, and the Austrian and Belgian Crowns. As a result, the so-called Second Mexican Empire was formed in 1864 with the dual goal of establishing a monarchist ally in the Americas and capturing South American markets. Napoleon created the Scientific Commission of Mexico to promote France's civilizing mission. Beyond the collection of botanical and zoological specimens, and the mapping of land, people, natural resources, and diseases, French scholars believed that "their work would 'regenerate' and 'civilize' Mexico through the retrieval and reconstruction of its past, through the cataloging and exploitation of its present resources, and by helping establish French cultural hegemony south of the Rio Grande." The mission was to conquest the Latin American country "through Science." The Second Mexican Empire lasted only until 1867, when Napoleon retired his army and, consequently, the emperor Maximilian was executed. Edison, "Conquest Unrequited," 459.

40. Phelan, "Pan-Latinism," 279–298.

41. Motivating these intellectuals' positions was the encounter between US migrants and the inhabitants of the territory then known as Nueva Granada (which included today's Colombia, Ecuador, Panama, Venezuela, and part of Peru), during the California gold rush of the late 1840s and 1850s. During those years, the Isthmus of Panama, already a main international trade route of commodities, became a territory of racial struggles.

42. McGuinness, "Searching for 'Latin America,'" 87–107.

43. Appelbaum, Macpherson, and Rosemblatt, "Racial Nations," 11.

44. Escobar, *Encountering Development*, xx–xxvii.

45. Ibid.

46. Miranda and Vallejo, *Darwinismo social*, 11–19. For a historiographic and critical approach to the use of the term "social Darwinism," see Girón Sierra, "Darwinismo, darwinismo social," 23–58.

47. Huyssen, "Geographies of Modernism," 203.

48. This definition of development—as a process of domestication and normalization—is one of ten definitions that Nikki Moore and I delineated for a glossary to be included in the forthcoming aggregate book, *Systems and the South*, edited by Arindam Dutta, M. Ijlal Muzaffar, and myself.

49. Boyer, *Le Corbusier*, 457.

50. Huyssen, "Geographies of Modernism," 203.

1. Francis Galton was a productive scientist who worked in such different fields as geography, genetics, sociology, psychology, anthropology, mathematics, and statistics, but he is mostly recognized as a pioneer of heredity and biometry. He is known as the founder of eugenics, coining and defining the term for the first time as "the science of improving inherited stock, which is by no means confined to questions of judicious mating, but which, especially in the case of man, takes cognizance of all the influences which give to the more suitable races or strains of blood a better chance of prevailing speedily over the less suitable than they otherwise would have had." He spent the last months of his life in 1910 writing his unpublished utopian novel. Galton died on January 17, 1911. For his definition of eugenics, see Galton, *Inquiries into Human Faculty*, 17.

2. While the utopian writer Thomas More had envisioned an ideal sixteenth-century society as an island without specific location, the title of Galton's utopia, *Kantsaywhere*, announced its own insularity and unknowable location. In 1516, when More coined the term "utopia" to identify his idealistic society, he collapsed two Greek words, *eu-topia* and *ou-topia* (*eu* meaning "good," *ou* meaning "no," and *topia* meaning "place"). Utopia was pictured by More as a good place that existed nowhere, as reflected in Galton's title. For the etymology of the word "utopia," see Marin, *Utopics: Spatial Play* and "Frontiers of Utopia."

3. "The Eugenic College of Kantsaywhere" was the complete title of Francis Galton's unpublished novel. As part of the eugenics proselytism that occupied his last years, Galton wanted his ideas to reach a wider public. However, when the book was rejected by publishers, Galton destroyed the novel. The surviving fragments were entrusted to Karl Pearson, Galton's student and biographer, and reproduced in Pearson's multivolume book, *The Life, Letters and Labours of Francis Galton*.

4. Pearson, *Life, Letters and Labours*, 3A:420.

5. Ibid. It is not surprising that the Malthusian fear of overpopulation, which haunted most European countries, was also a threat to Galton's Kantsaywhere.

6. Ibid., 416–418. Four equally important tests determined the ranking: an anthropometric test; an examination of one's knowledge of aesthetics and literature; a medical examination; and an examination of one's ancestry, searching for evidence of family talents or illnesses. As Pearson notes, the description of the anthropometric test and the place for this examination in Galton's novel are reminiscent of Galton's real laboratory in South Kensington. Regarding Galton's laboratory in South Kensington, see Pearson, *Life, Letters and Labours*, 2:257–262.

7. Ibid., 3A:414.

8. In fact, the nature versus nurture debate has been traditionally attributed to Galton. Cowan, "Nature and Nurture," 133–207.

9. Kevles, *In the Name of Eugenics*, 17. This emphasizes his own genealogy, connecting with his cousin Charles Darwin and stimulating the belief that "genius" was only the result of inherited aptitudes.

10. Pearson, *Life, Letters and Labours*, 3A:414.

11. On January 11, 1978, Michel Foucault devoted his lecture at the College de France to this topic. Foucault, *Security, Territory, Population*, 1–27.

12. Gisela Heffes had emphasized the importance of analyzing the relationship between discourse and practice. Heffes, *Las ciudades imaginarias*, 12. See also her introduction to *Utopías urbanas*, 13–45.

13. Heffes, *Las ciudades imaginarias*, 109–215.

14. From *Dos partidos en lucha: Fantasía científica*, the utopia written in 1875 by the Argentinian physician and naturalist Eduardo Ladislao Holmberg—which emerged from the debates generated by the reception of Darwinian theories in Argentina—to the utopias of the 1920s in which eugenics appears as the "science" that will solve all of Latin America's ailments, the list of utopias emphasizing scientific issues is quite numerous. Among these are Augusto Emílio Zaluar, *O Doutor Benignus* (Brazil, 1875); Achilles Sioen, *Buenos Aires en el año 2080: Historia verosímil* (Argentina: Igon Hermanos Editores, 1879); Luis V. Varela, *El doctor Whüntz: Fantasía* (Argentina: C. Casavalle, 1881), a novel dedicated to the well-known physician and eugenicist José María Ramos Mejía; Francisco Calcagno, *En busca del eslabón: Historia de monos* (Cuba: S. Manero, 1888); Enrique Vera y González, *La estrella del sur* (Argentina: La sin bombo, 1904); Eduardo Urzaiz, *Eugenia: Esbozo novelesco de costumbres futuras* (Yucatán, Mexico, 1919); Emilio Coni, "La ciudad argentina ideal o del porvenir," *La Semana Médica* 14 (1919): 342–345; Juan Manuel Planas y Sáinz, "Las teorías del Profesor Miliscenios," *El Fígaro* (Cuba, 1917), and *La corriente del Golfo* (Cuba: Imprenta O'Reilly, 1920).

15. Of course, Galton was neither the first nor the last to write about a utopian society based on the control of sexuality and human breeding; in *The Republic*, written in approximately 368 BC under its original Greek title *Politeia*, Plato also imagined a utopian society achieved through the implementation of highly effective eugenic practices. In 1602, inspired by Plato's *Republic* and his utopian island "Atlantis," the Dominican friar Tommaso Campanella visualized his *Città del sole* as an ideal republic in which births were organized according to the quality of citizens. See Riot-Sarcey, Bouchet, and Picón, *Dictionnaire des Utopies*, 33–37, 64–69, 176–179, 184–185, 201.

16. Choay, *The Rule and the Model*, 7–8.

17. In fact, in an article written for the exhibition "Utopie: La quête de la société idéale en Occident" (Utopia: The Search for the Ideal Society in the Western World), Choay identified three structural elements that constitute the utopian genre: a critique of a society, a model society, and a model space. See Choay, "Utopia and the Philosophical Status," 346, 348.

18. Ibid., 348.

19. Although the analysis of such spaces goes beyond the scope of this book, a brief comment on one of these utopian texts, *Hygeia: A City of Health*, is relevant—not only because of its influence on Latin American literary and medical circles but also because of its evocation of Lamarckian eugenics. As a medical utopia, the text describes a city planned with a primary focus on the moral and physical health of its inhabitants. It is clear that *Hygeia* reverberated beyond being a fictional narrative: it was presented by its author, the English physician Benjamin Ward Richardson, as a case study in a scientific meeting in Brighton, England, in 1862. Using the novel to visualize a kind of ideal hospital-city, an urban panopticon in which environment was regulated and controlled in order to eradicate most forms of diseases, Richardson was in fact one of the first to emphasize the detrimental effects of alcohol and tobacco in his book *Diseases of Modern Life* (1875). See Richardson, *Hygeia, a City of Health*, and Choay, *L'Urbanisme*. A Spanish version of *Hygeia* was published in *Revista Médico Quirúrgica*, no. 12, 1876.

20. Choay argues that at the end of the nineteenth century, the utopian genre practically disappeared from Western literature. Perhaps, as Choay observes, William Morris's *News from Nowhere*, written in 1890, was the last major utopia of the century in the Western world.

21. Foucault, "The Politics of Health in the Eighteenth Century," in *Power/Knowledge*, 172.

22. The utopias examined in this chapter were written between 1879 and 1926 in Argentina, Mexico, and Brazil—the three Latin American countries exemplary of eugenics in the region and home to three of the strongest traditions of utopian writing.

23. In his book *Encountering Development*, Arturo Escobar explains how development became a main preoccupation during the first half of the twentieth century for many countries of Asia, Africa, and Latin America—the so-called Third World. These countries in their process of modernization embarked "upon the task of 'un-underdeveloping' themselves by subjecting their societies to increasingly systematic, detailed and comprehensive interventions." Escobar, *Encountering Development*, 6.

24. Dubos, "Medical Utopias," 410–424.

25. Gilson and Levinson, *Latin American Positivism*.

26. Stepan, *The Hour of Eugenics*, 41–42.

27. Since classical antiquity, the conviction that good health and natural life were inseparable has been a common belief. But in modern times, beginning with the romanticism of the eighteenth century until the current obsession with sustainability in the twenty-first century, this conviction has grown to greater proportions. Even Edward Jenner (1749–1823), the so-called father of immunology, in his presentation of the "not so natural" practice of vaccination, argued that "the deviation of Man from the state in which he [was] originally placed by Nature seems to have proved to him a prolific source of Disease." Jenner, quoted in Dubos, *Mirage of Health*, 6.

28. Ibid., 20–21.

29. Lee, "Modern Architecture," 6–29.

30. Canguilhem, "Bichat," 122.

31. "La vie est l'ensemble des fonctions qui résistent a la mort." Bichat, *Recherches physiologiques*, 1.

32. Dubos, "Medical Utopias," 411.

33. As mentioned in this book's introduction, Georges Canguilhem, in his definition of "milieu," follows Lamarck to identify the absence of an intrinsic harmony between living organisms and the environment and a consequent mutual process of struggle and adaptation. For Michel Foucault, milieu was, in fact, a "field of intervention" where the objective was precisely the transformation of the population. See Canguilhem, *Knowledge of Life*, and Foucault, *Security, Territory, Population*, 21.

34. Dubos, "Medical Utopias," 411.

35. Mumford, "Utopia, the City and the Machine," 271–292.

36. Sicard de Plauzoles, *La Police des familles*, 178.

37. Urzaiz, *Eugenia*.

38. "Eugenia" was precisely one of the Spanish terms and also the Portuguese translation for eugenics used at the time in Cuba, Brazil, and other Latin American countries.

39. Born in Guanabacoa, Cuba, in 1876, Eduardo Urzaiz Rodríguez immigrated with his family to the city of Mérida on the Yucatán Peninsula of Mexico. After studying medicine in Mexico and the United States, Urzaiz gained recognition as a professor at the Universidad Autónoma de Yucatán, then known as the Universidad Nacional del Sureste. He became the first university president in 1922 and held other important public positions in Mexico, such as director of the Ayala psychiatric hospital, director of the Department of Public Education, and director of the State Health Council in Yucatán. Urzaiz's novel was first published in 1919 by Talleres Gráficos A. Manzanilla, but several later editions were published by the Universidad Autónoma de Yucatán and by the Universidad Autónoma Nacional de México. For a full summary of Urzaiz's trajectory, see Rachel Haywood Ferreira's most recent book, *The Emergence of Latin American Science Fiction*, 68.

40. Urzaiz, *Eugenia*, 35.

41. Ibid., 22.

42. Ibid., 13–14.

43. Alfonso L. Herrera, quoted in Stepan, *The Hour of Eugenics*, 135.

44. Urzaiz, *Eugenia*, 14.

45. Ernesto was basically what could be called a bon vivant, a playboy supported by his lover, with no regular job, only hobbies. He had won racing competitions on his "aerocicleta de motor de nitroglicerina coloidal" (colloidal nitroglycerine motor aerocycle), which allowed him to make the Villautopía-Havana-Villautopía trip in only forty minutes. Urzaiz, *Eugenia*, 36.

46. Ibid., 15.

47. Ibid., 24.

48. Ibid., 44.

49. Ibid.

50. At this time, the proposal made by Palaviccini for eugenic sterilization was approved with only seven votes, but one decade later, when the Mexican Eugenic Society had already strengthened its ties with eugenic societies in other countries, Mexican elites became much more enthusiastic about sterilization policies, which they considered very favorably in the modern countries they admired such as the United States and Sweden. Stepan, *The Hour of Eugenics*, 131.

51. On July 6, 1932, the government of the state of Veracruz authorized the first and only eugenics sterilization law in the country, legalizing sterilization not only for criminals but also for "undesirable human specimens with the capacity to reproduce," such as "the insane, the idiots, and the degenerated" and those whose disease or defect "is considered incurable or genetically transmissible." See Law 121, published in the appendix in Suárez y López Guazo, *Eugenesia y racismo en México*, 266–271.

52. After a decade of fighting (1910–1920), the revolution reclaimed not only the land of wealthy landowning oligarchies for rural communities of native peoples but also a place for indigenous peasants and mestizo workers in the process of Mexico's state formation. Understanding the need to manipulate symbols of national identity, the new postrevolutionary government set up a state-run political and cultural program to show to the international community Mexico's transformation from a semifeudal country into a modern industrialized nation. It also aimed to show the local rural and urban masses that the government had conceded to stand up for their rights, while preventing them from interfering with "efforts to turn Mexico into a modern, profit-making nation." Mexican muralism played a critical role in this process. Greeley, "Muralism and the State," 18.

53. Vasconcelos, *La raza cósmica / The Cosmic Race*, 5.

54. Ibid., 26.

55. Ibid., 32.

56. Zavala, "The *India Bonita* Contest," 283.

57. Ibid.

58. Ibid., 289; emphasis in original.

59. Ferreira, *Emergence of Latin American Science Fiction*, 70.

60. The described image of Celiana was not only featured on the cover of various editions of Urzaiz's novel, including the English translation recently published by the University of Wisconsin Press, but even on the cover of scholarly books on eugenics published in Mexico, such as Laura Luz Suárez y López Guazo's *Eugenesia y racismo en México*.

61. That is why the endless scientific debates on race classification and the impossibility for scientists to agree on specific racial types are clear and "powerful indicators that racial categories are not representations of pre-existing biological groups . . . but distinctions based on complex political-scientific and other kinds of conventions and discriminatory practices." Stepan, *The Hour of Eugenics*, 13.

62. Stepan argues that there is no similar term for "gender" that would indicate "the socially constituted character of the 'races' represented in European sciences and politics." Ibid.

63. This is the main thesis of Alexandra Minna Stern's extraordinary article. See Stern, "Responsible Mothers and Normal Children," 369–397.

64. Foucault, *The History of Sexuality*, 103–114.

65. Monteiro Lobato, *O presidente negro*, 78–79.

66. Ibid., 76.

67. Ibid., 81.

68. Ibid., 148.

69. Ibid., 163.

70. Ibid., 83.

71. As Skidmore defines it, "white superiority" arises from the belief that the white race was at the top of the racial hierarchy, whereas "white supremacy" advocates for the need to eliminate every other race but the white in the name of progress. See Skidmore, *Fact and Myth*.

72. The following note was included in the first page of the first edition of *Problema vital*: "Essays published in *Estado de S. Paulo* were included in this volume by the São Paulo Eugenics Society and the Pro-sanitation League of Brazil." Monteiro Lobato, *Problema vital*.

73. In Brazil, where medical education served as the equivalent of a liberal arts degree, and physicians were revered as leaders, medicine saturated every aspect of the social and political life of this modern nation. So it makes sense that, expressing his adherence to the sanitarian movement of the late 1910s, Monteiro Lobato calls for scientists to replace all politicians in state and federal government.

74. Monteiro Lobato, *Mr. Slang e o Brasil e Problema vital*, 121.

75. However, race continued to be a key issue in Monteiro Lobato's work, as expressed in his influential characters A Negrinha, Tia Nastácia, and Tio Barnabé.

76. Race was always a source of conflict in Monteiro Lobato's intellectual and personal life. After publishing *Problema vital*, in 1919 he still refers to Alberto Rangel and to his friend Leo Vaz in those racist terms, and almost ten years later, in 1928, he laments to the eugenicist Oliveira Vianna: "You know what I came to find in this country? . . . we [in Brazil] have no race . . . Gobineau, Gobineau . . ." Monteiro Lobato, quoted in Skidmore, *Black into White*, 271.

77. Borges, "Puffy, Ugly, Slothful and Inert," 235.

78. In a remarkable article published in *El País* in 2012, Mario Vargas Llosa criticizes the view of homosexuality as depravation or, in the best-case scenario, as illness, which still prevails in Latin America. He emphasizes how commonly this view "is taught in schools, transmitted within families, predicated from pulpits, forecast through mass media," and how the LGBT community is represented as abnormal and dangerous, "deserving the contempt and rejection of decent, normal, and ordinary people." Pointing out the way in which religious dogmas and moral codes have enthroned "an orthodox sexuality from which only perverts, crazy, and sick people deviate," Vargas Llosa argues that homophobes do not censor themselves in the same way racists do: homophobia runs free and unpunished. See Vargas Llosa, "La caza del gay."

79. Ibid.

80. Armus, commenting on Sioen's text, *La ciudad impura*, 33.

81. Sioen, *Buenos Aires en el año 2080*, 62.

82. The French criminologist Alexandre Lacassagne was the first to define *hygiène social* in his 1876 essay "Précis d'hygiène privée et sociale" as "the art of knowing the various influences that come from the milieu in which human beings develop themselves and modify themselves in the way most favorable for their physical, intellectual, and moral development." In 1902, Émile Duclaux, a disciple of Louis Pasteur, emphasized social hygiene's interdependence between body and disease by arguing how diseases were not considered in and of themselves but in relation to their repercussions in society. See Lacassagne, quoted in Drouard, *L'Eugénisme en questions*, 81. For Duclaux's definition, see Duclaux, *L'hygiène sociale*, 5.

83. Sicard de Plauzoles, *Principes d'hygiène sociale*, 44.

84. Sicard de Plauzoles, quoted in Donzelot, *The Policing of Families*, 178.

85. *Prévoyance*, from the Latin *praevidentĭa*, refers to an ability to see ahead, to have foresight, to prepare for the unexpected. Horne, *A Social Laboratory*, 29.

86. Gorelik, *La grilla y el parque*, and Berjman, *Plazas y parques de Buenos Aires*.

87. Forestier's blueprints for the urban transformation of Buenos Aires were published in 1925 by the Comisión de Estética Edilicia de la Municipalidad de la Ciudad de Buenos Aires (MCBA) under the title *Proyecto orgánico para la urbanización del municipio*. See Comisión de Estética Edilicia, *Proyecto orgánico para la urbanización del municipio*.

88. Coni, "La ciudad argentina ideal," 342–345.

89. Coni, *Progrès de l'hygiène dans la République Argentine*.

90. Coni, "La ciudad argentina ideal," 343.

91. Ibid., 344.

92. Sisto, preface to *La ciencia del niño*, 3–7.

93. I borrow this association between puericulture and agriculture from Jane Ellen Crisler, "Saving the Seed."

94. Of course, it was a required course for girls only. As late as the 1980s, when I was a high school student in Venezuela, puericulture was part of girls' curriculum in public and private schools. Rodríguez, *Civilizing Argentina*, 119.

95. Alberdi, *Bases y puntos de partida*.

96. Canguilhem, "The Normal and the Pathological," 18.

97. Rabinow, *French Modern*, 11.

98. Even at the end of the twentieth century, the Brazilian senator and anthropologist Darcy Ribeiro wrote a utopian novel titled "Yvy-Marãen: A terra sem males, ano 2997" (Ivy-Marãen: A land without diseases, year 2997). As its title indicates, Yvy-Marãen, meaning a "land without diseases" in the indigenous language of Tupí-Guaraní, was the name of a continental nation that a thousand years later would occupy all of the South American territory, from the borders of the Caribbean Sea to Patagonia. In this immense and diverse territory, Ribeiro imagined the largest population of Latinos in the world, the two billion *ivynos*, a mix of multiple races and cultures, the "products of the same civilization process." This homogenized population, almost white after so much mixture, lives in harmony with nature. According to Ribeiro, it does not matter if they are living in the tropical areas, in the middle of the Amazon, in the Andean altiplanos, along the coasts, or in the wetlands, here "climate stops commanding human life." While Brasília was the capital of Brazil, the people suffered immensely, as the city only served the powerful bureaucrats. However, when, Brasília became the capital of Yvy-Marãen, the formerly supermodern and segregated city offered humanity a commonwealth. In a world in which there were no more fossil fuels and pollutants, Brasília, "the area of the world better illuminated by the sun" with its millions of miles cultivated with bushes and trees, became the major source of energy in the world. By controlling the environment and homogenizing its population, Yvy-Marãen became the world's premiere eco-utopia. Ribeiro, "Yvy-Marãen," 37–58.

99. Rabinow, *French Modern*, 211.

CHAPTER 2

1. The Eiffel Tower and the Gallery of Machines were the architectural symbols of the 1889 World's Fair, built to embody France's vision of a new public environment constructed in accord with modern science and advanced industry.

2. In his report to the 11th Congrès de L'Alliance d'hygiène sociale, Eugène Gautrez differentiated social hygiene from public hygiene: "Public hygiene is the collection of measures in a country that aims at the general health and at the same time the defense of individuals and society against the risks of sickness and death. . . . Social hygiene has higher and further aims. Its objectives surpass the simple preservation of the race and extend to its constant improvement, to its perfection. It attacks, for example, diseases of a special order: tuberculosis, syphilis, and alcoholism, which affect the individual and his descendants." Gautrez, Rapport, "L'Organisation sanitaire," 45.

3. Although the term "social question" emerged in nineteenth-century France to refer primarily to the lives and working conditions of the industrial workers, and was present throughout public discourse at the time, it was at the turn of the twentieth century that the "social question" began to be seen not as a condition exclusively attributed to industrial society but as a compendium of issues related to society as a whole. As Janet Horne argues, it "captured a strong element of bourgeois fear, both of change itself and of the possibility of not being able to understand or harness change; it also embodied fear of workers and of labor militancy." Horne, *A Social Laboratory*, 17. See also Stone, *The Search for Social Peace*, 1–23.

4. Christian Topalov argues that at the beginning of the twentieth century, with the rise of social science, a transformation of the representation of the "other" occurred. Topalov, "Da questão social," 33. In English, see Topalov, "From the 'Social Question' to 'Urban Problems,'" 319–336.

5. Among these events it is relevant to mention the Congrès international de psychologie physiologique (International Conference of Psychological Psychology)—which was presided over by the renowned neurologist

Jean-Martin Charcot and counted among its participants Francis Galton, the English scientist who first coined the term "eugenics"; Charles Richet, the physiologist and Nobel Prize winner who systematically argued that heredity and milieu were not antagonistic but "synergistic"; Pierre Janet, one of the founding fathers of psychology; and also the polemical Cesare Lombroso—the Congrès international d'hygiène et de démographie (The International Conference of Hygiene and Demography) in which Louis Landouzy presented his reports associating hygiene and the protection of infancy; the Congressus Mundi Dermatologiae and Syphiligraphy (International Dermatology and Syphiligraphy Conference); and the mentioned II Congrès international d'anthropologie criminelle, biologie, et sociologie (Second International Conference of Criminal Anthropology).

6. Anonymous, "Anthropologie criminelle," 4.

7. Nye, *Crime, Madness, and Politics*, 97. As mentioned in the introduction to this book, recent research on molecular biology recognized the critical role played by the environment in human development, reinvigorating Lamarckian discourses. As the scholars Sara Shostak and Margot Moinester state, the environment has always been the "missing piece of the puzzle of human health and illness." In this postgenomic era, the environment has in fact become the imperative subject of scientific investigation to unravel "the processes and outcomes of gene action." Shostak and Moinester, "The Missing Piece of the Puzzle?," 194.

8. See Silverman, "The 1889 Exhibition," 71–91.

9. Although the main buildings at the Champ de Mars straightforwardly represented progress and evolution, a particular exhibition called "Histoire de l'habitation humaine," very close to the Eiffel Tower and designed by Charles Garnier, the well-known architect of the Opera de Paris, represented the habitat of forty-four different cultures with a dismissive view. Articles written at the time, and even Garnier's own book published in 1892, showed a kind of superiority complex that developed nations often displayed toward cultures different from their own. Near the Galerie des Machines, a well-known collector of Islamic art, Alphonse Delort de Gléon, undertook the reconstruction of a Cairo Street, featuring picturesque civil architecture, two mosques, a bazaar, shops, and cafés, all animated by Egyptian musicians, dancers, vendors, and artisans, and even by fifty Egyptian donkeys and their drivers representing themselves. After the Eiffel Tower, this was the second most popular attraction at the 1889 World's Fair. See Garnier and Amman, *Histoire de l'habitation humaine*, and Delort de Gléon, *L'architecture arabe des khalifes d'Égypte*. For an analysis of architectural representations of the Arab world and "exotic" performances at the 1889 World's Fair, see Mitchell, *Colonising Egypt*; Çelik, *Displaying the Orient*; and Çelik and Kinney, "Ethnography and Exhibitionism," 34–59.

10. Benedict, *The Anthropology of World's Fairs*, 48. See also Blanchard et al., *Zoos humains et exhibitions coloniales*; Palermo, "Identity under Construction," 285–301.

11. Scott, *Seeing Like a State*, 3.

12. Although the French philosopher of science Bruno Latour argues that it was not until Pasteur's discoveries in 1895 that hygiene gained serious scientific authority, public hygiene was already perceived as a scientific enterprise before that time. By the time the 1889 World's Fair opened, Pasteur was already considered a national hero. At the simultaneously held Congress of Hygiene in the Hôtel de Ville of Paris, Pasteur was welcomed with "La Marseillaise." According to the French historian Ann La Berge, "Hygiene was one of those areas that had to be transformed into a scientific discipline. . . . If the hygienists' method was scientific, their mission was hygienism, a kind of medical imperialism incorporating both the medicalization and moralization of society." La Berge, *Mission and Method,* 2. See also Latour, "Le Théâtre de la preuve."

13. See Janet R. Horne's section on the Social Economy Exhibition in *A Social Laboratory*, 70–76.

14. Cheysson, "L'Économie sociale," 1–19.

15. Picard, *Exposition universelle internationale*, 140–141.

16. Horne actually claims that "it was during this period [during the Third Republic], rather than during the revolution of 1848, that France built the lasting foundation of a social republic." Horne, *A Social Laboratory*, 58.

17. As is documented in the exhibition's "Rapports du jury international," the Social Economy Exhibition was organized according to the following fifteen sections: Section I: Remuneration of Labor (Rémunération du travail); Section II: Profit Sharing: Co-operative Associations of Production (Participation aux bénéfices: Associations coopératives de production); Section III: Professional Syndicates (Syndicats professionnels); Section IV: Apprenticeship (Apprentissage); Section V: Mutual Aid Societies (Sociétés de secours mutuels); Section VI: Banks of Pension and Life Annuities (Caisses de retraites et rentes viagères); Section VII: Accident and Life Insurance (Assurances contre les accidents et sur le vie); Section VIII: Savings (Épargne); Section IX: Consumptive Co-operative Associations (Associations coopératives de consommation); Section X: Co-operative Loan Associations (Associations coopératives de crédit); Section XI: Workers' Housing (Habitations ouvrières); Section XII: Workers' Clubs: Recreations and Plays (Cercles d'ouvriers: Récréations et jeux); Section XIII: Social Hygiène (Hygiène sociale); Section XIV: Institutions Created by Employers in Favor of Their Employees (Institutions diverses créées par les chefs d'exploitation en faveur de leur personnel); Section XV: Large and Small Industry and Large and Small Culture (Grande et petite industrie et grande et petite culture). See Picard, *Exposition universelle internationale*.

18. Sicard de Plauzoles, *Principes d'hygiène sociale*, 44.

19. See Lacassagne, quoted in Drouard, *L'Eugénisme en questions*, 81; and for Duclaux's definition, see Duclaux, *Hygiène sociale*, 5.

20. See Émile Neumann's official report, "Hygiène sociale," in Picard, *Rapports du jury international*, 283–302.

21. As noted in chapter 1, the term *prévoyance* (from the Latin *praevidentia*) refers to an ability to see ahead, to have foresight, to prepare for the unexpected. In France, the liberal idea of *prévoyance* became a republican value of self-help and individual thrift. For liberal ideas in Second Empire France, see Hazareesingh, *From Subject to Citizen*, 162–232; and Mitchell, *Socialism and the Emergence of the Welfare State*, 24–40.

22. Schneider, *Quality and Quantity*, 11.

23. The liberalist Léon Say was the first to call this institution the "Experimental Museum of the World." For the origins of the Musée social, see Horne, "Le Musée social à l'origine," 47–69.

24. Late-nineteenth-century France saw the emergence of a new kind of museum to collect, display, and discuss materials related to modern technology and culture, which traditionally were temporarily exhibited only at international fairs. For example, the first anthropological museum in France, the Musée d'Ethnographie du Trocadéro (which in the 1930s became the Musée de l'Homme), was first established as a temporary exhibition at the 1878 World's Fair; the Musée des Arts Décoratifs in Paris originated in 1882, in the wake of the Universal Exhibitions, when a group of collectors decided to promote the applied arts; and in 1904 the former Conservatoire national des arts et métiers, which later became the Musée des Arts et Métiers, created the new Musée de la prévention des accidents du travail et d'hygiène industrielle.

25. Crisler, "Saving the Seed," 76.

26. The year of the official inauguration of the Musée social, 1895, was also the year when Adolphe Pinard reactivated the term "puericulture." Previously, Charles Alfred Caron had coined this term to describe "the hygiene and physiological science of raising children" in his 1866 work, *La Puériculture, ou la Science d'élever hygiéniquement et physiologiquement les enfants*. Then, on November 26, 1895, at the Académie de Médecine in Paris, Pinard revisited the term in a talk titled "La Puériculture intrauterine." See Carol, *Histoire de l'eugénisme*, 41.

27. Sicard de Plauzoles, *La Police des familles*, 178.

28. Murard and Zylberman, *L'Hygiène dans la République*, 450.

29. Pitsos, *L'Alliance d'hygiène sociale*, 12.

30. Kahn, *L'Esthétique de la rue*, 299. See also Mory, "Architecture et hygiénisme à Paris," 145–162.

31. Alliance d'hygiène sociale, *Congrès de Roubaix*, 11.

32. Bourgeois, "Congrès d'hygiène sociale de Roubaix," 1.

33. Benoît-Lévy, "Lotissements modèles et cités-jardins," 64–74.

34. Agache, "La Cité-Jardin," 75–116.

35. The garden-city model, originally formulated by Ebenezer Howard in his 1898 book, *To-morrow: A Peaceful Path to Real Reform*, developed into a movement in its own right. Considering rural migration and the decline of cities as England's main social problems, Howard visualized a solution: the establishment of self-contained communities of around 30,000 inhabitants in the countryside living in a healthy environment that combines residential, industrial, agricultural, and recreational areas surrounded by greenbelts. Although the Musée social did not adopt the garden city as an official agenda, it did sponsor early investigations of the model by some of its members. Georges Benoît-Lévy traveled to England and the United States to participate in study missions about the garden-city movement with the museum's support; and even before the creation of the Alliance d'hygiène sociale, members of the Musée social were among the main leaders of the Association française des cités jardins, which was founded in 1903. Benoît-Lévy, *La Cité jardin.*

36. Horne, *A Social Laboratory*, 254.

37. As Anne Cormier argues, South America became a territory of application of the Musée social's theories in the same way as did the colonies and protectorates such as Indochina, Madagascar, and Morocco. Cormier, "Extension, limites, espaces libres," 51.

38. For the Musée social's urban projects outside of France, see Palacio, "Musée social et urbanistique"; Osti, "Il Musée social di Parigi"; and Novick, "Le Musée social et l'urbanisme en Argentine."

39. Carvalho, *Porous City*, 10.

40. The sanitary and urban reforms developed during the first decades of the twentieth century were not limited to sewage works and the construction of avenues; they also included medical policies that, among other actions, forced the population to be vaccinated for smallpox—a campaign widely rejected. Sevcenko, *A Revolta da Vacina*; Hochman, *A era do saneamento*; and Benchimol, "Reforma urbana e Revolta da Vacina."

41. In 1567, after the original settlement established by French Huguenots on Urca was destroyed, the Portuguese governor-general of Brazil, Mem de Sá, moved the city to the Morro do Castelo. The first historical buildings were built there, among them a military fort, the Convento dos Capuchinhos, the Colégio dos Jesuítas, the São Sebastião church, and more than four hundred residential buildings distributed along narrow streets. Evenson, *Two Brazilian Capitals*, 40; and Quelhas Paixão, "O Rio de Janeiro e o morro do Castelo," 25–26.

42. Pereira Passos' ambitious reforms have been extensively discussed in Rosso del Brenna, *O Rio de Janeiro de Pereira Passos*; Benchimol, *Pereira Passos;* and Needell, *A Tropical Belle Epoque.*

43. This information is included in documentation about Carlos Sampaio (in the Instituto Histórico Geográfico Brasileiro [IHGB], Coleção Carlos Sampaio, Lata 642, p. 25) quoted by Quelhas Paixão in "O Rio de Janeiro e o morro do Castelo," 30–33. The IHGB has played a crucial role in the construction of the memory of the country since its foundation in 1838.

44. Meade, *"Civilizing" Rio*, 66–74; and Chalhoub, *Cidade febril*, 54–56.

45. *Careta*, one of the most popular magazines of the time, frequently referred to the Morro do Castelo as "montanha de estrume." Quelhas Paixão, "O Rio de Janeiro e o morro do Castelo," 33.

46. The term "favela," which originally referred to a type of scruffy bush that proliferated on Rio's hills known as *faveleiro*, became a synonym for the word "slum." Vaz, "Dos cortiços às favelas e aos edifícios de apartamentos," 590–591.

47. Meade, *"Civilizing" Rio*, 123.

48. Quelhas Paixão, "O Rio de Janeiro e o morro do Castelo," 191.

49. Ibid., 41–48.

50. In 1798, the city senate, preoccupied with the sanitary conditions of the city's urban center, distributed an official questionnaire to determine the causes of endemic and epidemic diseases affecting Rio's population. In their response to this questionnaire, the physicians Manoel Joaquim Marreiros, Bernardino Antônio Gomes, and Antonio Joaquim de Medeiros blamed the "morros"—the hills that emerged along the city's bays and valleys—among the main causes that provoked the bad circulation of air and its consequent proliferation of miasmas and other diseases. The physicians also considered that some nonnatural factors contributed to the proliferation of diseases, such as the architecture of most of the buildings, which were too low-rise, humid, and poorly ventilated. They proposed the elimination of some of the hills and the construction of taller buildings. This questionnaire was first published in 1813, in the scientific and cultural newspaper *O Patriota*. See Ferreira, "Os periódicos médicos," 331–351.

51. Nonato and Santos, *Era uma vez o Morro do Castelo*, 67.

52. Meade, *"Civilizing" Rio*, 173.

53. Ibid., 175; Abreu, *A evolução urbana do Rio de Janeiro*, 77; and Sedrez, "'The Bay of all Beauties,'" 62–110.

54. Meade, *"Civilizing" Rio*, 31.

55. Although most people of color were displaced to the north of the city and the suburbs, a large number remained in the southern neighborhoods to serve the wealthy inhabitants of that zone. "According to [the Brazilian sociologist Luiz de Aguiar] Costa Pinto, 70 percent of the inhabitants of the favelas were people of color." Dávila, *Diploma of Whiteness*, 85.

56. Sampaio, *O arrasamento do Morro do Castelo*, 4. As early as 1891, Carlos Cesar de Oliveira Sampaio had founded the Cia. Do Arrasamento do Morro do Castelo, his own private corporation to study and execute the demolition of the mountain. In his first acceptance speech as mayor of Rio, Sampaio made very clear the nature of his government: "The present moment is of action . . ." However, accused of corruption, Sampaio was unable to continue his ambitious plans. It was not until the end of the municipal government of Sampaio's successor, Alaor Prata, that the debates about a master plan for the city would be reinitiated. See Silva, "Engenheiros, arquitetos e urbanistas," 397–410; and "A trajetória de Alfred Donat Agache no Brasil."

57. Sampaio, *O arrasamento do Morro do Castelo*, 4–5.

58. Sevcenko, *Literatura como missão*, 29. The year 1922 was an electoral year in Brazil. Epitácio Pessoa, the president of the country from 1919 to 1922, found relief from military rebellions and political conflicts in the Centennial Commemoration Exhibition of the Independence of Brazil. As Mauricio Tenorio argues, international exhibitions and politics complement each other, and "Pessoa's position in relation to the exhibition of the First Republic of Brazil was similar to the one assumed by French President Sadi Carnot during the 1889 World's Fair, in the no-less-vulnerable Third Republic of France." Tenorio, "Um Cuauhtémoc carioca," 125.

59. Topalov, "Da questão social," 23.

60. The First Republic, also known as the República Velha (Old Republic), was the period between November 15, 1889, when the Brazilian Army overthrew the monarchy of the Empire of Brazil, and the military coup d'état of October 1930, when Getúlio Vargas, a politician from Rio Grande do Sul and a wealthy pro-industrial nationalist, became the head of the Brazilian state. Vargas was in power from 1930 to 1945, and later from 1951 until his death in 1954. For a description of the Brazilian First Republic, see Fausto, "Brazil," 779–830.

61. Levy, *A Exposição do Centenário*, 63–121.

62. Nereo de Sampaio, "Sobre capiteis (Notas de aula)," 129.

63. Ibid., 130.

64. Ibid. In the second part of his article "Sobre capiteis," published that same year in the same journal, Nereo de Sampaio emphasizes Lamarckian connotations in his descriptions of the evolution of styles. See Nereo de Sampaio, "Sobre capitéis (Conclusão), 155–163.

65. Morales de los Rios Filho, *Teoria e filosofia da arquitetura*, 326. Later in this same book, Morales de los Rios argues that the neocolonial style represented by the Brazilian pavilions at the Centennial Exhibition "was not a copy or an integral reproduction but an adaptation" to the Brazilian milieu. Morales de los Rios Filho, quoted in Levy, *A Exposição do Centenário*, 91.

66. In his seminal essay "The Conditions of Artistic Creation," T. J. Clark argues: "We might say that 'style' is the form of ideology: and that indicates the necessity and the limitations of a history of styles." In other words, style is, in a sense, the very social and political context that constitutes it. Clark, "The Conditions of Artistic Creation," 251.

67. Dávila, *Diploma of Whiteness*, 5

68. *O Livro de Ouro*, 77. It was published in conjunction with the Exposição Internacional do Centenário do Brazil (Brazilian International Centennial Exhibition), held in Rio de Janeiro from September 7, 1922, to March 23, 1923.

69. Ibid.

70. The only exception is a brief mention, made by Monsignor Fernando Rangel in his article, of the abolition of slavery in Brazil. Rangel, "A igreja no Brasil," 287–288.

71. Advertisements featured a variety of products such as wine and other liquor, cigars, oils, olives, tea, metal artifacts, shoes, buttons, and medicines, as well as companies offering health insurance, importation and exportation, typesetting and printing, clinical laboratories, and pharmacies.

72. In 1921, the Mexican evolutionist Alfonso L. Herrera announced that through "science," humanity will be able to materialize a paradise on earth in which the ideal of "beauty of form, intellect and virtue" will be "Hellenic." Stepan, *The Hour of Eugenics*, 135.

73. Domingues, *Hereditariedade e eugenia*, 147.

74. *O Livro de Ouro*, 4–5.

75. The original Tijuca Forest, destroyed by the proliferation of coffee plantations, was replanted during the second half of the nineteenth century with the aim of protecting Rio de Janeiro's water resources. The Tijuca Forest in Rio covers 32 square kilometers, making it the largest urban forest in the world.

76. Although the idea of erecting a colossal image of Christ emerged in 1921 as part of the following year's commemoration of Brazilian independence, its construction did not start until 1926, and its final version was not inaugurated until 1931. Several design versions were proposed for the image of Christ. The statue as finally built is attributed to the Brazilian artist Carlos Oswald, the Brazilian engineer Heitor da Silva Costa, and the French sculptor Paul Landowski. In July 2007, the statue Cristo Redentor was named one of the New Seven Wonders of the World.

77. *O Livro de Ouro*, 367.

78. Sevcenko, *Literatura como missão*, 29.

79. Austregésilo, "A Escola Médica brasileira," 96.

80. *O Livro de Ouro*, 93.

81. Ibid., 94–95.

82. See, for example, Afrânio Peixoto's "O ensino público no Brasil" and Bernardino António Gomes' "A medicina e a hygiene ha cem annos" in *O Livro de Ouro*.

83. Under the influence of Pinard and Landouzy, puericulture—the form that characterizes eugenics in Latin America—was added to the curricula in almost every Latin American high school from Mexico to Patagonia, and institutes of puericulture and hominiculture were founded in countries as different as Brazil, Cuba, and Mexico.

84. In the exhibition catalogue, *O Livro de Ouro*, twenty-five congresses are mentioned as simultaneous events to the exhibition, including the First Brazilian Congress for the Protection of Infants (Primeiro Congresso Brasileiro de Proteção à Infância), the Third Pan-American Child Congress (III Congreso Americano da Criança), the First National Congress of Practitioners, and the First International Leprosy Conference. See *O Livro de Ouro*, 334.

85. The First Brazilian Congress for the Protection of Infants was held in Rio de Janeiro from August 27 to September 5 of 1922. Although for Brazil and the rest of Latin America, I use the term "Lamarckian" or "Lamarckianism" to reflect the steady reception of Lamarck's theories there, in France, though some Lamarckian traditions went unchallenged, I add the prefix "neo-" to acknowledge the reappropriation and reworking of certain Lamarckian concepts from the 1880s onward.

86. Pinard, "De la dépopulation de la France," 30, quoted in Carol, "Médecine et eugénisme en France," 618–631.

87. Bezerra Dantas, "A criança e a eugenia," published in the section on Sociology and Legislation in the *Primeiro Congresso Brasileiro de Proteção à Infância*, 175–179.

88. Schneider, "Puericulture," 265–277.

89. Stepan, *The Hour of Eugenics*, 135.

90. At the beginning of the 1950s, the scientific and aesthetic infiltration of puericulture was still clearly manifested in the fact that the very first modern building constructed on the new campus for the Federal University of Rio de Janeiro was the Instituto de Puericultura. Designed in 1949 by Jorge Machado Moreira, one of the young architects who collaborated with

Lúcio Costa in the design of the Ministry of Health and Education, the horizontal modern building of the Institute of Puericulture, with gardens by Roberto Burle Marx, received the first prize (Category: medical buildings) at the II São Paulo Bienal in 1953. A few years later, a Puericulture Dispensary designed by Marcello Fragelli in Alto de Boa Vista, Rio de Janeiro, was also recognized with an honorary citation at the VI São Paulo Bienal in 1961.

91. After the 1922 celebrations of the independence of Brazil and the public works executed in Rio de Janeiro between 1920 and 1922 by Carlos Sampaio, the municipality was submerged in a financial and political crisis. The idea of producing an urban master plan for the transformation of the city capital was undertaken by a new municipal committee, the Nova Comissão da Carta Cadastral, presided over by the new mayor, Alaor Prata (1922–1926), and directed by the engineer Armando Augusto de Godoy. This committee would later constitute an ad hoc committee devoted exclusively to the discussion and implementation of Rio's first comprehensive master plan. In 1926, when Antônio da Silva Prado Júnior (1926–1930) replaced Alaor Prata as mayor of the city, the discussion was no longer about the need to produce an urban plan but about who would be the best professional to undertake it, "an architect or an engineer, a local professional or a foreigner." To select the ideal professional to develop this urban plan, the ad hoc committee invited the participation of diverse institutions and civil organizations such as the Instituto Central dos Arquitetos (ICA) and the Rotary Club, perhaps the most influential institution in this process. See Silva, "A trajetória de Alfred Donat Agache no Brasil," 397–410; and Stuckenbruck, *O Rio de Janeiro em questão*.

92. Defending the idea of hiring an international well-known professional, they suggested four foreign architects: the German Joseph Stübben, the Englishman Thomas Bennett, and the Frenchmen Jaussely and Agache.

93. At the beginning of 1927, still in the middle of the debates, Prado Júnior was convinced that there was no local professional capable of undertaking such an urban project, so he invited Agache to deliver a series of lectures in Rio. Agache arrived on June 25, 1927, delivered his five lectures, and never left; in November of that same year, with the approval of the Municipal Council, he was hired to develop a comprehensive urban plan for the capital city and established his office in the Municipal Theater of Rio de Janeiro. For the polemical process of Agache's invitation and appointment, see Silva, "A trajetória de Alfred Donat Agache no Brasil," 397–410.

94. Only a year later, after the Portuguese royal family, escaping from Napoleonic invasions, established its court in Rio de Janeiro in 1808, a "French Artistic Mission" led by the architect Grandjean de Montigny (1776–1850) was invited to change the image of the city that in 1815 would be the new capital of the Portuguese Empire, transforming it into a new Paris. Other members included Auguste-Marie Taunay, Jean-Baptiste Debret, and Joachim Lebreton. From 1809, this mission established a century of Beaux-Arts aesthetics in the art and architecture of the city that lasted even after the independence of the country in 1822, when Rio became the capital of independent Brazil, and continued throughout the twentieth century with the urban Haussmannian transformation led by Mayor Francisco Pereira Passos, between 1902 and 1906. Rio was the capital of Brazil until 1960, the year in which the federal capital was transferred to Brasília, a city laboratory designed by Lúcio Costa in the midwest of the country. See Arestizabal, *Uma cidade em questão I*, and Rosso del Brenna, *O Rio de Janeiro de Pereira Passos*.

95. As the architectural historian Otavio Leonídio points out, this argument was basically the same one formulated by Monteiro Lobato, the writer of the utopian text *O presidente negro ou O choque das raças*, commented on in chapter 1, when he said that "style is the unique form of things. It is a way of being distinct. It is a physiognomy. It is a face. The lack of a face is so terrible that cities that hesitate to construct their own style import masks just to pretend they have a face." Monteiro Lobato, quoted in Leonidio, *Carradas de razões*, 31. See also Lemos, "O estilo que nunca existiu."

96. I am referring to the writers, artists, and intellectuals who participated in the art festival in São Paulo in February of 1922, known as the Week of Modern Art, and who openly attacked the faux modernity represented by the cultural establishment in Rio. The group included the poet Oswald de Andrade, the author of the influential "Anthropophagic Manifesto," which brought to center stage two elements associated with backwardness: primitive, untamed nature and those people whom the elites wanted to overlook—Indians and blacks. These two elements were in fact the territorial targets of transformation of the eugenics movement: tropical environment and nonwhite people. Tarsila do Amaral's painting *Abaporu*, whose title means "man who eats" in Tupí-Guaraní, the language of a tribe that was said to practice cannibalism, was the very painting selected to illustrate Andrade's manifesto. By adopting a metaphor for cannibalism and thus implying the need to eat the enemy to appropriate his best qualities, Andrade championed Brazil's digestion of European culture, metabolized now into something original, truly Brazilian. Later, this battle would again manifest during the Getúlio Vargas regime with the establishment of cultural institutions such as the Institution for the Preservation of the National Historical and Artistic Patrimony and the Imperial Museum. See Williams, *Culture Wars in Brazil*. See also Amaral, *Artes plásticas na Semana de 22*.

97. The neocolonial style was declared by the government to be the national style, the mandatory style to be adopted by every building that would represent Brazil abroad from 1922 to 1938. Perhaps the need to represent modern Brazil with a particular style as a homogeneous white society was behind the omission of race as a demographic factor in every national census from 1890 to 1940. This omission was not the result of a need to promote a race-neutral society but the fantasy of a much-desired white Brazil, and it is especially significant in a country that not only received more Africans than any other country in the world during the course of the slave trade but was also the last in the Americas to abolish slavery. See Skidmore, *Fact and Myth*.

98. Neoclassicism was incorporated into Rio's urban fabric from the first half of the nineteenth century by members of the French Artistic Mission.

99. In his 1923 "Decalogue for the Brazilian Architect" (Decálogo do arquiteto brasileiro), Mariano Filho refers to neocolonial architecture as "maternal architecture." His preoccupation with the neocolonial style was manifested not only in his innumerable articles published in the most popular periodicals of the period but also in the promotion of national architectural competitions and travel fellowships for young architects to travel to historical cities such as the baroque cities of Minas Gerais. Yet in 1921, taking advantage of his leadership position in the Central Institute of Architects and the Brazilian Society of Fine Arts, Mariano Filho also created prizes to recognize the work of architects who appropriated the language of the religious and civic architecture of colonial times. See Leonidio's section "O neocolonial: Lúcio Costa e José Mariano Filho (1924–1929)," in *Carradas de razões*, 31.

100. In 1936, on the eve of Vargas' Estado Novo (1937–1945), Andrade continued his support of the neocolonial as the national style and, in his preliminary project for the institutionalization of the National Services of Artistic Heritage (Serviço do Patrimônio Artístico Nacional), suggested Mariano Filho as a consultant.

101. Agache, *A cidade do Rio de Janeiro*, 5.

102. Ibid., 21.

103. At the core of the Musée social, Agache and a group of members of the Section d'hygiène urbaine et rurale had created the Société des architectes urbanistes (1913), the first professional organization in France devoted to city planning that later became the Société française des urbanistes (SFU; 1919).

104. Agache, *A cidade do Rio de Janeiro*, 3; italics mine.

105. Wolf, *Eugène Hénard and the Beginning of Urbanism*.

106. Agache, *A cidade do Rio de Janeiro*, 6. The plan was published in Paris, first in 1930 in Portuguese as *A cidade do Rio de Janeiro, remodelação, extensão e embelezamento*, and then, two years later, in French as *La remodelation d'une capitale*. Agache's lectures in Rio were included as the introduction to both editions.

107. The Morro do Castelo was almost entirely demolished by Sampaio for the exhibition of 1922, and then completely razed by Mayor Prado Júnior in 1929.

108. In fact, Agache pointed it out by drawing a dotted line from the center of the place that once was occupied by the Morro do Castelo to Urca, adding the caption "The axis of the Santos Dumont Avenue is aligned with the Pão de Acucar" (L'Axe de L'Avenue Santos Dumont est dans l'alignement du Pain de Sucre). In Agache's project, the new Santos Dumont Avenue was parallel to the Avenida Rio Branco, opened by Pereira Passos at the beginning of the century.

109. According to Agache, the demolition of the Morro de Santo Antônio was first considered by the engineers João Pedreira do Couto Ferraz and Libanio Lima during imperial times.

110. Roquette-Pinto, "Inaugural Session," 11–12.

111. Agache, *A cidade do Rio de Janeiro*, 160–161. In the early 1920s, the popular cartoonist J. Carlos published a series of cartoons openly presenting a critical position toward the demolition of the mountains. His cartoons refer to the economic and political agenda behind the government decision, as well as the consequences this decision would have for the people who would be displaced. One of the cartoons, titled "Negócio da China," a popular expression used to refer to a grand business deal, represents the dialogue between two technocrats (one of them probably Carlos Sampaio himself), who, pointing toward the water while standing in a little boat, talk about the "liquidity" that the sale of the new land would generate. In another cartoon titled "Os extremos se tocam," Neptune exclaims from the sea: "But what is this?," and a character representing the Centenary of the Independence of Brazil responds from the top of the hill being demolished: "This is a straight line from Calabouço to Glória." See J. Carlos, "Negócio da China," in *Careta* (Rio de Janeiro), August 27, 1921; and "Os extremos se tocam" on the cover of *Careta* (Rio de Janeiro), no. 621, August 27, 1921.

112. Agache, *A cidade do Rio de Janeiro*, 129–130.

113. Underwood, "Alfred Agache," 149.

114. Agache, *A cidade do Rio de Janeiro*, 4.

115. Mattos Pimenta led an anti-favela campaign that included lectures and articles published in the most popular newspapers of his time and even a film produced with the support of the Rotary Club. See Mattos Pimenta, "Para a remodelação do Rio de Janeiro"; and Valladares, *La favela d'un siècle à l'autre*, 32–33.

116. This quote from Mariano Filho's "O problema das 'favelas' do Rio de Janeiro" was referenced in Joel Outtes' article "Disciplinando a la sociedad a través de la ciudad," 62.

117. Roquette-Pinto, "Inaugural Session," 12.

118. "A domesticação é factor preponderante nas diferenciações raciais; mas é preciso acentuar que a influência não é do meio natural e sim de um meio artificial, criado pelo homem." Roquette-Pinto, "Second Session," 16.

119. Roquette-Pinto, "Inaugural Session," 12.

120. Lúcio Costa (1902–1998), a disciple of Mariano Filho and one of the main promoters of the neocolonial movement in Brazil, became the director of the National School of Fine Arts in December of 1930, and soon after, the leader of a radical transformation in architectural education in Brazil, which separated him from the hegemony of the neocolonial style as the national style. Costa became a pioneer of Brazilian modernist architecture. A renowned architect and city planner, he was the main author of the most celebrated icons of Brazilian architectural modernism, including the 1936 building for the Ministry of Health and Education in Rio, the 1939 Brazilian Pavilion for the World's Fair in New York, and Brasília—the new capital created ex nihilo in the center of the country.

121. "Sou apenas pessimista quanto à . . . arquitetura em geral e urbanismo. Toda arquitetura é uma questão de raça. Enquanto o nosso povo for essa coisa exótica que vemos pelas ruas a nossa arquitetura será forçosamente uma coisa exótica. Não e essa meia dúzia que viaja e se veste na rue de la Paix, mas essa multidão anónima que toma trens da central e

Leopoldina, gente de caras lívidas, que nos envergonha por toda a parte. O que podemos esperar de um povo assim? Tudo é função da raça. A raça sendo boa o governo é bom, será boa a arquitetura. Falem, discutam, gesticulem, o nosso problema básico é a imigração selecionada, o resto é secundário, virá por si." Costa, "O arranha-céu e o Rio de Janeiro."

122. For the urban transformation of Rio during the 1930s, see Conniff, *Urban Politics in Brazil*.

123. According to a note published on April 19, 1936, in the *Jornal do Commercio*, Minister Gustavo Capanema invited Le Corbusier and the Spanish endocrinologist Gregorio Marañón to deliver lectures on their respective disciplines in Rio de Janeiro. This note is attached to a letter, dated June 15, 1936, sent by Le Corbusier to the engineer Alberto Monteiro de Carvalho, whom he had met during his first trip to Brazil in 1929. This letter followed a series of letters in which they discussed and negotiated the purpose and conditions of Le Corbusier's new trip to Brazil. In the first letter, dated March 21, 1936, Monteiro de Carvalho informally announced to Le Corbusier that "[Lúcio Costa and Carlos Leão] as well as a group of modern comrades faithful to Le Corbusier, like Affonso Reidy, Jorge Moreira, Oscar Niemeyer, . . . think that the Minister [Capanema] might ask you to come here to give a course at the Escola de Bellas Artes and when you are here the Minister would certainly request your advice on the University campus as well, and it will be easy to arrange things so that you can at least manage to direct the project to the benefit of the young Brazilians." Weeks later, in a different letter, Monteiro de Carvalho also mentioned the possibility of consulting for the design of the new Ministry of Health and Education. In his responses, Le Corbusier pressed for a commission in Brazil, and though the official invitation he received from Minister Capanema did not offer an architectural project, Le Corbusier accepted the invitation. Le Corbusier, letter to Alberto Monteiro de Carvalho, dated June 15, 1936, FLC 13–3-15; and Monteiro de Carvalho, letter to Le Corbusier dated March 21, 1936, FLC 13–3-5, Fondation Le Corbusier, Paris.

124. For this understanding of the *brise-soleil*, I am thankful to Ayala Levin's talks and unpublished essay "The Thick Wall: Climate Control as a Cold War Aesthetics."

125. Of course, I refer to the evolutionary stance articulated by Adolf Loos in his famous series *Ornament and Crime* (1908). See Cogdell, *Eugenic Design*, 14.

126. This is the focus of chapter 4. "Dégénérescence du logis, dégénérescence de la famille, c'est tout un." Le Corbusier, Radio Broadcast (1941), FLC B3–12, No. 216, Fondation Le Corbusier, Paris.

127. In the first pages of his 1935 book *La Ville Radieuse*, Le Corbusier argues for the "rebirth of the human body." Le Corbusier, *La Ville Radieuse*. For an English translation, see Le Corbusier, *The Radiant City*, 7.

CHAPTER 3

1. Beatriz Colomina, in an interview with Anatxy Balbeascoa published in the Spanish newspaper *El País*, said that architecture has been studied from every point of view except from the most obvious: the clinical one. Colomina, "Los arquitectos buscamos dioses," *El País*, April 20, 2009. Regarding the connection between modern architecture and health, see Colomina, "The Medical Body in Architecture," 228–238.

2. See Domingo Faustino Sarmiento's 1845 seminal text, *Facundo, ó Civilización y barbarie en las pampas argentinas*. For the civilization-barbarism dichotomy, see Swanson, *Companion to Latin American Studies*, 69–85; and Mignolo, *La idea de América Latina*.

3. The French historian of medicine Jacques Léonard traced eugenics' preoccupations with early-nineteenth-century medical treatises devoted to the "Art de bien procréer," to "dégénération et regeneration," and to related concepts such as Adolphe Pinard's concept of puericulture and Louis Landouzy's concept of hominiculture. See Carol, *Histoire de l'eugénisme en France*, 364.

4. It was Michel Foucault who first defined *dispositif* as a heterogeneous ensemble of "discourses, institutions, architectural forms, regulatory decisions, laws, administrative measures, scientific statements, philosophical, moral and philanthropic propositions" that function as a system of power exercised over the social body. See Foucault, "The Confession of the Flesh," in *Power/Knowledge*, 194–228.

5. See Agamben, "What Is an Apparatus?," in *What Is an Apparatus?*, 14.

6. *Dégénérescence* as a social question appeared for the first time in medical debates about the relative quality of the population. "[B]y the 1890s degeneracy was no longer simply a clinical theory of abnormal individual pathologies, but a social theory of persuasive force and power" applied to the state of the nation. Nye, *Crime, Madness and Politics*, 143.

7. In her book *Art Nouveau in Fin-de-Siècle France*, Debora L. Silverman argues that there were two opposite characterizations of nineteenth-century France: one that emphasized the meliorist and progressive aspects of the period; the other, its dissension and degeneration. See Eugen Weber's *France, Fin de Siècle* as an example of the meliorist interpretation; and Robert A. Nye's *Crime, Madness and Politics in Modern France* as a work that emphasizes the national crisis of the country and its fear of degeneration. Silverman, *Art Nouveau in Fin-de-Siècle France*, 316–317.

8. Nye, *Crime, Madness and Politics*, 143.

9. These are Zola's own words from his article "De la description," published in *Le Roman expérimental*, and quoted by Chantal Pierre-Gnassounou in "Zola and the Art of Fiction," 89–90. See also Zola, *Le Roman expérimental*.

10. Zola's twenty novels are *La Fortune des Rougon* (1871), *La Curée* (1871), *Le Ventre de Paris* (1873), *La Conquête de Plassans* (1874), *La Faute de l'abbé Mouret* (1875), *Son Excellence Eugène Rougon* (1876), *L'Assommoir* (1877), *Une page d'amour* (1878), *Nana* (1880), *Pot-Bouille* (1882), *Au Bonheur des Dames* (1883), *La Joie de vivre* (1884), *Germinal* (1885), *L'Œuvre* (1886), *La Terre* (1887), *Le Rêve* (1888), *La Bête humaine* (1890), *L'Argent* (1891), *La Débâcle* (1892), and *Le Docteur Pascal* (1893).

11. In "Différences entre Balzac et moi," an article written simultaneously with the beginning of the *Rougon-Macquart* series, Zola argues: "I do not want to paint contemporary society, but a single family, by showing the play of race modified by the milieu." Zola, "Différences entre Balzac et moi," 1869, BnF, Manuscrits, NAF 10345, f. 14–15.

12. These plans and sketches were collected by Zola in his "dossiers préparatoires" for the novels of the *Rougon-Macquart* series. According to Henri Mitterand, who in 1986 published a selection of Zola's "dossiers préparatoires," what characterizes Zola's preparatory work for this series was the clear understanding of the three features of his *ethnographic method*: "observation of the characteristics of particular groups . . . , analysis and organization of the phenomena observed in order to produce descriptive documents, and syntheses." See Henri Mitterand, quoted in Nelson, "Zola and the Nineteenth Century," 5; and Mitterrand, *Le Regard et le signe*, 80.

13. Although his "dossiers préparatoires" appeared for the first time in 1986 in Mitterand's book, Zola did not intend to keep them secret; during his lifetime, he talked about them as illustrations of his naturalist method. Most of Zola's plans and sketches are at the Bibliothèque nationale de France in Paris. See Mitterand, *Carnets d'enquêtes*.

14. In fact, as a preface to the first volume, *La Fortune des Rougon* (1871), Zola warns the reader: "Physiologically the Rougon-Macquart represent the slow succession of accidents pertaining to the nerves or the blood, which befall a race after the first organic lesion, and, according to environment, determine in each individual member of the race those feelings, desires and passions—briefly, all the natural and instinctive manifestations peculiar to humanity—whose outcome assumes the conventional name of virtue or vice." Zola, *Les Rougon-Macquart*. For this English version, see Zola, *The Fortune of the Rougons*, 4.

15. Thiher, *Fiction Rivals Science*, 166.

16. Prosper Lucas's *Traité de la'hérédité naturelle* (1850) and Claude Bernard's *Introduction à l'etude de la médecine expérimentale* (1865) were among the scientific works that Zola cited as bases for his work.

17. It was in *Le Docteur Pascal*, the final novel in the cycle of *Les Rougon-Macquart*, that Zola anticipated what would be the focus of his following book, *Fecondité*: his concern about France's depopulation and his conviction that only through a sustained program to increase the birth of healthy children would degeneration in France be stopped. It is also in this novel that Pascal Rougon, a physician member of the family, collects, analyzes, and catalogues heredity patterns in an attempt to reconstruct the genetic history of the Rougon-Macquart family.

18. In *L'Assommoir*, Zola depicts the role of alcoholism in the suffering of the Parisian working class. He describes the social and moral degradation of urban proletarians in contemporary Paris by portraying the degeneration of Gervaise Macquart and her husband, with alcoholism as its vehicle.

19. In *Germinal*, Zola describes the physical reality of a coal-mining community in the northeast of France. The main character of this novel is Etienne Lantier, Gervaise Macquart's son with his lover and a worker in the mines, who becomes the leader of a strike against the bourgeois masters. Zola's detailed description of workers' houses, the illnesses that affect miners and their families, and the political demonstrations against the mines' owners represents the way in which working-class alienation and bourgeois domination complement each other.

20. In *Nana*, Zola traces the vicissitudes of Gervaise Macquart's daughter, Nana, a high-class prostitute, a kind of "femme fatale" who, as a moral metaphor for an uncontrollable disease, simultaneously consumes men and their families. Nana, the child but also the agent of degeneration, carries in her desirable body, in her incapacity to procreate, in her atavistic sexuality, a germ of degeneration that is passed on to her clients. Portrayed as a symbol of the depravity of the metropolis, Nana dies of *la petite vérole* (smallpox), in a clear allusion to syphilis (*la grande vérole*); thus, as Zola ends the novel, the decomposition of her body mirrors the decay of the French Empire. It has been said that, fascinated by Zola's *L'Assommoir*, the novel in which the degenerated girl Nana first appeared, Edouard Manet, the celebrated painter of nineteenth-century France, envisioned Nana's future by first depicting her as a prostitute. However, rather than portraying Nana as he did in his famous *Olympia*—lying naked in bed in her boudoir served by her "primitive" black maid—Manet painted Nana clothed but in a position that flaunts her ear—her Darwinian ear—that atavistic feature described by Darwin in *The Descent of Man*. As it is understood, in Manet's *Olympia*, the black maid represents the illness that invades the prostitute's bedroom as well as deviant sexuality (just as the naturalist Comte de Buffon, Lamarck's mentor, visualized black sexuality aligned with primitive deviation). In Manet's *Nana*, the degenerate and the primitive live inside of her own body. A few years later, Zola imagined his Nana, the child of alcoholics, who, true to medical patterns, falls into prostitution. See Gilman, "Black Bodies, White Bodies," 259–274.

21. In *La Bête humaine*, Jacques Lantier, a train driver of the Paris–Le Havre line, who was another of Gervaise Macquart's progeny, is afflicted by a hereditary madness that transforms him into a serial killer triggered by sexual contact with his victims. In this novel, Zola portrays the convergence between progress and regression by depicting his character's regression to primitive states against the backdrop of the mechanisms of a modern city and its moving trains.

22. In *La Curée* and *Pot-Bouille*, Zola confronts sexual deprivation and financial speculation in the life of the bourgeoisie during the Haussmannization of Paris and the development of new apartment houses. Zola portrays the new capitalists' sexual excesses vis-à-vis the speculation and corruption encouraged by Haussmann's urban transformation as the basis to criticize the Second Empire's decadent social morality. In *La Curée*, Zola also depicts the figure of the inverti (the homosexual), who refuses to procreate, as a menace to the family and, consequently, to the nation.

23. Zola became one of the founding members of the pro-natalist organization Alliance nationale pour l'accroissement de la population française. In 1896, in an article published in *Le Figaro*, Zola announced that "the tragic

theme of depopulation" would be the subject of his new book, *Fecondité*. See Zola's article "Dépopulation," *Le Figaro*, May 16, 1896; and his *Feconité*. For an English version, see *Fruitfulness*, translated by Ernest Alfred Vizetelly.

24. Zola was the main precursor to naturalism. Influenced by the positivist ideas of Comte, Taine, and Darwin, and convinced that human beings were part of the animal kingdom and so living under natural laws, Zola called for the adoption of the scientific principles of objectivity and detachment as they applied to the study of human beings.

25. Nouzeilles, "Pathological Romances and National Dystopias," 31.

26. Wallace, "Argentina's Centennial," 748.

27. Clemenceau, *South America To-Day*, 28.

28. Clemenceau described Buenos Aires as "a perfectly healthy city," exalting how "no expense has been spared to satisfy the demands of a good system of municipal sanitation. Avenues planted with trees, gardens and parks, laid out to ensure adequate reserves of fresh air, are available to all, and lawns exist for youthful sports." Clemenceau, *South America To-Day*, 38.

29. See Deutsch, *Las Derechas*.

30. Scobie, "The Paris of South America," 170–181.

31. Hipólito Yrigoyen, known as "the father of the poor," was cofounder of the Radical Civic Union (Unión Cívica Radical), the center-left political party, and a member of the Socialist International, which remained in power for fourteen years: Yrigoyen was president of Argentina from 1916 to 1922, and again from 1928 to 1930; Marcelo T. de Alvear, also a member of the Radical Civic Union, was the president between Yrigoyen's two presidencies. Rock, *Politics in Argentina*.

32. I am particularly thankful to Julia Rodríguez's extraordinary intellectual history of medical science in modern Argentina and her critical approach to this period, which enriched my own research. Rodríguez, *Civilizing Argentina*, 84.

33. Ramos Mejía, "The Modern Crowd," 183. This quote was originally published in Spanish in Ramos Mejía, *Las multitudes argentinas*, 289.

34. Ramos Mejía, "The Modern Crowd," 184. Emphasis here, as in the original Spanish version, was added to the English translation. Ramos Mejía, *Las multitudes argentinas*, 291–292.

35. A Comtean positivist, Élisée Reclus (1830–1905) believed that through environmental adaptation and scientific observation it would be possible to improve people's potential. As discussed in the introduction to this book, this idea was at the core of his conception of the Great Globe for the 1900 World's Fair in Paris—a representation of the inevitable interaction between the milieu of living beings and the dynamics of heredity. In *Las multitudes argentinas*, Ramos Mejía also cited the French social geographer Reclus to emphasize "the intimate correlation that should exist between land [the environment] and the living beings who inhabit it." Ramos Mejía, *Las multitudes argentinas*, 285.

36. Talak, "Eugenesia e higiene mental," 564.

37. Ramos Mejía contributed to "the peculiarly divisive mind-set" that Nicolas Shumway observes as Argentine nineteenth-century intellectuals' ideologic legacy, which is "in some sense a mythology of exclusion rather than a unifying national ideal, a recipe for divisiveness rather than consensual pluralism." Shumway, *The Invention of Argentina*, x.

38. Foucault, *The History of Sexuality*, 139.

39. The city of Buenos Aires did not have a hygiene council until 1871, when it was created by the leading hygienists Emilio Coni, Luis Agote, Eduardo Wilde, and, of course, Ramos Mejía. This hygiene council was mainly concerned with environmental influences and the living conditions of the population, "but also with behaviors and mental states as causes of disease." In 1880, this municipal council was converted into the National Department of Hygiene. Rodríguez, *Civilizing Argentina*, 181.

40. Foucault, *The History of Sexuality*, 139.

41. Neurasthenia, or nerve weakness, was a very common disease in Europe during World War I. It was understood as a disease associated with the dynamic of modern life that primarily affected the upper class. This new disease was also associated with the stress of the battlefields affecting men in the army. Its "discovery" was attributed to the neurologist George Miller Beard from New York, but it was Jean-Martin Charcot, the famous French neurologist at the Salpêtrière Psychiatric Hospital in Paris, who popularized neurasthenia in French and Argentine medical circles. Ferrari, "Historia cultural de la psiquiatría," 288–309.

42. Cholera killed more than 18,000 Parisians, of which more than 11,000 were workers and artisans and only 5,000 were professionals and members of the upper classes, demonstrating what Louis Chevalier called "the biological basis of class antagonism." This data revealed how "miserable conditions somehow provided an environment for weakening the character and body of the poor, making them susceptible to illness." The brutality of this epidemic was ironically accompanied by a significant state accomplishment: a new understanding of disease as a single entity, arising from society and space. Rabinow, *French Modern*, 30–39. For more details on the cholera epidemic of 1832, see Delaporte, *Disease and Civilization*.

43. At the turn of the century, France and Belgium had become the main sponsors of hygienic ideas. Some numbers make this clear: from fifteen international congresses of hygiene held between 1852 and 1912, Paris hosted three and Brussels hosted three; from fourteen international sanitary conferences celebrated between 1851 and 1938, Paris hosted seven. Chevallier, *Le Paris moderne*.

44. Latour, *The Pasteurization of France*, 17.

45. Ibid., 23.

46. Chevallier, *Le Paris moderne*, 13.

47. Penna and Madero, *La administración sanitaria*, 125.

48. Ibid., 211–260.

49. Ibid., 218.

50. Ibid., 220.

51. Foucault, *Power/Knowledge*, 176.

52. The term *casier* in French (or *casillero* in Spanish) is difficult to translate. It literally means a file cabinet or a compartment. David Barnes, in his book *The Making of a Social Disease: Tuberculosis in Nineteenth-Century France*, argues that this term conveys a sense of grid, an overlay of compartments extended over the city. By inspecting family houses, the Prefecture of the Seine's Casier sanitaire des maisons in Paris collected data, disinfecting between 7,000 and 11,000 houses per year between 1894 and 1905, and became France's premier institution to support the idea that a disease such as tuberculosis was caused by the lack of light and air in overcrowded urban areas. Barnes, *The Making of a Social Disease*, 117–118.

53. Penna and Madero, *La administración sanitaria*, 269–298.

54. Barnes, *The Making of a Social Disease*, 118.

55. As previously noted, the French natalist Sicard de Plauzoles defined social hygiene as "an economic science" that looks simultaneously to land and bodies, producing and reproducing human capital through eugenics and puericulture, conserving this capital through hygiene and medicine, while training and augmenting it through professional and physical education, for the sake of ever-increasing productivity. Sicard de Plauzoles, *Principes d'hygiène sociale*, 44.

56. López-Durán and Moore, "MEAT-MILIEU."

57. Silvestri, *El color del río*, 155–186.

58. Paraphrased from López-Durán and Moore, "MEAT-MILIEU."

59. Rose, "Medicine, History and the Present," 51.

60. Foucault, *Dits et écrits*, 3:510.

61. Foucault, *Discipline and Punish*, 220–221.

62. Miranda and Vallejo, "La eugenesia y sus espacios institucionales," 149–150.

63. Ibid.

64. Juan Vucetich was an immigrant from Croatia who arrived in Argentina in 1882, and less than ten years later conducted scientific research on human identification based on mathematical calculations, accurate representations of human body parts, and photography to develop a method of fingerprint identification known as dactyloscopy. In Argentina, his discovery was later used for "electoral laws, the admission of public workers and the creation of public records of immigrants, homeless, vagabonds, prostitutes, etc." Miranda and Vallejo, "Los sabores del poder," 427.

65. Sekula, "The Body and the Archive," 18.

66. Hecht, *The End of the Soul*, 159.

67. Sekula, "The Body and the Archive," 18–19.

68. Ibid., 22.

69. It is very telling that the sociologists Frédéric Le Play and Émile Durkheim argued that "the science of society, or 'social science' should be a normative science." Teyssot, *A Topology of Everyday Constellations*, 40.

70. Ibid., 52–53.

71. Hora, *The Landowners of the Argentine Pampas*, 69.

72. Rodríguez, *Civilizing Argentina*, 27.

73. Sekula, "The Body and the Archive," 33.

74. When Vucetich came across Galton's research on the scientific use of fingerprints in the French Journal *Revue Scientifique* in 1891, he claimed that Bertillon's anthropometric method of criminal identification was inaccurate and "too inconclusive." Hecht, *The End of the Soul*, 162. For Bertillon's influence in Argentina, see Rhodes, *Alphonse Bertillon*.

75. Cole, *Suspect Identities*, 130.

76. Stepan, *The Hour of Eugenics*, 116.

77. Teyssot's article "Norm and Type: Variations on a Theme" likely constitutes the very first elaboration on this topic.

78. As Nancy Stepan argues, in Latin America, Argentina "was the most conventionally racist in its eugenic ideology. In 1918, the country considered itself to be largely white and immigrant; its black population, once quite sizable, had by the 1880s been reduced to less than 2 percent of the national population. The indigenous 'Indians' were socially marginalized. Argentinians believed their country to be not at all like Mexico, which in 1911 believed itself to be 35 percent Indian, 50 percent mestizo (Indian-white) and 15 percent creole (white), or like Brazil, which was 15 percent black and 40 percent mestizo-mulatto, the rest being 'whites,' relatively few of whom could claim complete 'purity' of blood. Indeed, Argentina seemed to many Latin Americans to be the only country that had realized its elites' old dream of racial transformation by whitening and Europeanization." Stepan, *The Hour of Eugenics*, 139.

79. Rock, *Politics in Argentina*, 34–39; Botana, *El orden conservador*, 217–316; and Rodríguez, *Civilizing Argentina* 224–236.

80. The historian David Rock argues that between 1871 and 1914 some 5.9 million people arrived in Argentina, of whom 3.1 million stayed. From its origins, the Museo Social Argentino was interested in determining the characteristics of these immigrants, calling to extend the faculties of the Law of Social Defense "to increase to its maximum the difficulties that could oppose the immigration of inferior races." Stach, "La defensa social y la inmigración," 361–389. For immigration data, see Rock, *Argentina, 1516–1982*, 141.

81. Just like the Parisian Musée social, the Museo Social Argentino was created as an institution capable of collecting information on past and present social organizations and analyzing the country's socioeconomic issues, including its physical and social environment. Among its goals were the creation of an archive and a library, the publication of a monthly bulletin, and the organization of a permanent exhibition on social and economic topics. But, differentiating itself from the Parisian Musée social and other similar institutions in Europe, the Argentinean museum had another fundamental goal: to promote "an advanced and systematic Argentine propaganda elaborated with entire openness and accuracy, with the aim of promoting Argentina, as it is, inside and outside its borders." See Museo Social Argentino, "Orígenes y desenvolvimiento del Museo Social Argentino," 9.

82. Miranda and Vallejo, "La eugenesia y sus espacios institucionales," 155–156.

83. Pelosi, "El Centenario y la 'cuestión social,'" 89–93.

84. The agronomical engineer Tomás Amadeo was a well-known scholar in Argentina whose teaching around the country allowed him to learn in situ about the social and economic problems faced by agricultural sectors. At the time, there were no schools of economic sciences or social services, specialized libraries, or journals devoted to social studies in Argentina. Amadeo founded the Museo Social Argentino as an institute of both research and social activity. On the foundation of the Museo Social Argentino, see Amadeo, *Economía social: Museo Social de Buenos Aires.*

85. On the Section d'hygiène urbaine et rurale, see Horne, *A Social Laboratory for Modern France*; and on the work of the Musée social's members in Latin America, see Palacio, "Musée social et urbanistique sud-américaine."

86. Ballent and Gorelik, "País urbano o país rural," 143–200.

87. Novick, "Le Musée social et l'urbanisme en Argentine," 334.

88. Pelosi, *El Museo Social Argentino*, 42.

89. Stach, "La defensa social y la inmigración," 361–389.

90. Alberdi, *Bases y puntos de partida*, 14–24.

91. Alberdi, quoted in Shumway, *The Invention of Argentina*, 147.

92. Museo Social Argentino, "La inmigración después de la guerra."

93. Museo Social Argentino, "Problemas agrarios," 262–263.

94. Pelosi, *El Museo Social Argentino*, 107.

95. Ibid., 109.

96. Ibid., 108.

97. Girbal de Blacha and Ospital, "Sectores de opinión y trabajo femenino," 187–209.

98. See *Boletín del Museo Social Argentino* 21, no. 2 (1913): 41–49.

99. Stepan, *The Hour of Eugenics*, 87.

100. Ibid., 58.

101. When the Argentine Eugenics Society was founded by the physicians Victor Delfino, Ubaldo Fernández, and Gregorio Aráoz Alfaro, eugenics took a more conservative and racist direction. The fear of foreign people and the economic crisis left by the war provoked a more reactionary understanding of eugenics, calling for "national purification" and strict control of immigration. Ibid., 82.

102. The two periods of Hipólito Yrigoyen's populist government, which since 1916 gave rise to the demands of the working and middle classes and immigrant groups, ended with the military coup of 1930. A decade of extreme conservatism began, and the most extreme eugenic principles and policies emerged in conference debates, were welcomed by the Catholic Church, and then were implemented by new institutions, including the Argentine Association of Biotypology, Eugenics, and Social Medicine and the new Polytechnic School of Biotypology, Eugenics, and Social Medicine. O'Lery, "Aportes acerca de la relación iglesia-eugenesia," 366.

103. The ideology of eugenics was so crucial for the Museo Social Argentino that its leaders were actually planning to name the university the "Universidad de Eugenesia." It opened with two schools: the School of Integral Eugenics and Humanism (Facultad de Eugenesia Integral y

Humanismo) and the School of Education Science (Facultad de Ciencias de la Educación). Pelosi, *El Museo Social Argentino*, 318–333.

104. These different topics—immigration, human health, and the built environment—were protagonists in most of the Museo Social Argentino's sessions, in the pages of its official bulletin, and in the panels of the various conferences and symposiums organized during the first decades of the twentieth century. However, rural topics prevailed over urban interests, and people's "life conditions" over the specificities of the built environment. As Alicia Novick argues, the "urban question" as "an innovative aspect of the reform" was not the focus of the Museo Social Argentino. It was the Asociación de Amigos de la Ciudad, an organization founded in 1924, that became the leader in architectural and urbanist debates in Argentina. Novick, "La ciudad de la reforma social," 193–211.

105. Agamben, *What Is an Apparatus?*, 14.

106. Ibid.

107. Rabinow, *French Modern*, 15.

108. According to the census of 1889, the National Department of Hygiene (Departamento Nacional de Higiene) was created by decree on December 31, 1880, to replace the earlier national Public Hygiene Council (Consejo de Higiene Pública), and the Department of Public Welfare was created a month later on January 31, 1881. See chapter 11, "Gobierno sanitario," in *Censo general*, 1:194–198.

109. In her book on prostitution in France, Jill Harsin argues that the origin of the dispensary can be traced to the start of the nineteenth century. An ordinance dated March 3, 1802, decreed that prostitutes had to be regularly examined for venereal disease; and an ordinance dated May 21, 1805, created the dispensary itself as the new space for this examination. See Harsin, *Policing Prostitution*, 7–18.

110. José María Ramos Mejía and Emilio Coni, the main proponents of the creation of Asistencia Pública, the new municipal Department of Public Welfare, had studied at the University of Buenos Aires during the 1870s under the influence of French medical theories. Their project was inspired by the Public Assistant program presented by Adolphe Thiers to the French Assembly in the early 1870s. Crider, "Modernization and Human Welfare," 35–36.

111. Coni, *Progrès de l'hygiène dans la République Argentine*, ix.

112. Ibid.

113. Coni's *Progrès de l'hygiène dans la République Argentine*, written in French, was modeled after the report, *L'Étude et les progrès de l'hygiène en France de 1878 à 1882*, which was presented by the Société de médicine publique de Paris at the International Congress of Hygiene and Demography held in Geneva in 1882. Coni's 266-page book contains more than twenty plates, including urban and architectural plans along with sewerage infrastructure details. Some of these plans were designed by well-known architects such as Ernesto Bunge and Juan Antonio Buschiazzo and built in strategic areas of the city.

114. Milich, "Medicina argentina."

115. Built in an area of 72,000 square meters in Villa Ortuzar, this urban sanatorium was initially conceived for the treatment of male patients only. But in 1911, the Sanatorio Tornu became the only hospital in Buenos Aires that accepted tubercular women, and in 1925 a maternity pavilion was created, which allowed physicians to separate the newborns from their tubercular mothers. See Coni, "The Campaign against Tuberculosis," 59; and Armus, *La ciudad impura*, 331–336.

116. Occupying an area of 130,504 square meters (31,860 meters of construction and 98,644 meters of gardens) in the Chacarita neighborhood, this health complex of forty-one pavilions was organized in two geometrical restorative gardens: a triangular one for the "Asylum of the Indigents," and a rhomboidal one for the "Hospice of the Incurables." Berjman, *Plazas y parques de Buenos Aires*, 203–204.

117. Miranda and Vallejo, "La eugenesia y sus espacios," 183.

118. Sisto, preface to Feinmann, *La ciencia del niño*, v.

119. Lavrin, *Women, Feminism, and Social Change*, 110.

120. Ibid., 112.

121. The Museo Social Argentino, like the Musée social in Paris, influenced the state apparatus. The ideas debated at the heart of the Museo transcended the "un-museum" institution, materializing into public policies.

122. Rodríguez, *Civilizing Argentina*, 119.

123. Stepan, *The Hour of Eugenics*, 78.

124. Ibid.

125. Ibid., 80.

126. See Emilio Coni's description of Dispensary Rawson, a model dispensary with its own laboratory for bacteriological analysis, and of Dispensario Tornu, built at the center of Patricios Park, in his presentation at the International Tuberculosis Congress held in Paris in October 1905. Coni, "Higiene pública," 1059–1076.

127. I borrowed the expression *"loisir productif"* from Georges Vigarello. See his article "Le temps du sport" in Corbin, *L'avènement des loisirs 1850–1960*, and his book on the history of sport, *Une histoire culturelle du sport*.

128. Together with Jean-Charles Adolphe Alphand, the *ingénieur-jardinier* director of parks for the city of Paris; Eugène Belgrand, the director of the Water and Sewers Department; the horticulturist Pierre Barillet-Deschamps; and other collaborators, Haussmann sought to improve the health and morals of Parisians by laying out major public parks in the city. From 1858 to 1870, Alphand and Barillet-Deschamps completed the construction of Parc Bois de Boulogne for the western edge of Paris; and under Alphand's direction, Barillet-Deschamps and landscape architect Edouard André designed the Bois de Vincennes for the eastern edge, the Parc des Buttes-Chaumont for the north side, and the Parc Montsouris for the south, among others. Imbert, *The Modernist Garden in France*, 3.

129. Ortiz, de Paula, and Parera, *La arquitectura del liberalismo*, 32.

130. For an English version of Sarmiento's seminal book, see Domingo Sarmiento, *Facundo: Or, Civilization and Barbarism*.

131. Vernes, "Genèse et avatars du jardin publique," 4.

132. Eduardo Wilde was the director of the National Department of Hygiene during Sarmiento's government. See Wilde, quoted in Berjman, *Plazas y parques de Buenos Aires*, 41.

133. Pablo Pschepiurca, "Palermo, La Construcción del Parque," *SUMMA* Temática 3 (1983); and Pschepiurca's unpublished article "Buenos Aires: Los Parques," 5. Accessed online at http://www.asnnoise.com.ar/wp-content/uploads/los-parques-11–01.pdf.

134. Ibid.

135. Gorelik, *La grilla y el parque*, 59.

136. Ibid., 72–73. In this quote, Gorelik cited Sarmiento's own words during his speech at the inauguration of Parque Tres de Febrero in 1875. Located in the neighborhood of Palermo, this park (also known as Bosques de Palermo) is still Buenos Aires' largest park.

137. Berjman's book *Plazas y parques de Buenos Aires* is devoted to the work of these five French landscape architects.

138. Parks as "lungs for the city" was a clear metaphor about one of the social diseases—tuberculosis. As mentioned in chapter 1, many utopian texts advocated the construction of green spaces in the city of Buenos Aires, among them: Sioen's *Buenos Aires en el año 2080* (1879), Vera y González's *La estrella del sur* (1904), and Quiroule's *La ciudad anarquista americana* (1914). See also Heffes, *Políticas de la destrucción/Poéticas de la preservación*, 245–272; and López-Durán, "Utopía en práctica," 131–164.

139. Congreso Nacional, "Diario de Sesiones de 1874," 165.

140. Adolfo Bullrich, quoted in *El Diario*, September 11, 1902.

141. Ibid.

142. Patricios Park was designed by the French landscape designer Charles/Carlos Thays, a student and collaborator of Édouard André in Paris. He traveled to Argentina specifically to develop an urban park for the city of Córdoba but stayed in the country and became the director of Parks and Public Promenades for the municipality of Buenos Aires from 1891 to 1913. During these years, Thays developed innumerable public promenades and urban parks in the capital, including El Parque del Oeste, which, although never built, embodies the connection between nature, leisure, and production. To be located within the Universidad de Buenos Aires' School of Agronomy and Veterinary, the park was conceived to combine recreational areas with facilities for scientific experimentation: areas for the cultivation of indigenous and imported plants and for the exhibition of botanical collections were surrounded by examination and exhibition stalls for "fine animals" (horses, sheep, and cows) and by vaccination and research laboratories. Berjman, *Plazas y parques de Buenos Aires*, 137–140.

143. Carrasco, "Evolución de los espacios verdes," 497.

144. Since Sarmiento's time, the physician Guillermo Rawson championed little plazas, far away from the river and the city's center, "spreading out across the urban fabric that, according to him, was inexorably growing to the west of Buenos Aires." But it was Carrasco who sought "to orient, manage, and equip" the city in its expansion through the transformation of its existing parks and the creation of new ones in residential neighborhoods, all as "civic centers," as agents of "social action." Armus, *La ciudad impura*, 51.

145. In 1923, Jean-Claude Nicolas Forestier was invited by Carlos Noel, the mayor of Buenos Aires, to collaborate in the production of a modern city plan for Argentina's capital city. At the time of the Argentinean invitation, Forestier was already a global technocrat. His ideas had traveled beyond the borders of France to the French colonies by invitation of Hubert Lyautey, the governor-general of Morocco from 1912 to 1925; to Seville for the redesign of the María Luisa Park; to Barcelona to develop a system of parks, including the Montjuïc gardens and America Avenue, the main entrance to the 1929 World's Fair; and later to Havana for the development of the city's master plan. Forestier, *Grandes villes et systèmes de parcs*.

146. Forestier, "Los parques de juego o jardines de barrio."

147. Choay, Preface to *Jean Claude Nicolas Forestier*, 13.

148. Forestier, *Jardines*, 15.

149. The idea of the *cité jardin* had been popularized in France since 1903 by Georges Benoît-Lévy. See Benoît-Lévy, *La Cité jardin*.

150. Forestier, *Jardines*, 14.

151. That same year and in the same magazine, Forestier published his article "Los jardines modernos" (The modern gardens). In this article, Forestier argues for the simplicity of gardens, stating that "modern gardens must be simple, free of adornments and colors."

152. Carrasco, "La ciudad del porvenir."

153. Ibid.

154. Eugène Hénard's urban plan for Paris also included a proposal for new regenerative gardens distributed throughout the city. He was convinced that green spaces "constitute genuine sanatoriums intended to combat diseases." Hénard's parks and squares included sports facilities and other infrastructures not usually integrated into public spaces, such as playgrounds and ball courts that emphasize the value of physical education. For example, for Champ de Mars, the esplanade where the Eiffel Tower and the Galerie des Machines represented the triumph of industry and modernity at the World's Fair of 1889, Hénard visualized car racing and running tracks, tennis courts, soccer and rugby fields, and gymnasiums. Hénard, *Études sur les transformations de Paris*, 92.

155. Horne, *A Social Laboratory*, 258.

156. Ibid., 262. See also March, "Pour la race," 551–582.

157. As early as 1903, before the creation of the new section, the physician and Musée social member Albert Calmette proposed that all French cities surrounded by military fortification walls should dismantle them to transform those spaces into a green "hygienic strip," including parks, gardens, and public health facilities for the poor and working-class families. Horne, *A Social Laboratory*, 246–247. See also Cormier, "Extension, limites, espaces libres," 15.

158. On January 23, 1908, a few months after the creation of the Section of Rural and Urban Hygiene, its members created a subcommission to develop the project for open spaces in Paris, for which Eugène Hénard was named president and Forestier vice president. The part of Hénard's plan devoted to public parks and squares was officially transformed into the first mission of the Musée social's new section. Architects such as Augustin Rey and Robert de Souza also joined the "espaces libres" commission. See Cormier, "Extension, limites, espaces libres," 17.

159. Wright, *The Politics of Design*, 25.

160. Forestier, *Jardines*, 15.

161. Ibid., 14. In this book, Forestier published some of his works developed between 1912 and 1920, including a group of gardens designed for Havana in 1918.

162. Forestier was aware of these three lines of action; he attended the section's meeting on December 15, 1920, when Georges Risler, at the time president of the Section of Rural and Urban Hygiene, established these priorities. Forestier was particularly adamant about the development of the periphery and the importance of expropriating property for the construction of green spaces. Le Musée social, *Le Musée social, Annales: Revue mensuelle*, 18–19.

163. Rabinow, *French Modern*, 343.

164. Le Musée social, *Memoires et documents*, 328.

165. Novick, "Foreign Hires," 276.

166. Rabinow, *French Modern*, 268.

167. Risler, "Les Plans d'amenagement et d'extension," 304.

168. The members of the Comisión de Estética Edilicia included recognized professionals from the most important public institutions in Argentina, such as Carlos Morra, president of the Central Society of Architects, and Sebastián Ghigliazza, director of the Ministry of Public Works, as well as Forestier, whose mission was the integration and expansion of the series of urban green spaces scattered throughout the city. Novick, "Foreign Hires," 274–275.

169. The 2,500 hectares of green space represented 14 percent of the city's territory. At the time, when Forestier was working in Buenos Aires, the city's green space accounted for only 6 percent of its total territory. Berjman, *Plazas y parques de Buenos Aires*, 245.

170. Ibid., 245–246.

171. Comisión de Estética Edilicia, *Proyecto orgánico*, 163. In 1936, more than ten years later, the Concejo Deliberante decided to construct the Gran Parque del Sur, following some variants of the forest-park that Forestier had designed for this area and that were included in the *Proyecto orgánico*. This park was conceived to function like Palermo Park to the north of the city.

172. Nelson, "Las plazas de juego para niños," 241–307.

173. In 1936, the Concejo Deliberante decided to build a "physical education plaza" (*plaza de educación física*) in Parque Avellaneda, including soccer, basketball, and tennis courts; track fields; and other services considered in Forestier's project. See Concejo Deliberante de la Ciudad de Buenos Aires, Versión taquigráfica, 7a sesión ordinaria, October 6 (1936), 1719.

174. Lichtenberger, "La Lutte pour la race," 801–803.

175. In his extensive article, generously illustrated with examples from Europe and the United States, Nelson explains the relevance of this new "social typology." He states that these *plazas de juego* compensate for an important element that the compactness of the city took away from urban children—the backyard of the house with its gardens—and at the same time embody "a new ideal, the social education [that] has penetrated the very field of education." Nelson, "Las plazas de juego para niños," 286.

176. Ibid., 263.

177. The *Proyecto orgánico* also recommended the possibility of acquiring the area of Quinta Lezica, next to the Irish orphanage, and designating it as a green area. Forestier also projected the transformation of Parque Saavedra, for which he kept its original oval shape; restored the water line, the natural element that divided the park in two; and designed geometrical gardens in which he inserted tennis courts, a swimming pool with showers and lockers, and even a music pavilion. Comisión de Estética Edilicia, *Proyecto orgánico*, 163.

178. See the mentioned 1906 Forestier article "Los parques de juego o jardines de barrio en las grandes ciudades," published in *Revista Municipal* in Buenos Aires.

179. It is not a coincidence that *Proyecto orgánico* refers to ideas presented by Robert de Souza, Forestier's colleague at the Musée social, in his book *Nice, capitale d'hiver*. Souza's book was considered a notable synthesis of the Musée social's tenets of modern urban planning. Comisión de Estética Edilicia, *Proyecto orgánico*, 162.

180. Ibid., 215.

181. In his presentation in Paris, Forestier argued for considering the development of periphery areas to accommodate growth—detailing how the population of Buenos Aires grew from 177,000 inhabitants in 1869, to 1,400,000 in 1914, to 1,800,000 inhabitants in 1924. Forestier, "Quelques travaux d'urbanisation à Buenos Aires," 302–304.

182. Forestier, quoted in Comisión de Estética Edilicia, *Proyecto orgánico*, 423.

183. The creation of the Urban League was announced in "Pour la défense et la salubrité de Paris" (For the defense and health of Paris), a manifesto published in the journal *Le Temps* on March 17, 1928. Among the Urban League members were Henri Prost and Albert Tirman, Forestier's colleagues at the Musée social's Section of Urban and Rural Hygiene. The work of the Urban League was interrupted by Forestier's death in 1930, but it was revived in 1933 and reestablished in 1943 under the name Urban and Rural League for Environmental Planning of French Life (Ligue urbaine et rurale pour l'aménagment du cadre de la vie française). For an account on Forestier and the Urban League, see Chombart-Gaudin, "Forestier, président de la Ligue urbaine," 141–148.

184. Giraudoux called for the creation of a Minister of Race, and for the search for a "moral and cultural type" rather than a "physical type," like in Germany. As the British historian Julian Jackson argues in his book on the Vichy government, "Whatever this meant, it did not prevent Giraudoux . . . from asserting 'we are in full agreement with Hitler in proclaiming that a policy only achieves its highest place once it is racial.'" Giraudoux, quoted in Jackson, *France, The Dark Years*, 111–112; and in Fox Weber, *Le Corbusier: A Life*, 406–407.

185. Around the time Forestier and Giraudoux founded the Urban League, Le Corbusier and Giraudoux began to establish a close relationship. For more on Giraudoux's interest in urban planning and his collaboration with Le Corbusier, see also Eardley, "Giraudoux and the Athens Charter," 83–90; and chapter 4 in this book.

186. The Law 1420 of General Common Education (Ley 1420 de Educación Común) was a landmark law that dictated that elementary education in Argentina must be public, free, and secular. Consejo Nacional de Educación, *Cincuentenario de la Ley 1420*. This is one of the main arguments defended by Daniela Alejandra Cattaneo in her recent doctoral dissertation, "La arquitectura escolar como instrumento del Estado."

187. A couple of years later, the municipality of Buenos Aires offered land for the creation of two more schools for "weak" children, one in Parque Patricios, just between Parque Olivera (today Parque Avellaneda) and Parque Lezama, and the other one in Parque Tres de Febrero, in the affluent neighborhood of Palermo. Cassinelli, "Contribución al estudio de los niños débiles," 63.

188. Although the term "weak" was occasionally used to refer to "abnormal" children, the elites were emphatic in clarifying that "weak" children were only those whose condition could be improved. Ibid., 27–28.

189. Ibid., 59.

190. Created in 1888 by the National Council of Education, the Cuerpo Médico Escolar was responsible for the individual diagnosis of the student that should be transferred to the new schools of "weak" children, in addition to its regular functions of performing medical examination of students and inspection and disinfection of school facilities. See "Cuerpo Médico Escolar" (1888), 635–636; and "Cuerpo Médico Escolar" (1919), 235.

191. Champagne, "The Children of the Parque Lezama," 1033–1039.

192. Ibid., 1036–1037.

193. Cassinelli, "Contribución al estudio de los niños débiles," 67.

194. Champagne, "The Children of the Parque Lezama," 1037; emphasis mine.

195. Alfred Binet, quoted in Cassinelli, "Contribución al estudio de los niños débiles," 143.

196. Ibid., 140–143.

197. Ibid., 62.

198. The architecture historian Gina Marie Greene developed this argument in her PhD dissertation, "Children in Glass Houses," 34.

199. As Greene argues, the open-air schools had a very ambitious goal: to become therapeutic agents of rehabilitation for children's bodies and to reinvigorate the hereditary health of the "French race." Ibid., 39. See Châtelet, Lerch, and Noël, *L'école de plein air*.

200. "L'école de plein air est l'école de régénération." Petit, "L'Alliance et les Écoles de plein air," 45.

201. Rey, "L'École de l'avenir," 103–115.

202. Ibid., 105.

203. Greene, "Children in Glass Houses," 172.

204. As Beatriz Colomina argued, "Modern architecture was unproblematically understood as a kind of medical equipment, a mechanism for protecting and enhancing the body." Colomina, "The Medical Body in Architecture," 230.

205. In April of 1917, in an open letter addressed to Dr. Angel Gallardo, director of the National Council of Education, Emilio Coni claimed he had been the first to promote the open-air schools in Argentina, in the journal of the Argentine Anti-Tuberculosis League, *Alianza de Higiene Social*. In 1921, in an article on the importance of the open-air schools, Coni celebrates that "the publicity made by this journal produced good results because just a few years later the National Council of Education, under the presidency of Dr. José M. Ramos Mejía, decided to build two schools for weak children, one in Parque Lezama and the other in Parque Avellaneda." See Coni, "Campaña sanitaria escolar," 3–10; and "Escuelas al aire libre y al sol," 147.

206. In 1907, Coni also established the Argentine Society for Moral and Sanitary Prophylaxis, which created dispensaries for the control of venereal diseases and prostitution linked to antituberculosis facilities. Rodríguez, *Civilizing Argentina*, 180.

207. See, for example, Anonymous, "Sobre escuelas para niños débiles"; Corvalán Mendilaharsu, "La escuela argentina"; Ayres, "Escuelas al aire libre en Estados Unidos"; Soria, *En el surco*; Vignati, "Informe de la Colonia de Vacaciones para niños débiles del Parque Avellaneda"; Tonina, "Funciones de las escuelas al aire libre."

208. Coni, "Inspección higiénica y médica de las escuelas," 166.

209. Coni, "Escuelas al aire libre y al sol," 147–148.

210. Resolutions of the Second International Congress of Open-Air Schools, published anonymously under the title "Las escuelas al aire libre," 266.

211. Carrasco, "El urbanismo contemporáneo," 315. According to Frank G. Carpenter, a traveler in Buenos Aires in 1923, *conventillos* "were immense buildings of one or two stories set up along narrow passages or around small courts [with] scores upon scores of tiny one-room homes . . . A [single] room may be the dwelling-place of one or more families . . . There are no means of heating in such dwellings, which look more like caves than homes of twentieth-century human beings." [There were] "swarms of children of all ages and sizes." Carpenter, quoted in Crider, "Modernization and Human Welfare," 13.

212. Carrasco, quoting the French architect and Musée social member Donat-Alfred Agache, emphasizes the social character of urbanism. Carrasco said that urbanism was fundamentally a "social science" that requires "a methodological study of human geography and urban topography." Carrasco, "El urbanismo contemporáneo," 315.

213. Cattaneo, "La arquitectura escolar como instrumento del Estado," 68.

214. Law 1420 of General Common Education (Ley 1420 de Educación Común) was passed in 1884 during the presidency of Julio Argentino Roca. See Consejo Nacional de Educación, *Cincuentenario de la Ley 1420*.

215. Cattaneo, "La arquitectura escolar como instrumento del Estado," 68.

216. Ibid.

217. Consejo Nacional de Educación, *Cincuentenario de la Ley 1420*, 3:89.

218. Consejo Nacional de Educación, "Conceptos sobre edificación escolar," 62. In 1932, this same council commissioned the General Directorate of Architecture to develop an ambitious plan to build fifty-three schools in Buenos Aires alone, including open-air schools and gymnasiums. See Cattaneo, "La arquitectura escolar como instrumento del Estado," 79.

219. Fournié, "Escuelas y obras al aire libre," 67.

220. Ibid., 131.

221. As early as 1907, the influential Argentine physician and positivist José Ingenieros argued that the Colonia de Vacaciones was for children at risk from tuberculosis or defective children, not for healthy ones; its mission, Ingenieros argued, "was medico-pedagogical rather than recreational." Ingenieros, "Las colonias de vacaciones," 118–119.

222. Madrid Páez, *Sociedad de Beneficiencia de la Capital*. See also Silvia di Liscia, "Colonias y escuelas de niños débiles."

223. Leopoldo Lugones, quoted in García, "Colonias y escuelas de niños débiles," 180.

224. For instance, in his compelling book *Invention of Hysteria*, Georges Didi-Huberman shows how hysteria—a psychological disorder formerly regarded as a disease specific to women—was actually invented by the neurologist Jean-Martin Charcot within the confines of the Salpêtrière hospital in Paris, to keep women regarded as a threat to society out of circulation. Didi-Huberman exposes how photography was instrumentalized as a means to trigger, document, and therefore prove the reality of hysteria. In order to be photographed, women at Salpêtrière were required to perform their "hysterical nature." But these famous photographs do not show how women were stimulated to perform, how through hypnosis, electroshock, and other mechanical operations, including genital manipulation, they made visible the symptoms, thereby confirming Charcot's diagnosis. As Didi-Huberman explains: "The bribe went something like this: either you seduce me (showing yourself in this way to be hysterical), or else I will consider you to be an incurable, and then you will no longer be exhibited but hidden away, forever, in the dark." See Didi-Huberman, *Invention of Hysteria*, 30.

225. In his influential work on French prostitution, Alain Corbin argues that it was precisely to canalize "extramarital sexuality" that the regulation of prostitution was institutionalized. See the "Regulationist Argument," in Corbin, *Women for Hire*, 3–29; 341–349.

226. Corbin, "Commercial Sexuality in Nineteenth-Century France,"

209–219. See also "La tuberculosis en femenino" in Armus, *La ciudad impura*, 107–132.

227. This was "a building with a modest architectonic plan: . . . an inscription hall, a waiting and distribution hall, a cabinet for examination, a consultation room, [another] cabinet for examination, a laboratory (micrographic service), the offices of the director and the secretary, office of statistics, sterilization room, changing room, a kitchen, a latrine, and a dark room." Penna and Madero, *La administración sanitaria*, 390–391.

228. Corbin, *Women for Hire*, 9–18.

229. Ibid., 127.

230. Guy, *White Slavery and Mothers Alive and Dead*, 126. See also chapter 19, "Profilaxis de la sífilis y enfermedades venéreas," in Penna and Madero, *La administración sanitaria*, 384–394.

231. Of course, men were never the object of the reform. In *Sex and Danger*, Donna J. Guy insistently showed us how, despite the evidence of male prostitution as well as men as a "source of contamination" to healthy prostitutes, they were never regulated.

232. Penna and Madero, *La administración sanitaria*, 390.

233. Ibid.

234. There is no information about the use of the dark room, but it is well know that in some manifestations of syphilis, such as syphilitic retinitis, patients required confinement in dark rooms to protect their eyes from bright light. Ibid., 390–391.

235. Ibid.

236. Since it was believed that prostitutes were a main source not only of national infection and degeneration but also of moral degradation, zones of tolerance were demarcated to prevent prostitution in other public spaces. The ordinance of 1908 established neighborhoods of total exclusion in which bordellos were prohibited. Guy, *Sex and Danger*, 82–83.

237. Guy, *White Slavery*, 126–127.

238. Ibid.

239. Rodríguez, *Civilizing Argentina*, 97.

240. Donzelot, *The Policing of Families*, 48–95.

241. "The separation of grown-ups and children, the polarity established between the parents' bedroom and that of the children (it became routine in the course of the century when working-class housing construction was undertaken), the relative segregation of boys and girls, the strict instructions as to the care of nursing infants (maternal breast-feeding, hygiene), the attention focused on infantile sexuality, the supposed dangers of masturbation, the importance attached to puberty, the methods of surveillance suggested to parents, the exhortations, secrets, and fears, the presence—both valued and feared—of servants: all this made the family, even when brought down to its smallest dimensions, a complicated network saturated with multiple, fragmentary, and mobile sexualities." Foucault, *The History of Sexuality*, 46.

242. See Della Paolera in Della Paolera, Tello, et al., "Congreso Argentino de la Habitación," 412.

243. See Tello in Della Paolera, Tello, et al., "Congreso Argentino de la Habitación," 529.

244. A few years later, this same position was voiced by Georges Risler, the president of the Musée social in France: "Without healthy homes there are no healthy families; without healthy families there cannot be a healthy nation." Risler, "L'hygiène de la maison," 226.

245. Foucault, *The History of Sexuality*, 118.

246. Ballent and Liernur, *La casa y la multitud*, 24–25. The National Council of Low-Cost Houses was created by the Argentine state during the last year of Victorino de la Plaza's government, which ended a forty-two-year period (1874–1916) of the conservative National Autonomist Party (Partido Autonomista Nacional; PAN) being in power. This council's aim was to resolve the lack of housing for the poor and working classes and the inappropriate conditions in which these sectors of the population were living. With the passage of Law 9677 of 1915 and with the initial authorization for building low-cost houses in the city of Buenos Aires only, this organization operated from 1915 to 1944, building 972 units in the capital city. For more on the National Council of Low-Cost Houses, see Liernur, "El rol inicial del Estado," 195–213.

247. Ballent and Liernur, *La casa y la multitud*, 33.

248. Ibid., 34.

249. Vezzetti, "'Viva Cien Años,'" 5–10. Among the supporting institutions of *Viva Cien Años* were the National Department of Hygiene, the municipal Department of Public Welfare, the Argentinean League of Mental Hygiene, and the Museo Social Argentino.

250. Ibid., 5.

251. Miranda and Vallejo, "La eugenesia y sus espacios," 183. On December 6, 1934, at the Honorable Concejo Deliberante, Jorge Kálnay began the talk that he would deliver a year later at the First Argentine Congress of Urbanism with the following words: "Each construction presents the endless problem of the relationship between man and space. The principal factor of this problem is not the construction itself but man, who [through architecture] has fought one of the toughest battles to affirm his position vis-à-vis nature, space, and the universe." Kálnay, "Zoning y reglamento funcional," 2:95.

252. Ibid., 2:97.

253. Ibid.

254. Ibid., 2:102. The Primer Congreso Argentino de Urbanismo was held in Buenos Aires, from October 11 to 19, 1935. This was a significant event, and President Agustín Pedro Justo, three governors, the mayor of Buenos Aires, and many representatives of the parliament and other public and private organizations attended the opening session. It was sponsored by various organizations, including the Sociedad Central de Arquitectos and Los Amigos de la Ciudad, under the leadership of the Museo Social Argentino. The conference was accompanied by an exhibition on urbanism in which Kálnay's stand presenting his ideas on zoning and green spaces was awarded first prize. For more on the Primer Congreso de Urbanismo, see Anonymous, "En breve se realizará en Buenos Aires el Primer Congreso Nacional de Urbanismo, *Revista de Architectura* 146 (1933): 77–78; and, for more on Kálnay, see Liernur, "Fragmentos de un debate tipológico y urbanístico en la obra de Jorge Kálnay," 405–406.

255. In Argentina, Wladimiro Acosta's Helios System constitutes a paradigmatic example. See Acosta, *Vivienda y clima.*

256. Primer Congreso Argentino de la Población, 1ra Parte, *Boletín del Museo Social Argentino* 28 (1940): 371–385. Jorge Kálnay also participated at the First Argentine Congress on Population, representing the organization Amigos de la Ciudad (Friends of the City).

257. The very first section of the congress, titled Birth, Marriage, Morbidity, and Mortality, was devoted to issues of puericulture and hominiculture, including a presentation titled "Eugenic Marriage" by Enrique Díaz de Guijarro. The sections were: Section I, Birth, Marriage, Morbidity and Mortality; Section II, Racial Problems; Section III, Culture and Population; Section IV, Agrarian Regime and Population; Section V, Urbanism; and Section VI, Migratory Movements and Immigration Politics.

258. Stepan, *The Hour of Eugenics*, 103.

259. Carlos Bernaldo de Quirós emphasized the importance of legal statutes to assist and protect women, highlighting the Estatuto de la Mujer Argentina of 1937, which, according to him, "would guarantee the constitution of the national type, the perfection of future generations, and the welfare of maternity and childhood." Bernaldo de Quirós, *Inquietudes al margen de mi lucha*, 121.

260. Primer Congreso Argentino de la Población, 2da. Parte, 71–73.

261. Ibid., 173–174. Pinard had already started this campaign within medical circles at the Academy of Medicine in Paris when he presented a 1900 book by the poet Henri Cazalis, titled *Science et marriage*, hoping that this book would become a marriage manual "in the hands of everyone." The book called for a mandatory medical examination before marriage in order to prevent the transmission of social diseases. Schneider, *Quality and Quantity*, 51.

262. Vezzetti, "'Viva Cien Años,'" 5.

263. It is curious that the designer commissioned by the French National Office of Social Hygiene to design the campaign poster was Leo Fontan, one of the illustrators of popular magazines such as *La vie parisienne*, *Le Sourire*, and *Fantasio*, who also followed Toulouse Lautrec in the design of posters for celebrated divas and shows at the Folies Bergère in Paris. I found a copy of this poster at the Archives Départemental des Bouches-du-Rhône, Marseille-France, Box 5M210, Propagande anti-syphilitique 1923–1936.

CHAPTER 4

1. According to the website of the Fondation Le Corbusier, just in the last five years, 181 books have been published and dozens of exhibitions about his work have been organized worldwide, including the magnificent blockbuster exhibition curated by Jean-Louis Cohen and organized by MOMA in New York in 2013.

2. To my knowledge, while I was writing and researching this book there was one exception: Nicholas Fox Weber's biography *Le Corbusier: A Life*, in which he includes references to Le Corbusier's relationship with the French eugenicist Alexis Carrel and other technocrats collaborating with the Vichy regime. See Fox Weber, *Le Corbusier: A Life*. More recently, when this book was about to go to press, three general-audience books on Le Corbusier's right-wing politics and his collaboration with the Vichy regime opened a controversial debate. This controversy was fueled in Paris by an exhibition on Le Corbusier at the Centre Georges Pompidou, which, though titled *Le Corbusier: Mesures de l'homme*, failed to acknowledge how this ideology in fact infiltrated his architectural work and theories. The three books are Xavier de Jarcy, *Le Corbusier: Un fascisme français*; Marc Perelman, *Le Corbusier, une froide vision du monde*; and François Chaslin, *Un Corbusier*.

3. After puericulture took its official form at the French Eugenics Society in 1912, the lovable goal of producing healthy children was tainted by the racial prejudice that characterized mainstream eugenics. Schneider, *Quality and Quantity*, 83.

4. Le Corbusier, *The Radiant City*, 115. In the original version in French, Le Corbusier uses the term *puériculture*, later translated as "scientific child-rearing." The original quote reads: "sont confiées à des infirmières spécialisées surveillées par des médecins: sécurité-sélection-puériculture."

5. Le Corbusier, "Aménagement d'une journée équilibrée," unpublished article, dated May 1932, FLC UE-5, 64–139.

6. In his 1945 book, *Les Trois établissements humains*, Le Corbusier argues that "l'eugénisme, la puériculture, assurant l'élevage d'une race." Le Corbusier, *Les Trois établissements humains*, 116.

7. Understood as a "self-reproducing force," transmitted from generation to generation and dragging the individual body and society down to decay and final extinction, degeneration, as described in chapters 2 and 3, became the largest fear haunting French society at the turn of the twentieth century. Pick, *Faces of Degeneration*, 21.

8. *L'Esprit nouveau: Revue internationale illustrée de l'activité contemporaine* published twenty-eight issues between 1920 and 1925, covering the European cultural scene and new discoveries in the fields of medicine, physics, psychology, and psychoanalysis.

9. Le Corbusier, letter to his friend and mentor William Ritter, dated July 5, 1911. See Fox Weber, *Le Corbusier: A Life*, 177–178.

10. Ibid.

11. The L'Esprit Nouveau Pavilion is a reproduction of a cell of the *immeuble-villas*, the 1922 multifamily housing project presented at the Salon d'Automne with its assembly of two hundred living cells, each with a narrow space open at both ends, a two-story living room, and its own garden. These cells, conceived as "Citröhan" houses, were modest living spaces that, according to Le Corbusier, could be as inexpensive as the Citroën automobile. The name, in fact, brings together the idea of mass production and Le Corbusier's conception of the house as a "machine for living." The L'Esprit Nouveau Pavilion also included a terraced garden and a diorama to present two of his urban projects: his Contemporary City for Three Million Inhabitants of 1922, and his Plan Voisin for the center of Paris of 1925, funded by the automobile and aircraft industrialist Gabriel Voisin.

12. In an interview originally published in 1977 in the *Annales historiques de la Révolution française*, Michel Foucault argues that "to analyze 'regimes of practices' means to analyze programs of conduct that have both prescriptive effects regarding what is to be done (effects of 'jurisdiction') and socializing effects regarding what is to be known (effects of 'veridiction'). So I was aiming to write a history, not of the prison as an institution but of the practice of imprisonment." Foucault, "Questions of Method," 103. I borrow the term "normatize" from Jonathan Turner. See Turner, "Analytical Theorizing," 156–194.

13. Foucault, *Discipline and Punishment*, 184.

14. Teyssot, *A Topology of Everyday Constellations*, 2–5. See also Agamben, *What Is an Apparatus?*, 1–24.

15. As Elizabeth Stephens observes, the word "normal" first appears in the Oxford English Dictionary in 1848, but as a concept it only appears at the very end of the nineteenth century in the theory of "normal distribution" in statistics, which is attributed to Galton. Stephens, "Normal," 141–145.

16. It is interesting to note that "synthesis," a key concept for Le Corbusier, appears in the introduction to the first issue of *L'Esprit nouveau*. It evokes the concept of a "total work of art," or *Gesamtkunstwerk*, seeing painting, sculpture, and other artistic expressions within the domain of architecture; but most importantly, it points to the intersection of modernization and governmentality. As Nicola Pezolet argues in his study of French modernism, the *synthesis of the arts* is part of a universalizing discourse "linked to modernist art and to the nascent welfare state notion of public space and its correlative rhetoric of beauty, hygiene, functionality and accessibility." Pezolet, "Spectacles Plastiques," 44; von Moos, *Le Corbusier*, 265.

17. In 1927, Le Corbusier said that these four volumes "were the theory of which the Pavilion ought to be the materialization." Le Corbusier, "Du Pavillon de L'Esprit Nouveau" in *Almanach d'architecture moderne*, 150. See Boyer, *Le Corbusier, Homme de Lettres*, 360. For more information on the International Exhibition of Modern Industrial and Decorative Arts, see Sutcliffe, *Paris: An Architectural History*.

18. Le Corbusier, *The Decorative Art of Today*, 72–79.

19. Hermann Muthesius was a German architect, architectural historian, and theorist who, in 1907, founded the Deutscher Werkbund, an influential movement that simultaneously embraced craft and industry as a means to fulfill the needs of modern society, as opposed to the English Arts and Crafts movement that rejected machine production. Muthesius, quoted in Kruft, *History of Architectural Theory*, 371. See also Muthesius, "Die Werkbund-Arbeit der Zukunft," 32–49.

20. Le Corbusier, *The Decorative Art of Today*, 79.

21. Ibid., 72.

22. Ibid., 72–73.

23. Teyssot, "Norm and Type," 141–142.

24. Muthesius, quoted in Kruft, *History of Architectural Theory*, 371.

25. "La vie est l'ensemble des fonctions qui résistent à la mort." Bichat, *Recherches physiologiques sur la vie et la mort*, quoted in Canguilhem, *Knowledge of Life*, 104.

26. Lee, "Modern Architecture and the Ideology of Influence," 13–14.

27. Geroulanos and Meyers, "Introduction," 10.

28. Lamarck, "The Influences of Circumstances"; Darwin, *On the Origin of Species*; Spencer, *Principles of Biology*.

29. "Ornament and Crime" was the title used by Adolf Loos to present a series of lectures, which he retrospectively dated to 1908. The first publication of "Ornament and Crime" is unknown, but lectures with this title were mentioned for the first time in *Fremden Blatt* in January 22, 1910. French translations were published in *Cahiers d'aujourd'hui* in June 1913, and in Le Corbusier's own magazine, *L'Esprit nouveau*, in November 1920. For an English version, see Loos, *Ornament and Crime*. See also Canales and Herscher, "Criminal Skins," 235–256.

30. Cogdell, *Eugenic Design*, 12. As Cogdell observes, Haeckel's recapitulation theory, which was based on Lamarck's theory of the "inheritance of acquired characteristics," was foundational for Loos' essay "Ornament and Crime."

31. Cogdell, *Eugenic Design*, 13–14. Moreover, in 1924, when Loos was asked if ornamentation should be eliminated from the art school curriculum, he replied: "Ornament will disappear of its own accord, and school should not interfere in this natural process, which humanity has been going through ever since it came into existence." Tying ornamentation to the primitive and also the feminine, Loos further states: "In the final analysis, women's ornament goes back to the savage," and that "the lower the cultural level, the greater the degree of ornamentation." See Loos' articles "Ladies' Fashion (1898–1902)" and "Ornament and Education (1924)" in *Ornament and Crime*.

32. Le Corbusier, *The Decorative Art of Today*, 96. Both Loos and Le Corbusier assigned ornamentation a low rung on the evolutionary ladder.

33. Forestier, "Les jardins à l'exposition des arts décoratifs," quoted in Imbert, *The Modernist Garden*, 40.

34. Ibid. The master plan for the 1925 International Exhibition of Modern Industrial and Decorative Arts was implemented by the architect and decorator Charles Plumet and by the Musée social member Louis Bonnier, the same architect who designed Élisée Reclus' Great Globe for the 1900 World's Fair—the monument that represented the inevitable interaction between milieu and heredity, described in the opening of this book. The supervisor of the garden section at the 1925 exhibition was Forestier, also a member of the Musée social, whose participation in the modernization of Buenos Aires is examined in chapter 3.

35. "Le Corbusier opposed the sophistication of the pavilion with only a lame image of nature. The shrubs and sparse flowers were scattered irregularly on the lawn; their configuration did not compete with the elevation of the cell. Rather than extending the plan of the unit to the site, Le Corbusier instead brought the garden inside." Imbert, *The Modernist Garden*, 35.

36. The International Exhibition of Modern Industrial and Decorative Arts closed in October 1925, and in December, Forestier arrived for the first time in Havana. Invited by the recently elected president Gerardo Machado (1925–1933) to transform the still-colonial city of Havana into a modern Antillean metropolis, Forestier assembled a binational working team. The comprehensive urban plan for the modernization of Cuba's capital, the *Plano del Proyecto de La Habana*, was assumed by five young architects from France, Eugene E. Beaudoin, Jean Labatut, Louis Heitzler, Theo Levau, and the landscape architect Jeanne Sorugue; and by an interdisciplinary group of Cuban architects, artists, and engineers, Emilio Vasconcelos, Raúl Hermida, Raúl Otero, J. I. del Alamo, Manuel Vega, and Diego Guevara. Although Forestier's plan for Havana was disrupted by the Great Depression of 1929 and the revolution of 1933, which took Machado out of power and paved the way for Fulgencio Batista's 1935 coup d'état, it created the unique urban character that Havana is still known for today. On Forestier's plan for Havana, see Leclerc, *Jean-Claude-Nicolas Forestier*, and Coyula, Scarpaci, and Segre, *Havana: Two Faces of the Antillean Metropolis*.

37. Hyde, *Constitutional Modernism*, 121.

38. According to historical accounts, the original ceiba tree planted in today's Habana Vieja, the historical colonial center of the city, was the site of the first Mass and the first *cabildo* (administrative council of the city); and the ceiba tree planted at the Plaza de la Fraternidad was grown from a seed planted in 1902 during a ceremony to inaugurate the new republic—recalling both the foundation of the city and the foundation of the republic.

39. In his book *La picota en América*, Bernaldo de Quirós revealed that the first old tree, replaced in 1828 by a neoclassical pavilion to commemorate the spot, also served as a *picota*—the infamous post placed in the main plazas of towns for punishment. In step with Quirós, in his fascinating book on modern architecture and civil society in prerevolutionary Cuba, Timothy Hyde argues that the Árbol de la Fraternidad Americana carries a distilled significance, associated not only with its symbolic lineage but also with the civil authority of the law. Hyde, *Constitutional Modernism*, 111–112. See also Bernaldo de Quirós, *La picota en América*.

40. Boyer, *Le Corbusier, Homme de Lettres*, 457. See also Martin, "Remembering the Jungle," 310–325.

41. In the first pages of his 1935 book *La Ville Radieuse*, Le Corbusier argues for the "rebirth of the human body." For an English translation, see Le Corbusier, *The Radiant City*, 7.

42. Le Corbusier, Notes and Sketch (n/d), Fondation Le Corbusier, document F2–17, No. 275.

43. Alexis Carrel's 1935 book was simultaneously published in French with the title *L'Homme cet inconnu* by Plon in Paris, and in English with the title *Man, the Unknown* by the American publisher Harper and Brothers, who also sold the rights to publish condensed chapters of the book in the popular American magazine *Reader's Digest* (which, by the mid-1930s, had a circulation of over 1.5 million copies), contributing to the commercial success of the book. Before the end of the 1930s, Carrel's book was translated into fourteen languages, and by 1940, Harper and Brothers had sold 50,000 copies, and Plon, 168,000. In *Man, the Unknown*, Carrel explicitly defends the elimination of defectives and criminals, and even recommends the use of gas chambers to accomplish this goal. See Reggiani, "Alexis Carrel, the Unknown," 331–356; and Carrel, *Man, the Unknown*.

44. As mentioned in chapter 2, Rio de Janeiro was moved from the base of the Pão de Açúcar mountain in Urca to a new site on the top of a hill on the coast of Guanabara Bay in 1567. This hill, called Morro do Castelo, was recognized from that moment on as Rio de Janeiro's original urban setting. However, in 1920, alleging hygienic and eugenic reasons, the mountain was demolished, its inhabitants expelled, and 815,000 square meters of flat land—the result of the demolition of the mountain and the new esplanade landfill reclaimed from the sea—was occupied first by neocolonial pavilions (at the time emblems of the modern nation) and then by modern buildings, including the Ministry of Health and Education, for which Le Corbusier was the principal consultant.

45. Agache, *A cidade do Rio de Janeiro*.

46. Getúlio Vargas' first regime lasted from 1930, the year of the coup d'état that marked the end of the First Republic (1889–1930), to 1945, when a bloodless coup took Vargas out of power. Following the corporatist authoritarian regime installed in Portugal in 1933 called Estado Novo, on November 10, 1937, Vargas announced the Brazilian Estado Novo, the authoritarian-nationalist New State that abolished the forthcoming 1938 presidential elections, dissolved the congress, and built its power on the state's use of violence to suppress any supposed threat to the nation. In 1951, Vargas came back to power, as a democratically elected president, and governed his country until his suicide in 1954. For more on Getúlio Vargas' first regime and its struggles over art, architecture, and culture, see the fascinating book by Daryle Williams, *Culture Wars in Brazil*.

47. Costa, "O arranha-céu e o Rio de Janeiro."

48. Although Costa did not closely collaborate with eugenicists in Brazil, he contributed to the internalization of the eugenics ideology that fueled modernization in Brazil.

49. The titles of the six lectures were: "La révolution architecturale accomplie apporte la solution à l'urbanisation des villes"; "La dénaturalisation du phénomène urbain"; "Les loisirs: Occupations véritable de la civilisation machiniste"; "Le logis considéré comme prolongement des services publics"; "Les Temps Nouveaux et la vocation de l'architecte"; and "L'autorité n'est pas renseignée." In his opening remarks, Le Corbusier briefly described each lecture. Le Corbusier, Manuscript Lecture I, "La civilisation machiniste" (July 31, 1936), Rio de Janeiro, FLC F2–17, 2–3.

50. Ibid., 1–2.

51. Ibid., 1.

52. Ibid.

53. Le Corbusier, "L'autorité devant les tâches contemporaines," 22–23.

54. Ibid.; emphasis mine.

55. Ibid.

56. Ibid.

57. Ibid.

58. Le Corbusier, *The Radiant City*, 5.

59. Christine Boyer argues that "the tree epitomizes the radiant city," it is the "ruling sign of the entire book." Boyer, *Le Corbusier, Homme de Lettres*, 504–506.

60. Le Corbusier has given this title, *Urbanisme totale*, to one of the two sections of *The Radiant City*'s conclusion, and to an unpublished essay written in January 1935. Le Corbusier, Manuscript Lecture I, 2–3.

61. Ibid.

62. Ibid., 4.

63. Here we see how Le Corbusier's words and images were an echo of the language of Carrel's book, which Le Corbusier was reading in Rio at the time of his talks. Le Corbusier owned Carrel's bestseller and read it during the summer of 1936. The following note appears, in Le Corbusier's handwriting, on the first page of his own copy of Carrel's book, held at the Fondation Le Corbusier: "Eté 1936, Rio + Le Piquey" (Summer 1936, Rio + Le Piquey). Carrel, *Man, the Unknown*, 3.

64. In *The Radiant City*, in a section titled "The Biological Unit," Le Corbusier declares that the conception of a living cell—a 14-square-meter human unit—is the very justification for his studies. Announcing that one day people will understand that "only architecture and city planning can provide [society] the exact prescription for its ills," Le Corbusier visualizes a new form of living in "a magnificently disciplined machine" capable of producing "a serene soul in a healthy body." Le Corbusier, *The Radiant City*, 143.

65. Le Corbusier, Manuscript Lecture I, 5.

66. Carrel, introduction to the 1939 edition of *Man, the Unknown*, accessed July 19, 2014, http://archive.org/details/TheManTheUnknownByNobelPrizeWinnerDr.AlexisCarrel.

67. Ibid. In the early 1930s, when Carrel was still working as a scientist at the Rockefeller Institute for Medical Research, the president of the Rockefeller Foundation Warren Weaver reconfigured the trajectory of Rockefeller-sponsored research under a single initiative called The Science of Man. Asking "Why do we seem to know so much more about atoms than we do about men?," Warren began to steer the foundation toward support for research into "bodily processes, including metabolism, genetics, disease, viruses, and cellular development." The urge to change the human from the ground up was what tied Carrel and the Rockefeller Foundation together, but it was in the understanding of this science of man as a comprehensive science and in his reliance on neo-Lamarckian ideas that Le Corbusier found alignment with Carrel. Carrel worked at the Rockefeller Institute from 1906 to 1939. Anonymous, "Molecular Biology," accessed January 11, 2017, http://www.rockefeller100.org/exhibits/show/natural_sciences/molecular-biology.

68. Winter, "Pour une science de l'homme," 37–42.

69. Carrel, *Man, the Unknown*, 2.

70. Ibid., 43.

71. Ibid., 43–44.

72. In this instance, I refer to the tree metaphor elaborated upon in Le Corbusier, "L'autorité devant les tâches contemporaines," 22–23.

73. Carrel, quoted in Drouard, *Une inconnue des sciences sociales*, 82. The term *genre de vie* refers to the human capacity to make life choices.

74. In his article "What Is America's Problem?," written while returning home from New York in December of 1935, Le Corbusier used the term "psycho-physiological" in pointing to the two interrelated models that he had brought together in *The Radiant City*: "the functional-rational" and "the biological." For Le Corbusier, these two models would foster a more "human-centered second machine age." Le Corbusier's "What Is America's Problem?" was first published in *American Architect* 148 (1936): 17–22. See also Bacon, *Le Corbusier in America*, 141.

75. Le Corbusier used a similar expression when in "What Is America's Problem?" he demands a human dwelling, a "radiant dwelling" that will combine "all the benefits of progress, of organization and of a plan designed in terms of the most profound needs of human nature, sun, sky, space, and trees—essential joys." Le Corbusier, "What Is America's Problem?," in *When the Cathedrals Were White*, 201.

76. Le Corbusier, Manuscript Lecture I, 7.

77. Le Corbusier, "What Is America's Problem?," 201.

78. Le Corbusier, Manuscript Lecture I, 7.

79. Ibid.

80. As Paula Young Lee explained: "The influence of the natural environment might be thwarted by the intervention of architecture, which would do the same job in its place." Lee, "Modern Architecture and the Ideology of Influence," 9.

81. Le Corbusier, Manuscript Lecture I, 14.

82. Carrel, *Man, the Unknown*, 1–29.

83. Le Corbusier, Manuscript Lecture II, "La dénaturalisation du phénomène urbain" (August 5, 1936), Rio de Janeiro, FLC C3–18; published in Tsiomis, *Conférences de Rio*, 69–95.

84. Ibid.

85. The Front Populaire was an alliance of left-wing movements that won the May 1936 legislative elections, which led to the leftist government of André Léon Blum and its socialist policies.

86. Le Corbusier' notes for the prologue of his Rio Talks, Manuscript FLC F2–17, published in Tsiomis, *Conférences de Rio*, 66–68.

87. Le Corbusier, Manuscript Lecture I, 6.

88. Carrel, *Man, the Unknown*, 222.

89. Le Corbusier, *The Radiant City*, 64.

90. Le Corbusier, Manuscript Lecture III, "Les loisirs considérés comme occupation véritable de la civilisation machiniste" (August 7, 1936), Rio de Janeiro, FLC C3–18; published in Tsiomis, *Conférences de Rio*, 96–117.

91. Ibid.

92. McLeod, *Urbanism and Utopia*, 248.

93. Udovicki-Selb, "Le Corbusier and the Paris Exhibition of 1937," 51–52.

94. McLeod, *Urbanism and Utopia*, 248.

95. Le Corbusier, Manuscript Lecture III, published in Tsiomis, *Conférences de Rio*, 96–117.

96. In the early 1930s, François de Pierrefeu and Le Corbusier were actively involved in the neo-syndicalist movement. Both were members of the editorial boards of *Plans*, *Prélude*, and *L'Homme réel*. During the 1930s, de Pierrefeu also became a technical and economic adviser to Le Corbusier on his plans for Algiers and Nemours (today Ghazaouet) in Algeria. In the early 1940s, de Pierrefeu joined Le Corbusier in his efforts to find a commission in the Vichy regime, to materialize his urban plans in North Africa, and to produce *The Home of Man*, the book Le Corbusier would present to his mother and brother as "a brief and brilliant revelation of a doctrine." Le Corbusier, letter to his mother, Marie-Charlotte Jeanneret Perret, and to his brother, Albert Jeanneret, dated June 2, 1941, Vichy; published in Baudouï and Dercelles, *Le Corbusier Correspondance*, 768–770.

97. Alexis Carrel, letter to Le Corbusier, dated August 31, 1937, FLC E1–12, Dossiers Nominatifs, 4 pages.

98. Jean Giraudoux, quoted in McLeod, *Urbanism and Utopia*, 380.

99. Giraudoux and Le Corbusier collaborated on several projects: In 1933, Giraudoux wrote the introduction to Le Corbusier's *Athens Charter*, CIAM's most famous manifesto, which was a very influential document on urban planning after World War II; in 1939, invited by the office of the Marshal Pétain, both participated on the Vichy Committee for the Study of Habitation and Urbanism. Their other collaborators were none other than Gaston Bergery, a left-wing dissident who in 1940 had published a pro-fascist declaration calling "for collaboration with Germany, and the organization of a new authoritarian order in France," and Alexis Carrel, the French eugenicist—Le Corbusier's champion at the time. Fox Weber, *Le Corbusier: A Life*, 447–449. For more on Giraudoux's interest in urban planning and his collaboration with Le Corbusier, see also Eardley, "Giraudoux and The Athens Charter," 83–90.

100. Carrel, *Man, the Unknown*, 222.

101. Le Corbusier, letter to his mother and brother, dated December 18, 1939, Vézelay; published in Baudouï and Decelles, *Le Corbusier Correspondance*, 641–644.

102. Le Corbusier, letter to his mother and brother, dated October 14, 1939, Vézelay, FLC R2-I-160.

103. Ibid. Giraudoux, the president of the Comité d'Études Préparatoires d'Urbanisme, considered France an "invaded country." Although, he prioritized moral and cultural qualities over physical ones, he manifested his agreement with Hitler "in proclaiming that a policy only achieves its highest place once it is racial." Giraudoux, quoted in Fox Weber, *Le Corbusier: A Life*, 407.

104. In a 1942 unpublished article slated to present *The Home of Man* in *Comodeia*—a French popular journal co-opted by the Vichy regime into a vehicle of Nazi propaganda—Le Corbusier presented the tree drawing for the first time. Le Corbusier, "Architecture et urbanisme: La Maison des hommes" (text manuscript and dactilograph written for *Comodeia* in August 1942), FLC B3–3/615 g 630, Paris. This article was unpublished until 1985, when the text was included by Giuliano Gresleri in his introduction to the first Italian edition of Le Corbusier's book *La Maison des hommes*. See Gresleri, introduction to *La casa degli uomini*, 22–24.

105. I am thankful to Marilyn Levine for introducing me to this connection. See also Charles Darwin, "Natural Selection; or The Survival of the Fittest," in *On the Origin of Species*, 7–43.

106. Le Corbusier and de Pierrefeu, *The Home of Man*, 139.

107. Ibid., 13.

108. Carrel, introduction to the 1939 edition of *Man, the Unknown*.

109. Le Corbusier and de Pierrefeu, *The Home of Man*, 14–15.

110. Le Corbusier, *Destin de Paris*, 60.

111. "Dégénérescence du logis, dégénérescence de la famille, c'est tout un. Dégénérescence du logis paysan, abandon de la terre, c'est tout un encore." Le Corbusier, Radio Broadcast (1941), Document: B3–12, No. 216, Fondation Le Corbusier, Paris.

112. Le Corbusier and de Pierrefeu, *The Home of Man*, 15.

113. Ibid., 14. The book includes Le Corbusier's preliminary planning ideas for Rio de Janeiro, São Paulo, and Montevideo.

114. Ibid.

115. Ibid., 17.

116. Ibid.

117. Le Corbusier, "Commentaires relatifs à Moscou et à la 'Ville Verte,'" 286.

118. Le Corbusier, *The Radiant City*, 115.

119. Le Corbusier, "Aménagement d'une journée équilibrée," unpublished article, dated May 1932, FLC UE-5, 64–139.

120. Le Corbusier, "Volonté," in *Des Canons, des munitions*, 53. See also Jarcy, *Le Corbusier: Un fascism français*, 178–179.

121. In his 1945 book, *Les Trois établissements humains*, Le Corbusier argues: "l'eugénisme, la puériculture, assurant l'élevage d'une race." Le Corbusier, *Les Trois établissements humains*, 116.

122. Carrel, quoted in Reggiani, "Alexis Carrel, the Unknown," 336.

123. For more on Le Corbusier's efforts to collaborate with Pétain's regime, see Fox Weber, *Le Corbusier: A Life*, 413–465.

124. In 1948, Le Corbusier stated that the elements of his doctrine were to be found in the books he wrote during World War II. He did not mention *Destin de Paris* (1941) or *Sur les quatres routes* (1941), but, as Christine Boyer argues, "Any attempt to abstract the elements of Le Corbusier's doctrine is incomplete without them." Boyer, *Le Corbusier, Homme de Lettres*, 617–618.

125. Fox Weber, *Le Corbusier: A Life*, 447.

126. Alexis Carrel, postcard to Le Corbusier, dated February 19, 1942, Paris, FLC B3–12, No. 219.

127. The French Foundation for the Study of Human Problems, also known as the Carrel Foundation, was a pluridisciplinary center that had as its main goal the "improvement" of the French population. This organization, with three hundred researchers, was created in 1941 by decree of the Vichy regime and lasted until 1944 under the joint supervision of the Ministry of Finances and the Ministry of Public Health. For more on the Carrel Foundation, see Drouard, "A propos de l'interface médecine-sciences sociales," 49–56.

128. Ibid.

129. This sketch is an adaptation of the one Costa sent to Le Corbusier in July 1937. However, the colossal seated and naked man was already included in a report Le Corbusier submitted to Minister Capanema regarding the construction of the Ministry of Health and Education and the University City Campus for Rio de Janeiro. In this report, dated August 10, 1936, Le Corbusier argues that the ministry building should be built off the coast (at Praia de Santa Luzia), rather than on the site of the esplanade proposed by Rio's director of Public Works João Gualberto Marques Porto, the site where the Morro do Castelo once stood. Fundação Getúlio Vargas, Archive Gustavo Capanema, Série F, 34.10.19, II-30, Rio de Janeiro.

130. Reggiani, *God's Eugenicist*, x. The colossal sculpture surrounded by tropical nature also evokes a painting emblematic of Brazilian modernism: *Abaporu* by Tarsila do Amaral, the very painting selected to illustrate Oswald de Andrade's influential 1928 "Anthropophagite Manifesto."

131. In a letter to President Getúlio Vargas, Capanema states that the new ministry's main goals were to "prepare, compose, and perfect the Brazilian man" (preparar, compor e afeiçoar o homem do Brasil). Gustavo Capanema, letter to Getúlio Vargas, dated June 14, 1937, Archive Gustavo Capanema, Série F, 34.10.19, III-9, Fundação Getúlio Vargas, Rio de Janeiro.

132. Celso Antônio was Costa's collaborator in his effort to reform the National School of Fine Arts' curriculum in the early 1930s. Previously, in the 1920s, he was a disciple of the celebrated French sculptor Antoine Bourdelle. Costa and Bourdelle recommended Celso Antônio as the project's sculptor, and in his letter to Capanema, Le Corbusier approved the selection of the Brazilian sculptor to model the "Brazilian Man." "Estou feliz também por saber que o grande escultor Celso Antônio estuda a figura monumental que será colocada diante do edíficio." Le Corbusier, letter to Capanema dated December 30, 1937, published in Lissovsky and Moraes de Sá, *Colunas da educação*, 139–140.

133. Gustavo Capanema, letter to Oliveira Vianna dated August 30, 1937, published in Lissovsky and Moraes de Sá, *Colunas da educação*, 225.

134. Lissovsky and Moraes de Sá, *Colunas da educação*, 225–229.

135. As noted in chapters 1 and 2, Brazilians saw miscegenation not as a menace but as a solution—as the vehicle for "wiping out the black" and consequentially "whitening" the country. Skidmore, *Fact and Myth*.

136. Edgard Roquette-Pinto, letter to Gustavo Capanema dated August 30, 1937, published in Lissovsky and Moraes de Sá, *Colunas da educação*, 226.

137. Roquette-Pinto was the first anthropologist to create a system of classification of racial types in Brazil. In his paper "Note on the Anthropological Types of Brazil" presented at the First Brazilian Congress of Eugenics in 1929, Roquette-Pinto classifies the Brazilian population in four main groups: the "white type," or Leucodermo, representing 51 percent of the population; the "mulatto type" (descendants of mixing whites and blacks), or Phaiodermo, representing 22 percent; the "caboclo type" (descendants of mixing whites and Indians), or Xanthodermo, representing 11 percent; and the "black type," or Melanodermo, representing 14 percent of the population. As opposed to Oliveira Vianna, Roquette-Pinto rejected the idea that mixed races were degenerated, although he accepted that they were, along with the blacks and the indigenous, less beautiful than the Caucasian type. Influenced by positivism and Lamarckian ideas, Roquette-Pinto was convinced that miscegenation contributes to the process of formation "of anthropological and eugenic healthy types," under environmental improvement. His work was so influential that it was cited by Gilberto Freyre in his famous 1933 book, *The Masters and the Slaves* (*Casa-grande e senzala*), which has been considered the most important sociological work on the formation of Brazilian society. Roquette-Pinto, "Nota sobre os typos antropológicos do Brasil," 119–148.

138. Rocha Vaz, letter to Capanema dated September 14, 1937, published in Lissovsky and Moraes de Sá, *Colunas da educação*, 229.

139. M. Paulo Filho, "Homem brasileiro," *Correio da Manhã*, September 23, 1938, 4.

140. Gustavo Capanema, in a document dated December 14, 1937, published in Lissovsky and Moraes de Sá, *Colunas da educação*, 230.

141. This was the first time that a modern building with no historical or stylistic references represented Brazil at an international fair. By 1922, the year of the centennial celebration of Brazilian independence in Rio de Janeiro, the neocolonial style had become the mandatory style for representing Brazil abroad. But for this occasion, historical styles were reserved for the organizers in New York, and the Brazilian government under Getúlio Vargas' new authoritarian regime—the Estado Novo—had to find a new vocabulary capable of representing Brazil as a modern and reliable nation. Vargas' government abolished the decree that President Epitácio Pessoa had promulgated in 1922 to make neocolonial the national style, announcing an architectural competition for the modern Brazilian pavilion to be built in New York.

142. This was in stark contrast to the pavilion's museological program, which portrayed Brazil not as a modern industrialized country but as a coffee-producing agricultural one, also associated with its natural resources of wood, rubber, and oil. Williams, *Culture Wars in Brazil*, 207–221.

143. Ibid., 207. Among the specialized magazines were *Architectural Forum, Architectural Record, The Magazine of Arts, Architectural Review, Architettura,* and *Casabella.* Quezado Deckker, *Brazil Built*, 60–61.

144. New York's newspapers, featuring photos of Brazilian modern architecture, announced the opening of the exhibition *Brazil Builds* at MOMA. Celebratory headlines such as "Brazil Builds for the Future," "Brazil Has Much to Offer US," "Brazil Leads U.S. in Modern Architecture," "Brazil Goes Ultra-Modern," and many more filled mass-media outlets. Widely circulated US architectural magazines, such as *Architectural Record* and *Architectural Forum*, covered the show. And during the following years, prestigious architectural journals in Europe, including *Architectural Review*, the *Journal of the Royal Institute of British Architects*, and *L'Architecture d'aujourd'hui*, dedicated articles and special issues to Brazilian architecture. See Quezado Deckker's chapter "Brazil Builds and the Press" in *Brazil Built*, 147–163.

145. In a letter to Pietro Maria Bardi, director of the Museum of Art of São Paulo, Le Corbusier narrates how the show at the École des Beaux-Arts exhibited the works of Niemeyer and Reidy with his own signature design elements, "pilotis, brise-soleil, pans de verre, terrain libre, ville verte," and how the invited young lecturer from Rio presented them as Brazilian inventions. "I was present at his side enjoying myself by seeing such a striking nationalization of my thoughts," Le Corbusier said. Letter from Le Corbusier to Pietro Maria Bardi, October 18, 1949, FLC C1–18, 67–69.

146. Scott, *Seeing Like a State*, 104; and Boyer, "Aviation and the Aerial View," 96.

147. Boyer, "Aviation and the Aerial View," 109.

148. Scott, *Seeing Like a State*, 347.

149. Le Corbusier, handwritten notes on Alexis Carrel's lecture, February 19, 1943, FLC U3–06.

150. The Unité d'habitation in Marseille, the first commission given to Le Corbusier by the French state, was conceived to resolve the housing problem of those who lost their home during the war. It took five years to be built, from 1947 to 1952.

151. Le Corbusier, handwritten notes on Alexis Carrel's lecture, FLC U3–06.

152. "A Commissariat à la Normalisation was established to coordinate the work of the committee for standards of the Order of Architects, the organization committee for the building trade and civil engineering, and the committee for producers of materials. Shortly after its creation, the committee for standards of the Order of Architects issued the norm NFP01–001 regarding 'modulation,' which was made public in September 1942, establishing a module of ten centimeters, which was the first step toward deliberate policies of modular coordination." Cohen, "Le Corbusier's Modulor."

153. Le Corbusier, *The Modulor*, 76–80.

EPILOGUE

1. From its creation in 1956 to 1980, the School of Integral Eugenics and Humanism (Facultad de Eugenesia Integral y Humanismo) at the Universidad del Museo Social Argentino actually offered a major in eugenics.

2. As James C. Scott observes in his book *Seeing Like a State*, "The city itself was an exercise in planned functional segregation—an exercise that became standard urban-planning doctrine until the late 1960s." As Scott argues, a rigid segregation of functions facilitates planning—separating zones for workplaces, residences, recreational facilities—and made standardization possible. Scott, *Seeing Like a State*, 109–111.

3. Duster, *Backdoor to Eugenics*, 130–131. As some scholars have observed, Darwin also recognized the way natural selection led to the development of human society by eliminating the unfit. For more on this view, see Rogers, "Darwinism and Social Darwinism," 265–280.

4. Shostak and Moinester, "The Missing Piece of the Puzzle?," 192–209.

5. Ibid., 193–194.

6. Ibid., 194.

7. Ibid.

8. Ibid., 202–204.

9. I refer to the series of impoverished peripheral nuclei—the so-called *cidades satélites*—that were created by the government to host a marginal population (mostly those who migrated from the poorest regions of the country and the very workers who built Brasília) even before the inauguration of the city. Clearly, as Hugo Segawa argues, there was no desire to admit this population into "the noble residential area of the new capital." In fact, two decades after its inauguration, the city that was conceived to host 500,000 residents actually ended up excluding 1.5 million inhabitants, or more than two-thirds of its population. Rather than becoming a social laboratory for destratification, the Plan Piloto designed by Lúcio Costa for Brasília guaranteed the preservation of the city's elitist configuration and its immunity from alteration. In 1987, further cementing this immutability, UNESCO declared Brasília and its plan a World Heritage site. See Segawa, *Arquiteturas no Brasil, 1900–1990*, 541.

10. Schindler, "Architectural Exclusion," 2024.

11. Scott, *Seeing Like a State*, 92.

BIBLIOGRAPHY

ARCHIVES AND REPOSITORIES

ARGENTINA

Archivo Dirección de Paseos, Municipalidad de la Ciudad de Buenos Aires (MCBA), Buenos Aires

Archivo Familia Borra, Colección Enrique Broszeit-Borra, Buenos Aires

Archivo General de la Nación (AGN), Buenos Aires

Archivo Histórico de la Ciudad de Buenos Aires, Buenos Aires

Archivo Museo Social Argentino, Buenos Aires

Biblioteca Facultad de Medicina, Universidad de Buenos Aires (UBA)

Biblioteca Nacional Mariano Moreno, Buenos Aires

Centro de Documentación, Facultad de Arquitectura, Diseño y Urbanismo, Universidad de Buenos Aires (FADU/UBA), Buenos Aires

Dirección General Centro Documental de Información y Archivo Legislativo (CEDOM), Buenos Aires

Museo de la Inmigración in partnership with Museo de la Universidad Nacional de Tres de Febrero (MUNTREF), Buenos Aires

Sociedad Central de Arquitectos (SCA), Buenos Aires

BRAZIL

Acervo Biblioteca da Faculdade de Arquitetura e Urbanismo da Universidade de São Paulo (FAU USP), São Paulo

Acervo Fundação Museu da Imagem e do Som (MIS), Rio de Janeiro

Arquivo Academia Nacional de Medicina (ANM), Rio de Janeiro

Arquivo Geral da Cidade do Rio de Janeiro (AGCRJ), Rio de Janeiro

Arquivo Histórico, Museu Histórico Nacional (MHN), Rio de Janeiro

Arquivo Noronha Santos, Instituto do Patrimônio Histórico e Artístico Nacional (IPHAN), Rio de Janeiro

Arquivo Público do Estado do Rio de Janeiro (APERJ), Rio de Janeiro
Arquivo Roberto Segre, private archive, Rio de Janeiro
Biblioteca Instituto de Pesquisa e Planejamento Urbano e Regional (IP-
    PUR), Universidade Federal do Rio de Janeiro (UFRJ), Rio de Janeiro
Biblioteca Lúcio Costa da Faculdade de Arquitetura e Urbanismo,
    Universidade Federal do Rio de Janeiro (UFRJ), Rio de Janeiro
Biblioteca Nacional (BN), Rio de Janeiro
Biblioteca Pontifícia Universidade Católica do Rio de Janeiro (PUC-Rio),
    Rio de Janeiro
Centro de Arquitetura e Urbanismo (CAU) do Rio de Janeiro, Prefeitura
    do Rio de Janeiro
Centro de Pesquisa e Documentação de História Contemporânea do Brasil
    (CPDOC), Gustavo Capanema Collection, Fundação Getúlio Vargas
    (FGV), Rio de Janeiro
Fundação Oswaldo Cruz (COC-Fiocruz), Rio de Janeiro
Instituto Histórico e Geográfico Brasileiro (IHGB), Rio de Janeiro
Instituto Moreira Salles (IMS), Rio de Janeiro
Museu Nacional de Bellas Artes, Rio de Janeiro

FRANCE

Archives départementales des Bouches-du-Rhône, Marseille
Archives nationales d'outre-mer, Aix-en-Provence
Bibliothèque historique de la Ville de Paris (BHVP), Paris
Bibliothèque des Arts Décoratifs, Paris
Bibliothèque interuniversitaire de médecine et d'odontologie (BIUM),
    Paris
Bibliothèque nationale de France (BnF), Département de Manuscrits,
    Paris
CEDIAS-Centre d'études, de documentation, d'information et d'action
    sociales (Le Musée social), Paris
Centre d'archives d'architecture du XXe siècle (Cité de l'architecture et du
    patrimoine, Institut français d'architecture), Paris
Fondation Le Corbusier (FLC), Paris

NORTH AMERICA (UNITED STATES AND CANADA)

Canadian Centre for Architecture (CCA), Montreal
Countway Library of Medicine, Harvard University, Cambridge, MA
Frances Loeb Library, Special and Visual Collections, Harvard Graduate
    School of Design, Cambridge, MA
Houghton Library, Harvard University, Cambridge, MA
Library of Congress, Prints and Photographs Division, Washington, DC
National Gallery of Art, Washington, DC
New York Public Library, William Williams Collection, New York
Widener Library, Harvard University, Cambridge, MA

NEWSPAPERS, JOURNALS, AND BULLETINS

Alliance d'hygiène sociale

Anales de Biotipología, Eugenesia y Medicina Social

Anales del Departamento Nacional de Higiene

L'Architettura

Architectural Forum

Architectural Record

Architectural Review

Architectura no Brasil—Engenharia/Construção

AU–Arquitetura e Urbanismo

Boletín del Honorable Concejo Deliberante, Municipalidad de Buenos Aires

Boletín del Museo Social Argentino

Caras y Caretas

Casabella

Correio da Manhã

El Diario

El Hogar

El Monitor de la Educación Común

El País

Jornal do Brasil

Jornal do Commercio

Journal of the Royal Institute of British Architects

L'Architecture d'aujourd'hui

La Revue des Vivantes

La Semana Médica

Le Musée social, Annales: Revue mensuelle

Le Musée social, Memoires et documents

L'Esprit nouveau

L'Homme réel

The Magazine of Art

The National Magazine

Nuestra Arquitectura

O Cruzeiro

O País

Plans

Prelude

Punto de Vista

Revista de Arquitectura (Argentina)

Sur

Viva Cien Años

OFFICIAL PUBLICATIONS

Alliance d'hygiène sociale. *Congrès de Roubaix, 19–22 octobre 1911: De la ville-taudis à la cité-jardin.* Agen, France: Imprimerie Moderne, 1911.

Bulletin officiel de l'exposition universelle de 1889 148, September 14, 1889.

Censo general de población, edificación, comercio e industria de la ciudad de Buenos Aires. Vol. 1. Buenos Aires: Compañía Sud-Americana de Billetes de Banco, 1889.

Comisión de Estética Edilicia. *Proyecto orgánico para la urbanización del municipio: El plano regulador y de reforma de la capital federal.* Buenos Aires: Talleres Peuser, 1925.

Concejo Deliberante de la Ciudad de Buenos Aires. Versiones taquigráficas del Honorable Concejo Deliberante (1920–1941).

Congreso Nacional. "Diario de Sesiones de 1874," Cámara de Senadores. Buenos Aires: Congreso Nacional, 1874.

Consejo Nacional de Educación. *Cincuentenario de la Ley 1420.* Vol. 3. Buenos Aires: Imprenta Oficial, 1941.

———. "Conceptos sobre edificación escolar en la República Argentina." *Revista de Arquitectura* 170 (1935): 60–67.

O Livro de Ouro: Comemorativo do Centenário da Independência do Brasil e da Exposição Internacional do Rio de Janeiro. Rio de Janeiro: Edição do Annuario do Brasil, 1923.

Primeiro Congresso Brasileiro de Eugenia: Actas e Trabalhos. Vol. 1. Rio de Janeiro, n.p., 1929.

Primer Congreso Argentino de la Población: Sesiones, trabajos y resoluciones, 1ra Parte. *Boletín del Museo Social Argentino* (Buenos Aires), no. 28 (1940): 371–385.

Primer Congreso Argentino de la Población: Sesiones, trabajos y resoluciones, 2da Parte. *Boletín del Museo Social Argentino* (Buenos Aires), no. 28 (1940).

Teses oficiaes, memórias e conclusões do Primeiro Congresso Brasileiro de Proteção á Infância, 7º Boletim. Rio de Janeiro: Empresa Graphica Editora, 1924.

Transactions of the Fifteenth International Congress on Hygiene and Demography. Washington, DC: Government Printing Office, 1913.

ART COLLECTIONS

Kunsthalle, Hamburg
Musée d'Orsay, Paris
Museum of Modern Art, New York

BOOKS, ARTICLES, AND THESES

Abreu, Mauricio de Almeida. *A evoluçao urbana do Rio de Janeiro.* Rio de Janeiro: IPLAN/J. Zhar, 1987.

Acosta, Wladimiro. *Vivienda y clima.* Buenos Aires: Ediciones Nueva Visión, 1976.

Adams, Mark B., ed. *The Wellborn Science: Eugenics in Germany, France, Brazil, and Russia.* New York: Oxford University Press, 1990.

Agache, Donat-Alfred. *A cidade do Rio de Janeiro, remodelação, extensão e embelezamento, 1927–1930.* Paris: Foyer Brésilien, 1930.

————. "La Cité-Jardin." In Alliance d'hygiène sociale, *Congrès de Roubaix, 19–22 octobre 1911: De la ville-taudis à la cité-jardin*, 75–116. Agen, France: Imprimerie Moderne, 1911.

————. *La remodelation d'une capitale*. Paris: Société coopérative d'architectes, 1932.

Agache, Donat-Alfred, J. Marcel Auburtin, and Edouard Redont. *Comment reconstruire nos cités détruites: Notions d'urbanisme s'appliquant aux villes, bourgs et villages*. Paris: Armand Colin, 1915.

Agamben, Giorgio. *What Is an Apparatus? and Other Essays*. Stanford: Stanford University Press, 2009.

Alberdi, Juan Bautista. *Bases y puntos de partida para la organización política de la República Argentina*. Buenos Aires: La Cultura Argentina, 1915.

Alberti, Leon Battista. *De re aedificatoria*. Manuscript. Florence: Biblioteca Digital Dioscórides, Universidad Complutense de Madrid, 1485.

Almandoz, Arturo. *Planning Latin America's Capital Cities, 1850–1950*. London: Routledge, 2002.

Aly, Gotz, Peter Chroust, and Christian Pross. *Cleansing the Fatherland: Nazi Medicine and Racial Hygiene*. Baltimore: Johns Hopkins University Press, 1994.

Amadeo, Tomás. *Economía Social. Museo Social de Buenos Aires: Fundamentos y anteproyecto*. Buenos Aires: Imprenta de Coni Hermanos, 1910.

Amaral, Aracy. *Artes plásticas na Semana de 22*. São Paulo: Martins, 1970.

Anonymous. "Anthropologie criminelle." *Bulletin officiel de l'exposition universelle de 1889* 145 (1889): 4.

————. "Cuerpo Médico Escolar." *El Monitor de la Educación Común*. Buenos Aires: Consejo Nacional de Educación, 1888.

————. "Cuerpo Médico Escolar." *El Monitor de la Educación Común*. Buenos Aires: Consejo Nacional de Educación, 1919.

————. "En breve se realizará en Buenos Aires el Primer Congreso Nacional de Urbanismo." *Revista de Architectura* 146 (1933): 77–78.

————. "Las escuelas al aire libre." Resolutions of the Second International Congress of Open-Air Schools. In *Boletín del Museo Social Argentino* 22 (1934), 265–266.

————. "Molecular Biology." Accessed January 11, 2017. http://www .rockefeller100.org/exhibits/show/natural_sciences/molecular-biology.

————. "Sobre escuelas para niños débiles." *El Monitor de la Educación Común*. Buenos Aires: Consejo Nacional de Educación, 1908.

Appelbaum, Nancy P., Anne S. Macpherson, and Karin Alejandra Rosemblatt. "Racial Nations," introduction to *Race and Nation in Modern Latin America*, edited by Nancy P. Appelbaum, Anne S. Macpherson, and Karin Alejandra Rosemblatt, 1–31. Chapel Hill: University of North Carolina Press, 2003.

Arestizabal, Irma, ed. *Uma cidade em questão I: Grandjean de Montigny e o Rio de Janeiro*. Rio de Janeiro: Pontifícia Universidad Católica, 1979.

Armus, Diego. *La ciudad impura: Salud, tuberculosis y cultura en Buenos Aires, 1870–1950*. Buenos Aires: Edhasa, 2007.

Austregésilo, Antônio. "A Escola Médica brasileira (1822–1922)." In *Comemorativo do Centenário da Independência do Brasil e da Exposição Internacional do Rio de Janeiro*. Rio de Janeiro: Edição do Annuario do Brasil, 1923.

Ayres, Leonard P. "Escuelas al aire libre en Estados Unidos." *El Monitor de la Educación Común*. Buenos Aires: Consejo Nacional de Educación, 1913.

Bacon, Mardges. *Le Corbusier in America: Travels in the Land of the Timid*. Cambridge, MA: MIT Press, 2001.

Ballent, Anahi, and Adrián Gorelik. "País urbano o país rural: La modernización territorial y su crisis." In *Nueva Historia Argentina*, Vol. 7, edited by Alejandro Cataruzza, 143–200. Buenos Aires: Sudamericana, 2001.

Ballent, Anahi, and Jorge Francisco Liernur. *La casa y la multitud: Vivienda, política y cultura en la Argentina moderna*. Buenos Aires: Fondo de Cultura Económica, 2014.

Barnes, David S. *The Making of a Social Disease: Tuberculosis in Nineteenth-Century France*. Berkeley: University of California Press, 1995.

Baudouï, Rémi, and Arnaud Dercelles, eds. *Le Corbusier Correspondance: Lettres à la famille 1926–1946*. Gollion: Infolio éditions, 2013.

Beal, Sophia. *Brazil Under Construction: Fiction and Public Works*. New York: Palgrave Macmillan, 2013.

Benchimol, Jaime. *Pereira Passos: um Haussmann tropical: A renovação urbana da cidade do Rio de Janeiro no início do século XX*. Rio de Janeiro: Biblioteca Carioca, 1990.

———. "Reforma urbana e Revolta da Vacina na cidade do Rio de Janeiro." In *O Brasil republicano: O tempo do liberalismo excludente—da Proclamação da República à Revolução de 1930*, edited by Jorge Ferreira and Lucilia de Almeida Neves Delgado, 231–186. Rio de Janeiro: Civilização Brasileira, 2003.

Benedict, Burton. *The Anthropology of World's Fairs*. London and Berkeley: Scholar Press, 1983.

Benoît-Lévy, Georges. *La Cité jardin*. Paris: Henri Jouve, 1904.

———. "Lotissements modèles et cités-jardins." In Alliance d'hygiène sociale, *Congrès de Roubaix, 19–22 octobre 1911: De la ville-taudis à la cité-jardin*, 64–74. Agen, France: Imprimerie Moderne, 1911.

Berjman, Sonia. *Plazas y parques de Buenos Aires: La obra de los paisajistas franceses, André, Courtois, Thays, Bouvard, Forestier, 1860–1930*. Buenos Aires: Fondo de Cultura Económica, 1998.

Bernaldo de Quirós, Carlos. *Inquietudes al margen de mi lucha: Sociología, derecho eugenésico, legislación*. Buenos Aires: Editorial Difusión, 1939.

Bernaldo de Quirós, Constancio. *La picota en América: Contribución al estudio del derecho penal indiano*. Havana: Jesús Montero, 1948.

Bernard, Claude. *Introduction à l'étude de la médecine expérimentale.* Paris: J. B. Baillière et Fils, 1865.

Bezerra Dantas, Christovam. "A criança e a eugenía." *Primeiro Congresso Brasileiro de Protecção á Infancia,* Boletim 7 (1924): 175–179.

Bichat, Marie-François Xavier. *Recherches physiologiques sur la vie et la mort.* Paris: Brosson-Gabon, 1805.

Blanchard, Pascal, et al., eds. *Zoos humains et exhibitions coloniales: 150 ans d'inventions de l'Autre.* Paris: La Découverte, 2011.

Borges, Dain. "Puffy, Ugly, Slothful and Inert: Degeneration in Brazilian Thought, 1880–1940." *Journal of Latin American Studies* 25, no. 2 (1993): 235–256.

Botana, Natalio. *El orden conservador: La política argentina entre 1880 y 1916.* Buenos Aires: Sudamericana, 1977.

Bourgeois, Léon. "Congrès d'hygiène sociale de Roubaix, October 19–22, 1911." *Bulletin Alliance d'hygiène sociale* 21 (1911): 1.

Boyer, M. Christine. "Aviation and the Aerial View: Le Corbusier's Spatial Transformations in the 1930s and 1940s." *Diacritics* 33, no. 3–4 (2003): 93–116.

———. *Le Corbusier, Homme de Lettres.* New York: Princeton Architectural Press, 2011.

Brackman, Arnold C. *A Delicate Arrangement: The Strange Case of Charles Darwin and Alfred Russel Wallace.* New York: Times Books, 1980.

Bragos, Oscar. "O Museu Social Argentino e a formação e difusão das idéias do urbanismo." In *Cidade, povo e nação: Gênese do urbanismo moderno,* edited by Luiz Cesar de Queiroz Ribeiro and Robert Pechman, 259–283. Rio de Janeiro: Civilização Brasileira, 1996.

Bretonne, Réstif de la. *La Découverte australe par un homme volant.* Imprimé à Leïpsick, se trouve à Paris, 1781.

Broberg, Gunnar, and Nils Roll-Hansen, eds. *Eugenics and the Welfare State: Sterilization Policy in Denmark, Sweden, Norway, and Finland.* East Lansing: Michigan State University Press, 1996.

Burkhardt, Richard W. *The Spirit of the System: Lamarck and Evolutionary Biology.* Cambridge, MA: Harvard University Press, 1977.

Burns, Bradford. *A History of Brazil.* New York: Columbia University Press, 1993.

Cabet, Etienne. *Voyage en Icarie.* Paris: H. Souverain, 1840.

Calcagno, Francisco. *En busca del eslabón: Historia de monos.* Barcelona: S. Manero, 1888.

Campanella, Tommaso. *La città del sole.* Turin, Italy: Chiantore, 1945.

Canales, Jimena, and Andrew Herscher. "Criminal Skins: Tattoos and Modern Architecture in the Work of Adolf Loos." *Architectural History* 48 (2005): 235–256.

Canguilhem, Georges. "Bichat, Marie-François-Xavier." In *Dictionary of Scientific Biography,* edited by Charles Gillispie, 2: 122–123. New York: Charles Scribner's Sons, 1979.

———. *Knowledge of Life.* New York: Fordham University Press, 2008.

————. *La connaissance de la vie*. Paris: Librairie philosophique J. Vrin, 1992.

————. "The Normal and the Pathological." In *A Vital Rationalist: Selected Writings from Georges Canguilhem*, edited by François Delaporte, 321–350. New York: Zone Books, 2000.

Carol, Anne. *Histoire de l'eugénisme en France: Les médecins et la procréation XIXe–XXe siècle*. Paris: Éditions du Seuil, 1995.

————. "Les médecins français et l'eugénisme: Un champ de recherche ouvert par Jacques Léonard." In *Pur l'histoire de la médecine*, Autour de l'œuvre de Jacques Léonard, directed by Michel Lagrée and François Lebrun, 39–47. Rennes, France: Presses universitaires de Rennes, 1994.

Caron, Charles Alfred. *La Puériculture, ou la Science d'élever hygiénique-ment et physiologiquement les enfants*. N.p.: Impr. de E. Orville, 1866.

Carrasco, Benito. "El urbanismo contemporáneo es una función de carácter social." *Boletín Museo Social Argentino* 22 (1934): 315.

————. "Evolución de los espacios verdes." *Boletín del Honorable Concejo Deliberante* 31 (1942): 497.

————. "La ciudad del porvenir." *Caras y Caretas* (Buenos Aires), no. 490, February 22, 1908.

Carrel, Alexis. Introduction to the 1939 edition of *Man, the Unknown*. Accessed July 19, 2014, http://archive.org/details/TheManTheUnknown ByNobelPrizeWinnerDr.AlexisCarrel.

————. *Man, the Unknown*. New York: Harper and Brothers, 1935.

Carvalho, Bruno. *Porous City: A Cultural History of Rio de Janeiro*. Liverpool, UK: Liverpool University Press, 2013.

Cassinelli, Hamilton. "Contribución al estudio de los niños débiles y retardados en edad escolar." PhD diss., Universidad de Buenos Aires, Facultad de Ciencias Médicas, 1912.

Cattaneo, Daniela Alejandra. "La arquitectura escolar como instrumento del Estado: Contrapuntos nación-provincias en la década de 1930." PhD diss., Universidad Nacional de Rosario, Argentina, Facultad de Arquitectura, Planeamiento y Diseño, 2015.

Cavalcanti, Lauro. "Moderno e brasileiro: Uma introdução ao guia de arquitetura." In *Quando o Brasil era moderno: Guia de arquitetura 1928–1960*, 8–25. Rio de Janeiro: Aeroplano Editora, 2001.

————. "When Brazil Was Modern: From Rio de Janeiro to Brasilia." In *Cruelty and Utopia: Cities and Landscapes of Latin America*, edited by Jean-François Lejeune, 161–169. New York: Princeton Architectural Press, 2005.

Çelik, Zeynep. *Displaying the Orient: Architecture of Islam at Nineteenth-Century World's Fairs*. Berkeley: University of California Press, 1992.

Çelik, Zeynep, and Leila Kinney. "Ethnography and Exhibitionism at the Expositions Universelles." *Assemblage* 13 (1990): 34–59.

Chalhoub, Sidney. *Cidade febril: Cortiços e epidemias na Corte Imperial*. São Paulo: Companhia das Letras, 1996.

Champagne, Mildred. "The Children of the Parque Lezama." *The National Magazine* 43 (1916): 1033–1039.

Chaslin, François. *Un Corbusier*. Paris: Éditions du Seuil, 2015.

Châtelet, Anne-Marie, Dominique Lerch, and Jean-Noël Luc, eds. *L'école de plein air: Une expérience pédagogique et architecturale dans l'Europe du XXe siècle / Open-Air Schools: An Educational and Architectural Venture in Twentieth-Century Europe*. Paris: Éditions Recherches, 2003.

Chevallier, Fabienne. *Le Paris moderne: Histoire des politiques d'hygiène, 1855–1898*. Rennes, France: Presses universitaires de Rennes, 2010.

Cheysson, Émile. "L'Économie sociale a l'Exposition universelle de 1889." *La Reforme sociale* 2 (1889): 1–19.

Choay, Françoise. *L'Urbanisme: Utopies et réalités: Une anthologie*. Paris: Éditions du Seuil, 1965.

———. Preface to *Jean Claude Nicolas Forestier 1861–1930: Du jardin au paysage urbain*, edited by Bénédicte Leclerc, 13–15. Paris: Picard, 1994.

———. *The Rule and the Model: On the Theory of Architecture and Urbanism*. Cambridge, MA: MIT Press, 1997.

———. "Utopia and the Philosophical Status of Constructed Spaces." In *Utopia: The Search for the Ideal Society in the Western World*, edited by Roland Schaer, Gregory Claeys, and Lyman Tower Sargent, 346–353. New York: The New York Public Library/Oxford University Press, 2000.

Chombart-Gaudin, Cécile. "Forestier, président de la Ligue urbaine." In *Jean Claude Nicolas Forestier, 1861–1930: Du jardin au paysage urbain. Actes du Colloque international sur J. C. N. Forestier, Paris 1990*, edited by Bénédicte Leclerc, 141–148. Paris: Picard, 1994.

Clark, Meri. "The Emergence and Transformation of Positivism." In *A Companion to Latin American Philosophy*, edited by Susana Nuccetelli. New York: Wiley Blackwell, 2010.

Clark, T. J. "The Conditions of Artistic Creation." In *Art History and Its Methods*, edited by Eric Fernie, 245–253. London: Phaidon Press, 1995.

Clemenceau, Georges. *South America To-Day: A Study of Conditions, Social, Political, and Commercial in Argentina, Uruguay and Brazil*. New York and London: The Knickerbocker Press, 1911.

Cogdell, Christina. *Eugenic Design: Streamlining America in the 1930s*. Philadelphia: University of Pennsylvania Press, 2004.

Cohen, Jean-Louis. *Algiers: Paysage urbain et architectures 1800–2000*. Paris: Éditions de l'imprimeur, 2003.

———. "Le Corbusier's Modulor and the Debate on Proportion in France." *Architectural Histories* 2, no. 1 (2014). http://doi.org/10.5334/ah.by.

Cohen, Jean-Louis, and Monique Eleb. *Casablanca: Mythes et figures d'une aventure urbaine*. Vanves, France: Éditions Hazan, 1998.

Cole, Margaret. *Robert Owen of New Lanark*. New York: A. M. Kelley, 1969.

Cole, Simon A. *Suspect Identities: A History of Fingerprinting and*

Criminal Identification. Cambridge, MA: Harvard University Press, 2001.

Colomina, Beatriz. "Los arquitectos buscamos dioses para adorarlos." *El País*, April 20, 2009, accessed April 20, 2009, http://elpais.com /diario/2009/04/20/ultima/1240178402_850215.html.

———. "The Medical Body in Architecture." In *AnyBody*, edited by Cynthia Davidson, 228–238. Cambridge, MA: MIT Press, 1997.

Coni, Emilio R. "The Campaign against Tuberculosis in the Argentine Republic." In *Transactions of the Sixth International Congress on Tuberculosis*, Vol. 4. Philadelphia: William F. Fell Company, 1908.

———. "Campaña sanitaria escolar: Carta abierta." *El Monitor de la Educación Común*. Buenos Aires: Consejo Nacional de Educación, 1917.

———. "Escuelas al aire libre y al sol." *El Monitor de la Educación Común*. Buenos Aires: Consejo Nacional de Educación, 1921.

———. "Higiene pública: La lucha antituberculosa en la República Argentina." *La Semana Médica* 42 (1905): 1059–1076.

———. "Inspección higiénica y médica de las escuelas." *El Monitor de la Educación Común*. Buenos Aires: Consejo Nacional de Educación, 1917.

———. "La ciudad argentina ideal o del porvenir." *La Semana Médica* 14 (1919): 342–345.

———. *Progrès de l'hygiène dans la République Argentine*. Paris: Libraire J—B. Baillière et Fils, 1887.

Conniff, Michael. *Urban Politics in Brazil: The Rise of Populism, 1925–1945*. Pittsburgh, PA: Pittsburgh University Press, 1981.

Corbin, Alain. "Commercial Sexuality in Nineteenth-Century France: A System of Images and Regulations." *Representations* 14 (1986): 209–219.

———. *Women for Hire: Prostitution and Sexuality in France after 1850*. Cambridge, MA: Harvard University Press, 1990.

Cormier, Anne. "Extension, limites, espaces libres: Les travaux de la Section d'hygiène urbaine et rurale du Musée social." Mémoire pour le CEA d'architecture urbaine. Master's thesis, École d'architecture Paris-Villemin, 1987.

Corvalán Mendilaharsu, Dardo. "La escuela argentina: De 'la letra con sangre entra' a la escuela al aire libre." *El Monitor de la Educación Común*. Buenos Aires: Consejo Nacional de Educación, 1910.

Costa, Lúcio. "O arranha-céu e o Rio de Janeiro." *O País* (Rio de Janeiro), July 1, 1928.

Cowan, Ruth Schwartz. "Nature and Nurture: The Interplay of Biology and Politics in the Work of Francis Galton." *Studies in the History of Biology* 1 (1977): 133–207.

Coyula, Mario, Joseph L. Scarpaci, and Roberto Segre. *Havana: Two Faces of the Antillean Metropolis*. Chapel Hill: University of North Carolina Press, 2002.

Crider, Ernest A. "Modernization and Human Welfare: The Asistencia Pública and Buenos Aires 1883–1910." PhD diss., Ohio State University, 1976.

Crisler, Jane Ellen. "Saving the Seed: The Scientific Preservation of Children in France during the Third Republic." PhD diss., University of Wisconsin-Madison, 1984.

Darwin, Charles. *On the Origin of Species*. Cambridge MA: Harvard University Press, 2003. Originally published in 1859.

———. *The Variation of Animals and Plants under Domestication*. London: John Murray-Albemarle Street, 1868.

Dávila, Jerry. *Diploma of Whiteness: Race and Social Policy in Brazil, 1917–1945*. Durham, NC: Duke University Press, 2003.

Delaporte, François. *Disease and Civilization: The Cholera in Paris, 1832*. Cambridge, MA: MIT Press, 1986.

Della Paolera, Carlos María, Wenceslao Tello, et al. "Congreso Argentino de la Habitación: Celebrado bajo los auspicios del Museo Social Argentino en la ciudad de Buenos Aires, durante los días 5 al 13 de septiembre de 1920." *Boletín del Museo Social Argentino*, Special Edition 96 (1921).

Delort de Gléon, Alphonse. *L'Architecture arabe des khalifes d'Égypte à l'Exposition universelle de Paris en 1889: La rue du Caire*. Paris: Plon, Nourrit et Cie, 1989.

Deutsch, Sandra Mcgee. Las Derechas: *The Extreme Right in Argentina, Brazil, and Chile, 1890–1939*. Stanford: Stanford University Press, 1999.

Didi-Huberman, Georges. *Invention of Hysteria: Charcot and the Photographic Iconography of the Salpêtrière*. Cambridge, MA: MIT Press, 2003.

Domingues, Otávio. *Hereditariedade e eugenía: Suas bases, suas teorias, suas aplicaçoes práticas*. Rio de Janeiro: Civilização Brasileira, 1936.

Donzelot, Jacques. *La Police des familles*. Paris: Minuit, 1920.

———. *The Policing of Families*. Baltimore, MD: Johns Hopkins University Press, 1997.

Drouard, Alain. "A propos de l'interface médecine-sciences sociales: La Fondation Française pour l'Etude des Problèmes Humains dite Fondation Carrel." *Histoire des sciences médicales* 28, no. 1 (1994): 49–56.

———. "Aux origines de l'eugenisme en France: Le neo-Mathusianisme (1896–1914)." *Population: Revue Bimestrielle de l'Institut National d'Etudes Demographiques* 47 (1992): 435–460.

———. *L'Eugénisme en questions: L'Exemple de l'eugénisme français*. Paris: Ellipses, 1999.

Dubos, Rene J. "Medical Utopias." *Daedalus* 88, no. 3 (1959): 410–424.

———. *Mirage of Health: Utopias, Progress, and Biological Change*. New Brunswick, NJ: Rutgers University Press, 1987.

Duclaux, Emile. *Hygiène sociale*. Paris: Félix Alcan, 1902.

Duster, Troy. *Backdoor to Eugenics*. New York: Routledge, 2003.

Eardley, Anthony. "Giraudoux and the Athens Charter." *Oppositions* 3 (1974): 83–90.

Edison, Paul N. "Conquest Unrequited: French Expeditionary Science in Mexico, 1864–1867." *French Historical Studies* 26 (2003): 459–495.

Escobar, Arturo. *Encountering Development: The Making and Unmaking of the Third World*. Princeton, NJ: Princeton University Press, 2011.

Esposito, Roberto. *Bios: Biopolitics and Philosophy*. Minneapolis: University of Minnesota Press, 2008.

Evenson, Norma. *Two Brazilian Capitals: Architecture and Urbanism in Rio de Janeiro and Brasilia*. New Haven: Yale University Press, 1973.

Fausto, Boris. "Brazil: The Social and Political Structure of the First Republic (1889–1930)." In *The Cambridge History of Latin America*, edited by Leslie Bethell, 779–830. Cambridge: Cambridge University Press, 1986.

Ferrari, Fernando José. "Historia cultural de la psiquiatría en Córdoba, Argentina: Recepción y decadencia de la neurastenia, 1894–1936." *Trashumante: Revista Americana de Historia Social*, no. 5 (2015): 288–309.

Ferreira, Luiz Otávio. "Os periódicos médicos e a invenção de uma agenda sanitária para o Brasil (1827–1843)." *História, Ciências, Saúde—Manguinhos* 6, no. 2 (1999): 331–351.

Ferreira, Rachel Haywood. *The Emergence of Latin American Science Fiction*. Middletown, CT: Wesleyan University Press, 2011.

Filho, Mariano. "Decalogue for the Brazilian Architect" ("Decalogo do arquiteto brasileiro"), 1923. First published in *Philosophie zoologique*. Paris: Dentu, 1809.

Filho, M. Paulo. "Homem brasileiro." *Correio da Manhã*, September 23, 1938.

Forestier, Jean-Claude Nicolas. *Grandes villes et systèmes de parcs*. Paris: Norma Editions, 1997.

———. *Jardines: Cuaderno de dibujos y planos*. Barcelona: Editorial Stylos, 1991. Originally published as *Jardins, carnet de plans et de dessins*. Paris: Emile-Paul frères, 1920.

———. "Les jardins à l'exposition des arts décoratifs" (August 22, 1925): 19–24.

———. "Los jardines modernos." *Caras y Caretas* (Buenos Aires), no. 461, August 31, 1907.

———. "Los parques de juego o jardines de barrio en las grandes ciudades." *Revista Municipal* (Buenos Aires), no. 146, November 5, 1906.

———. "Quelques travaux d'urbanisation à Buenos Aires: L'Avenida Costanera." Section d'hygiène urbaine et rurale et de prévoyance sociale, séance of June 15, 1928. *Le Musée social, Annales: Revue mensuelle* (1929): 302–304.

Foucault, Michel. *Discipline and Punish: The Birth of the Prison*. New York: Vintage Books, 1995.

———. *Dits et écrits*, vol. 3: *1976–1979*. Paris: NRF Gallimard, 1994.

———. *The History of Sexuality*. New York: Vintage Books, 1990.

———. *Power/Knowledge: Selected Interviews and Other Writings 1972–1977*. Edited by Colin Gordon. New York: Pantheon Books, 1972.

———. "Questions of Method: An Interview with Michel Foucault." In *After Philosophy: End or Transformation?*, edited by Kenneth Baynes,

James Bohman, and Thomas A. McCarthy, 100–118. Cambridge, MA: MIT Press, 1987.

———. *Security, Territory, Population: Lectures at the Collège de France, 1977–1978*. Edited by Michel Senellart. New York: Palgrave Macmillan, 2007.

———. *"Society Must Be Defended": Lectures at the Collège de France, 1975–1976*. Edited by Mauro Bertani and Alessandro Fontana. New York: Picador, 2003.

Fourier, Charles. *La phalange*. Paris: Imprimerie L. Lévy, 1845–1849.

Fournié, Emilio. "Escuelas y obras al aire libre en América." *El Monitor de la Educación Común*. Buenos Aires: Consejo Nacional de Educación, 1937.

Fox Weber, Nicholas. *Le Corbusier: A Life*. New York: Knopf, 2008.

Freyre, Gilberto. *The Masters and The Slaves (Casa-grande e Senzala): A Study in the Development of Brazilian Civilization*. New York: Knopf, 1956.

Galton, Francis. "Eugenics: Its Definition, Scope, and Aims." *The American Journal of Sociology* 10, no. 1 (1904): 1–25.

———. *Inquiries into the Human Faculty and Its Development*. London: Dent and Sons, 1907.

García, María Nélida. "Colonias y escuelas de niños débiles." *El Monitor de la Educación Común*. Buenos Aires: Consejo Nacional de Educación, 1919.

Garnier, Charles, and Auguste Amman. *Histoire de l'habitation humaine*. Paris: Hachette, 1892.

Gautrez, Eugène. Rapport, "L'Organisation sanitaire et l'Armement d'Hygiène sociale du Puy-de-Dôme." In *Alliance d'hygiène sociale: Congrès de Clermont-Ferrand, 30 septembre, 1er et 2 octobre 1921*. Clermont-Ferrand, France: Impr. G. Mont-Louis, 1921.

Gemelli, Giuliana, ed. *Big Culture: Intellectual Co-operation in Large-Scale Cultural and Technical Systems*. Bologna, Italy: Clueb, 1994.

Geroulanos, Stefanos, and Todd Meyers. "Introduction: Georges Canguilhem's Critique of Medical Reason." In Georges Canguilhem, *Writings on Medicine*, 1–24. New York: Fordham University Press, 2012.

Gilman, Sander L. "Black Bodies, White Bodies: Toward an Iconography of Female Sexuality in Late Nineteenth-Century Art, Medicine, and Literature." *Critical Inquiry* 12, no. 1 (1985): 204–242.

Gilson, Greg, and Irving Levinson, eds. *Latin American Positivism: New Historical and Philosophical Essays*. New York: Lexington, 2013.

Giraudoux, Jean. *Pleins pouvoirs*. Paris: Gallimard, 1939.

Girbal de Blacha, Noemí M., and María Silvia Ospital. "Sectores de opinión y trabajo femenino: La experiencia del Museo Social Argentino, 1911–1930." In *III Jornadas de Historia de la Ciudad de Buenos Aires*. Buenos Aires: Instituto Histórico de la Ciudad de Buenos Aires, 1988.

Girón Sierra, Álvaro. "Darwinismo, darwinismo social e izquierda política (1859–1914): Reflexiones de carácter general." In *Darwinismo social y eugenesia en el mundo Latino*, edited by Marisa Miranda and Gustavo

Vallejo, 23–58. Buenos Aires: Siglo Veintiuno de Argentina Editores, 2005.

Gissis, Snait B., and Eva Jablonka. *Transformations of Lamarckism: From Subtle Fluids to Molecular Biology*. Cambridge, MA: MIT Press, 2015.

Gomes, Bernardino António. "A medicina e a hygiene ha cem annos." In *O Livro de Ouro: Comemorativo do centenário da independência do Brasil e da Exposição Internacional do Rio de Janeiro*, 290–292. Rio de Janeiro: Edição do Annuario do Brasil, 1923.

Gómez Díaz, Francisco. *De Forestier a Sert: Ciudad y arquitectura en La Habana (1925–1960)*. Barcelona: Abada Editores, 2008.

Gorelik, Adrián. *La grilla y el parque: Espacio público y cultura urbana en Buenos Aires, 1887–1936*. Buenos Aires: Universidad Nacional de Quilmes, 2004.

Greeley, Robin Adèle. "Muralism and the State in Post-Revolution Mexico, 1920–1970." In *Mexican Muralism: A Critical History*, edited by Alejandro Anreus, Robin Adèle Greeley, and Leonard Folgarait, 13–36. Berkeley: University of California Press, 2012.

Greene, Gina Marie. "Children in Glass Houses: Toward a Hygienic, Eugenic Architecture for Children during the Third Republic in France, 1870–1940." PhD diss., Princeton University, 2012.

Gresleri, Giuliano. Introduction to *La casa degli uomini* by Le Corbusier and François de Pierrefeu. Milan, Italy: Jaca Book, 1985.

Gutiérrez, Ramón. "Modelos e imaginarios europeos en urbanismo americano, 1900–1950." *Revista de Arquitectura* 8 (1996): 2–3.

Guy, Donna J. *Sex and Danger in Buenos Aires: Prostitution, Family, and Nation in Argentina*. Lincoln: University of Nebraska Press, 1991.

———. *White Slavery and Mothers Alive and Dead: The Troubled Meeting of Sex, Gender, Public Health, and Progress in Latin America*. Lincoln: University of Nebraska Press, 2000.

———. *Women Build the Welfare State: Performing Charity and Creating Rights in Argentina, 1880–1955*. Durham, NC: Duke University Press, 2009.

Hardoy, Jorge E., and R. M. Morse, eds. *Repensando la ciudad de América Latina*. Buenos Aires: Grupo Editor Latinoamericano, 1988.

Harsin, Jill. *Policing Prostitution in Nineteenth-Century Paris*. Princeton, NJ: Princeton University Press, 1985.

Hazareesingh, Sudhir. *From Subject to Citizen: The Second Empire and the Emergence of Modern French Democracy*. Princeton, NJ: Princeton University Press, 1998.

Hecht, Jennifer Michael. *The End of the Soul: Scientific Modernity, Atheism, and Anthropology in France*. New York: Columbia University Press, 2003.

Heffes, Gisela. Introduction to *Utopías urbanas: Geopolíticas del deseo en América Latina*, edited by Gisela Heffes. Madrid and Frankfurt: Iberoamericana/Vervuert, 2013.

———. *Las ciudades imaginarias en la literatura latinoamericana*. Buenos Aires: Beatriz Viterbo Editora, 2008.

———. *Políticas de la destrucción / Poéticas de la preservación: Apuntes para una lectura (eco)crítica del medio ambiente en América Latina.* Buenos Aires: Beatriz Viterbo Editora, 2013.

Hénard, Eugène. *Études sur les transformations de Paris.* Paris: Librairies-Imprimeries Réunies, 1904.

Hochman, Gilberto. *A era do saneamento: As bases da política de saúde pública no Brasil.* São Paulo: Hucitec/Anpocs, 1998.

Holmberg, Eduardo Ladislao. *Dos partidos en lucha: Fantasía científica.* Buenos Aires: Corregidor, 2005.

Holmes, Samuel J. *A Bibliography of Eugenics.* Berkeley: University of California Press, 1924.

Hora, Roy. *The Landowners of the Argentine Pampas: A Social and Political History, 1860–1945.* Oxford: Oxford University Press, 2001.

Horne, Janet R. "Le Musée social à l'origine: Les Métamorphoses d'une idée, 1889–1900." *Le Mouvement social* 171 (1995): 47–69.

———. *A Social Laboratory for Modern France: The Musée Social and the Rise of the Welfare State.* Durham, NC: Duke University Press, 2002.

Howard, Ebenezer. *Garden Cities of To-morrow.* London: Swan Sonnenschein, 1902.

———. *To-morrow: A Peaceful Path to Real Reform.* London: Swan Sonnenschein, 1898.

Huyssen, Andreas. "Geographies of Modernism in a Globalizing World." *New German Critique* 34, no. 1 100 (2007): 189–207. Accessed February 28, 2015, doi:10.1215/0094033X-2006–023.

Hyde, Timothy. *Constitutional Modernism: Architecture and Civil Society in Cuba, 1933–1959.* Minneapolis: University of Minnesota Press, 2013.

Imbert, Dorothée. *The Modernist Garden in France.* New Haven: Yale University Press, 1993.

Ingenieros, José. "Las colonias de vacaciones." *El Monitor de la Educación Común.* Buenos Aires: Consejo Nacional de Educación, 1907.

Jablonka, Eva, and Marion Lamb. *Epigenetic Inheritance and Evolution: The Lamarckian Dimension.* Oxford: Oxford University Press, 1999.

Jackson, Julian. *France, The Dark Years, 1940–1944.* Oxford: Oxford University Press, 2001.

Jarcy, Xavier de. *Le Corbusier: Un fascisme français.* Paris: Éditions Albin Michel, 2015.

Kahn, Gustave. *L'Esthétique de la rue.* Paris: Eugène Fasquelle Editeur, 1901.

Kálnay, Jorge. "Zoning y reglamento funcional." In *Primer Congreso Argentino de Urbanismo: Trabajos aprobados en las reuniones plenarias.* Vol. 2. Buenos Aires: Imprenta Mercatali, 1937.

Kevles, Daniel J. *In the Name of Eugenics: Genetics and the Uses of Human Heredity.* New York: Knopf, 1999.

Kjellén, Rudolph. *Staten som livsform.* Stockholm, Sweden: Hugo Geber, 1916.

Kruft, Hanno-Walter. *History of Architectural Theory From Vitruvius to the Present.* New York: Princeton Architectural Press, 1994.

La Berge, Ann. *Mission and Method: The Early Nineteenth-Century French Public Health Movement*. Cambridge: Cambridge University Press, 1992.

Lamarck, Jean-Baptiste. "The Influence of Circumstances." In *Lamarck to Darwin: Contributions to Evolutionary Biology, 1809–1859*, edited by Henry Lewis McKinney. Lawrence, KS: Coronado Press, 1971. First published in *Philosophie zoologique*. Paris: Dentu, 1809.

———. *Philosophie zoologique, ou Exposition des considérations relatives à l'histoire naturelle des animaux*. Cambridge: Cambridge University Press, 2011.

Latour, Bruno. "Le Théâtre de la preuve." In *Pasteur et la révolution pastorienne*, edited by Claire Salomon-Bayet. Paris: Payot, 1986.

———. *The Pasteurization of France*. Cambridge, MA: Harvard University Press, 1993.

Lattes, Alfredo E., and Ruth Sautu. "Inmigración, cambio demográfico y desarrollo industrial en la Argentina." *Cuadernos del CENEP* 5 (1978): 2–3.

Lavrin, Asunción. *Women, Feminism, and Social Change in Argentina, Chile, and Uruguay, 1880–1940*. Lincoln: University of Nebraska Press, 1998.

Le Bon, Gustave. *The Crowd: A Study of the Popular Mind (Psychologie des foules)*. New York: Viking Press, 1960.

Leclerc, Bénédicte. *Jean-Claude-Nicolas Forestier: Du jardin au paysage urbain*. Paris: Picard, 1994.

Le Corbusier. *Almanach d'architecture moderne*. Paris: Editions Crès, 1926.

———. "Commentaires relatifs à Moscou et à la 'Ville Verte.'" In Jean-Louis Cohen, *Le Corbusier et la mystique de l'URSS: théories et projets pour Moscou, 1928–1936*. Brussels, Belgium: Éditions Mardaga, 1987.

———. *The Decorative Art of Today* (1925). Translated by James I. Dunnett. London: Architectural Press, 1987. First published in French as *L'Art décoratif d'aujourd'hui*. Paris: Éditions Crès, 1925.

———. "Dégénérescence du logis, dégénérescence de la famille, c'est tout un." Radio Broadcast, FLC B3–12, no. 216. Paris: Fondation Le Corbusier, 1941.

———. *Des Canons, des munitions . . . non merci! Des logis, S.V.P.* Boulogne, France: Éditions de L'Architecture d'Aujourd'hui, 1938.

———. *Destin de Paris*. Clermont-Ferrand, France: Fernand Sorlot, 1941.

———. *The Four Routes*. London: Dennis Dobson, 1947.

———. "La révolution architecturale accomplie apporte la solution a l'urbanisation des villes"; "La dénaturalisation du phénomène urbain"; "Les loisirs: occupations véritable de la civilisation machiniste"; "Le logis considéré comme prolongement des services publics"; "Les Temps Nouveaux et la vocation de l'architecte"; and "L'autorite n'est pas renseignée." In Le Corbusier, Manuscript Lecture I, "La civilisation machiniste" (July 31, 1936), Rio de Janeiro, FLC F2–17, 2–3.

———. *L'Art décoratif d'aujourd'hui*. Paris: G. Crès, 1925.

———. "L'Autorité devant les tâches contemporaines." *L'Architecture d'aujourd'hui*, no. 9 (September 1935): 22–23.

———. *La Ville Radieuse*. Boulogne-sur-Seine, France: Éditions de L'Architecture d'aujourd'hui, 1935.

———. "Les loisirs considérés comme occupation véritable de la civilisation machiniste." Manuscript Lecture III (August 7, 1936), Rio de Janeiro, FLC C3–18. In Tsiomis, *Conférences de Rio*, 96–117.

———. *Les Trois établissements humains*. Paris: Denoël, 1945.

———. *L'Urbanisme des trois établissements humains*. Paris: Minuit, 1957.

———. *Manière de penser l'urbanisme*. Boulogne-sur-Seine, France: Editions de L'Architecture d'aujourd'hui, 1946.

———. *The Modulor: A Harmonious Measure to the Human Scale Universally Applicable to Architecture and Mechanics*. London: Faber and Faber, 1956.

———. Notes and Sketch (n/d). Fondation Le Corbusier, document F2–17, no. 275.

———. *Oeuvre complète 1934–1938*. Zurich: Éditions Girsberger, 1953.

———. *Précisions sur un état présent de l'architecture et de l'urbanisme*. Paris: G. Crès, 1930.

———. *Propos d'urbanisme*. Paris: Bourrelier, 1946.

———. *The Radiant City*. New York: Orion Press, 1967.

———. *Sur les quatres routes*. Paris: Gallimard, 1941.

———. *Urbanisme*. L'Esprit nouveau. Paris: Éditions Crès, 1925.

———. *Vers une architecture*. L'Esprit nouveau. Paris: Éditions Crès, 1923.

———. "Volonté." *Volonté* 1 (1937). Reprinted in Le Corbusier, *Des Canons, des munitions . . . non merci! Des logis, S.V.P.* Boulogne, France: Éditions de L'Architecture d'aujourd'hui, 1938.

———. "What Is America's Problem?" *American Architect* 148 (1936): 17–22. Reprinted in *When the Cathedrals Were White: A Journey to the Country of Timid People*. New York: McGraw-Hill, 1964.

Le Corbusier and Amédée Ozenfant. *La Peinture moderne*. Paris: Éditions Crès, 1926.

Le Corbusier and François de Pierrefeu. *The Home of Man*. Translated by Clive Entwistle and Gordon Holt. London: The Architectural Press, 1948.

———. *La Maison des hommes*. Paris: Plon, 1942.

Lee, Paula Young. "Modern Architecture and the Ideology of Influence." *Assemblage*, no. 34 (1997): 6–29.

Lemos, Carlos. "O estilo que nunca existiu." In *Arquitectura neocolonial: América Latina, Caribe, Estados Unidos*, edited by Aracy Amaral, 147–164. São Paulo: Memorial/Fondo de Cultura Económica, 1994.

Le Musée social, Section d'Hygiène Urbaine et Rurale et de Prévoyance Sociale, séance 16 de December 1920. *Le Musée social, Annales: Revue mensuelle* (1923): 18–19.

———. *Mémoires et documents* (1907): 328.

Léonard, Jacques. "Eugénisme et Darwinisme: Espoirs et perplexités chez des médecins français du XIXe siècle et du début du XXe siècle." In *De Darwin au Darwinisme: Science et Idéologie*, edited by Yvette Conry, 187–207. Paris: Vrin, 1983.

———. "Les origines et les consequences de l'eugenique en France." *Annales de Démographie Historique* (1985): 203–214.

Leonídio, Otavio. *Carradas de razões: Lucio Costa e a arquitetura moderna brasileira*. Rio de Janeiro: PUC-Rio Edições Loyola, 2008.

Levy, Ruth. *A Exposição do Centenário e o meio arquitetônico carioca do início dos anos 20*. Rio de Janeiro: Seba Publicações, 2010.

Lichtenberger, André. "La Lutte pour la race, espaces libres et terrains de jeux." *L'Opinion* 24 (1910): 801–803.

Liernur, Jorge Francisco. "El rol inicial del Estado: La Comisión Nacional de Casas Baratas." In Anahi Ballent and Jorge Francisco Liernur, *La casa y la multitud*, 195–213. Buenos Aires: Fondo de Cultura Económica, 2014.

———. "Fragmentos de un debate tipológico y urbanístico en la obra de Jorge Kálnay." In Anahi Ballent and Jorge Francisco Liernue, *La casa y la multitud*, 405–406. Buenos Aires: Fondo de Cultura Económica, 2014.

Lissovsky, Mauricio, and Paulo Sérgio Moraes de Sá. *Colunas da educação: A construção do Ministério da Educação e Saúde, 1935–1945*. Rio de Janeiro: Fundação Getúlio Vargas, CPDOC, 1996.

Loos, Adolf. *Ornament and Crime: Selected Essays*. Riverside, CA: Ariadne Press, 1997.

López-Durán, Fabiola. "Utopía en práctica: Eugenesia y naturaleza en la construcción de la ciudad moderna latinoamericana." In *Utopías urbanas: Geopolíticas del deseo en América Latina*, edited by Gisela Heffes, 131–164. Madrid and Frankfurt: Iberoamericana/Vervuert, 2013.

López-Durán, Fabiola, and Nikki Moore. "MEAT-MILIEU: Medicalization, Aestheticization and Productivity in The Pampas, 1868–1940." Paper presented at the 12th International Conference on Urban History-EAUH, Lisbon, Portugal, September 4, 2014.

Madrid Páez, Samuel. *Sociedad de Beneficiencia de la Capital: Su misión y sus obras, 1823–1923*. Buenos Aires: Sociedad de Beneficiencia de la Capital, 1923.

March, Lucien. "Pour la race: Infertilité et puericulture." *Revue du mois* 10 (1910): 551–582.

Marin, Louis. "Frontiers of Utopia: Past and Present." *Critical Inquiry* 19 (1992): 397–420.

———. *Utopics: Spatial Play*. London: Macmillan, 1984.

Martin, Wendy. "Remembering the Jungle: Josephine Baker and Modernist Parody." In *Prehistories of the Future: The Primitivist Project and the Culture of Modernism*, edited by Elazar Barkan and Roland Bush, 310–326. Stanford: Stanford University Press, 1995.

Mattos Pimenta, João Augusto de. "Para a remodelação do Rio de Janeiro:

Discursos pronunciados no Rotary Club do Rio de Janeiro." Lectures. Rio de Janeiro: Rotary Club, 1926.

McGuinness, Aims. "Searching for 'Latin America': Race and Sovereignty in the Americas in the 1850s." In *Race and Nation in Modern Latin America*, edited by Nancy P. Appelbaum, Anne S. Macpherson, and Karin Alejandra Rosemblatt, 87–107. Chapel Hill: University of North Carolina Press, 2003.

McLaren, Angus. *Our Own Master Race: Eugenics in Canada, 1885–1945*. Toronto: McClelland and Stewart, 1990.

McLeod, Mary Caroline. *Urbanism and Utopia: Le Corbusier from Regional Syndicalism to Vichy*. Ann Arbor, MI: University Microfilms, 1985.

Meade, Teresa A. *"Civilizing" Rio: Reform and Resistance in a Brazilian City, 1889–1930*. University Park: Pennsylvania State University Press, 1999.

Mignolo, Walter. *La idea de América Latina: La herida colonial y la opción decolonial*. Barcelona: Gedisa, 2007.

Milich, Juan E. "Medicina argentina: Ligero bosquejo histórico y evolución de la higiene en la República Argentina 1906–1910." PhD diss., Facultad de Ciencias Médicas de la Universidad Nacional de Buenos Aires, 1911.

Miranda, Marisa, and Gustavo Vallejo, eds. *Darwinismo social y eugenesia en el mundo latino*. Buenos Aires: Siglo XXI de Argentina Editores, 2005.

———. "La eugenesia y sus espacios institucionales en Argentina." In *Darwinismo social y eugenesia en el mundo latino*, edited by Marisa Miranda and Gustavo Vallejo, 145–192. Buenos Aires: Siglo XXI de Argentina Editores, 2005.

———. "Los sabores del poder: Eugenesia y biotipología en la Argentina del siglo XX." *Revista de Indias* 64, no. 231 (2004): 427. Doi: 10.3989/revindias.2004.i231.547.

Mitchell, Allan. *Socialism and the Emergence of the Welfare State: A Concise History*. Bloomington, IN: Trafford Publishing, 2012.

Mitchell, Timothy. *Colonizing Egypt*. Berkeley: University of California Press, 1988.

Mitterand, Henri. *Le Regard et le signe: Poétique du roman réaliste et naturaliste*. Paris: Presses Universitaires de France, 1987.

Monteiro Lobato, José Bento. *Mr. Slang e o Brasil e Problema vital*. São Paulo: Editora Brasiliense, 1972.

———. *O presidente negro ou O choque das raças: Romance americano do ano 2228*. São Paulo: Editora Brasiliense, 1979.

———. *Problema vital*. São Paulo: Revista do Brasil, 1918.

Morales de los Rios Filho, Adolfo. *Teoria e filosofia da arquitetura*. Rio de Janeiro: A Noite, 1955.

More, Thomas. *Utopia*. New Haven: Yale University Press, 1964.

Morris, William. *News from Nowhere, or, An Epoch of Rest: Being Some Chapters from a Utopian Romance*. New York: Cambridge University Press, 1995.

Morse, Richard M., Michael L. Conniff, and John Weibel, eds. *The Urban Development of Latin America, 1750–1920*. Stanford: Center for Latin American Studies, Stanford University, 1971.

Mory, Pascal. "Architecture et hygiénisme à Paris au début du XXe siècle: L'Architecte entre savoir médical et pouvoir politique." In *Les hygiénistes: Enjeux, modèles et pratiques*, edited by Patrice Bourdelais, 145–162. Paris: Éditions Belin, 2001.

Mumford, Lewis. "Utopia, the City and the Machine." *Daedalus* 94, no. 2 (1965): 271–292.

Murard, Lion, and Patrick Zylberman. *L'Hygiène dans la République: La Santé publique en France, ou l'utopie contrariée, 1870–1918*. Paris: Fayard, 1996.

Museo Social Argentino. "La inmigración después de la guerra: Encuesta realizada por el Museo Social Argentino." *Boletín Mensual del Museo Social Argentino* 8 (1919): xvii, 186.

———. "Orígenes y desenvolvimiento del Museo Social Argentino." *Boletín Mensual del Museo Social Argentino* 1 (1912): 5–72.

———. "Problemas agrarios: Nuestra Encuesta sobre la inmigración." *Boletín Mensual del Museo Social Argentino* 27 (1939): 262–263.

Muthesius, Hermann. "Die Werkbund-Arbeit der Zukunft." In *Der Werkbund-Gedanke in den germanischen Ländern*. Jena, Germany: Eugen Diederichs Verlag, 1914.

Nachman, Robert G. "Positivism, Modernization, and the Middle Class in Brazil." *The Hispanic American Historical Review* 57, no. 1 (1977): 1–23.

Needell, Jeffrey. *A Tropical Belle Epoque: Elite Culture and Society in Turn-of-the-Century Rio de Janeiro*. New York: Cambridge University Press, 1987.

Nelson, Brian. "Zola and the Nineteenth Century." In *The Cambridge Companion to Emile Zola*, edited by Brian Nelson, 1–18. Cambridge: Cambridge University Press, 2007.

Nelson, Ernesto. "Las plazas de juego para niños." *Boletín del Museo Social Argentino* 20 (1913): 241–307.

Nereo de Sampaio, Fernando. "Sobre capiteis (Conclusão). *Architectura no Brasil—Engenharia/Construção* 5 (1922): 155–163.

———. "Sobre capiteis (Notas de aula)." *Architectura no Brasil—Engenharia/Construção* 4 (1922): 129–135.

Newton, Sir Isaac. "Milieu." In *Encyclopédie*, edited by Denis Diderot and Jean le Rond d'Alembert. New York: Abrams, 1978.

Nonato, Jose Antonio, and Nubia Melhem Santos. *Era uma vez o Morro do Castelo*. Rio de Janeiro: IPHAN, 2000.

Nouzeilles, Gabriela. "Pathological Romances and National Dystopias in Argentine Naturalism." *Latin American Literary Review* 24 (1996): 23–39.

Novick, Alicia. "Foreign Hires: French Experts and the Urbanism of Buenos Aires, 1907–1932." In *Urbanism: Imported or Exported? Native*

Aspirations and Foreign Plans, edited by Joe Nasr and Mercedes
Volait, 263–289. Chichester, West Sussex, UK: Wiley-Academy, 2003.
———. "La ciudad de la reforma social bajo el prisma del Museo Social
Argentino." In *Pensar Buenos Aires: X Jornadas de Historia de la
Ciudad de Buenos Aires*. Buenos Aires: Municipalidad de la Ciudad de
Buenos Aires, 1994.
———. "Le Musée social et l'urbanisme en Argentine, 1911–1923."
In *Le Musée social en son temps*, edited by Collette Chambelland,
331–358. Paris: Presses de l'École Normale Superieure, 1998.
Nye, Robert A. *Crime, Madness and Politics in Modern France: The Medi-
cal Concept of National Decline*. Princeton, NJ: Princeton University
Press, 1984.
O'Lery, María de las Mercedes. "Aportes acerca de la relación iglesia-
eugenesia en Argentina, 1930–1940." In *Políticas del cuerpo: Estrate-
gias modernas de normalización del individuo y la sociedad*, edited by
Marisa Miranda and Gustavo Vallejo, 365–376. Buenos Aires: Siglo
XXI Editora Iberoamericana, 2007.
Ortiz, Federico, Alberto S. J. de Paula, and Ricardo Gregorio Parera. *La
arquitectura del liberalismo en la Argentina*. Buenos Aires: Editorial
Sudamericana, 1968.
Osti, Giovanna. "Il Musée social di Parigi e gli inizi dell'urbanistica
francese (1894–1914)." Tesi di laurea, Istituto universitario di architet-
tura di Venezia, 1982–1983.
Outtes, Joel. "Disciplinando la sociedad a través de la ciudad: El origen
del urbanismo en Argentina y Brasil (1894–1945)." *Portafolio* 13 (2006):
50–65.
Overy, Paul. *Light, Air and Openness: Modern Architecture Between the
Wars*. London: Thames and Hudson, 2007.
Palacio, Michel. "Musée social et urbanistique sud-américaine." Mémoire
de DEA Politiques urbaines. Thesis, Université de Paris XII, 1993.
Palermo, Lynn E. "Identity under Construction: Representing the
Colonies at the Paris 'Exposition Universelle' of 1889." In *The Color of
Liberty: Histories of Race in France*, edited by Sue Peabody and Stovall
Tyler, 285–301. Durham, NC: Duke University Press, 2003.
Pearson, Karl. *The Life, Letters and Labours of Francis Galton*. Vol. 3A.
Cambridge: Cambridge University Press, 1930.
Peixoto, Afrânio. "O ensino público no Brasil." In *O Livro de Ouro:
Comemorativo do Centenário da Independência do Brasil e da
Exposição Internacional do Rio de Janeiro*, 115–121. Rio de Janeiro:
Edição do Annuario do Brasil, 1923.
Pelosi, Hebe Carmen. "El Centenario y la 'cuestión social': Una iniciativa
académica." In *Temas de historia argentina y americana*, 81–104.
Buenos Aires: Universidad Católica Argentina e Instituto de Historia
Argentina y Americana, 2004. http://bibliotecadigital.uca.edu.ar
/repositorio/revistas/temas-de-historia05.pdf.
———. *El Museo Social Argentino y la Universidad del Museo Social
Argentino*. Buenos Aires: Universidad del Museo Social Argentino, 2000.

Penna, José, and Horacio Madero. *La administración sanitaria y Asistencia Pública de la Ciudad de Buenos Aires*. Buenos Aires: Imprenta, Litografía y Encuadernación de G. Kraft, 1910.

Perelman, Marc. *Le Corbusier, une froide vision du monde*. Paris: Michalon Éditeur, 2015.

Petit, Edouard. "L'Alliance et les Écoles de plein air." *Bulletin Alliance d'Hygiene Sociale* 21 (1911): 45.

Pezolet, Nicola. "Spectacles Plastiques: Reconstruction and the Debates on the 'Synthesis of the Arts' in France, 1944–1962." PhD diss., MIT, 2013.

Phelan, John L. "Pan-Latinism, French Intervention in Mexico (1861–1867) and the Genesis of the Idea of Latin America." In *Conciencia y autenticidad históricas*, edited by Juan Ortega y Medina, 279–298. Mexico City: Universidad Nacional Autónoma de México, 1968.

Picard, Alfred, ed. *Exposition universelle internationale de 1889 à Paris: Rapport du jury international: Groupe de l'économie sociale*. Paris: Imprimerie nationale, in association with Ministère du commerce, de l'industrie et des colonies, 1891–1892.

Pick, Daniel. *Faces of Degeneration: A European Disorder, c. 1848–1918*. Cambridge: Cambridge University Press, 1989.

Pierre-Gnassounou, Chantal. "Zola and the Art of Fiction." In *The Cambridge Companion to Emile Zola*, edited by Brian Nelson, 86–104. Cambridge: Cambridge University Press, 2007.

Pinard, Adolphe. "De la dépopulation de la France." *Revue Scientifique*, July 30, 1910, 30. In Anne Carol, "Médecine et eugénisme en France, ou l rêve d'une prophylaxie parfaite (XIXe–première moitié du XXe siècle)." *Revue d'histoire moderne et contemporaine* 4, no. 43–44 (1996): 618–631.

Pitsos, Nikolaos. *L'Alliance d'hygiène sociale: L'Histoire d'une association entre l'hygiénisme et le solidarisme, 1904–1955*. Mémoire de DEA: Politiques sociales et société, Université Paris I, 2005.

Planas y Sáinz, Juan Manuel. *La corriente del Golfo*. Havana: El Fígaro, 1920.

———. "Las teorías del Profesor Miliscenios." *El Fígaro* (Cuba), 1917.

Plato. *The Republic*. Reprint. Champaign, IL: Project Gutenberg, 1990s.

Primeiro Congresso Brasileiro de Eugenia. *Primeiro Congresso Brasileiro de Eugenia: Actas e Trabalhos*, Vol. 1. Rio de Janeiro: N.p., 1929.

Pschepiurca, Pablo. "Buenos Aires: Los parques." Unpublished manuscript, accessed online. http://www.asnnoise.com.ar/wp-content/uploads/los-parques-11–01.pdf.

———. "Palermo, la construcción del parque." *SUMMA Temática* 3 (1983).

Quelhas Paixão, Cláudia Míriam. "O Rio de Janeiro e o morro do Castelo: Populares, estratégias de vida e hierarquias sociais." Master's thesis, Universidade Federal Fluminense, 2008.

Quezado Deckker, Zilah. *Brazil Built: The Architecture of the Modern Movement in Brazil*. London: Spon Press, 2001.

Quiroule, Pierre. *La ciudad anarquista americana.* Buenos Aires: La Protesta, 1914.

Rabinow, Paul. *French Modern: Norms and Forms of the Social Environment.* Chicago: University of Chicago Press, 1995.

Rama, Ángel. *La ciudad letrada.* Hanover, NH: Ediciones del Norte, 1984.

———. *The Lettered City.* Durham, NC: Duke University Press, 1996.

Ramos Mejía, José María. *Las multitudes argentinas: Estudio de psicología colectiva para servir de introducción al libro "Rosas y su tiempo."* Buenos Aires: Félix Lajouane, 1899.

———. "The Modern Crowd." In *The Argentina Reader: History, Culture, Politics,* edited by Gabriela Nouzeilles and Graciela Montaldo, 182–187. Durham, NC: Duke University Press, 2002.

Rangel, Fernando. "A igreja no Brasil." In *O Livro de Ouro: Comemorativo do Centenário da Independência do Brasil e da Exposição Internacional do Rio de Janeiro,* 287–288. Rio de Janeiro: Edição do Annuario do Brasil, 1923.

Reclus, Elisée. "A Great Globe." *The Geographical Journal* 12, no. 4 (1898): 401–406.

Reggiani, Andrés Horacio. "Alexis Carrel, the Unknown: Eugenics and Population Research under Vichy." *French Historical Studies* 25, no. 2 (2002): 331–356.

———. *God's Eugenicist: Alexis Carrel and the Sociobiology of Decline.* New York: Berghahn Books, 2007.

Rey, M. A. Augustin. "L'École de l'avenir." *Transactions of the 15th International Congress on Hygiene and Demography* 3 (September 1912): 103–115.

Rhodes, Henry T. F. *Alphonse Bertillon: Father of Scientific Detection.* New York: Abelard-Schuman, 1956.

Ribeiro, Darcy. "Yvy-Marãen: A terra sem males, ano 2997." In Darcy Ribeiro, *Utopia Brazil,* edited by Isa Grinspum Ferraz, 37–58. São Paulo: Hedra, 2008.

Richardson, Benjamin Ward. *Diseases of Modern Life.* New York: D. Appleton, 1876.

———. *Hygeia* (Spanish version). *Revista Médico Quirúrgica, Publicación Quincenal: Órgano de los Intereses Médicos Argentinos,* no. 12 (1876).

———. *Hygeia, a City of Health.* London: Macmillan, 1876.

Richet, Charles. *La sélection humaine.* Paris: F. Alcan, 1922.

Riot-Sarcey, Michèle, Thomas Bouchet, and Antoine Picon. *Dictionnaire des utopies.* Paris: Larousse, 2002.

Risler, Georges. "Les Plans d'amenagement et d'extension des villes." *Memoires et documents du Musée Social* 11 (1912): 304.

———. "L'hygiène de la maison." *Le Musée Social* 8 (1925): 226.

Rock, David. *Argentina 1516–1987.* Berkeley: University of California Press, 1987.

———. *Argentina, 1516–1982: From Spanish Colonization to the Falklands.* Berkeley: University of California Press, 2003.

———. *Politics in Argentina, 1890–1930: The Rise and Fall of Radicalism.* Cambridge: Cambridge University Press, 1975.

Rodríguez, Julia. *Civilizing Argentina: Science, Medicine, and the Modern State.* Chapel Hill: University of North Carolina Press, 2006.

Rogers, James Allen. "Darwinism and Social Darwinism." *Journal of the History of Ideas* 33 (1972): 265–280.

Romero, José Luis. *Latinoamérica: Las ciudades y las ideas.* Buenos Aires: Siglo XXI Editores, 2005.

Roquette-Pinto, Edgard. "Inaugural Session." *First Brazilian Congress of Eugenics (Congresso Brasileiro de Eugenia), Actas e Trabalhos.* Vol. 1. Rio de Janeiro: N.p., 1929.

———. "Nota sobre os typos antropológicos do Brasil." *Primeiro Congresso Brasileiro de Eugenia: Actas e trabalhos* (Rio de Janeiro) 1 (1929): 119–148.

———. "Second Session." *First Brazilian Congress of Eugenics (Congresso Brasileiro de Eugenia), Actas e Trabalhos.* Vol. 1. Rio de Janeiro: N.p., 1929.

Rose, Nikolas. "Medicine, History and the Present." In *Reassessing Foucault: Power, Medicine and the Body*, edited by Colin Jones and Roy Porter, 48–72. London: Routledge, 1994.

Rosso del Brenna, Giovanna. *O Rio de Janeiro de Pereira Passos.* Rio de Janeiro: Index, 1985.

———. *O Rio de Janeiro de Pereira Passos: Uma cidade em questão II.* Rio de Janeiro: PUC/RJ/Shell, 1985.

Sampaio, Carlos. *O arrasamento do Morro do Castelo.* Paris: Société Française d'Imprimerie, n.d., ca. 1920.

Santos-Dumont, Alberto. *My Airships: The Story of My Life.* London: G. Richards, 1904.

Sarmiento, Domingo F. *Facundo, ó Civilización y barbarie en las pampas argentinas.* Buenos Aires: Stock Cero, 2003.

———. *Facundo: Or, Civilization and Barbarism.* English translation. New York: Penguin, 1998.

Schindler, Sarah. "Architectural Exclusion: Discrimination and Segregation through Physical Design of the Built Environment." *Yale Law Journal* 124, no. 6 (2015): 1937–2024.

Schneider, William H. "Puericulture, and the Style of French Eugenics." *History and Philosophy of the Life Sciences* 8, no. 2 (1986): 265–277.

———. *Quality and Quantity: The Quest for Biological Regeneration in Twentieth-Century France.* Cambridge: Cambridge University Press, 1990.

Scobie, James. "The Paris of South America." In *The Argentina Reader: History, Culture, Politics*, edited by Gabriela Nouzeilles and Graciela Montaldo, 170–181. Durham, NC: Duke University Press, 2002.

Scott, James C. *Seeing Like a State: How Certain Schemes to Improve the Human Condition Have Failed.* New Haven: Yale University Press, 1998.

Sedrez, Lise Fernanda. "'The Bay of All Beauties': State and Environment in Guanabara Bay, Rio de Janeiro, Brazil, 1875–1975." PhD diss., Stanford University, 2004.

Segawa, Hugo. *Arquiteturas no Brasil, 1900–1990.* São Paulo: EDUSP, 1999.

Sekula, Allan. "The Body and the Archive." *October* 39 (1986): 3–64.

Sevcenko, Nicolau. *A Revolta da Vacina: Mentes insanas em corpos rebeldes.* São Paulo: Scipione, 2003.

———. *Literatura como missão: Tensões sociais e criação cultural na Primeira República.* São Paulo: Brasiliense, 1983.

Shostak, Sara, and Margot Moinester. "The Missing Piece of the Puzzle? Measuring the Environment in the Postgenomic Moment." In *Postgenomics: Perspectives on Biology after the Genome*, edited by Sarah Richardson and Hallam Stevens, 192–209. Durham, NC: Duke University Press, 2015.

Shumway, Nicolas. *The Invention of Argentina.* Berkeley: University of California Press, 1993.

Sicard de Plauzoles, Justin. *Principes d'hygiène sociale.* Paris: Editions médicales, 1927.

Silva, Lúcia Helena Pereira da. "A trajetória de Alfred Donat Agache no Brasil." In *Cidade, povo e nação: Gênese do urbanismo modern*, edited by Luiz Cesar de Queiroz Ribeiro and Robert Pechaman, 397–410. Rio de Janeiro: Civilização Brasileira, 1996.

———. "Engenheiros, arquitetos e urbanistas: A historia da elite burocratica na cidade do Rio de Janeiro, 1920–1945." Master's thesis, IPPUR/Universidade Federal do Rio de Janeiro, 1995.

Silverman, Debora L. *Art Nouveau in Fin-de-Siècle France: Politics, Psychology, and Style.* Berkeley: University of California Press, 1992.

———. "The 1889 Exhibition: The Crisis of Bourgeois Individualism." *Oppositions* 8 (1977): 71–91.

Silvestri, Graciela. *El color del río: Historia cultural del paisaje del Riachuelo.* Quilmes, Argentina: Universidad Nacional de Quilmes, 2004.

Silvia Di Liscia, María. "Colonias y escuelas de niños débiles: Los instrumentos higiénicos para la eugenesia: primera mitad del siglo XX en Argentina." In *Instituciones y formas de control social en América Latina, 1840–1940*, edited by María Silvia Di Liscia and Ernesto Bohoslavsky, 93–113. Buenos Aires: Prometeo, 2005.

Sioen, Aquilles. *Buenos Aires en el año 2080: Historia verosímil.* Buenos Aires: Igon Hermanos, 1879.

Sisto, Genaro. Preface to Enrique Feinmann, *La ciencia del niño: Nociones de puericultura e higiene infantil.* Buenos Aires: Cabaut, 1915.

Skidmore, Thomas E. *Black into White: Race and Nationality in Brazilian Thought.* Durham, NC: Duke University Press, 1998.

———. *Fact and Myth: Discovering a Racial Problem in Brazil.* São Paulo: Instituto de Estudos Avançados, 1992.

Skidmore, Thomas E., and Peter H. Smith. *Modern Latin America.* New York: Oxford University Press, 2005.

Soria, Benito. *En el surco: Gimnasios públicos y escuelas al aire libre para niños débiles*. Córdoba, Argentina: Imprenta Argentina V. Rossi, 1917.

Souza, Robert de. *Nice, capitale d'hiver*. Paris: Berger-Levrault, 1913.

Spencer, Herbert. *Principles of Biology*. Ithaca: Cornell University Library, 2009. Originally published in 1864.

Stach, Francisco. "La defensa social y la inmigración." *Boletín del Museo Social Argentino* 5 (1916): 361–389.

Stepan, Nancy Leys. *The Hour of Eugenics: Race, Gender, and Nation in Latin America*. Ithaca, NY: Cornell University Press, 1991.

———. *Picturing Tropical Nature*. London: Reaktion Books, 2001.

Stephens, Elizabeth. "Normal." *TSQ: Transgender Studies Quarterly* 1, nos. 1–2 (2014): 141–145. doi:10.1215/23289252-2399848.

Stern, Alexandra Minna. "Responsible Mothers and Normal Children: Eugenics, Nationalism, and Welfare in Post-revolutionary Mexico, 1920–1940." *Journal of Historical Sociology* 12, no. 4 (1999): 369–397.

Stone, Judith. *The Search for Social Peace: Reform Legislation in France, 1890–1914*. Albany: University of New York Press, 1985.

Stuckenbruck, Denise Cabral. *O Rio de Janeiro em questão: O Plano Agache e o ideário reformista dos anos 20*. Rio de Janeiro: IPPUR/FASE, 1996.

Suárez y López Guazo, Laura Luz. *Eugenesia y racismo en México*. Mexico City: Universidad Nacional Autónoma de México, 2005.

Sutcliffe, Anthony. *Paris: An Architectural History*. New Haven: Yale University Press, 1993.

Swanson, Philip. *The Companion to Latin American Studies*. London: Arnold, 2003.

Talak, Ana María. "Eugenesia e higiene mental: Usos de la psicología en la Argentina, 1900–1940." In *Darwinismo social y eugenesia en el mundo latino*, edited by Marisa Miranda and Gustavo Vallejo, 563–600. Buenos Aires: Siglo XXI de Argentina Editores, 2005.

Tenorio, Mauricio. "Um Cuauhtemoc carioca: Comemorando o Centenário da Independência do Brasil e a raça cósmica." *Revista Estudos Históricos* 7, no. 14 (1994): 23–148.

Teyssot, Georges. "Norm and Type: Variations on a Theme." In *Architecture and the Sciences: Exchanging Metaphors*, edited by Antoine Picon and Alessandra Ponte, 150–151. New York: Princeton Architectural Press, 2003.

———. *A Topology of Everyday Constellations*. Cambridge, MA: MIT Press, 2013.

Thiher, Allen. *Fiction Rivals Science: The French Novel from Balzac to Proust*. Columbia: University of Missouri Press, 2001.

Tonina, Dr. "Funciones de las escuelas al aire libre." *El Monitor de la Educación Común*. Buenos Aires: Consejo Nacional de Educación, 1924.

Topalov, Christian. "Da questão social aos problemas urbanos: Os reformadores e a população das metrópoles em princípios do século XX." In *Cidade, povo e nação: Gênese do urbanismo moderno*, edited by Luiz

Cesar de Queiroz Ribeiro and Robert Pechman, 23–52. Rio de Janeiro: Civilização Brasileira, 1996.

———. "From the 'Social Question' to 'Urban Problems': Reformers and the Working Classes at the Turn of the Twentieth Century." *International Social Science Journal* 125 (1990): 319–336.

Tsiomis, Yannis. *Conférences de Rio: Le Corbusier au Brésil-1936*. Paris: Flammarion, 2006.

Turner, Jonathan. "Analytical Theorizing." In *Social Theory Today*, edited by Anthony Giddens and Jonathan Turner, 156–194. Stanford: Stanford University Press, 1987.

Udovicki-Selb, Danilo. "Le Corbusier and the Paris Exhibition of 1937: The Temps Nouveaux Pavilion." *Journal of the Society of Architectural Historians* 56 (1997): 51–52, accessed February 28, 2014, DOI:10.1086/599247.

Underwood, David K. "Alfred Agache, French Sociology, and Modern Urbanism in France and Brazil." *Journal of the Society of Architectural Historians* 50, no. 2 (1991): 130–166.

Urzaiz Rodríguez, Eduardo. *Eugenia: A Fictional Sketch of Future Customs*. Madison: University of Wisconsin Press, 2016. Originally published in 1919.

———. *Eugenia: Esbozo novelesco de costumbres futuras*. Mexico City: Premiá Editora de Libros, 1982. First edition: Mérida, Yucatán: Talleres Gráficos A. Manzanilla, 1919. Later editions: Universidad Autónoma de Yucatán and the Universidad Autónoma Nacional de México.

Valladares, Licia. *La favela d'un siècle à l'autre: Mythe d'origine, discours scientifiques et représentations virtuelles*. Paris: Fondation Maison des sciences de l'homme, 2006.

Varela, Luis V. *El doctor Whüntz: Fantasía*. Buenos Aires: N.p., 1881.

Vargas Llosa, Mario. "La caza del gay." *El País*, April 8, 2012, accessed June 25, 2012. http://elpais.com/elpais/2012/04/04/opinion/1333540547_113226.html.

Vasconcelos, José. *La raza cósmica / The Cosmic Race*. Baltimore: Johns Hopkins University Press, 1979.

Vaz, Lilian Fessler. "Dos cortiços às favelas e aos edifícios de apartamentos—a modernização da moradia no Rio de Janeiro." *Análise Social* 29, no. 127 (1994): 590–591.

Ventura Santos, Ricardo. "Guardian Angel on a Nation's Path: Contexts and Trajectories of Physical Anthropology in Brazil in the Late Nineteenth and Early Twentieth Centuries." *Current Anthropology* 53 (2012): S17–S32.

Vera y González, Enrique. *La estrella del sur*. Reprint. Buenos Aires: Instituto Histórico de la Ciudad de Buenos Aires, 2000. Originally published in 1904.

Vernes, Michel. "Genèse et avatars du jardin publique." *Monuments Historiques* 142 (1986): 4–10.

Vezzetti, Hugo. "'Viva Cien Años': Algunas consideraciones sobre familia y matrimonio en la Argentina." *Punto de Vista*, no. 27 (1986): 5–10.

Vigarello, Georges. "Le temps du sport." In Alain Corbin, *L'avènement des loisirs, 1850–1960*. Barcelona: Flammarion, 2009.

———. *Une histoire culturelle du sport: Techniques d'hier et d'aujourd'hui*. Paris: Laffont et Revue EPS, 1988.

Vignati, Juan. "Informe de la Colonia de Vacaciones para niños débiles del Parque Avellaneda: Temporada 1920–1921." *El Monitor de la Educación Común*. Buenos Aires: Consejo Nacional de Educación, 1921.

Violich, Francis. *Cities of Latin America: Housing and Planning to the South*. New York: Reinhold Publishing, 1944.

Virey, Julien-Joseph. "Vie ou force vitale." In *Dictionnaire des sciences médicales*. 60 vols. Paris: Panckoucke, 1812.

von Moos, Stanislaus. *Le Corbusier: Elements of a Synthesis*. Rotterdam: 010 Publishers, 2009.

Wallace, Alfred Russel. "On the Law Which Has Regulated the Introduction of New Species." *Annals and Magazine of Natural History* 16 (1855): 184–196.

———. "On the Tendency of Varieties to Depart Indefinitely from the Original Type." *Journal of the Proceeding of the Linnaean Society of London (Zoology)* 3 (1858): 52–62.

Wallace, R. W. "Argentina's Centennial." *The Journal of Education* 71–72 (1910): 747–748.

Weber, Eugen. *France, Fin de Siècle*. Cambridge, MA: Harvard University Press, 1986.

Welter, Volker M. *Biopolis: Patrick Geddes and the City of Life*. Cambridge, MA: MIT Press, 2002.

Williams, Daryle. *Culture Wars in Brazil: The First Vargas Regime, 1930–1945*. Durham, NC: Duke University Press, 2001.

Winter, Pierre. "Pour une science de l'homme." *L'Homme réel* 1 (1934): 37–42.

Wolf, Paul. *Eugène Hénard and the Beginning of Urbanism in Paris, 1900–1914*. The Hague, Netherlands: Ando, 1968.

Wolfe, Cary. "Life: Neovitalism and Biopolitical Thought." Lecture, Townsend Center for the Humanities Forum on the Humanities and the Public World, University of California-Berkeley, Berkeley, August 31, 2011. Filmed [August 2011], Townsend Center video, 01:25:30. Posted [August 2011], http://townsendcenter.berkeley.edu/media /cary-wolfe-english-rice-university.

Wright, Gwendolyn. *The Politics of Design in French Colonial Urbanism*. Chicago: University of Chicago Press, 1991.

Zavala, Adriana. "The *India Bonita* Contest: Gender, Tradition and Modernity in Mexico City, 1921." In *Seeing and Beyond: Essays on Eighteenth- to Twenty-First-Century Art in Honor of Kermit S. Champa*, edited by Deborah J. Johnson and David Ogawa, 277–306. New York: Peter Lang, 2005.

Zola, Émile. *Au Bonheur des Dames*. Philadelphia: T. B. Peterson and Bros., 1883.

———. *Carnets d'enquêtes: Une ethnographie inédite de la France*. Edited by Henri Mitterand. Terre Humaine. Paris: Librairie Plon, 1986.

———. "De la description." In *Le Roman expérimental*. Paris: Charpentier, 1880.

———. "Dépopulation." *Le Figaro*, May 16, 1896.

———. *Fecondité*. Paris: Charpentier, 1899.

———. *The Fortune of the Rougons: A Natural and Social History of a Family under the Second Empire*. London: Chatto and Windus, 1898.

———. *Fruitfulness*. Translated by Ernest Alfred Vizetelly. London: Chatto and Windus, 1900.

———. *Germinal*. Paris: Fasquelle, 1885.

———. *La Bête humaine*. Paris: Charpentier, 1890.

———. *La Conquête de Plassans*. Paris: Charpentier, 1874.

———. *La Curée*. Paris: A. Lacroix Verboeckhoven, 1871.

———. *La Débâcle*. Paris: N.p., 1892.

———. *La Faute de l'abbé Mouret*. Paris: Fasquelle, 1876.

———. *La Fortune des Rougon*. Paris: Charpentier, 1879.

———. *La Joie de vivre*. Paris: Charpentier, 1884.

———. *L'Argent*. Paris: Charpentier, 1891.

———. *L'Assommoir*. Paris: Charpentier, 1877.

———. *La Terre*. Paris: Charpentier, 1888.

———. *Le Docteur Pascal*. Paris: Charpentier et E. Fasquelle, 1893.

———. *Le Rêve*. Paris: Charpentier, 1888.

———. *Le Roman expérimental*. Paris: Charpentier, 1880.

———. *Le Ventre de Paris*. Paris: Charpentier, 1873.

———. *L'Œuvre*. Paris: Charpentier, 1886.

———. *Nana*. Paris: F. Mackar, 1879.

———. *Pot-Bouille*. Paris: Charpentier, 1882.

———. Preface to *La Fortune des Rougon*. In Emile Zola, *Les Rougon-Macquart: Histoire naturelle et sociale d'une famille sous le Second Empire*, edited by Henri Mitterand, 5 vols. Paris: Tchou, 'Cercle du Livre Precieux,' 1966–1970.

———. *Son Excellence Eugène Rougon*. Paris: Charpentier, 1876.

———. *Une page d'amour*. Paris: Charpentier, 1878.

INDEX

Note: Page numbers in *italics* refer to figures.

La administración sanitaria y Asistencia Pública de la Ciudad de Buenos Aires (Penna and Madero), 93–102, *94–96, 98–100*

Agache, Donat-Alfred: anthropogeography and, 78; chosen for Rio de Janeiro master plan, 70; garden city and, 54–55; "human plant," 55; Kahn and, 54; lectures in Rio, 71–72, 214n93; as positivist missionary, 73; Rio de Janeiro Master Plan, 56–57, 72–79, *73–76, 79, 157*

Agamben, Giorgio, 84

Agote, Luis, 223n39

agricultural home (*hogar agrícola*) project, 110

Alberdi, Juan Bautista, 41, 109

Alberti, Leon Battista, 23

alcoholism. *See* "social diseases"

Alliance d'hygiène sociale (Musée social), 53–54

Alliance nationale pour l'accroissement de la population française, 221n23

Almandoz, Arturo, 197n30

Alphand, Jean-Charles Adolphe, 118, 119, 228n128

Amadeo, Tomás, 108, 226n84

Amaral, Tarsila do, 2?

Andrade, Mário de, 71, ?

Andrade, Oswald de, 215n

André, Édouard, 119, 228n1?

anthropogeography, 78–79

"Anthropophagic Manifesto" (Andrade), 215n96, 248n130

anthropotechnology (*anthropotechn?* 47

Antônio, Celso, 180–181, *182*, 248n132

Antônio Gomes, Bernardino, 211n50

architectural styles: clinical agenda of, 102; as ideology, 212n66; International Style, 81–82; neoclassicism, 215n98; propagation of, 63–64. *See also* neocolonial style

architecture: biopolitics and, 107; body-environment dynamic and, 27; as handmaiden of health and reform, 138; Kálnay on urbanism and, 140; Lamarck and, 5; Le Corbusier and Pierrefeu on stability and, 176; Le Corbusier on architect as technocrat and architectural revolution, 158–161; Le Corbusier's link between agriculture and, 159–160; modern architecture as medical equipment, 234n204; Musée social and social function of, 54; as primary vehicle for remaking every aspect of human life, 130;

bordellos, 137. *See also* prostitutes, regulation and spatialization of
Borges, Dain, 36
"born criminal" thesis, 47
Bourdelle, Antoine, 248n132
Bouvard, Joseph Antoine, 39, 115, 119
Boyer, Christine, 247n124
Brasília, 192, 206n98, 215n94, 251n9
brasilidade, 183
Brazil: African population in, 197n34; capitals of, 215n94; Centennial Exhibition (1922), *62–66*, 62–68, 211n58; Department of Infancy, 68; Estado Novo, 243n46, 249n141; First Republic, 62, 211n58; modernist pavilion, 1939 World's Fair (New York), 183–184; in Monteiro Lobato's *O presidente negro ou O choque das raças*, 34; neocolonial as national style, 71, 215n97, 249n141; "Ordem e Progresso" (Order and Progress) motto, 194n13; physical transformation of, 12; puericulture in, 68–70; reverence for medicine in, 204n73; Roquette-Pinto's racial typology of, *180*, 249n137; São Paulo, 167, 197n33, 215n96; urban population growth in, 11, 197n33; whitening policy, 35; "white only" decree (1921), 61. *See also* Rio de Janeiro
Brazil Builds exhibition (MOMA), 183, 250n144
"Brazilian Man" ideal, *180*, 180–182
brise-soleil, 81, 183–184
Buenos Aires: Avenida Costanera, 128, *128*, *129*; Casas de Socorro (miniature hospitals), 115; centennial celebration and fears of degeneration, 90–91; as centerless city (Carrasco), 121; clinical agenda of architecture and, 102–103; Coni's "La ciudad argentina ideal o del porvenir," 40–41; Cosme Argerich Hospital, 115; Department of Public Welfare, 95, 113, 227n110; economic boom and political and social conflicts in, 91–92; Forestier's Master Plan (1924), 40, 56, *56*, *57*, 123–128, *124*, *126–129*; Gran Parque del Sur, 231n171; hygiene council, 223n39; immigration to, *20*, *21*, 91; Jardín

de los Irlandeses, 127, *127*; medical diagnosis sought for, 93; municipal baths, *38*, *39*; Parque Avellaneda, *124*, 125–126, 231n173; Parque del Oeste (planned), 229n142; Parque de los Patricios, 120, 229n142; Parque Saavedra, *126*, 232n177; Parque Tres de Febrero, 229n136; Penna and Madero report on modern pathogenic city, 93–102, *94–96*, *98–100*, 137–138; population growth, 197n33; productivity focus, 101–102; Ramos Mejía's "biology of the crowd" and, 92–93; restorative gardens, 118–121, 125–128; La Rotonda immigrants' hotel, *20*; as sanitary utopia in Sioen's *Buenos Aires en el año 2080*, 37; Torcuato de Alvear Hospital, 115; Tornu Sanatorium, 115
Buenos Aires en al año 2080 (Sioen), 37, 39
Buffon, Georges-Louis Leclerc, Comte de, 193n5, 221n20
Bullrich, Adolfo, 120
Bunge, Carlos Octavio, 116
Burle Marx, Roberto, *81*, 214n90

Cabet, Étienne, 23, *25*
Calmette, Albert, 230n157
Campanella, Tommaso, 200n15
Canguilhem, Georges, 7, 149, 202n33
Capanema, Gustavo, 180–181, 248n131
Caracas, 57
Carlos, J., *77*, 217n111
Carnot, Sadi, 211n58
Carol, Anne, 195n22
Caron, Charles Alfred, 209n26
Carpenter, Frank G., 234n211
carpetas de casas (house folders), 101
Carrasco, Benito, *38*, 39, 120, 121, 124, 135, 230n144, 234n212
Carrel, Alexis: *Athens Charter* and, 246n99; Le Corbusier and, 155–156, 161–166, *170*, 171–172, 174, *178*, 178–179, 184–188, *185*; *Man, the Unknown*, 156, 161, 163, 164–165, 172, 197n29, 242n43; at Rockefeller Institute, 244n67
Carrel Foundation (French Foundation for the Study of Human Problems), 178, 248n127

criminality: "born criminal" thesis, 47;
children's playground to prevent,
126; criminal typing and biotypology in Argentina, 103–108; Loos's
"Ornament and Crime," 150
criminal typing, 103–104
crowd, biology of (Ramos Mejía), 92–93
Cruz, Oswaldo, 67
Cuba: Forestier's comprehensive plan
for Havana, 242n36; Plaza de la
Fraternidad, Havana (Forestier),
153, 154, 242n38
Cuerpo Médico Escolar (medical
academic committee), 130, 233n190
La Curée (Zola), 88, 221n22

dactyloscopic analysis, 104–106
Daladier, Édouard, 171
Darwin, Charles: Galton and, 19,
199n9; naturalism and, 222n24;
natural selection and society,
251n3; Pangenesis theory, 196n25;
Tree of Life, 172; Wallace and,
194n9
Darwinism, social, 14, 190
De Condorcet, Nicolas, 1
degeneration (*dégénérescence*): first
appearance of term, 219n6; French
obsession with, 84, 239n7; Le
Corbusier and Pierrefeu on French
population and, 174–175; Manouvrier on Lombroso's "born criminal"
thesis and, 47; social diseases as
explanation for, 84; three culprits
of, 51; Zola's *Les Rougon-Macquart*
and *Fecondité*, 84–90
Delort de Gléon, Alphonse, *48*, 207n9
Department of Infancy, Brazil, 68
Dermée, Paul, 145
Deutscher Werkbund, 240n19
development: agricultural, 109; of
children, 141; defined, 198n48;
Le Corbusier on master
plan as rational tool for, 175;
modernization and, 13–14; Social
Economy Exhibition and, 49;
"un-underdevelopment," 26, 201n23
Didi-Huberman, Georges, 235n224
disease and illness: Jenner on naturalness and, 201n27; *Livro de Ouro*
on eradication of, 67–68; Penna
and Madero maps of distributions

of, in Buenos Aires, *94–96*, 96–97;
as relationship, 94; social hygiene
and fear of, 37. *See also* "social
diseases"
disinfection, 98–100, *98–100*
dispensaries, 117–118, 137–138
dispositifs: *casillero sanitario / casier
sanitaire*, 100–101; criminal
typing and biotypology, 103–108;
definitions of, 84, 111, 219n4;
family house, 139–142; restorative
gardens, 118–129; schools for
"weak" children (Escuelas de Niños
Débiles), 129–136, *133*, *134*; spaces
of quarantine and reproduction for
women, 136–142
Le Docteur Pascal (Zola), *85*, 87, 88,
220n17
Dubos, René J.: "Medical Utopias," 26
Duclaux, Émile, 50, 205n82
Dupont, Benjamin, 137
Durkheim, Émile, 224n69

École des Beaux-Arts, 183, 250n145
Écoles de Plein Air (France), 132,
233n199–234n200. *See also*
open-air schools
eco-utopias, 36–41
education for women and children, 116
Eiffel Tower, 1, *5*, *45*, 206n1
Ellis Island, *21*
environment: body-environment
dynamic, 26–28; epigenetics research and, 191; French worldview
of importance of, 47; molecular
biology and, 207n7; Roquette-Pinto
and built environment, 80. *See also*
specific places and topics, such as
milieu
epigenetics, 9, 191
Escobar, Arturo, 201n23
"Les Espaces libres à Paris" workshop
(Musée social), 121–123
Esposito, Roberto, 7
L'Esprit Nouveau magazine, 145–146,
239n8, 240n16
L'Esprit Nouveau Pavilion, *146*,
146–147, *152*, 153, 239n11
Estado Novo, Brazilian, 243n46,
249n141
Eugenia (Urzaiz), 28–33, *32*
eugenics: institutionalization of, in

233n199–234n200; Family Code, 171; history of eugenics in, 6; influence in Latin America, 12; as "invaded country," 246n103; Le Corbusier's tree and the French state, 172–174, *173*; Mexico, invasion of, 198n39; "social question," 43, 44, 48, 50, 206n3; Third Republic, 44; Vichy regime, 177, 239n2, 246n99. *See also* Paris; World's Fair, Paris

Freimann, Elvira, 116

French Artistic Mission, 214n94, 215n98

French Eugenics Society, 69, 239n3

French Foundation for the Study of Human Problems (Carrel Foundation), 178, 248n127

Freyre, Gilberto, 249n137

Gallery of Machines, World's Fair (Paris, 1899), *45*, 47, 206n1

Galton, Francis: about, 199n1; bioengineering laboratory, 27–28; coining of term "eugenics" by, 6, 19, 28, 199n1; Darwin and, 19, 199n9; fingerprint research and identification system, 103–104, 225n74; International Conference of Psychological Psychology and, 206–207n5; *Kantsaywhere*, 19–23, 199nn2–3; nature-nurture dichotomy, 9, 199n8; pictorial statistics of, 103–104; "Specimens of Composite Portraiture," *106*; theory of normal distribution, 147, 240n15

garden-city model: Buenos Aires garden-city worker village plan (Coni), 113, *114*; Forestier and, in Buenos Aires, 121; idea of, 54–55, 209n35

gardens, restorative: in Buenos Aires, 118–121, 125–128; Forestier's "neighborhood garden" concept, 120–121; forest-parks, 125, 231n171; Hénard's plan for Paris, 230n154

garitas de desinfección (chambers of disinfection), 100

Garnier, Charles, *46*, 207n9

Geddes, Patrick, 4–5

gender: ambiguity of, 31–33; Indian race, gendering of, 31; in Monteiro Lobato's *O presidente negro ou O*

choque das raças, 35; prostitution and men not object of reform, 236n231; social construction of, 33; Urzaiz's *Eugenia* and, 30, 32–33. *See also* women

General Common Education Law 1420 (1884), 129–130, 233n186

General Directorate of Architecture (Argentina), 135, 235n218

genetics: contemporary risks with, 190; Galton and, 9, 20; Mendelian, 3, 9, 11, 117

Germinal (Zola), 88, 220n19

Ghigliazza, Sebastián, 231n168

giraffe example of environmental adaptation, 194n10

Giraudoux, Jean, 129, 171–172, 232n184–233n185, 246n99, 246n103

globe of Reclus, *xvi*, 1–2, *2–4*, 4–5, 193n1, 222n35

Godoy, Armando Augusto de, 70, 214n91

Gorelik, Adrián, 119, 229n136

"Great Globe" (Reclus, Bonnier, and Marey), *xvi*, 1–2, *2–4*, 4–5, 193n1, 222n35

Greene, Gina Marie, 233n199

Guy, Donna J., 236n231

habits, everyday, 149

Haeckel, Ernst, 241n30

Harsin, Jill, 227n109

Haussmann, Georges-Eugène, 41, 43, 72, 118, 228n128

Havana: Forestier's comprehensive plan for, 242n36; Plaza de la Fraternidad (Forestier), *153*, 154, 242n38

Hénard, Eugène, 53, 55, 121–122, 230n154, 231n158

heredity: Galton and, 9, 19, 199n1; in Galton's *Kantsaywhere*, 21; Lamarckian environmental adaptation and, 63–64, 93, 110; Lamarckian eugenics and, 27, 93; nature-nurture debate and, 191; puericulture and, 52–53, 68–69; Reclus' globe and, 1; tree image and, 172; "weak" children and, 130; Zola on milieu and, *85*; Zola's diagrams and family trees, *85*, 86, *86*, 88

Jardin zoologique d'acclimatation, Paris World's Fair (1889), *49*
Jaussely, Léon, 55
Jeanneret, Charles-Édouard. *See* Le Corbusier
Jeanneret, Pierre, 167–169
"Jeca Tatu: A ressurreição" (Monteiro), 36
Jenner, Edward, 201n27
Jewish immigrants, 109
Justo, Agustín Pedro, 237n254

Kahn, Gustave, 53–54
Kálnay, Jorge, 140–141, 237n251, 237n254, 238n256
Kantsaywhere (Galton), 19–23, 199nn2–3
Kjellén, Rudolf, 195n15

La Berge, Ann, 207–208n12
Lacassagne, Alexandre, 50, 204n82
"La ciudad del porvenir" (Carrasco), 121
Lamarck, Jean-Baptiste: architecture and, 5; evolutionary theory of, 193n5; giraffe example of environmental adaptation, 194n10; "milieu" and, 149–150, 195n17; theories of heredity, 93; theory of inheritance of acquired characteristics, 3, 8–9, 111–112, 241n30
Landouzy, Louis: Argentine League of Social Prophylaxis and, 110–111; at "Les Espaces libres à Paris" workshop, 122; "hominiculture," 39–40, 53; International Conference of Psychological Psychology and, 207n5; Musée social and, 52, 55; social hygiene and, 38
Landowski, Paul, 213n76
La Plata, Argentina, 103, *112*
Latin America: Belle Époque, 11; history of term, 12–13; influence of France in, 12; migration of scientific modernism from France to, 10–14; positivism, influence of, 194n12; positivism and evolutionary theories in, 6; racial delineation from North America, 13. *See also specific countries and cities*
Latin race, 13
Latour, Bruno, 97, 207n12

Law of Residence (Argentina, 1902), 107–108
Law of Social Defense (Argentina, 1910), 107–108, 225n80
Leão, Carlos, *81*
Le Bon, Gustave, 92
Le Corbusier, *187*; aerial view and, 184; "Aménagement d'une journée équilibrée," 144; anthropogeography and, 78–79; on architect as technocrat and architectural revolution, 158–161; *Athens Charter*, 246n99; "L'autorité devant les tâches contemporaines," 159; the biological unit, 161, *161*, 244n64; Carrel and, 155–156, 161–166, *170*, 171–172, 174, *178*, 178–179, 184–188, *185*; "Commentaires relatifs à Moscou et à la 'Ville Verte,'" 176; connection between puericulture and eugenics, advocacy for, 144–145; Costa and, 155, 157–158; on decorative arts in decline, 150–151; *Destin de Paris*, 175; doctrine of, 177–178, 187–188; L'Esprit Nouveau Pavilion, *146*, 146–147, *152*, 153, 239n11; first articulation of eugenics, 82; *The Four Routes*, 171; Giraudoux and, 129, 233n185; *The Home of Man*, 171, 172–176, 184, 246n96, 247n104; *immeuble-villas*, 239n11; Kahn and, 54; lectures in Rio de Janeiro, 158–159, 165–167, 171, 218n123; on Martel brothers and Mallet-Stevens's "Winter Garden and Concrete Trees," *150*, *151*, 151–153; "Modulor," 188; neo-syndicalist movement and, 246n96; on "psycho-physiologique," 163–164, 245n74; *The Radiant City*, *157*, 160, 166, 167, 244n64; "rebirth of the human body," 154, 161; Reclus' globe and, 2; retreat to Vézelay, 171–172; in Rio de Janeiro, 82; "science of man" and, 162–163; sketch connecting the simple man, Rio, Costa, and Carrel's eugenics, 155–158, *156*; sketches made in Rio, *155*, *164*, *165*, 180; sketch for Ministry of Health and Education building, Rio de Janeiro, *179*, 179–180; on

Paris World's Fair, 44–45; environment as primary in construction of, 110; undesirable immigrants to Argentina as threat to, 103; as worldwide phenomenon, 14
modernization, defined, 13–14
"Modulor," 188
Moinester, Margot, 207n7
Monteiro de Carvalho, Alberto, 218n123
Monteiro Lobato, José Bento: "Jeca Tatu: A ressurreição," 36; *O presidente negro ou O choque das raças*, 33–35, 215n95; *Problema vital*, 35–36; race as issue for, 204n75; on scientists replacing politicians, 204n73
Montevideo, 167
Montigny, Grandjean de, 214n94
Morales de los Rios Filho, Adolfo, 64, 212n65
More, Thomas, 23, 28, 199n2
Moreira, Jorge, *81*
Moreira, Juliano, 67
Morra, Carlos, 231n168
Morris, William, 201n20
Morro do Castelo demolition, Rio de Janeiro, 57–62, *59*, *60*, 74–76, 210n41, 216n107, 216n109
Morro do Santo Antônio demolition, Rio de Janeiro, 74–76
mother-child unit. *See* puericulture
Mumford, Lewis, 27
Musée de la prévention des accidents du travail et d'hygiène industrielle (Paris), 209n24
Musée des Arts Décoratifs (Paris), 209n24
Musée d'Ethnographie du Trocadéro (Paris), 209n24
Musée social: Alliance d'hygiène sociale, 53–54; born at Paris World's Fair, 52; Congrès d'hygiène sociale (Roubaix, 1911) and garden-city model, 54–55; "Les Espaces libres à Paris" workshop, 121–123; "espaces libres" commission, 231n158; Forestier and, 39; Latin American master plans, *56*, 56–57, *57*; Museo Social Argentino and, 108–109, 225n81; Pinard and Landouzy's puericulture and hominiculture

concepts and, 52–53; Section on Urban and Rural Hygiene, 121–122, *122*, 231n158; Société des architectes urbanistes, 216n103; urbanism and Société française des urbanistes, 55–56
Museo Social Argentino, 108–111, 116, 139, 141–142, 225nn80–81, 226n84, 226n103, 227n104, 228n121
Museum of Modern Art (MOMA), 183, 250n144
Muthesius, Hermann, 147–148, 240n19

Nana (Manet), *89*
Nana (Zola), 88, 221n20
Napoleon III, 12, 118, 198n39
natalism: Alliance nationale pour l'accroissement de la population française, 221n23; Zola and, 87, 90, 221n23
National Council of Education (Argentina), 129–130, 135, 234n205
National Council of Low-Cost Houses (Argentina), 140, 237n246
National Department of Hygiene, Argentina, 95, 113
National School of Fine Arts (France), 248n132
naturalism, 90, 222n24
natural monuments in Rio de Janeiro, 65–67
naturalness, 22, 201n27
natural selection, 4, 14, 30, 150, 163, 190, 194n9, 251n3
nature-nurture dichotomy, 9, 191, 199n8
"Negócio de China" cartoon (Carlos), *77*, 217n111
Neiva, Arthur, 36
Nelson, Ernesto, *125*, 125–126, 232n175
neoclassicism, 215n98
neocolonial style: Agache's Rio de Janeiro and, 70–71; as Brazilian national style, 71, 215n97, 249n141; at Centennial Exhibition (Rio de Janeiro, 1922), 62–64, *63*, 212n65; as "maternal architecture," 71, 216n99; whiteness and, 71
neo-Lamarckians, 9, 68, 196n26
neo-syndicalist movement, 246n96

Nereo de Sampaio, Fernando, 63–64
neurasthenia, 223n41
Niemeyer, Oscar, *81*, 182–184, 250n145
Noël, Carlos, 123, 230n145
normalization: architecture as key tool for, 102; development and, 198n48; L'Esprit Nouveau Pavilion and, 147; Foucault on, 146; in Monteiro Lobato's *O presidente negro*, 34–35; Museo Social Argentino and, 111; neocolonial style and, 71; open-air schools and, 136; puericulture and hominiculture in Argentina and, 115; Quetelet and, 104; Vichy regime and, 188; of white heterosexual society, 36–37
North America and South America, racial delineation between, 13
Nouzeilles, Gabriela, 90
Novick, Alicia, 227n104
Nueva Granada, 198n41

Obregón, Álvaro, 31
Olmsted, Frederick Law, 119
Olympia (Manet), *88*, 221n20
open-air schools, 129–136, 234n205
"Ordem e Progresso" (Order and Progress) motto, 194n13
Order of Architects, 250n152
"Ornament and Crime" (Loos), 150, 241n29, 241n31
"orthopedics," 148
"Os extremos se tocam" cartoon (Carlos), *77*, 217n111
Oswald, Carlos, 213n76
Outtes, Joel, 78, 217n116
Ozenfant, Amédée, 145

Palaviccini, Félix, 30, 31, 202n50
Pangenesis theory, 196n25
pan-Latinist movement, 12
Paolera, Carlos María Della, 139
Paris: *casier sanitaire*, 100–101, 224n52; Champs de Mars, 47, 207n9, 230n154; cholera epidemic (1832), 97, 223n42; Committee for the Study of Habitation and the Urbanism of Paris (Vichy), 178, 246n99; Congress of Hygiene, 208n12; "Les Espaces libres à Paris" workshop (Musée social), 121–123; Esplanade des Invalides,

47–48, 50, *50*; Haussman public parks plan, 228n128; Hénard's garden plan, 230n154; Landouzy report on tuberculosis in, 122; new museums, emergence of, 209n24; Salpêtrière hospital, 235n224. *See also* Musée social; World's Fair, Paris (1889)
Pasteur, Louis, 49, 97, 208n12
"peasant family" ideal, 109–110
Penna, Belisário, 36, 115, 137–138
Penna, José, 93–102
Pereira Passos, Francisco, 57–58, 61, 72, 158, 215n94
Pessoa, Epitácio, 211n58, 249n141
Pezolet, Nicola, 240n16
La Phalange (Fourier), 23
pictorial statistics, 103–104
Pierrefeu, François de, 171, 172, 174–176, 246n96
Pinard, Adolphe: Argentine League of Social Prophylaxis and, 110–111; on marriage regulation, 238n261; mother-child unit and, 115–116; puericulture, 40–41, 52–53, 68, 209n26; social hygiene and, 38
plasma theory, 9
Plato, 200n15
playgrounds for children, 125, *125*, 126, 232n175
Plaza de la Fraternidad, Havana (Forestier), *153*, 154, 242n38
Plumet, Charles, 241n34
Poëte, Marcel, 55
population growth: Agache on control of, 71–72; from immigration, 197n34; from industrialization and urbanization, 11, 197n33; in Rio de Janeiro, 58, 71–72; Zola on depopulation in *Fecondité*, 89–90, 222n23
portraiture, composite (Galton), 103–104, *106*
positivism: Agache as missionary of, 73; Brazil's "Ordem e Progresso" (Order and Progress) motto, 194n13; evolutionary theories and, in Latin America, 6; medicalization of urban fabric and, 93; naturalism and, 222n24; Roquette-Pinto and, 80; science, trust in, 26; Zola and, 86
Pot-Bouille (Zola), 88, 221n22

for hereditary acquired characteristics, 111–112

Spencer, Herbert, 150, 190

standardization, 146–148

Stepan, Nancy Leys, 8, 117, 194n12, 203n62, 225n78

Stephens, Elizabeth, 240n15

sterilization, eugenic: Carrel's "science of man" and, 163; dispensaries and, 138; Mexico and, 30–31, 202n50–203n51; in Monteiro Lobato's *O presidente negro ou O choque das raças*, 34, 35; in Urzaiz's *Eugenia*, 30–33

syphilis. *See* "social diseases"

Tello, Wenceslao, 139

Temps Nouveaux pavilion (Le Corbusier and Jeanneret), 167–171, *169*

Tenorio, Mauricio, 211n58

Thays, Charles (Carlos), 119, 124, 229n142

Thiers, Adolphe, 227n110

"Third World," 193n4, 201n23

Tijuca Forest, Rio de Janeiro, 67, 212n75

Tirman, Albert, 232n183

Topalov, Christian, 206n4

Torres Caicedo, José María, 13

tree image and metaphor: Darwin's Tree of Life, 172; Forestier's ceiba, Plaza de la Fraternidad, Havana, *153*, 154; Le Corbusier and, 159–160, *160*, 172–174, *173*, 247n104; "Winter Garden and Concrete Trees" (Martel brothers and Mallet-Stevens), *150*, *151*, 151–153

tuberculosis. *See* "social diseases"

24-hour solar cycle, 164–166

"type-needs" and "type-objects" (Le Corbusier), *147*, 147–149

Underwood, David, 77

Unité d'habitation, Marseille (Le Corbusier), *186*, 187–188

United States: *Brazil Builds* exhibition (MOMA), 183, 250n144; Ellis Island, *21*; in Monteiro Lobato's *O presidente negro ou O choque das raças*, 34–35; neo-Lamarckians

in, 9, 196n26; New York World's Fair (1939), 183–184

Universidad del Museo Social Argentino, 190, 250n1

Urban and Rural League for Environmental Planning of French Life, 129, 232n183

urban hygiene, 43

urbanism: Agache master plan for Rio de Janeiro, 72–79, *73–76, 79*; Agache's "What is Urbanism?," 71–72; Brazil Centennial Exhibition (1922) and, 62–68; Carrasco on social character of, 234n212; demolition of Morro do Castelo, Rio de Janeiro, 57–62, *59, 60*, 74–76, 210n41, 216n107, 216n109; Forestier's Buenos Aires master plan and, 124; Kálnay on architecture and, 140; Musée social and, 52–57; as racial-class technology, 57; World's Fair (1889, Paris) and, 44–52

Urban League, 129, 232n183

"urbanología," 140

urban planning. *See* Buenos Aires; Musée social; Paris; Rio de Janeiro

Urzaiz Rodríguez, Eduardo, 28–33, *32*, 202n39

Utopia (More), 23

utopian narratives: Argentine eco-utopias, 36–41; Campanella's *Città del sole*, 200n15; Coni's "La ciudad argentina ideal o del porvenir," 40–41; Dubos' "Medical Utopias," 26; Galton's *Kantsaywhere*, 19–23; medicalization and beautification of bodies in bio-utopias, 26–28; medical origin of, 24–26; Monteiro Lobato's *O presidente negro ou O choque das raças*, 33–35, 215n95; Monteiro Lobato's *Problema vital* and "Jeca Tatu: A ressurreição," 35–36; origin of term "utopia," 199n2; Plato's *Republic*, 200n15; proliferation of, 23; relationship between the city, eugenics, and utopia, 41–42; Ribeiro's "Yvy-Marãen," 205n98; Richardson's *Hygeia*, 23, 200n19; science, space, and ideology in, 22–23, 200n14; Sioen's *Buenos Aires en al año*